Hatching Results for Secondary School Counseling

Hatching Results for Secondary School Counseling

Implementing Core Curriculum, Individual Student Planning, and Other Tier One Activities

Trish Hatch, Whitney Triplett,
Danielle Duarte, and Vanessa Gomez

Foreword by Carl A. Cohn

FOR INFORMATION:

Corwin

A SAGE Company

2455 Teller Road

Thousand Oaks, California 91320

(800) 233-9936

www.corwin.com

SAGE Publications Ltd.

1 Oliver's Yard

55 City Road

London EC1Y 1SP

United Kingdom

SAGE Publications India Pvt. Ltd.

B 1/I 1 Mohan Cooperative Industrial Area

Mathura Road, New Delhi 110 044

India

SAGE Publications Asia-Pacific Pte. Ltd.

18 Cross Street #10-10/11/12

China Square Central

Singapore 048423

Program Director: Jessica Allen

Content Development Editor: Lucas Schleicher

Senior Editorial Assistant: Mia Rodriguez

Production Editor: Tori Mirsadjadi

Copy Editor: Pam Schroeder

Typesetter: C&M Digitals (P) Ltd.

Proofreader: Talia Greenberg

Indexer: Maria Sosnowski

Cover Designers: Alexa Turner and Juliana YipOno

Marketing Manager: Deena Meyer

Printed in the United States of America

Library of Congress Cataloging-in-Publication Data

Names: Hatch, Trish, author.

Title: Hatching results for secondary school counseling : implementing core curriculum, individual student planning, and other tier one activities / Trish Hatch, Whitney Triplett, Danielle Duarte, and Vanessa Gomez ; Foreword by Carl A. Cohn.

Description: Thousand Oaks, California : Corwin, [2019] | Includes bibliographical references and index.

Identifiers: LCCN 2018057267 | ISBN 9781544342078 (pbk. : alk. paper)

Subjects: LCSH: Counseling in secondary education—United States. | Student counselors—United States. | Educational counseling—United States. | Common Core State Standards (Education)

Classification: LCC LB1620.5 .H395 2019 | DDC 373.14—dc23

LC record available at https://lccn.loc.gov/2018057267

This book is printed on acid-free paper.

19 20 21 22 23 10 9 8 7 6 5 4 3 2

Contents

Visit hatchingresults.com
for downloadable resources.

Foreword

Fifty years ago this month, after studying to be a priest for 9-plus years, I walked out of a Roman Catholic seminary into the unknown world of public schools. As a 23-year-old in 1968, I thought I would have good rapport with high school students in the inner city and that I might be able to make a difference in their lives. In addition to my misgivings about a life of celibacy, I was answering the call of recently assassinated Robert F. Kennedy to "give a damn about the plight of urban America."

I thought I would use my privileged parochial school education to become an outstanding high school counselor. Although I was "young, gifted, and Black," I had no idea what I was doing or what my future might hold as a secondary school counselor. So, I walked into the personnel office of the Compton Unified School District in Southern California and was sent out to Dominguez Senior High School as a day-to-day substitute teacher. By January, I had a long-term assignment replacing a social studies teacher who had been run out of the school by disruptive students who were wreaking havoc in many of the classrooms on the sprawling, chaotic campus.

Knowing that I wanted to be a high school counselor, I enrolled in an MA in School Counseling and Pupil Personnel Credential program at what was then Chapman College. And, I really enjoyed all of the counseling, psychology, and other behavioral science courses that were absent from my seminary training. After only a year and a half as a teacher, I got my first full-time assignment as a high school counselor at the very same high school where I started. Again, I had no idea what I was doing. It seemed that the school administration wanted me to handle everything associated with keeping the peace on a campus that was filled with racial tension and an emerging "Black power" movement.

After only a single year as a full-time counselor, I was offered my "dream job" as a counselor at the flagship high school of the Long Beach Unified School District, Polytechnic High School, an academic and sports powerhouse that has been around for more than 120 years. Once again, I had no real organized idea about what I was supposed to be doing but a much more focused assignment from the Polytechnic administration in the area of "make sure that we don't have any more riots." Toward that end, I was freed from the usual scheduling and programming responsibilities that the regular contingent of high school counselors were saddled with in a 3,000-student high school. Whatever success I had during those turbulent days, in terms of ensuring that there weren't any more riots, served to advance my own career, resulting in ever higher levels of leadership responsibility and ultimately becoming superintendent of schools in Long Beach and San Diego, and federal court monitor in Los Angeles. I believe strongly that the listening skills that I learned and practiced as a high school counselor were a critical factor in whatever success I have had as a leader of school systems.

But, I didn't do anything to advance the profession of school counseling or to better define the important work of school counselors in an organized, relevant, and consistent way, and that's why this new volume by the Hatch team is so valuable, important, and timely. They take seriously "the art and science" of school counseling and are capable of explaining it to practitioners in the field in ways that are both compelling and urgent.

There is nothing more disheartening during times of economic distress and school district budget cutting than the phenomenon of school counseling sometimes heading the list of possible places to cut. These co-authors capture throughout this volume all of the reasons why that is a singularly horrible idea. They lift up the profession of secondary school counseling by showing in rich detail the vital importance of what counselors do, first and foremost, to reach *all* kids—an idea that sometimes gets lost in the old notion that sometimes counselors are in schools to serve only some or the few.

This new approach requires new skills for secondary counselors with regard to core curriculum lesson planning, classroom management, family engagement, transitions, discipline, and its alternative—all functions that current higher education preparation programs may not do an adequate job of preparing secondary counselors for. For example, the authors point out that 74% of counselors indicated that their university preparation program provided no training in classroom management while, at the same time, respondents said that 82% of teachers had specifically asked for their help in this area of need. This new book provides practical help and tips in many of these important areas of need if secondary counselors are going to play these key leadership roles on school campuses.

For the past 7 years, I have played a significant leadership role in both education policy-making and its execution here in our nation's most populous state: first, as a member of the State Board of Education, and most recently as the first executive director of the California Collaborative for Educational Excellence, a new small state agency whose mission is to get the right kind of help to school districts, charter schools, and county offices of education. This is consistent with ESSA's devolution of authority to states and, in turn, our own former governor Brown's efforts to further return control to the local level, providing substantially more education funding for students who are poor, learning English, or in foster care. Part of that bargain is to bring new, bottom-up voices to the table, those of students, parents, and community in defining how monies are going to spent and how youngsters are going to be better served. The changing roles of school counselors, carefully outlined here, are absolutely critical to the execution of that new vision for improving schools and districts here in California and throughout the nation.

Trish Hatch, Whitney Triplett, Danielle Duarte, and Vanessa Gomez have done an outstanding job of placing school counselors at the center of these necessary and vital changes that are designed to define the important work of secondary school counselors for decades to come. We are all in their debt for crafting a bright future for all students and how school counselors make that happen in this groundbreaking and timely new book.

Carl A. Cohn
Professor Emeritus
Claremont Graduate University

Acknowledgments

With the release of the elementary version of this book in 2018, we are so excited to make available *Hatching Results for Secondary School Counseling: Implementing Core Curriculum, Individual Student Planning, and Other Tier One Activities* to equip secondary school counselors with greater tools and resources around Tier 1 activities. As former school counselors we are fully aware of the attitude, knowledge, and skill gaps in the profession around the delivery of Tier 1 school counseling supports. Based on the varied experiences of the co-authors, we wrote this book to close those gaps so that secondary school counselors are better resourced to improve student outcomes. We have many to thank for their contributions.

We are grateful to those who provided testimonials, examples, and samples either in the text or the online appendix of additional resources including Dr. Carolyn Stone from University of North Florida, Dr. Robin Hausheer from Plymouth State University, Megan Jansen from Brea Olinda School District, Ashley Hansen from the Ohio State, Becky Love from Shasta County, Michele Howard, Dr. Heidi A. Traux, and the Chicago Public Schools Office of School Counseling and Postsecondary Advising, who contributed several strategies outlined in Chapters 8 and 11. Inelda Luna, former teacher on special assignment in Fallbrook Union Elementary School District and current Principal in San Jacinto Unified School District, is thanked for providing inspiration for the engagement strategy pictures and descriptions within Chapter 5. Special thanks to Dr. Norm Gysbers, Dr. Carolyn Magnuson, Dr. Bragg Stanley, Carolyn Roof, and Linda Lueckenhoff for the collaborative effort in outlining the development of statewide core curriculum in Missouri and Nancy Sandoval for the investigative work to create the core curriculum and national awareness campaign downloadable resources.

Sincerest thanks to school counselors-in-training Zoe Leshner and Araminta Koppenheffer for their formatting, technical, and administrative assistance—we are grateful for your time and talent and know you are going to be phenomenal school counselors! Special thanks also to Lisa De Gregorio, who was instrumental to the success of this text through her co-authorship of the elementary version, which set the framework for the secondary text. Lisa, we owe you a Tropical Bay Breeze! Finally, a giant thank-you also goes out to Carl Cohn for not only for his kind words in the foreword but most importantly for being a huge advocate for the school counseling profession.

From Trish: When I first began in my role as Coordinator of Student Services in Moreno Valley Unified (MVUSD), I had years of experience as an elementary counselor but not as many at secondary. I learned a great deal from the counselors at high school, which cultivated what later would become the impetus for ideas shared in this and other texts (particular thanks to Lori Holland and posthumously to Pat Chandler for their mentorship). Since that time 15 years ago, it has been my honor to teach and learn from hundreds of graduate students at SDSU and thousands of secondary counselors and administrators in hundreds of districts nationwide. Continuing to support their professional development is the purpose of this text. Humble thanks to Greg Darneider for the opportunity to serve at a national level as consultant and advisor on school counseling for the White House and the USDOE during the Obama administration. I am grateful to Jami Parsons, Mayu Iwatani, and the Orange County Department of Education for their advocacy and partnership to educate school counselors and administrators statewide in MTMDSS and the ASCA National Model. Special thanks to the entire Hatching Results Team for supporting this secondary text. To my co-authors, Whitney, Danielle, and Vanessa, thank you for your complete and uncompromising commitment to excellence, for taking the *Use of Data* concepts and applying them within your respective districts, and for sharing them within this text. You are all phenomenal leaders, and I am so grateful for your collaboration on this project. As always, I'm grateful to Corwin Press (Jessica Allen, Lucas Schleicher, and Mia Rodriguez) for their support, assistance, and belief in the importance and value of school counseling texts. On a personal note, I'd like to offer tender, loving thanks to my dear parents (John and Kathleen Meyers), who at 90 and 86 continue to support my love of school counseling, Mom always asking about every district I am training in and Dad reading each text cover to cover. Finally, to my three sons (Brian, Michael, and Greg) and my two beautiful grandchildren (Nolan and Emery), who ground and inspire me every day.

From Whitney: I would first like to thank my best friend, partner, and husband, Adam, for his humor and unending support throughout the development of this book over the last few years, although in his words even *he* "could have written it by now" LOL! I also thank Grady and Everson for their patience as Mommy was writing, sometimes while one or both were sitting on my lap :). To my parents, the Rev. Dr. Doug and Debbie Danner, who after 40 years of marriage are still my biggest sources of advice, counsel, and encouragement to "change the world." I am ever grateful to Trish for believing in me and mentoring me toward becoming a more effective school counselor advocate, and our co-authors, Danielle and Vanessa, for their dedication and positivity throughout this writing experience. Thank you to Barbara Karpouzian, whose mentorship has helped me stay centered and focused on what's really important. Thank you to my rock-star "cubicle buddies" at OSCPA, whose mission-driven mindsets make miracles happen for school counselors and students every day; Angela Shanahan, Michele Howard, Laura Herbert, Eugene Robinson, Imah Effiong—you inspire me to be the best version of myself, and I wouldn't have survived without you. Thank you to my amazing school counselor mentors at various points throughout my life and career: Lisa De Gregorio, Angela Bridges, Carol Alexander, Thalistine Morris, Sally Goodwin, Joyce Brown, Sandy Sloane, Cathy Brown (a school counselor in spirit), and many others. I am also grateful to Dr. Vince Walsh-Rock, the Illinois School Counselor Association, Dakota Beavers, and the Illinois State Board of Education, who supported the statewide rollout of MTMDSS through the 2018 update of the Developmental Counseling Model for Illinois Schools. And finally, to the phenomenal school counselors in Chicago Public Schools: You taught me to be fearless and relentless in my advocacy because "the stakes are just too high." Continue to rise up, persist, and blaze the halls with your endless enthusiasm, student-centered energy, and vision-driven passion for student success. You are true servant leaders, and it has been one of my life's greatest joys to learn from and serve alongside you.

From Danielle: I want first to thank my dad, who was always my biggest cheerleader and encouraged me to take on any challenge, including writing a book. Although he passed away during the writing process, his love and support are still so present and will be felt evermore when the book is released. A huge thank-you to my amazing middle school counseling partner in crime, Megan Jansen, for supporting all my crazy ideas, leading the way for our RAMP application, listening as we talked through the walls of the counseling office, and overall being a phenomenal teammate. Additionally, thank you to the students, teachers, administrators, school counseling interns, and support staff I worked with at Potter Junior High School for your support of our school counseling program. I am also so grateful to Tawnya Pringle's mentorship when I interned with her, which has continued and developed into friendship. Once again, Malia Altieri from San Marcos Unified and Inelda Luna from San Jacinto Unified are given huge hugs for sharing exceptional classroom lesson tools and engagement strategies, which provided inspiration for content in Chapters 4 through 6. I am also grateful for Melissa Lafayette, who began co-teaching with me at San Diego State University (SDSU) and who continues to pave the way for similar, much-needed courses for school counselors to learn about designing, teaching, and evaluating classroom lessons. Thank you to the many cohorts of SDSU school counseling graduate students I both taught and learned from, the amazing school counseling leaders I worked with on the California Association of School Counselors (CASC) Board of Directors, and the school counseling staff developers from AVID (and AVID's amazing content!). Gratitude is forever given to Ian Bradley, for his love and support of my career ambitions, which often leave him doing the dishes, flying across the country, and patiently waiting while I read or write one more thing! Finally, thank you to my co-authors—my forever mentor and co-conspirator Trish; the amazing Whitney, who is doing great work in my former position; and Vanessa, who encouraged my school counseling leadership, which helped me get involved with CASC and so much more!

From Vanessa: First I would like to thank God for allowing me to live my purpose and blessing me with all of the wonderful people in my life. I would also like to thank Trish Hatch for being an amazing mentor and friend. Your dedication to students and the school counseling profession is inspiring. A special thank-you to Diane Perez, superintendent of San Jacinto Unified, who had the vision of what the school counseling program could be, and to Sherry Smith, assistant superintendent, and Karen Kirschinger, director of Student Support, for all of your support. Thank you to the school counselors, administrators, staff, and students whom I have worked with in San Jacinto Unified School District and in Moreno Valley Unified School District; I do not have enough words to express my gratitude for all you do for our students. I am eternally grateful to have worked with the best school counselors and staff around and am always inspired by your dedication to your students. A special thank-you to my first school counselor mentors: Lori Holland, Nancy Stimson, Bob McDonald, and Paul Andersen. You were my very first school counseling family and took me under your wings, providing me with a strong foundation. A special thank-you to Jordan Reeves, Monica Loyce, April Phillips, Sophia De La Rocha, and Hugo Gonzalez for putting in the time, support, dedication, and systems into place that created a strong foundation for the Tigers' school counseling program. A huge thank-you to the current SJUSD school counselors for the work you do, for always putting our students first, and for having the willingness to think outside of the box. Finally, I want to provide a huge thank-you to my mom and dad for their love and support; to all of my siblings for being the best role models; to Kevin, Brittany, Olivia, and Sophia for always inspiring me and for your unending support of my passion.

About the Authors

Trish Hatch, PhD, is a Professor at San Diego State University (SDSU), where she was Director of the School Counseling Program from 2004 until 2015. She is the best-selling author of *The Use of Data in School Counseling: Hatching Results for Students, Programs, and the Profession* (2013) and co-author of *Evidence-Based Practice in School Counseling: Making a Difference With Data-Driven Practices* (Dimmit, Carey, & Hatch, 2007) and the *ASCA National Model: A Framework for School Counseling Programs* (ASCA, 2003, 2005). This text and her most recent text, *Hatching Results for Elementary School Counseling: Implementing Core Curriculum and Other Tier One Activities* (Hatch, Duarte, & De Gregorio, 2018), are used throughout the nation for professional learning and the preparation of school counselors.

Dr. Hatch is the President and CEO of Hatching Results®, LLC, an educational consulting company providing professional development, consultation, grant writing, and program evaluation services to support school counselors, administrators, and school districts in designing, implementing, and evaluating school counseling programs. She served as a national consultant and advisor on school counseling and educational issues for the White House and the U.S. Department of Education under the Obama administration. In 2014, she co-led the organization and planning of the second "invitation-only" White House Convening on School Counseling at San Diego State University. A former school counselor, site and central office administrator, state association president, and ASCA Vice President, Hatch has received multiple national awards including the American School Counselor Association (ASCA) Administrator of the Year Award, and its highest honor, the Mary Gehrke Lifetime Achievement Award. She most recently received the National Association for College Admission Counseling's (NACAC's) Excellence in Equity Award (2015) and the inaugural California Association of School Counselors' School Counselor Educator of the Year (2016).

Whitney Triplett, MA, NCC, the Director of Professional Development for Hatching Results, trains school counselors and administrators across the nation. Previously at Chicago Public Schools, Whitney supported the district's 850+ school counselors and college and career coaches while serving on the board for the Illinois School Counselor Association and instructing school counseling students at Loyola University Chicago. It was through these roles that she was recognized in 2018 as the School Counseling Advocate of the Year for the state of Illinois. Having received RAMP recognition in 2011, Whitney is a former Lead RAMP Reviewer for the American School Counselor Association. As a school counselor, Whitney received a Counselor Leadership Award and an Oppenheimer Recognition Award for her collaborative work in raising the Freshmen-on-Track rate at her school. A former Education Pioneers Visiting Fellow, Whitney is passionate about school reform, closing achievement gaps, and school counseling to promote equity, access, and the success of *all* students!

Danielle Duarte, MS, is passionate about supporting students' academic success, college and career readiness, and social/emotional development while using data to show the positive impact of school counselors. She is currently a doctoral student in the Education Leadership Program at Harvard University and co-author of the book *Hatching Results for Elementary School Counseling: Implementing Core Curriculum and Other Tier One Activities.* Formerly a school counselor, counseling grant project director, adjunct faculty member at San Diego State University, and Director of Professional Development for Hatching Results, Danielle continues to train counselors and administrators in developing comprehensive, data-driven school counseling programs. Danielle was featured in *San Diego Magazine*'s "17 Big Ideas for 2017: Let's Implement More School Counseling Programs" and earned Recognized ASCA Model Program (RAMP) status in her previous district. Additionally, Danielle served on the board of directors for the California Association of School Counselors for 7 years including as president (2015–2016) and was also involved in Michelle Obama's Reach Higher Initiative, attending all national convenings representing California's Reach Higher Team.

Danielle is an AVID Staff Developer, frequent presenter at state and national conferences, and author of multiple articles featured in school counseling publications, including ASCA's *Professional School Counseling Journal*.

Vanessa Gomez, EdD, is the Coordinator of Student, Community, and Personnel Support in San Jacinto Unified School District, where she oversees the development and implementation of an award-winning, comprehensive school-counseling program that was the recipient of the Golden Bell Award sponsored by the California School Board Association and the Riverside Model of Excellence Award. Vanessa has 22 years of experience as a school counselor at all levels, including alternative education. During her career Vanessa has experience in developing and implementing comprehensive, data-driven school counseling programs, creating and implementing student assistance programs. She co-created the New Insight Group curriculum and has vast experience with crisis response counseling, including creating and designing suicide prevention protocols. Vanessa earned her doctorate degree from San Diego State University and completed her dissertation study on implementing trauma-informed approaches in schools.

Vanessa has served as the president of the California Association of School Counselors. For 9 years Vanessa served as adjunct faculty at San Diego State University in the School Counseling and School Psychology Department. In 2011 Vanessa was awarded the Most Influential Faculty award. She was also the recipient of the American School Counselor Association's 2009 top 10 school counselors. Vanessa enjoys providing local, state, and national trainings on implementing the ASCA National Model, student assistance programs, new insight curriculum, developmental assets, trauma-informed approaches, and crisis response.

Introduction

As a first-year school counselor, Trish recalls arriving at her school and being shown to her office. When she opened the desk drawers, she found one file with the names of children identified as "gifted" inside. She had no curriculum, lesson plans, materials, or brochures—nothing. When Whitney landed her first job as a school counselor, she was expected to teach core curriculum lessons in the classroom. However, she had not received any graduate training or professional development in core curriculum design, lesson planning, student engagement strategies, or classroom management and was ill prepared to address the Tier 1 needs of her students. When Danielle first began at Potter Junior High School, she was the only full-time school counselor for 900 middle school students. Although there were fires to be put out left and right, Danielle knew she needed to create a counseling program that included prevention to address the problems at their core. Similarly, when Vanessa entered the school counseling profession, there was a lack of consistency in terms of Tier 1 services that school counselors provided, which caused confusion and inequities for students.

These experiences are why we all made the daunting commitment to spend evenings and weekends writing this book—because we believe that school counselors need high-quality materials to design a strong Tier 1 program to meet the diverse needs of all students. Additionally, we believe that measuring and sharing the impact of school counseling programs through collecting and analyzing process, perception, and outcome data is essential.

The purpose of *Hatching Results for Secondary School Counseling: Implementing Core Curriculum, Individual Student Planning, and Other Tier One Activities* is to provide secondary school counselors, administrators, district-level leaders, and graduate students with a hands-on guide to creating and implementing high-quality Tier 1 school counseling systems of support. The frame of this book originated from *Hatching Results for Elementary School Counseling: Implementing Core Curriculum and Other Tier One Activities* by Trish, Danielle, and Lisa K. De Gregorio (2018) and was built on content from *The Use of Data in School Counseling: Hatching Results for Students, Programs, and the Profession* (Hatch, 2013). This new text focuses on Tier 1 activities at the secondary level within what we call a Multi-Tiered, Multi-Domain System of Supports (MTMDSS). Tier 1 focuses on core curriculum classroom lessons and schoolwide activities provided to all students in the academic, social/emotional, and college/career domains aligned with the American School Counselor Association (ASCA) National Model. Additionally, a new chapter provides extensive details about individual student planning specifically for counselors at the secondary level. This text provides specific information and examples to directly support middle and high school counselors as they design, implement, and evaluate preventative Tier 1 activities to support the development and needs of all students schoolwide.

Within implementation of the MTMDSS, school counselors, like teachers, provide core subject matter in the three counseling domains for students at the secondary level. *Hatching Results for Secondary School Counseling: Implementing Core Curriculum, Individual Student Planning, and Other Tier One Activities* provides clear direction for today's middle and high school counselors on how to design, teach, assess, and improve core curriculum classroom lessons. The text provides content on other schoolwide (Tier 1) programs and activities, such as implementing schoolwide college application and FAFSA completion activities, coordinating family education programs, planning schoolwide prevention weeks, organizing peer mediation programs, leading College Signing Day, and more. Also included in the text are best practices from school counselors throughout the United States, including some who are now professional development specialists for Hatching Results®. The strategies in the text have been proven to be effective through measuring the impact on students' attitudes, knowledge, skills, and behaviors.

Today's middle and high school counselors are expected to create lesson plans, teach classroom curriculum, deliver engaging content, manage classroom behaviors, and provide assessments. Unfortunately, they often receive minimal training in their graduate programs on executing these responsibilities. This text closes the new and practicing school counselor's knowledge and skill gaps in teaching, learning, and instruction. Through this step-by-step guide on how to measure the impact of school counseling programs, readers will improve their skills and increase buy-in for their own programs.

The content within this book is applicable for use in school counseling graduate courses, such as Introduction to School Counseling; Learning, Achievement, and Instruction for School Counselors; Counseling Children and Adolescents; Secondary School Counseling; Program Evaluation; and any course that teaches prevention and intervention, including implementation of Multi-Tiered System of Supports (MTSS) for school counselors. This text will be of benefit to supervisors and students interning or completing fieldwork hours at the middle and high school levels. Through this resourceful guide for Tier 1 programs and services, school counselors will ensure that all students are benefitting from a comprehensive school counseling program.

Administrators, along with district and state school counseling coordinators, will value this text as it can assist them in understanding the appropriate role of secondary school counseling within Tier 1 and provides tools, examples, and helpful tips that can be useful for supporting and evaluating school counselors' implementation of the schoolwide program. This text can be further utilized for online learning to support school counselors in their attainment of additional continuing education units (CEUs) for maintenance of state certification or licensure.

Three key areas of focus within the text, in which school counselors often have limited or no training, are *effective teaching strategies*, *using measurement tools*, and *individual student planning*. This text provides school counselors with strong skills for teaching core content (a major component of Tier 1), which will lead to better outcomes for both counselors and students. Measuring and quantifying the success of such outcomes is also a critical skill for counselors to have. Additionally, individual student planning for *all* secondary level students is essential to ensure their completion of coursework for graduation and to attain postsecondary goals.

When school counselors are competent in using data, they can more accurately measure the impact of their services. There is still a lack of evidence-based materials for the school counseling profession, including for Tier 1 lessons, individual student planning, and schoolwide activities. The need is so great that thousands of counselors have started Facebook groups to share information. Unfortunately, much of the core curriculum and materials shared in these forums are not vetted through any evidence-based approach, and data-driven practices are rarely discussed. As educators, school counselors are held to similar standards and expectations as teachers in terms of setting measurable goals, objectives, and outcomes when providing instruction in the classroom. This text emphasizes using data to measure the impact of school counseling services and evaluate the students' outcomes aligned with the school counseling program.

The federal funding regulations in the Every Student Succeeds Act (ESSA) currently indicate that funds can be spent on hiring and supporting school counselors. As federal accountability measures shift, many states are supporting local control of funding decisions. In California, for instance, there has been a 30% improvement in student-to-counselor ratios over 5 years with the release of local control funding formulas (from 1,016 in 2010–2011 to 708 in 2015–2016). Now, more than ever, school counselors must be held accountable to show how their programs and services positively impact academic achievement, school climate, graduation, attendance, behavior, college going, parent and student engagement, and so on. This text provides examples of how to measure results in all areas within Tier 1. Readers can assess their growth and progress relative to these outcomes by utilizing the multiple assessment tools presented throughout the text, including applied activities, check-for-understanding tools, and reader self-assessments. Finally, readers will learn to use data for program improvement as they share results and recommendations with faculty and other stakeholders.

Hatching Results for Secondary School Counseling: Implementing Core Curriculum, Individual Student Planning, and Other Tier One Activities includes a variety of pedagogical formats, including vignettes from practicing school counselors, templates and samples for developing lesson plans, action plans, PowerPoint slides, pre- and post-assessments, and Flashlight Results along with sample individual learning plans, case studies with processing questions, and a variety of graphs and other ways to present school counseling program data. Additional resources are available in the online appendix.

online resources

The text will prepare readers in the following areas:

ATTITUDES

- *Believe* all students deserve to receive school counseling core curriculum (classroom lessons).
- *Believe* each and every student deserves an Individual Learning Plan (4-year plan).
- *Believe* in the importance of secondary school counselors taking an active role in core curriculum implementation, individual student planning, and schoolwide programs and activities.
- *Believe* in the importance of developing schoolwide school counseling core curriculum action plans.

- *Believe* in the importance of including families in prevention education to support their children.
- *Feel* confident and competent as they deliver school counseling core curriculum lessons, implement schoolwide programs and activities, and support students in developing their Individual Learning Plans.
- *Believe* secondary school counselors must assess the impact of their lessons.

KNOWLEDGE

- *Understand* the secondary school counselor's role in MTSS.
- *Describe* the components of an Individual Learning Plan.
- *Explain* appropriate ways to garner staff input on school counseling core curriculum.
- *Differentiate* among the different types and uses of data as they pertain to core curriculum.
- *Understand* a wide range of student engagement and classroom management strategies.

SKILLS

- *Locate, compare,* and *select* an appropriate core curriculum and individual student planning framework for a school/district.
- *Write* high-quality lesson plans with measurable objectives.
- *Develop* high-quality Individual Learning Plans.
- *Create* a school counseling core curriculum action plan for a school/district and align it to the individual student planning process.
- *Create* pre/post-tests for assessing students' attitudes, knowledge, and skills.
- *Align* the Individual Student Planning process to student outcomes.
- *Implement* appropriate student engagement and classroom management strategies.
- *Share* results from the school counseling core curriculum.

1

Multi-Tiered, Multi-Domain System of Supports

A Framework for Tier 1

> *Angela is a school counselor in a district that recently adopted the Multi-Tiered System of Supports (MTSS) as their framework for ensuring that students receive appropriate services aligned to their needs. The district is gearing up with a marketing strategy, resources, and tons of professional development for administrators, teachers, support staff, and even students and families. Angela has heard of MTSS before and has a general idea about what it is but wonders about her role as school counselor in this framework.*

This text is designed to guide the school counselor in developing, implementing, evaluating, and improving Tier 1 core curriculum, individual student planning, and schoolwide programs and activities within the Multi-Tiered System of Supports (MTSS). As we begin, it will be helpful to provide an overall contextual framework regarding MTSS and introduce the new Multi-Tiered, *Multi-Domain* System of Supports (MTMDSS) that aligns with the role of the school counselor at any grade level and the American School Counselor Association (ASCA) National Model (ASCA, 2012).

AN INTRODUCTION TO MTSS IN EDUCATION

The Multi-Tiered System of Supports (MTSS) is a comprehensive framework that addresses the *academic and behavioral* needs of all students within the educational system (Cowan, Vaillancourt, Rossen, & Pollitt, 2013; Hawken, Vincent, & Schumann, 2008). Research shows that schools benefit from multiple evidence-based interventions of varying intensity to meet the range of behavioral, social-emotional, and academic needs of all students (Anderson & Borgmeier, 2010). Combining Response to Intervention (RTI) and Positive Behavior Intervention and Supports (PBIS), MTSS is a tiered systems approach of increasingly intensive interventions. Like RTI, MTSS facilitates effective universal implementation that focuses on core academic and differentiated interventions to support the academic success of all students. Similar to PBIS, MTSS is a problem-solving model that employs a continuum of positive, proactive, multi-tiered behavioral interventions (Kennelly & Monrad, 2007). (See Figures 1.1 and 1.2 for illustrations of the RTI, and PBIS and MTSS models.)

Within the MTSS framework utilized in general education programs, MTSS Tier 1 is the foundation for both academic and behavioral systems of support. Tier 1 contains universal support and core instruction that *all* students receive from their classroom teacher. For example, all students receive world history education in high school. Similarly, school counselors can ensure all students participate in universal instruction on FAFSA completion in high school as well. Preventative in nature, Tier 1 curriculum, student planning, and schoolwide programs and activities are implemented with the entire student population. Typically, general education teachers proactively differentiate (modify or adapt) their instructional practices to support students' specialized needs, providing a more challenging or more supportive learning environment as necessary. Tier 2 within MTSS is comprised of supplemental interventions in addition to Tier 1 core instruction for students identified through the use of data indicators as needing additional supports, such as small-group practice and skill building. Teachers and others collaborate to determine the data-driven identifiers that will serve as the mechanism for the students to receive a Tier 2–level intervention (e.g., scoring less than proficient on a benchmark assessment). Tier 3 addresses the students with the highest level of need, providing supports of a greater intensity specifically tailored to meet the needs of individual students (Illinois State Board of Education, 2010).

Students who are not responsive to the Tier 1 supports may receive a Tier 2 intervention. These students continue to receive the Tier 1 intervention, but more structure and guidance are provided to assist them in meeting schoolwide expectations. Students receiving Tier 2 supports typically exhibit behavior that is not dangerous to themselves or others but is disruptive to their learning or the learning of their peers. Tier 2 interventions are implemented similarly across groups of students who exhibit comparable behavior problems and are therefore likely to benefit from the same type of intervention. For example, students who exhibit deficits in social competence (e.g., conflict resolution skills) might participate in a skills group in which all students in the group receive the same level and intensity of instruction as well as similar feedback on their behavior (Anderson & Borgmeier, 2010).

Figure 1.1 Traditional Tiered Educational Models: RTI and PBIS

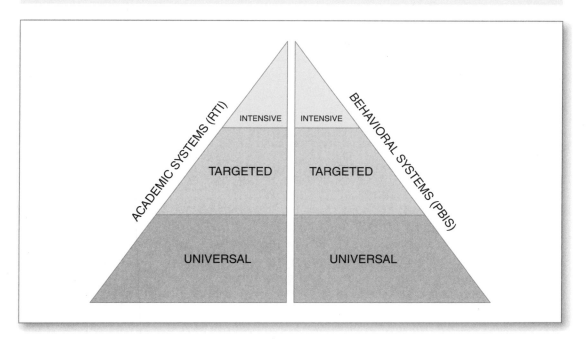

Figure 1.2 Traditional Tiered Educational Models: MTSS

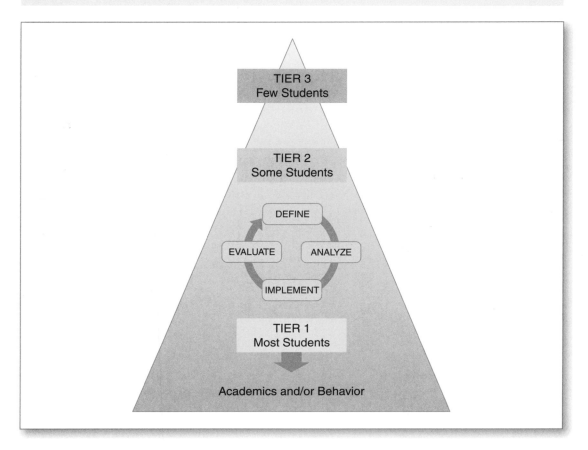

CONNECTING MTSS TO SCHOOL COUNSELING: MTMDSS

ASCA calls on school counselors to assist in the academic and behavioral development of students through the implementation of a comprehensive developmental school counseling program based on the ASCA National Model in the following ways:

- Providing all students with a standards-based school counseling core curriculum to address universal academic, career, and social/emotional development
- Analyzing academic, career, and social/emotional development data to identify struggling students
- Identifying and collaborating on research-based intervention strategies implemented by school staff
- Evaluating academic and behavioral progress after interventions
- Revising interventions as appropriate
- Referring students to school and community services as appropriate
- Collaborating with administrators, other school professionals, community agencies, and families in the design and implementation of MTSS
- Advocating for equitable education for all students and working to remove systemic barriers (ASCA, 2018a)

While MTSS is focused on *two* areas (academic and behavioral), school counselors focus on *three* domains: 1) academic, 2) college/career, and 3) social/emotional development. To align with the work of the school counselor, the MTMDSS (see Figure 1.3) was designed to align with MTSS as a decision-making framework that utilizes evidence-based practices in core instruction and assessments to address the universal and targeted (data-driven) intervention needs of *all* students in *all* school counseling domains. Note that for purposes of this text, from this point forward, we will simply refer to the three school counseling domains of academic, college/career, and social/emotional development as the three domains.

School counseling programs are an integral part of the total educational program for student success. The entire school community is invested in student academic achievement, college and career readiness, and social/emotional well-being. Schoolwide proactive, preventative, and data-driven intervention services and activities belong to the entire school. Therefore, it is recommended that schools *add the third domain* (college and career readiness) to their MTSS program and create a comprehensive, schoolwide MTMDSS.

MULTI-TIERED, MULTI-DOMAIN SYSTEM OF SUPPORTS (MTMDSS)

The MTMDSS is a framework (see Figure 1.3) designed specifically for school counseling programs to organize a continuum of core activities, instruction, and interventions to meet students' needs with the goals of 1) ensuring that all students receive

Figure 1.3   Multi-Tiered, Multi-Domain System of Supports (MTMDSS)

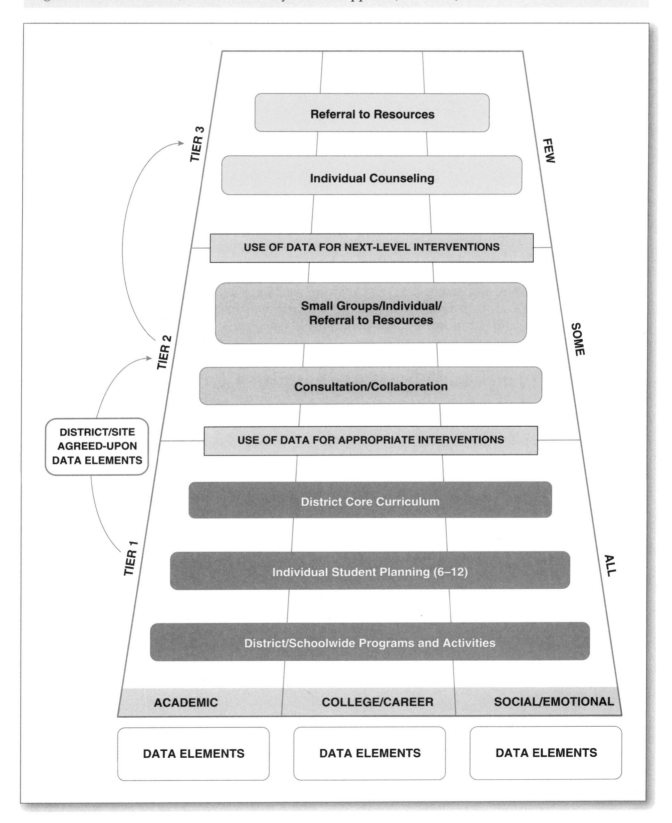

developmentally appropriate core instruction in all three domains; 2) increasing the academic, social/emotional, and college/career competencies of all students; 3) ensuring guaranteed interventions for students demonstrating a data-driven need; and 4) maximizing student achievement. The MTMDSS model organizes school intervention services into three levels, or tiers.

Tier 1: Core Program (Universal Supports) (100%)—For All Students

The core program is comprised of the delivery of services that *all students* receive (curriculum, individual student planning, and schoolwide programs and activities). A standards- and competency-based school counseling *core curriculum* (formerly called "guidance curriculum") is developmental in nature, preventative and proactive in design, and comprehensive in scope. *Individual student planning* includes a comprehensive approach to ensuring all students receive 4- and/or 6-year college/career planning and career readiness (generally for Grades 6–12). *Schoolwide programs and activities* for all students, such as national awareness, pride, or celebration campaigns; postsecondary exploration and planning events; activities designed to promote a positive and inclusive culture and climate; and family education programs, are provided to all students and/or families, aligned with classroom lesson content and standards, and support the core program.

Tier 2: Targeted Interventions (20%)—For Some Students

Similar to what general education teachers do when designing Tier 2 interventions, targeted data-driven interventions (small-group counseling/instruction, referral to interventions on campus, etc.) are designed for students who are identified by prescheduled and predetermined data-screening elements. At the elementary level, these include, for example, attendance rates, behavior infractions, and work skills/study habits (report card marks). In Grades 6–12, these might also include course failures or credit deficiencies in the academic domain. In the college and career domain, data elements may be related to ensuring subgroups are provided additional resources to ensure college and career readiness, or activities to address equity and access issues. Tier 2 interventions include *short-term* progress monitoring and collaboration among teachers, parents/guardians, and the school counselor until improvement and/or referral to appropriate services can be identified and implemented. Tier 2 activities are also designed for students who 1) exhibit barriers to learning; 2) are struggling to achieve academic success; and/or 3) are identified as deserving of instruction and/or supports in addition to Tier 1 curriculum activities (foster youth, dual-language learners, etc.).

Tier 3: Intensive Interventions (5–10%)—For a Few Students

Individualized student interventions (e.g., one-on-one counseling or advisement) are designed for students to address emergency and crisis-response events. In the social/emotional domain, these include short-term, solution-focused counseling sessions to address life-changing events (divorce, death, imprisonment of a parent, etc.) or unresolved challenges unaffected within Tier 1 and Tier 2. In the academic domain at the secondary level, these may also include students who enroll severely credit deficient and are in need of advisement to appropriate alternative educational resources. In the college/career domain, these may include students who are at risk of losing a scholarship or admissions due to unforeseen circumstances. These types of crisis response sessions are typically provided on a limited basis and, if issues are unresolved, lead to referrals to outside resources. Tier 3 interventions include *short-term* consultation and collaboration among teachers, families, administrators, outside agencies or resources, and the school counselor until the crisis is resolved and/or referral to appropriate responsive services can be identified and implemented. Figure 1.4 on the next page provides an example of an MTMDSS for the secondary school level.

MTMDSS ALIGNMENT TO TEXT

The purpose of this text is to provide thorough instruction on the activities that secondary school counselors provide within Tier 1. Throughout this text, we will dive deeply into planning, implementing, evaluating, and improving Tier 1 activities, those provided to *all* students "because they breathe." These include school counselor core curriculum classroom lessons at all grade levels, focusing on developmentally appropriate and needs-based topics.

Tier 1 at the secondary level also includes individual student planning and schoolwide programs and activities that are provided and coordinated systematically throughout the entire school. These include, for example, restorative practices, College Signing Day, FAFSA Challenges, Suicide Prevention Week, social media/anti-bullying campaigns, and Individual Learning Plans as well as family education, school transition supports, and others.

Tier 1 instructional content is developmentally appropriate and standards based, similar to the curriculum provided by teachers. Rather than conducting "random acts" of Tier 1 lessons and activities, school counselors assess the developmental and data-driven needs of the school and create schoolwide action plans. School counseling activities within the three domains (academic, college/career, and social/emotional) are calendared prior to the start of the year (see Chapter 11). The previous year's data may be used to identify schoolwide and grade-specific needs. The calendar is then shared with faculty, families, and other stakeholders.

Figure 1.4   Multi-Tiered, Multi-Domain System of Supports (MTMDSS) Secondary Example

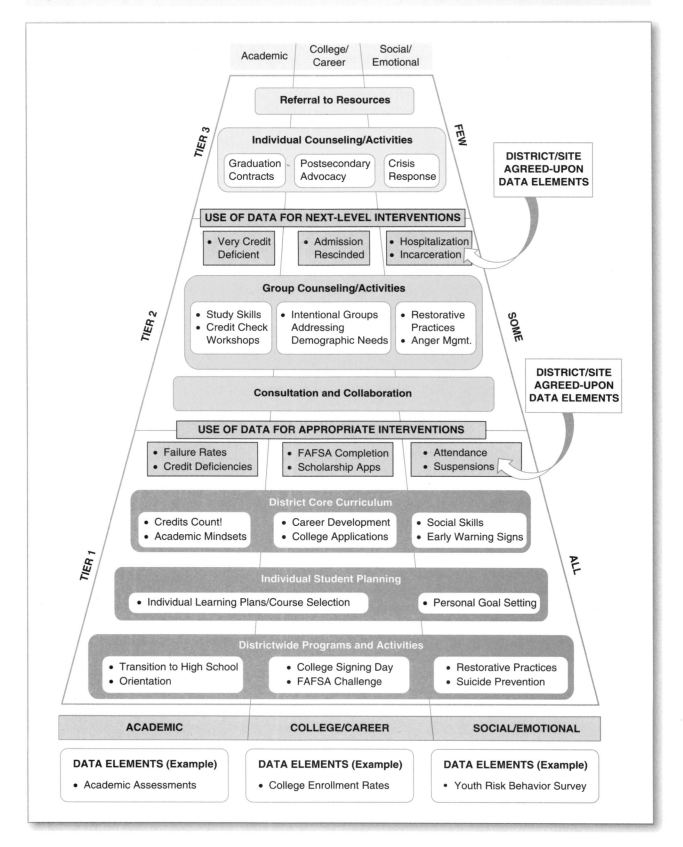

ALIGNING MTMDSS WITH THE ASCA NATIONAL MODEL

Figure 1.5   ASCA National Model Diamond

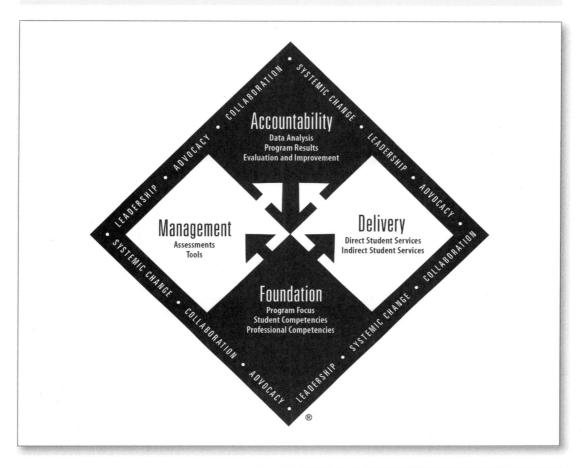

Source: American School Counselor Association (ASCA). (2012). *ASCA national model: A framework for school counseling programs* (3rd ed.). Alexandria, VA: Author.

Note: The ASCA National Model diamond used in this graphic represents the ASCA National Model, third edition. Readers are advised that the American School Counselor Association is revising the ASCA National Model, to be released June 2019, and are strongly encouraged to research and utilize the new version. The ASCA National Model is trademarked by the American School Counselor Association and reprinted with permission.

Activities in the MTMDSS fall within several components of the ASCA National Model (3rd edition), with a recommendation that 80% of time be spent on direct and indirect student services. Previous versions of the ASCA National Model suggested that school counselors spend between 15% and 45% of their time on guidance curriculum (now called core curriculum classroom lessons), depending on their level. Elementary school counselors typically teach more lessons (35–45%), whereas middle and high school counselors teach fewer (15–35%). Although the newest edition of the ASCA National Model has removed specific recommendations for time within each direct delivery method (see Figure 1.6), the authors still encourage school counselors to consider the 15–35% time frame as a guide when first beginning to design and implement their programs (ASCA, 2012, p. 136), but they do not give this as a prescription.

Providing a strong prevention-oriented framework is key to teaching students foundational and developmentally appropriate skills, such as treating others with respect, learning organizational and study strategies, understanding the college readiness and application process, resolving minor conflicts, and beginning career exploration. Devoting significant time to teaching classroom lessons, facilitating individual student planning, and coordinating schoolwide programs and activities within the Tier 1 framework provide a strong foundation of evidence-based prevention education programs and services that students need to succeed, which reduces the likelihood of students qualifying for Tier 2 and 3 interventions.

Figure 1.6   ASCA National Model Suggested Use of Time

	Delivery System Component	Elementary School % of Time	Middle School % of Time	High School % of Time	ASCA Recommendation
Direct Services	Core Curriculum **(Tier 1)**	35%	30%	20%	
	Individual Student Planning **(Can be Tier 1/2/3)**	5%	15%	25%	
	Responsive Services **(Can be Tier 1/2/3)**	25%	20%	20%	80% or more
Indirect Services	Referrals, Consultation, Collaboration **(Can be Tier 1/2/3)**	20%	20%	20%	
	System Support **(Can support Tiers 1/2/3)**	15%	15%	15%	20% or less

Source: Adapted from Gysbers & Henderson (2000).

ALIGNING MTMDSS WITH THE ASCA POSITION STATEMENTS

The *School Counselor and Multitiered System of Supports* position statement was adopted in 2008 and revised in 2014 and 2018 by ASCA (see Figure 1.7). It calls on school counselors to be stakeholders in developing and implementing an MTSS that includes but is not limited to RTI and behavioral interventions and supports such as PBIS. According to the position statement, the school counselor's role is to provide *all* students with a standards-based school counseling core curriculum to address universal academic, college/career, and social/emotional development. As school counselors align their work with MTSS and comprehensive school counseling programs designed to improve student achievement and behavior, the MTMDSS model in this text adds the third domain of college and career readiness to MTSS, which typically addresses only academics and behavior. Ensuring an informed, intentional approach to the student core curriculum in all three domains at the Tier 1 level is important, along with helping students with challenges by providing Tier 2 and 3 interventions. In 2018, the position statement was updated to reference the *Hatching Results for Elementary School Counselors* text as well as the Hatching Results video at our website (www.hatching results.com/videos) aligning the role of the school counselor at any grade level across multiple domains (academic, college/career, and social/emotional).

online resources

Figure 1.7   ASCA Position Statement

The School Counselor and Multitiered System of Supports
(Adopted 2008, revised 2014, 2018)

American School Counselor Association (ASCA) Position
School counselors are stakeholders in the development and implementation of a Multitiered System of Supports (MTSS), including but not limited to response to intervention (RTI) and responsive positive behavioral interventions and supports (PBIS). School counselors align their work with MTSS through the implementation of a comprehensive school counseling program designed to affect student development in the academic domain (achievement), the career domain (career exploration and development) and the social/emotional domain (behavior).

The Rationale
MTSS is a culturally responsive, evidence-based framework implemented in K–12 schools using data-based problem solving to integrate academic and behavioral instruction and intervention at tiered intensities to improve the learning and social/emotional functioning of all students (Sink, 2016). Guided by student-centered data, MTSS teams engage in cyclical data-based problem solving; make informed decisions about general, compensatory and special education; and assist in the creation of a well-integrated and seamless system of instruction and intervention (Ehren, Montgomery, Rudebush, & Whitmire, 2006).

Within the framework of a data-driven, comprehensive school counseling program school counselors augment their collaboration, coordination and leadership skills (Shepard et al., 2013) to meet the needs of all students and identify students who are at risk for not meeting academic and behavioral expectations. School counselors collaborate across student service disciplines with teachers, administrators and families to design and implement plans to address student needs and to promote students' academic, career social/emotional success (American School Counselor Association [ASCA], 2012). Data are collected and analyzed to determine the effectiveness of the learning supports for continual improvement efforts over time.

MTSS offers school counselors opportunities to have a lasting impact on student academic success and behavior development while integrating the framework within a comprehensive school counseling program (Ziomek-Daigle, Goodman-Scott & Donohue, 2016). The application of MTSS aligns with the role of school counseling at any grade level and can be used across multiple domains (Hatch, 2018; Hatch, Duarte, & Degregorio, 2017), such as academic, college/career and/or social/emotional development, based on the ASCA National Model.

The School Counselor's Role
The ASCA National Model serves as the foundation that assists school counselors in the academic, career and social/emotional development of students through the implementation of a comprehensive developmental school counseling program by:
  • Providing all students with a standards-based school counseling core curriculum to address universal academic, career and social/emotional development
  • Analyzing academic, career and social/emotional development data to identify struggling students
  • Identifying and collaborating on research-based intervention strategies implemented by school staff
  • Evaluating academic and behavioral progress after interventions
  • Revising interventions as appropriate
  • Referring to school and community services as appropriate
  • Collaborating with administrators, other school professionals, community agencies and families in the design and implementation of MTSS
  • Advocating for equitable education for all students and working to remove systemic barriers

Where MTSS interacts with school counseling programs the school counselor can serve in roles of supporter and/or intervener (Ockerman, Mason, & Feiker-Hollenbeck, 2012). In the supporting role, the school counselor may provide indirect student service by presenting data or serving as a consultant to a student support team. In intervener role, the school counselor may provide direct student service through the delivery component of the ASCA National Model.

(Continued)

Figure 1.7 (Continued)

Summary

School counselors implement a comprehensive school counseling program addressing the needs of all students. Through the review of data, school counselors identify struggling students and collaborate with other student services professionals, educators and families to provide appropriate instruction and learning supports within an MTSS. School counselors work collaboratively with other educators to remove systemic barriers for all students and implement specific learning supports that assist in academic and behavioral success.

References

American School Counselor Association. (2012). *The ASCA National Model: A framework for school counseling programs.* (3rd Ed). Alexandria, VA: Author.

Ehren, B., Montgomery, J., Rudebusch, J., & Whitmire, K. (2006). *New roles in response to intervention: Creating success for schools and children.* Retrieved from https://www.asha.org/uploadedFiles/slp/schools/prof-consult/rtiroledefinitions.pdf

Hatch, T. (2018) Multi-tiered, multi-domain system of supports (MTMDSS) video https://www.hatchingresults.com/videos/

Hatch, T., Duarte, D., & DeGregorio, L. (2017). Hatching results for elementary school counseling: Implementing core Curriculum and Other Tier One Activities. Thousand Oaks, CA: Corwin/Sage.

Ockerman, M.S., Mason, E.C., & Feiker-Hollenbeck, A. (2012) Integrating RTI with school counseling programs: Being a proactive professional school counselor. *Journal of School Counseling 10*(15).

Shepard, J.M., Shahidullah, J.D., & Carlson, J.S. (2013). Counseling Students in Levels 2 and 3: A PBIS/RTI Guide. Thousand Oaks, CA: Corwin/Sage

Sink, C. (2016). Incorporating a multi-tiered system of supports into school counselor preparation. Retrieved from http://tpcjournal.nbcc.org/wp-content/uploads/2016/09/Pages203-219-Sink.pdf

Ziomek-Daigle, J., Goodman-Scott, E., Cavin, J., & Donohue, P. (2016). Integrating a multi-tiered system of supports with comprehensive school counseling program. http://tpcjournal.nbcc.org/integrating-a-multi-tiered-system-of-supports-with-comprehensive-school-counseling-programs/

Resources

Hatch, T. (2018). Multi-tiered, multi-domain system of supports. https://www.hatchingresults.com/blog/2017/3/multi-tiered-multi-domain-system-of-supports-by-trish-hatch-phd

McIntosh,K. & Goodman, S. (2016). Integrated Multi-Tiered Systems of Support: Blending RTI and PBIS. Guilford Press.

Source: Reprinted with permission from the American School Counselor Association, 2019.

MTMDSS aligns with the framework of a comprehensive, data-driven school counseling program to meet the needs of all students and to identify students who are at risk. School counselors collaborate with stakeholders and collect and analyze data to determine the effectiveness of the learning supports. More information on ASCA position statements can be found here: www.schoolcounselor.org/school-counselors-members/about-asca-(1)/position-statements.

ALIGNING MTMDSS WITH THE ASCA ETHICAL STANDARDS

The purpose of the *ASCA Ethical Standards for School Counselors* (ASCA, 2016) document is to guide the ethical practices of school counselors. Guidelines that align with Tier 1 in the MTMDSS model include the following:

A.3. Comprehensive Data-Informed Program

School counselors:

a. Provide students with a comprehensive school counseling program that ensures equitable academic, career, and social/emotional development opportunities for all students (ASCA, 2016, p. 3).

A.4. Academic, Career, and Social/Emotional Plans

b. Provide and advocate for individual students' PreK–postsecondary college and career awareness, exploration, and postsecondary planning and decision-making, which supports the students' right to choose from the wide array of options when students complete secondary education.

d. Provide opportunities for all students to develop the mindsets and behaviors necessary to learn work-related skills, resilience, perseverance, an understanding of lifelong learning as a part of long-term career success, and a positive attitude toward learning and a strong work ethic (ASCA, 2016, p. 3).

Activity 1.1

Review the ASCA ethical standards with your administrator. Discuss how a comprehensive school counseling program provides tiered supports to meet the needs of all students. The ASCA ethical guidelines document can be found on the ASCA website: www.schoolcounselor.org/asca/media/asca/Ethics/EthicalStandards2016.pdf.

Dr. Carolyn Stone, ASCA Ethics Chair, Answering Ethical Dilemmas About Core Curriculum

Question from a School Counselor:

My principal has asked me to teach a 9th grade life skills class two periods a day as a way to provide counseling curriculum to students. All 9th graders would rotate through the class during different quarters throughout the year. I would be the teacher on record (even though I don't have a teaching credential) and would also have to assign grades. Is that permitted? Does that create a dual relationship? How do I respond to my principal?

Dr. Stone's Answer:

It is not uncommon to hear about school counselors being asked to serve in incongruous roles that stratify their effectiveness such as the recent inquiry to the American School Counselor Association's (ASCA) Ethics Chair in which a school counselor was being asked to act as both principal and school counselor. The more common scenario is that school counselors teach part of the day. Sometimes the school counselor is not even dually certified and out of field for one of the roles. These scenarios pose considerable problems of dual relationships that compromise both roles the school counselor is serving, confuse students, and dent the school counseling program and counselor's effectiveness.

I view this scenario as problematic, but on the positive side the course content is far less troublesome than the curriculum dual role counselors are being required to deliver. The problem is not the content of the curriculum but the structure. The content and recipients of the curriculum are a plus. Ninth grade is a critical year for graduation prediction. Students who finish freshman year with an F grade point average have only an 18% chance to graduate from high school on time; those with a D grade point average have about a 60% chance of graduating on time. Nearly all of their peers earning C through A grade point averages, on the other hand, will graduate in 4 years (Easton, Johnson, & Sartain, 2017). One of the barriers school counselors often express is access to classrooms for core curriculum delivery. The structure of this class provides an opportunity to work with the group most at risk for dropping out. Student motivation is enhanced when the school counselor closes the information gap and helps these 9th graders understand the interrelatedness between what they are doing now and their future economic opportunities and job satisfaction. Structure for classroom curriculum in which we can meet the needs of 100% of our students is a win, but the downside of this scenario is real and troublesome. It is not the curriculum but the shifting of the role between teacher and counselor and all that comes with a teaching role that causes this scenario on balance to be inappropriate.

When tied to a fixed schedule, the counselor is no longer able to respond to the unpredictable nature of a school counselor's day, eliminating or delaying the chance to engage in timely responses for students needing immediate support. If it is reported that a student is suicidal and skipping class, the school counselor does not have two hours to wait to notify parents so the student can be found and helped. A child has been sexually abused and her friends have given her the courage to come to talk to the counselor; two hours is too long to make that connection. Yes, we are often pulled in many different directions and may not be available immediately, but a consistent daily removal of two hours that can never be flexed is too much.

Discipline and classroom management are always part of delivering the school counselor's core curriculum, but discipline takes on a different nature when the "teacher" counselor is present daily in a classroom. The shifting of roles is further exacerbated because the counselor is put in the role of evaluating students: a role likely to supersede and overshadow in students' minds the counselor's primary role of student advocate and purveyor of unconditional positive regard.

What should be said to the principal? If possible, negotiate out of the role of teacher for this or any class. You might stress the obstructive nature this will cause to your primary role, but a better approach might be to cite case law. If you are not a certified teacher, stress that liability to the district goes up when something happens in a classroom manned by an uncertified teacher. There are many solid arguments against this teaching assignment, but using case law will be heard by administrators as a more authentic argument and not self-serving. Failing this approach, advocate for delivery of core curriculum with a different structure in which at least half of the quarter a teacher covers the regular life skills curriculum, grades this portion, and assigns the report card grade, and therefore, you do not have to grade. This approach is unlikely, as if they had a life skills teacher, they would put the teacher in full time, but there may be a way to trade off classes or courses to make such a schedule work. If in line with school board policy, make the course pass/fail, with failure tied to objective measures such as absences. The point would be to try to strike some compromise in which the counselor is not having to evaluate student performance for a report card grade. If all efforts to compromise are futile, use the course to help raise student knowledge and motivation for postsecondary success.

Table 1.1 Myths versus Facts About School Counselors' Role in a Multi-Tiered, Multi-Domain System of Supports

Myth	Fact	Learn More
School counselors only provide Tier 2 and 3 supports	School counselors provide all students with a standards-based school counseling core curriculum to address universal academic, college/career, and personal/social/emotional development	ASCA position statement about the school counselor in MTSS: http://bit .ly/2n3ouaY
School counselors provide Tier 3 individual counseling to all students	Tier 3 consists of short-term, highly structured interventions and wraparound services defined as "intensive, individual interventions for students at high risk"	ASCA position statement about the school counselor in MTSS: http://bit .ly/2n3ouaY
School counselors provide supports in only one domain (i.e., social/emotional or college/career)	Today's school counselors are vital members of the education team, helping all students in the areas of academic achievement, social/emotional development, and college/career readiness	ASCA executive summary: http://bit .ly/2fZJNqO
Most of the school counselor's time is spent on Tier 2 and 3 supports	The greatest amount of the school counselor's time should be spent on implementing Tier 1 with a high degree of integrity, which is the most efficient means for serving the greatest number of students	"Integrating RTI with School Counseling Programs: Being a Proactive Professional School Counselor," by Ockerman, Mason, and Hollenbeck (2012) Researchers indicate that around 75% to 80% of children should be expected to reach successful levels of competency through Tier 1 delivery (Shapiro, n.d.) "Spending 90% of the school counselor's time with 10% of the students is not the philosophy of intentional guidance." (Hatch, 2013)

Source: Triplett, W. (2017). *Utilizing a multi-tiered system to implement your school counseling program* [PowerPoint slides]. Created for Chicago Public Schools.

Babies in the River

"Babies in the River" is a wonderful parable often told to illustrate the difference between prevention and intervention. Co-author Trish adapted this version from Pat Martin, a dear friend and colleague.

On a spring afternoon, after the students had left at the end of a minimum day, a group of high school counselors walked to a nearby park area next to a river to eat lunch together for the first time all year. Considering that they rarely even ate lunch at all, this was a treasured event. After a few minutes of talking and eating, Mariana (the school counselor with alphabet A–Hi) noticed a baby floating down the river. Alarmed, she jumped up to assess the situation. As she did, she noticed several babies floating. She screamed for her colleagues to help, and for the next 20 minutes, they retrieved dozens of babies out of the river, until finally the babies stopped floating by. Exhausted, Mariana returned to her picnic and realized that Bob (the school counselor with alphabet Mx–Sm) was missing. Where was Bob? He hadn't been helping rescue the babies? Pretty soon Bob was heard whistling down the walkway. The rest of the group inquired, "Where were you? We were busy retrieving babies, and you were nowhere to be found!"

"Well," he commented, "I decided to go up the river to see how they were getting in! Turns out someone, in their wisdom, decided to build a nursery/preschool next to the river! I noticed that the door had a broken lock, so first I fixed that. Then I realized that the babies didn't know how to swim, so I taught them. Then I learned that the teachers had no floaties, so I bought floaties and put them near the exit so that if any babies fall in again, they can throw a floaty in the water for the babies to assist themselves. Finally, I filed a complaint with the city to ensure that no one ever builds a nursery or preschool within a mile of a river again!"

Although the prevention approach is almost always the most appealing, it can be difficult for counselors if they think that shifting to prevention education means turning their back on those students currently in need. It is also not always obvious how to work within the system to redesign how it functions—to build it differently and to partner to train those on the front lines and assist them in understanding how to provide first-level interventions and supports. But this is a requirement if school counselors are going to meet the needs of *all* students because there is not enough time to rescue every drowning student (hypothetically) and there are far too many in the caseload.

The bottom portion of the MTMDSS pyramid (see Figure 1.3) is the largest section and reflects the importance of prevention education. Just as in this story, school counselors can either fill their days with reactive services (i.e., rescuing the babies one after another), or they can get out in front of things and engage in proactive prevention (i.e., teaching the babies how to swim). When counselors spend 80% of their day mired in Tier 2 and 3 reactive services, they may feel like they are in an emergency room rather than a school, and they won't have time for teaching prevention education and for designing systems of support to catch students early. Without a strong prevention system in place, the need for responsive services will continue to grow. By implementing a strong Tier 1 program, complete with classroom lessons, individual student planning, and schoolwide programs and activities, students will gain the attitudes, knowledge, and skills necessary to prevent them from needing Tier 2 and 3 services, thereby reducing the time spent in these tiers.

Shifting school counselor program activities from being primarily responsive to being proactive takes commitment, planning, time, and cooperation from administration and faculty alike. As school counselors begin to shift the pyramid to focus more on Tier 1, consideration should be given to addressing the potential challenges of finding balance between the time spent in classrooms and the number of reactive services they previously provided. School counselors will benefit from scaffolding the transitions at their school site to a proactive approach by adding lessons to their Tier 1 action plans each year or by beginning with just one grade level and adding a grade level each year. In addition, when collaborating with teachers and administrators to gain support for Tier 1 classroom lessons and participating on leadership teams to create necessary systemic processes, school counselors will improve efficiency and effectiveness as they determine which students are referred for additional Tier 2 and 3 data-driven interventions.

For more information on the school counselor and MTMDSS, please refer to:

- Ockerman, M.S., Mason, E.C., & Feiker-Hollenbeck, A. (2012). Integrating RTI with school counseling programs: Being a proactive professional school counselor. *Journal of School Counseling, 10*(15).
- Patrikakou, E., Ockerman, M.S., & Hollenbeck, A. F. (2016). Needs and contradictions of a changing field: Evidence from a national response to intervention implementation study. *The Professional Counselor, 6*(3).
- Sink, C. A., & Ockerman, M. S. (2016). School counselors and a multi-tiered system of supports: Cultivating systemic change and equitable outcomes. *The Professional Counselor, 6*(3).
- Ziomek-Daigle, J., Goodman-Scott, E., Cavin, J., & Donohue, P. (2016). Integrating a multi-tiered system of supports with comprehensive school counseling programs. *The Professional Counselor, 6*(3).

NOTES

_____

_____

_____

_____

_____

_____

MULTI-TIERED, MULTI-DOMAIN SYSTEM OF SUPPORTS (MTMDSS) ASSESSMENT

Activity 1.2

Please review the MTMDSS diagram (Figure 1.3) regarding school counselor activities within an MTMDSS. Next, complete the blank MTMDSS (see Figure 1.8, also available online) by listing your current Tier 1, 2, and 3 activities, lessons, and interventions per each domain: academic, college/career, and social/emotional. Look for strengths and potential areas for growth.

Figure 1.8 Blank MTMDSS Diagram

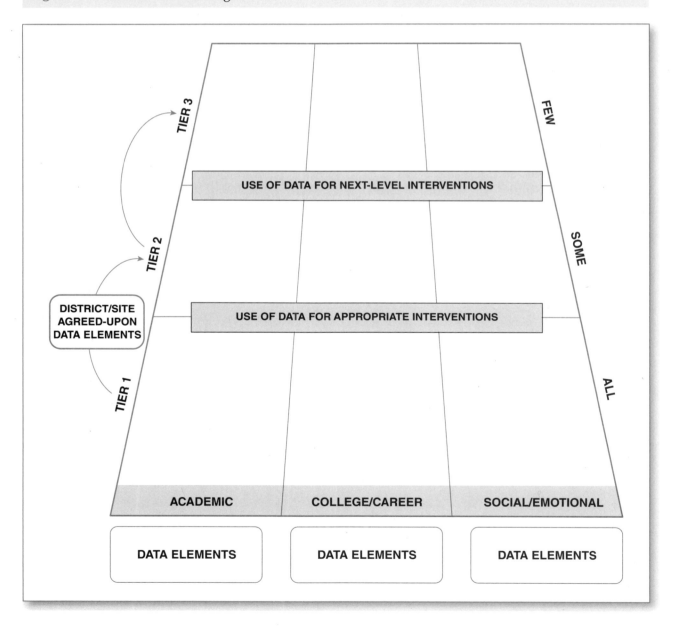

2

Franchising Core Curriculum

Figure 2.1   MTMDSS—Core Curriculum

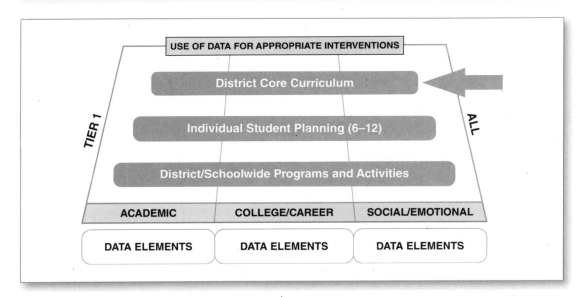

On a recent trip to Santorini, Greece, I saw what I thought would be the demise of the island: McDonald's (see Figure 2.2). How could they ruin my favorite city with a franchise? No one

(Continued)

(Continued)

Figure 2.2   Trish Sees the McDonald's Franchise in Greece

would eat there, or so I thought. Soon it was filled with customers from every country purchasing Big Macs, Chicken McNuggets, Filet-o-Fish, fries, chocolate shakes, and, yes, apple pie. Why would people come to Greece and order McDonald's? You guessed it—because they knew what they could count on. No matter where you go in the world, McDonald's has a guaranteed menu—it's part of the franchise requirements. In addition to the franchise menu, there are culturally appropriate items to satisfy local needs, such as pineapples and Spam on burgers in Hawaii, Ebi filet-o-shrimp burgers in Japan, taro-root pie in China, McCurry in India, and the dreaded McGyro in my beloved Santorini (I have not tried it—yet).

McDonald's is a franchise business. Private entrepreneurs purchase rights to open and run a location of the larger parent company and sign a contractual agreement to follow the company's rules for operation. When a franchisee signs the agreements, they agree to the terms of operating according to the franchisor's requirements, which are dictated by the parent company. The benefits of owning a franchise include the familiarity of the company name and image and training from the parent company on operating the franchise successfully. Failure rates among franchises tend to be lower than among other new businesses, largely because customers generally recognize the company name and know what to expect (Lorette, n.d.).

WHAT IS FRANCHISING?

In secondary school counseling, there is not currently a national "franchisable" core curriculum (see Figure 2.1) ready to purchase and implement (at the time of publication). There's nothing that parents can "count on" when they come into a middle or high school counseling office. School counseling standards and curricula often vary from state to state, district to district, site to site, and counselor to counselor. Some states have set up common expectations and provide sample curriculum recommendations, but most leave decisions about expectations for consistent delivery up to individual districts, schools, and counselors. Imagine if this happened at McDonald's. It would cease to be a franchise and would be more like a mom-and-pop hamburger shop, where prices and expectations of food quality and preparation vary from place to place. Although local control gives power to schools and districts to select the curriculum best suited for their students' needs, the fact that school counselors provide inconsistent curriculum in schools affects what the "customer"—in this case, students and families—can count on.

Alignment With the ASCA National Model

The purpose of this text is to provide thorough instruction on the activities that secondary school counselors provide within Tier 1, including core curriculum, individual student planning, and schoolwide programs and activities. Rather than conducting "random acts" of Tier 1 lessons and activities, school counselors assess the developmental and data-driven needs of the school and create schoolwide action plans within the three ASCA domains and aligned to school and district goals.

The ASCA position statement on the school counselor's role in MTSS states,

> The ASCA National Model serves as the foundation that assists school counselors in the academic, career and social/emotional development of students through the implementation of a comprehensive developmental school counseling program by . . . providing all students with a standards-based school counseling core curriculum to address universal academic, career and social/emotional development. (ASCA, 2018b)

Additionally, the ASCA Ethical Standard A.3.b. states that school counselors "provide students with a comprehensive school counseling program that ensures equitable academic, career and social/emotional development opportunities for all students" (ASCA, 2016). A.3.e. goes further: "School counselors ensure the school counseling program's goals and action plans are aligned with district's school improvement goals" (ASCA, 2016). However, aligning the school counseling program to the districtwide goals is just one step. Developing a "franchised" school counseling core curriculum ensures consistency across the district, provides a standard and developmentally appropriate scope and sequence, and better serves students who transfer across schools.

> An aligned curriculum is a coherent and consistent progression of content, instruction and assessment within and across a course of study. In an aligned system, common rigorous expectations for student learning in any one grade level are consistent across the district, grade level expectations build on the prior year's work and feed into the next year, and [educators] have the materials and training to teach the content to their students. (Seattle Public Schools, n.d.)

Indeed, curriculum for various subject areas are often "franchised" districtwide; so too can school counseling core curriculum be "franchised"!

WHAT CAN STUDENTS, FAMILIES, AND TEACHERS EXPECT (COUNT ON) FROM SCHOOL COUNSELING PROGRAMS?

The purpose of a Schoolwide Core Curriculum Action Plan is to ensure that every student gets every *thing*! By virtue of breathing, all students are guaranteed to receive instruction from the school counseling program, and all students get everything (i.e., the entire curriculum designed for their grade level). The Schoolwide Core Curriculum Action Plan, which is used when creating and presenting the school counseling core curriculum, is similar to a teacher's scope and sequence. Just as teachers collaborate to determine grade-level expectations, scope and sequence, and pacing charts for timely delivery of subject content, school counselors are called on to collaborate and create similar documents to ensure that all students are on target to receive common instruction from school counseling programs.

Just as a standardized curriculum exists for math, science, and English, a "franchisable" core curriculum is intended to provide a message of consistency regarding expectations for student learning among schools and across districts and states. Just as parents come to know that English 1 and world history will be taught to all freshmen, so too will they understand that the 9th grade school counseling lesson taught to all students in January contains content on understanding credits and what's required to graduate, learning to analyze Semester 1 transcripts and where to locate support if students are credit deficient. Teachers will meet regularly to agree on "essential standards" or "power standards" for each grade level; similarly, school counselors will collaborate with other secondary counselors in the district and share with site administrators to discuss and determine which content is most appropriate for students at each grade level. During planning, school counselors will take students' developmental levels into consideration, along with site-specific and data-driven needs in all three domains (academic, college/career, and social/emotional).

The 80/20 Approach

Ideally, approximately 80% of the curriculum should be created as franchisable, school to school, within a district (see Figure 2.3). When selecting the 80% franchisable curriculum topics that will be consistent school to school within a district, school counselors are encouraged to follow the same process of standards-based educational expectations as teachers do. Therefore, school counselors are encouraged to include a thorough review of the American School Counselor Association (ASCA) domains (academic, college/career, and social/emotional) and Mindsets & Behaviors for Student Success standards in creating developmentally appropriate scaffolding of attitudes, knowledge, and skills in the areas of academic, college/career, and social/emotional learning. When developing the school counseling franchisable curriculum districtwide, attention is paid to what every student needs to know at each grade level. Counselors create "skeleton" lessons that can be revised with the school's colors or mascot. Additionally, site-specific needs can be built into lesson planning. For example, if "learning strategies" is scheduled to be taught to all 9th grade students districtwide, a school counselor in a school that provides academic planners might incorporate additional lesson content on using planners in the curriculum or add an additional lesson (see what follows). Similarly, many districtwide curriculum action plans call for all students to receive classroom instruction from school counselors on requirements to graduate college ready and the course selection process. Districts creating generic lessons to be utilized by all high schools would want to provide space for schools with pathways (or other models) to replace or add additional content ensuring all of their students acquire the knowledge they need to make informed decisions on the pathway course selection process.

As mentioned, 80% of the core curriculum should be consistent school to school within the district. The subsequent 20% of the curriculum delivered is reserved for specific schoolwide curriculum based on local and/or school site needs. Note that on the MTMDSS High School Example in Chapter 1 (Figure 1.4) the words "Data Elements" are included in boxes at the bottom of the figure. These are provided to remind the school counselor to consider data elements when designing curriculum. In reviewing schoolwide data, a youth behavior risk survey may indicate a high percentage of students who report that they are experimenting with marijuana or other drugs. In this scenario, the school counselor may want to add lessons to address this data-driven need. Similarly, if discipline/suspension data indicate high levels of cyber-bullying or sexual harassment, it would be more efficient and effective to conduct curriculum in classes or grade levels with high numbers of offenders than it would be to remove students from class to conduct multiple group or individual interventions.

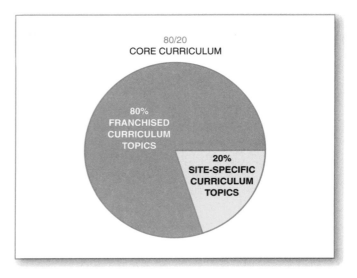

Figure 2.3   The 80/20 Approach

When Tier 2 or 3 Becomes Tier 1

Sometimes an overabundance of Tier 2 referrals suggests that a more efficient and effective way of addressing students' needs would be to add additional classroom lessons (or units) to the action plan. This may or may not be temporary, depending on your student population, but should always be based on school site data (as already described). There is no magic number or percentage that determines when a school counselor should stop seeing students in small groups and instead conduct additional classroom curriculum; this is a conversation best discussed among the team and ideally with school administration.

Systemic thinking could also be applied to 9th grade failure rates. Imagine, for example, that report cards indicate a high percentage of students in the 9th grade are failing two or more classes. A school counselor might be tempted to facilitate multiple, time-consuming, small counseling groups or individual sessions for these students. When Tier 2 or 3 interventions become all-encompassing, it may be time to consider a Tier 1 curricular or more schoolwide programmatic approach to address this systemic need for additional content on study habits, academic perseverance, and/or other academic mindsets and behaviors.

WHITNEY'S STORY

"Tier 1 Looks Different at My School"

When I was a newborn school counselor at a small but mighty high school on Chicago's west side ("One Team, One Family!"), I was excited to get into the classroom and teach Tier 1 lessons. Home to some of the best teachers I've ever met even to this day, I had great mentors to help me learn this new skill of teaching, having never taught in the classroom before. When determining what lessons to deliver, it was important to us to teach lessons that were developmental, preventative, and highly tailored to our student population's unique needs. I was often humbled by the resiliency, strength, grit, and perseverance of our students and their families, who commonly faced issues associated with poverty and systematic oppression, such as unemployment, gang violence, trauma, teen pregnancy, and a myriad of other challenges. I often heard folks say things like "all of our students need wraparound supports" or "we have all Tier 3 kids" (a common misnomer, as no student "is Tier 3" or otherwise—they may just need Tier 3 supports from time to time to be successful at school).

The reality is that Tier 1 at our school looked different from Tier 1 supports at schools in other parts of the city. Whereas about 80% of our school counseling core curriculum was pretty standard (i.e., how to read a transcript, building healthy relationships, managing stress, college match, etc.), about 20% of our curriculum was specific to our student population's needs, including growth mindset, safe sex, code-switching, self-advocacy, and grief and loss. Taking into account that our students often reported feeling unsafe walking to and from school, we implemented schoolwide programs, activities, and systems (discussed in Chapter 8), such as greater adult presence outside the school, bringing in self-defense instructors, and offering workshops on personal safety. When we learned that our school was situated in a zip code with one of the highest rates of HIV in the city, we brought in community agencies regularly to talk to our entire student body (and their families) about safe sex and provide free sexually transmitted infection testing and treatment. We implemented trauma-informed and restorative practices schoolwide to better meet the needs of our students.

When we talk about "franchising," it doesn't mean ignoring the unique needs of a particular school. The 80/20 approach beautifully describes an inclusive and culturally sensitive approach for meeting the developmental and/or data-driven needs of students. Whether we work at a school with students who are incarcerated, pregnant/parenting, working full time, diverse learners, high achieving, or who report higher levels of stress on a youth behavior risk survey, freshmen everywhere need to know how to calculate their GPAs. Seniors everywhere need to create a plan for after high school. These are developmental needs common to all teenagers. This is the "80%." The remainder—the "20%"—is where school counselors meet the unique needs of their school's population.

Don't Forget About Alternative Education! :)

It is important that school counselors collaborate *between and across levels* (elementary, middle, and secondary) to determine what Tier 1 core classroom lessons will be provided within the district. This helps ensure that core curriculum is developmental in design and scaffolded across grade levels, K–12. Because not all students attend traditional schools, it is important to remember to include school counselors from alternative education sites so that classroom lesson content is consistent across *all* school sites.

In San Jacinto Unified School District (SJUSD), school counselors at both the traditional and alternative schools collaborate across grade levels to develop and implement a districtwide "franchised" school counseling core curriculum. This ensures that all students in the district, even those enrolled at alternative education sites, receive consistent Tier 1 supports. What follows is the list of core classroom lessons

	Traditional Core Curriculum at SJUSD	Alternative Ed Core Curriculum at SJUSD
9th	Counselor Connection Bullying Prevention College & Career: Making It Happen 4-Year Plan Course Selection Naviance	- No Students Enrolled -
10th	Counselor Connection Early Warning Signs for Violence College & Career: Making It Happen 4-Year Plan Course Selection A–G Help Naviance	Meet the Counselor Early Warning Signs for Violence College & Career: Making It Happen 4-Year Plan Orientation/Transcript Review A–G Help Career Planning
11th	Counselor Connection College & Career: Making It Happen Course Selection A–G Help Mini Lessons PSAT/SAT Postsecondary Plan Scholarships	Meet the Counselor College & Career: Making It Happen Orientation/Transcript Review A–G Help Career Trends/Planning Mini Lessons PSAT/SAT Khan Academy Postsecondary Plan Scholarships

(Continued)

(Continued)

	Traditional Core Curriculum at SJUSD	Alternative Ed Core Curriculum at SJUSD
12th	Counselor Connection	Meet the Counselor
	College & Career: Making It Happen	College & Career: Making It Happen
	Course Selection	Orientation/Transcript Review
	A–G Help	A–G Help
	Mini Lessons	FAFSA Lesson
	PSAT/SAT	Mini Lessons
	Postsecondary Plan	PSAT/SAT
	Scholarships	Khan Academy
	FAFSA Link Lessons	Postsecondary Plan
		Scholarships

provided in SJUSD at both the traditional high schools and the alternative schools. Notice that the lessons topics are similar, although the grade level may vary due to the fact that there are no freshmen at the alternative sites.

Although the content is similar across school sites, the mode or time of delivery may differ in the alternative settings to best serve the unique needs of the students. Often, alternative education school counselors have to be creative in ensuring that classroom lessons occur. Justin Ryan, an innovative school counselor in SJUSD, serves two alternative schools—Mt. View High and Mt. Heights Academy (an Independent Studies Program). Mr. Ryan wanted to ensure that his Independent Studies students had access to the school counseling program, so he created online counselor lessons using Power Schools to reach his goal, such as his "Meet the School Counselor" lesson (https://youtu.be/3043f373ULw). This video provides an overview of the school counseling services and provides a flexible way to ensure that *all* students—even those who are not regularly on campus—have an understanding of the school counseling program. He also schedules in-person lessons during the time frame that the Independent Studies students are on campus.

Schoolwide Core Curriculum Action Plans

The ASCA National Model: A Framework for School Counseling Programs (ASCA, 2012) presents the use of three types of action plans, one of which is the School Counseling Core Curriculum Action Plan. Schoolwide Core Curriculum Action Plans are standards driven and ensure that every student gets every *thing* (again, the whole curriculum designed for his or her grade level). What content will every student receive because they came through the front door? What can we tell each parent and student that each student will receive from the school counseling program as a 7th, 9th, 11th, or 12th grader?

Developmental in design, preventative in nature, and comprehensive in scope, the Schoolwide Core Curriculum Action Plan guarantees that families, students, teachers, and other stakeholders know exactly what curriculum students will receive and at what time throughout the year. The curriculum, much like math or science, is competency driven, created by school counselors and student service professionals to address the standards and competencies (ASCA, 2014). The school counselors, in collaboration with site administrators (or, in some cases, district coordinators), determine what content will be covered in each lesson and align it with standards. School counselors create an action plan, calendar these lessons, and collect process, perception, and outcome data. Lessons are either selected or designed by school counselors to become consistent (or franchisable) from school to school to ensure that when students transfer within a district, they will receive the same curriculum from the school counseling program. For example, just as all 9th graders take physical education, so too are all 11th grade students taught a proactive lesson on filling out the FAFSA.

Although different districts approach the development of the core curriculum differently, collaboration is key. Within one school district, the junior high school counselors may choose to use the pre-developed Second Step Middle School Program and design additional lessons that align with the academic and college/career domains. In another district, the entire curriculum may be self-generated by the school counselors. At the high school level most, if not the entire curriculum, is school counselor generated. In either case, school counselors within a district work collaboratively to ensure consistency in the lesson content that they develop and deliver.

The table that follows provides an example of a Schoolwide Core Curriculum Action Plan indicating the specific curriculum that every student in the district will receive from the school counseling program in secondary school (in this school these are Grades 6–12). Care is also taken to ensure that all three school counseling domains are addressed, with attention to a minimum number of agreed-upon lessons for each grade level.

Guidelines for Creating Schoolwide Core Curriculum Action Plans

Schoolwide Core Curriculum Action Plans contain:

1. Grade(s)
2. Lesson topic(s)
3. The ASCA domain and Mindsets & Behaviors standards to be addressed
4. A description of the curriculum and materials that the school counselor or counseling team will provide
5. A timeline for the start and completion of each activity (projected start and end)
6. When class lessons will be taught (by class and/or subject)
7. Process data (i.e., the number of students impacted)
8. Perception data (attitudes, skills, and knowledge)
9. Outcome data (achievement-related and achievement results)
10. The name of the individual responsible for making sure the lesson is created and ready for delivery (contact person)
11. An indication that the plan has been reviewed and signed by the administrator

Tier 1 Core Curriculum Action Plan Agreements - Shasta County (Representing Five Districts)

Grade Level	Lesson Topic	ASCA Mindsets & Behaviors	Curriculum Content and Materials	When?	Presented in Which Subject?	Process Data # Students	Perception Data Type of Surveys/Assessments to Be Used Attitudes (A), Knowledge (K), Skills (S)	Outcome Data Achievement-Related (AR) Achievement (A)	Contact Person
9	**High School 101**	M2 B-LS10 B-SS3 NOSCA Component 3	Traits of a Successful Learner (attendance, communication, etc.); Credits Count; Importance GPA to Your Academic Future; Academic Resources; Student Involvement; Assessing Aeries (Student Information System)	Q1	To be determined and entered here by each school site	To be determined and entered here by each school site	A: Importance of passing with a C or better the first time A: Importance of communicating with teachers, staff, school counselor A: Importance of good attendance K: Where to go for tutoring K: Involvement opportunities S: Ability to access Aeries S: Create/update Khan Academy	AR: Attendance rate AR: Student involvement in activities A: 9th grade credit efficiency rate A: % of 9th graders with 2.0 or higher GPA	Name of the school counselor coordinating this lesson at each site
9	**4 Year Plan**	M4 B-LS7 NOSCA Component 2	Graduation & A-G Requirements; Credits & GPA (community college, state university, university systems); Creating Flexibility in Schedule	Q1/Q2	To be determined and entered by each school site	To be determined and entered by each school site	A: Success requires planning K: Course selection according to goals K: Impact of a D S: Use of technology to complete a 4 Year Plan	AR: Course enrollment patterns A: 9th grade credit deficiency rate A: % of 9th successfully completing A-G sequence	Name of the school counselor coordinating this lesson at each site
9	**Course Selection**	M4 B-LS4 B-LS9 NOSCA Component 4	Transcript Analysis; Edit 4-Yr. Plan; Course Selection; Typical Schedules (showing a wide variety of schedules); Eligible, Non-Eligible, Competitive (including CTE in all 3 sample schedules); Grade Enhancement (Tutoring; Credit Recovery)	Q3	To be determined and entered by each school site	To be determined and entered by each school site	A: Importance of keeping all doors open K: Impact of a D or F grade K: Options for credit recovery and grade enhancement S: Analyze transcript	AR: Course enrollment patterns A: 9th graders on track for graduation & A-G A: % of GPA 2.0 and above	Name of the school counselor coordinating this lesson at each site
9	**Career Exploration**	M4 M5 B-LS9 NOSCA Component 5	CA Career Zone/ONet/ Cacolleges.edu; Interest Inventory; Career Industry Sectors; Holland Codes; Degrees & Certificates	Q4	To be determined and entered by each school site	To be determined and entered by each school site	A: Taking a career exploration survey will help them make postsecondary choices K: Identify career industry sectors aligning with personal interests K: Identify necessary education/training S: Create profile in web-based tool for career development	AR: # completing career exploration survey AR: # using Naviance (or other tool) AR: (Long-range) postsecondary reporting on senior exit surveys	Name of the school counselor coordinating this lesson at each site

Grade Level	Lesson Topic	ASCA Mindsets & Behaviors	Curriculum Content and Materials	When?	Presented in Which Subject?	Process Data # Students	Perception Data Type of Surveys/Assessments to Be Used Attitudes (A), Knowledge (K), Skills (S)	Outcome Data Achievement-Related (AR) Achievement (A)	Contact Person
10	**Keeping Doors Open**	M4 B-LS9 NOSCA Component 5	Specific Tests: PSAT, SAT, ACT, ASVAB (why/when and their differences); Fee Waivers; Test-Taking Strategies & Test Prep; Importance of GPA	Q1	To be determined and entered here by each school site	To be determined and entered here by each school site	A: Belief taking prep tests are important K: Benefits of free & reduced lunch program K: How to register for tests S: Create ACT or Collegeboard account	AR: # of students who took PSAT, SAT, ACT, and ASVAB tests AR: # of fee waivers used A: PSAT, SAT, ACT, ASVAB scores	Name of the school counselor coordinating this lesson at each site
10	**Strategies for Success**	M1 B-SMS7 B-SS9 NOSCA Component 3	Organizational Skills; Time & Stress Management; Healthy Relationships; Emotional Intelligence; Social Media	Q2	To be determined and entered here by each school site	To be determined and entered here by each school site	A: Organizational skills contribute to academic/career success & personal health K: How to use electronic calendars K: Physical preparation for tests S: Ability to prioritize activities given different scenarios	AR: Attendance rate AR: Discipline referrals AR: Assignment completion A: % students with a GPA of 2.0 and higher	Name of the school counselor coordinating this lesson at each site
10	**Course Selection**	M4 M5 B-LS4 NOSCA Component 2	Transcript Analysis; CTE/Regional Occupational Program (ROP) Pathways; AP/Concurrent/Dual Enrollment; Credit Recovery; Grade Enhancement; Edit 4 Yr. Plan	Q3	To be determined and entered here by each school site	To be determined and entered here by each school site	A: Responsibility for graduation and postsecondary readiness K: Know how to analyze transcript for graduation S: Analyzing transcripts & individual course selection	AR: Course enrollment patterns A: % on track for graduation A: % on track for A-G	Name of the school counselor coordinating this lesson at each site
10	**Career Assessments**	M4 B-LS5 NOSCA Component 5	Naviance, CA Career Zone, ONet, Cacolleges.edu; Interest Inventory; Career Industry Sectors; Holland Codes; Degree Options & Certificates; CTE Pathways	Q4	To be determined and entered here by each school site	To be determined and entered here by each school site	A: CTE/Regional Occupational Program (ROP) pathways and A-G pathways can both be completed A: CTE/ROP is for everyone K: CTE Pathways S: Add favorite careers to profile in web-based career exploration tool	AR: Course enrollment patterns AR # students with postsecondary plan A: CTE completer rate	Name of the school counselor coordinating this lesson at each site

(Continued)

(Continued)

Grade Level	Lesson Topic	ASCA Mindsets & Behaviors	Curriculum Content and Materials	When?	Presented in Which Subject?	Process Data # Students	Perception Data Type of Surveys/Assessments to Be Used Attitudes (A), Knowledge (K), Skills (S)	Outcome Data Achievement-Related (AR) Achievement (A)	Contact Person
11	Post-Secondary Deadlines and Testing	M2 M4 B-SMS1 NOSCA Component 5	Inclusive Calendar: Deadlines & Activities; Postsecondary Admission/ Placement Testing (PSAT, SAT, ACT, ASVAB, EAP); Fee Waivers; Khan Academy; Marketing for Parent Night	Q1	To be determined and entered here by each school site	To be determined and entered here by each school site	A: Belief in using calendar A: Importance of taking CCR assessments A: Belief in importance of families attending parent night K: Important dates S: Calendaring appointments S: Link PSAT/create account in Khan Academy	AR: # PSAT test takers AR: # parents attending parent night AR: # fee waivers used A: PSAT/SAT/ACT scores	Name of the school counselor coordinating this lesson at each site
11	College Knowledge	B-LS1 B-LS9 NOSCA Component 4	Career Assessments; College Systems (Community, Four Year, Trade, Vocational Programs); Exploring College Majors; College Applications; Match & Fit	Q2	To be determined and entered here by each school site	To be determined and entered here by each school site	A: Believe that taking career assessments will assist in postsecondary planning K: Differences between certificates and degrees K: Different college applications S: Researching college major, internship, or trade schools according to career interest results	AR: # College applications A: On track for grad. A: A-G readiness rate A: # CTE completers A: College enrollment rate (National Student Clearinghouse data)	Name of the school counselor coordinating this lesson at each site
11	Course Selection	B-SMS1 B-LS4 NOSCA Component 2	Transcript Analysis; Graduation & A-G Requirements; Credit Recovery and Grade Enhancement; CTE Completer Courses; Dual Enrollment/Concurrent; NCAA	Q3	To be determined and entered here by each school site	To be determined and entered here by each school site	A: Responsibility for graduation and postsecondary readiness K: Know how to analyze transcript K: Credit Recovery K: Graduation/A-G Requirements S: Analyzing transcripts & course selection	AR: # Enrolled in Credit Recovery AR: # Enrolled in Grade Enhancement A: # On Track for Grad. A: A-G Readiness Rate A: # CTE completers	Name of the school counselor coordinating this lesson at each site
11	Post-Secondary Planning	M4 B-LS1 NOSCA Component 7	Job Apps.; Internship Apps.; Resume Building; Military Branches (finding sites, forms to be completed, contact numbers for recruiter); Creating a Proper Email Address	Q3/4	To be determined and entered here by each school site	To be determined and entered here by each school site	A: Importance of planning and researching K: Social Security Number K: Components of a resume; how to complete a college/job/military application S: Completing a college/job/military application S: Creating a proper email address	AR: # Resumes completed AR: # College/job/military applications AR: Senior Exit Survey data: # students with a postsecondary plan and # with no plan A: # College enrollments, jobs obtained, military enlistments	Name of the school counselor coordinating this lesson at each site
11	Pre-Senior Summer	M2 B-LS1 NOSCA Component 7	FSA ID; FAFSA/CADAA (Dream Act); Scholarships, Letters of Rec., College Visits, College Application Essays; Engagement Activities; Free college at CA Community Colleges and specifics about Shasta Community College	Q4	To be determined and entered here by each school site	To be determined and entered here by each school site	A: Importance of starting college readiness over the summer before senior year K: Essay prompts K: How to research college visits S: Locate college websites & scholarships S: Student portion FAFSA/CADAA (Dream Act)	AR: # Completing the FAFSA AR: # College applications A: College acceptance rate A: College enrollment rate A: Scholarship dollars earned	Name of the school counselor coordinating this lesson at each site

Grade Level	Lesson Topic	ASCA Mindsets & Behaviors	Curriculum Content and Materials	When?	Presented in Which Subject?	Process Data # Students	Perception Data Type of Surveys/Assessments to Be Used Attitudes (A), Knowledge (K), Skills (S)	Outcome Data Achievement-Related (AR) Achievement (A)	Contact Person
12	**Senior Timeline**	M4 B-LS1 NOSCA Component 7	Senior Year Activities; Calendars & Deadlines; Letters of Recommendation; All the "to-do's" (transcript requests, sending scores, etc.) Marketing parent nights	Q1	To be determined and entered here by each school site	To be determined and entered here by each school site	A: Belief in importance of team approach with students, families, & school counselors K: Important dates S: Identify key people to complete letters of recommendation	AR: Family attendance at parent events AR: # of applications submitted (CC, CSU, UC, Common App., military, jobs) A: Acceptance rates	Name of the school counselor coordinating this lesson at each site
12	**Apply, Apply, Apply!**	M5 B-LS5 NOSCA Component 7	College Application for CCC, CSU, UC, Common App. (students choose); Military Applications Job Applications	Q1	To be determined and entered here by each school site	To be determined and entered here by each school site	A: Importance of applying to a diverse array of postsecondary opportunities K: Differences between systems & accessing their websites S: Transferring transcript to application	AR: # of applications submitted (CC, CSU, UC, Common App., military, job) A: # College enrollments, jobs obtained, military enlistments	Name of the school counselor coordinating this lesson at each site
12	**Money Matters**	M4 B-SS8 NOSCA Component 6	FAFSA/CADAA (Dream Act) Cal Grant; Shasta Community College (1st year free); Community Force Scholarship Application; Community Scholarship App.	Q2	To be determined and entered here by each school site	To be determined and entered here by each school site	A: Importance of applying to a wide range of financial aid K: FSA ID, FAFSA, scholarship apps. K: FAFSA Deadline S: Locating on web S: Creating FSA ID	AR: # Completing FAFSA A: Student Aid Reports and other award letters (Cal Grant) A: Scholarship dollars earned	Name of the school counselor coordinating this lesson at each site
12	**Successful Transitions**	M2 B-SMS10 NOSCA Component 8	Social/Emotional Independence; Managing Portals; Submitting Student Intent to Register (SIR) Overcoming Summer Melt Risks; Support Resources at College; Employment Supports; Next Steps—To Do's Up Next, Better Make Room	Q4	To be determined and entered here by each school site	To be determined and entered here by each school site	A: Take responsibility K: How to use portals K: Summer support available K: Navigating "The Labyrinth" S: Access UpNext S: Connect with postsecondary support personnel before graduation	AR: # Student Intent to Register Submitted A: College enrollment rates (National Student Clearinghouse data) A: College persistence rates (National Student Clearinghouse data)	Name of the school counselor coordinating this lesson at each site

The number of lessons delivered may vary depending on the student-to-counselor ratio or the extent to which the school counselors deliver all lessons or assist others in the delivery of the curriculum (such as when school counselors supervise interns or paraprofessionals or when secondary teachers deliver part of the curriculum as a portion of a seminar, a colloquium, or advisory lessons). Because the school counseling curriculum is delivered to all students, the numbers per grade level appear under "Projected Number of Students Impacted." Most curricula at the secondary level are generated by the school counselor, and some may come from pre-packaged programs, but all include a method for evaluation that will be discussed later in this text.

Although some lessons include immediate and/or long-term evaluation tools, this is not to imply that the school counselor would measure every lesson in every way annually. Rather, the Schoolwide Core Curriculum Action Plan may provide a list of which perception and outcome data might be reviewed or examined as significant data points that align with each curriculum lesson. The school counseling team selects a few lessons each year to evaluate and improve based on their alignment with schoolwide and/or program goals (discussed further in Chapter 3).

Instructions for Completing an Action Plan

When completing an action plan, refer to these guidelines:

1 *Grade(s)*

It is important to ensure that every student receives access to the achievement of competencies; therefore, school counselors must teach (or partner with others to teach) core curriculum classroom lessons to all students within each grade level.

2 *Lesson Topic*

When deciding which content you'll provide to every student, it will be helpful to draw from the collective professional wisdom of school counselors as well as review your developmental crosswalk of the *ASCA Mindsets & Behaviors for Student Success* standards (discussed further in Chapter 4) and the three domains of academic, college/career, and social/emotional development. Which standards do you want to be certain to address? Which of the three domains are taught within each grade level throughout the year? Ideally, and with a low ratio, school counselors want to address each domain, but this may not be possible. Consider your counseling program SMART goals and priorities and begin in that domain. Priorities might include areas that the data indicate need the most attention. Perhaps your college-going rate and/or FAFSA completion rate is far below other schools in your district. Based on these data, you might prioritize these lessons and therefore begin by strongly addressing the college/career domain. School counselors can then add on a few core curriculum lessons each year until all domains are addressed.

3 *ASCA Domain and Mindsets & Behaviors Standards*

In this section school counselors will list the appropriate counseling domain(s) covered by the lesson—academic, college/career, and/or social/emotional. Then the school counselor will add the ASCA Mindsets & Behaviors standards that align with each lesson. In this section write in the abbreviations of the most important standards to be covered by the lessons. In some states, school counseling standards may be added to this section as well.

4 *Curriculum and Materials*

This column asks you to identify the specific content to be taught in the classroom lesson. For example, the competency might be career exploration, but the content will vary by grade level and student population. Seventh grade students may receive a lesson on interest inventories. In 9th grade the lesson might be aligning interests to career pathways and in 11th grade might include discovering the educational requirements for different careers and matching these to colleges. By scaffolding developmentally appropriate lessons in career exploration on a continuum of lessons throughout middle and high school, students have the opportunity to build on what they have learned. Tracking the different curricula being used and measuring and comparing the results of lessons allow school counseling teams also to determine which curriculum and materials are most effective. These formal and informal assessments allow for program improvement and prevent costs associated with purchasing ineffective curriculum. In addition, if the curriculum to be used is documented, it can be easily referenced each academic year.

5 *Projected Start/End*

Knowing when a lesson or activity will occur and when it will be completed is essential to team planning. This facilitates intelligent planning of when events will take place within the school year. For example, teaching the course selection process is most effective when done just prior to registration, and teaching 9th graders that credits count is best done early in the 9th grade. Waiting until students are in second semester is too late for freshmen. Similarly, teaching how to make healthy choices a couple weeks before prom or spring break is always a smart idea.

6 *Lesson Presented During Time/Subject*

When school counselors are deciding the subject area in which to deliver their core curriculum lessons, it is important to recognize and appreciate the standards and competencies that the classroom teachers are required to address. Effort should be made to infuse lesson activities across the curriculum, as opposed to impacting only one academic area, if applicable at secondary schools. This section can also be used to include the time of recurring lessons. Through collaboration and alignment of lessons, school counselors gain staff buy-in and mutual support for lessons. Many school counselors find that career development lessons they provide in 11th grade align well with the teaching standards in language arts. Additionally, the Common Core State Standards for English Language Arts, Speaking and Listening Standards 6–12, include components that may align with counseling lessons. School counselors are highly encouraged to review their state standards and other standards utilized by the district (i.e., social and emotional learning, health, etc.) for alignment.

7 *Process Data*

The number of students impacted by each classroom lesson is indicated in this section. School counselors will document the approximate number of students in each grade level and add it to this section, and school counselors are advised to schedule their lessons when all students are present.

8 *Perception Data*

Before the delivery of classroom lessons, it is important for the school counselor to consider the criteria by which success will be measured. What are the *attitudes*, *knowledge*, and *skills* to be taught? Will the perception data be measured by a pre- and post-test? In this section, counselors will fill out what they hope students will believe, know, and be able to do after the lesson is taught. Much more on pre-post assessments will be provided in Chapter 8.

9 *Outcome Data*

What outcome data align with your lesson? Achievement-related (AR) and achievement (A) data are the ultimate outcomes aligned with school counseling core curriculum lessons. Student achievement data consist of outcome data focusing on academic achievement; at the secondary level these measures include graduation rates, college-going rates, GPA, scores on SAT/ACT, and so on. Achievement-related data are the data elements, determined by research, that support student achievement. In secondary school, student achievement data include course enrollment patterns, behavior (referrals/suspension), parent engagement, completing college applications, and so on (Hatch, 2013).

10 *Contact Person*

At the secondary level, where there are often (though not always) multiple counselors, team members may split up the responsibility for preparing lesson content and materials for different lessons. In this section, write the name(s) of the counselor(s) responsible for ensuring specific lessons are ready and perhaps scheduling times within the agreed-upon time frame to present the lessons. Generally multiple, if not all, members of the counseling team present lessons; the contact person is listed to ensure everything is prepared to do so.

11 *Administrator's Signature*

The signature of the administrator ensures collaboration and agreement with the proposed core curriculum lessons, individual student planning, and school-wide programs and activities of the comprehensive school counseling program. Although this section is not included in the ASCA template, it is added in the plan provided here to encourage support and awareness from school leadership. Additionally, a date scheduled for a faculty presentation to share this information is also included on the action plan so that counselors can discuss their program and provide a calendar indicating when the lessons will be delivered, allowing time for teachers to prepare in advance. Additional discussion about the importance of utilizing planning calendars is presented in Chapter 11. The action plan can also be shared with families and is included on the school counseling program website.

Figure 2.4 is an ASCA Action Plan Template adapted to add the time or subject during which the lesson will be presented and signature items at the bottom. Additional templates are available online. School counselors are encouraged to use and adapt these templates to meet the needs of their school counseling program.

online resources

Figure 2.4   Core Curriculum Action Plan Template

SCHOOL COUNSELING CORE CURRICULUM ACTION PLAN

Templated Adapted from:

AMERICAN SCHOOL COUNSELOR ASSOCIATION

School Counseling Program Goals:

Core Curriculum Lessons and Related to Goals:

Grade Level	Lesson Topic	ASCA Domain and Mindsets & Behaviors Standard(s)	Curriculum and Materials	Projected Start/End	Lesson Presented During Time/ Subject	Process Data (Projected number of students affected)	Perception Data (Type of surveys/ assessments to be used)	Outcome Data (Achievement, attendance, and/or behavior data to be collected)	Contact Person

Principal's Signature   Date   Date of Staff Presentation   Prepared by

A Districtwide Franchising Story

Contributed by Becky Love

Shasta County is a rural area in the far northern region of California. In the fall of 2017, high school and middle school counselors, along with district and site administrators, began a professional development academy with Hatching Results, with the goal of implementing the ASCA National Model across Shasta County. Those participating included four high school districts with 10 high schools and two middle school districts with five middle schools. Shasta County's Superintendent of Schools, Judy Flores, worked with the districts to design a unique infrastructure with multiple districts pooling funds for a full-time counseling coordinator to lead the work and collaborate among districts. As the newly hired counseling coordinator, I was relieved of my caseload and worked from the county office. In addition to my role as the coordinator, each school selected a school counselor identified as a co-lead, and their role was to represent their school counseling department in monthly meetings with the counseling coordinator.

In October, the Hatching Results School Counseling Academy began by leading counselors and administrators through updates in the profession and an exploration of the major differences between guidance counselors and 21st century school counselors. The learning curve was steep, and there were varying perspectives and motivations throughout the room. However, one common belief was that the school counselors would be able to reach *all* students if they were to embrace and implement a comprehensive, evidenced-based school counseling program based on the ASCA National Model. Toward the end of the first professional development, the concept of Tier 1 Core Curriculum was introduced, and school counselors were split into developmental study groups: middle school (sixth through eighth), freshmen, sophomores, juniors, and seniors. School counselors in each study group were to discuss and brainstorm as to which content was most important for students to receive at each grade. At the end of the activity, the content for number of lessons per grade ranged from 6 to 10, with topic titles such as: "High School 101," "College Knowledge," "Suicide Awareness & Prevention," and "Money Matters." The conversations were lively as school counselors collaborated on age-appropriate content from the academic, social/emotional, and college/career domains as well as, of course, each school's favorite lessons. As the counseling coordinator, I worked with counselors between trainings to reduce the number of lessons and finalize the Tier 1 core curriculum topics. Co-leads across districts collaborated about the value of each lesson by grade level and shared curriculum resources with one another. In listening to the district co-leads, caution was expressed by counselors across the county that we not rush to fully endorse the curriculum too quickly and that more thoughtfulness was needed. At the December training, the Hatching Results professional development (PD) specialists explained to school counselors that deciding on lesson topics and subsequently creating them are processes that take time and that they were in exactly the growth place they needed to be.

Additionally, a decision was made to focus on the art and science of *teaching* as opposed to *presenting*. Most school counselors were skilled presenters but, as a group, had little teaching experience. The PD specialists provided them with examples of engagement strategies and even modeled a classroom lesson using these skills to show them what teaching counseling concepts at the secondary level looks like.

The December training also introduced school counselors and administrators to analyzing data to identify needs for Tier 1 lessons; writing core curriculum action plans; understanding process, perception, and outcome data through the Hatching Results Conceptual Diagram; creating effective pre/post questions, and aligning class lessons to the ASCA Mindsets and Behaviors standards. At the close of the day, school counselors agreed to teach *one* common lesson by the end of February. The co-leads and I were charged with developing one agreed-upon, grade-level-appropriate lesson that would be delivered across Shasta County. Administrators agreed to provide feedback via the Hatching Results Core Curriculum Classroom Lesson Feedback Tool (see our website). The assignment was designed to assist administrators in participating in the process of supporting their counselors in this work. In this way, counselors would then become more familiar with the expectations of an effective and engaging Tier 1 core curriculum lesson.

online resources

When training continued in March, the countywide lesson had been delivered, and most administrators had provided feedback to their school counselors. Once the teams of counselors debriefed about their experiences teaching a complete lesson, Dr. Hatch announced that the goal of the day was to gain consensus (counselors and administrators) around the Tier 1 core curriculum that *all* Shasta County students would receive. We were led through the following process:

1. The original curriculum discussed in October for each school's team was shared to review, discuss, and, if necessary, prioritize up to four lessons per grade level.

2. One counselor from each school's team would be joining a grade level study group, and with a clean poster they would begin to list the most important lessons for their assigned grade. The PD specialists explained that the school counselor assigned to each grade level study group was going to be considered the "expert" and was to be trusted to advocate for the school's positions and priorities.

3. The newly appointed "experts" and administrators collaborated within each grade level and made impassioned pleas for specific lessons. Ideas were written on a fresh poster, and a new list of four lessons per grade level was created (even though it was difficult to reduce the list to only four). Administrators recognized that counselors were, indeed, experts in their field and expressed appreciation and enthusiasm for their work. The growth that occurred during this phase was palatable!

4. Educators returned to their district teams. The PD specialists gave a pep talk about the work underway being difficult but honorable. We were reminded that our endeavor was unique because we were building a countywide curriculum, but the potential for growth in our students' attitudes, knowledge, and skills, and the benefits for our community would be extraordinary!

5. The next step was to participate in a gallery walk and for everyone to review all lessons for each grade level. All participants received two star stickers to place on the lessons they felt were the most important at each grade level. The "winning" two lessons (with the most stars) would be developed and implemented with fidelity in the 2018–2019 school year. The remaining two lessons for each grade would be listed in the Shasta County School Counseling Program Handbook, to be taught in future years, as agreed upon by the group.

(Continued)

(Continued)

6. The gallery walks gave *all* school counselors and administrators an opportunity to provide input and was instrumental in gaining support and commitment from everyone. Administrators expressed an enlightened understanding of the content school counselors would be delivering and vowed to advocate for counselors having access to teach students in a variety of classrooms. Appreciation and excitement was seen by all by giving and getting a thumbs-up signaling agreement to implementing the Shasta County Tier 1 Core Curriculum!

Our process to "franchise" core curriculum classroom lessons across Shasta County continues as we are designing lessons, teaching and assessing with pre-/post-tests, reevaluating and updating the curriculum based on feedback, and adding new lessons each year. We understand and are grateful for the opportunity to teach in the classroom setting, which allows us the chance to broaden a child's vision for academic and career goals; empower students with the attitudes, knowledge, and skills to make educated decisions about their health and their friendships; and positively impact a school's climate and culture. Additionally, we feel positive about the direction we are moving to bring consistency to the curriculum we are delivering across schools and districts, which also helps clarify our roles as school counselors.

Source: Created by Becky Love, adapted by Hatching Results.

School counselor: How many lessons should counselors teach per grade level?

Trish's answer: Many districts we work with provide four to five lessons per grade level per year, but it depends. Imagine that your school counseling program is like a house. All houses have kitchens, bathrooms, and bedrooms. Some houses have only two bedrooms, whereas other larger homes have four or five bedrooms. But they all have bedrooms. Similarly, all school counseling programs have similar components—core lessons, small-group interventions, family education, and so forth. If a school counselor has a larger caseload, it doesn't mean that they give up on one of the components of the program. Rather, the counselor provides fewer small-group interventions or lessons if they have a larger caseload. Depending also on the curriculum taught and available resources, some school counselors may collaborate to co-teach curriculum with teachers or consider an advisory program.

WAYS TO DELIVER CORE CURRICULUM

As part of the planning process, school counselors will collaborate with teachers to determine the best times to present classroom lessons. Note that in Figure 2.4, the core curriculum action plan includes specific subject areas for scheduled lessons. Ideally, school counselors will select subject areas that allow for the most number of students to be impacted. Typically this means delivering lessons in English, history, or physical education. It's always best when teachers can be present and involved in the lessons so that they can enhance and reinforce the content after school counselors leave. However, school counselors may have to be flexible to ensure that content is taught in a way that best serves everyone. In some situations, the school calendar will require counselors to be flexible in their scheduling of lessons. What follows are some suggestions for secondary counselors as they are planning to teach the core curriculum:

- Integrate the school counseling curriculum into core subjects to deliver counselor-led lessons or co-teach lessons. In this case, it can be especially helpful to align lesson content to subject content whenever possible (i.e., a lesson on calculating GPA during math; a lesson on cultural diversity during social studies, or a lesson on résumé building in English). In this way school counselors support the academic core learning standards.
- Prerecord a video to be shown by classroom teachers and provide a lesson plan and/or activity for students to complete during or after the video. This option works well to enhance schoolwide activities such as an introduction to school resources, financial aid completion challenges, or even course registration introductions when the school counselor may not have time to be present in all classrooms. Not all of the curriculum has to be delivered by the school counselor face-to-face. If a counselor has a large caseload that limits the number of lessons they can teach, video lessons may be an option. In this case, utilizing students in video lessons (with the proper permissions) often increases attention and engagement!
- Advisory or homeroom teachers can participate in the delivery of the school counseling curriculum at the secondary level. Counselors can collaborate with advisory teachers to provide lesson plans; however, care must be taken to ensure the quality of content and instruction through the assessment process. Advising and homeroom can support the school counseling program as one delivery model within the core curriculum, but this method is not intended to be the sole means of delivery. School counselors are advised to create detailed lesson plans and provide them to teachers prior to the lesson along with methods for evaluation.
- Depending on class size and space, combining two classes of students together can be another means to teach core curriculum. Grouping students can double the school counselor's time—but a note of caution—assess student outcomes to ensure that the same level of learning is taking place compared to teaching each class individually. More students mean that fewer individuals are able to share answers with the group, and students may be more likely to get distracted. Strong classroom management skills on the part of the school counselor are also important to prevent off-task behaviors. Additionally, consider which lesson topics are best suited for only one class, such as creating 4-year plans, during which students may have many individual questions.
- Offer to take half the class from two teachers on two back-to-back days. In this way the teachers can continue to teach the same instruction with smaller class sizes, and the school counselor can still see all students over a two-day period (win-win!). Remember to also provide a copy of the lesson plan and/ or PowerPoint to the teachers so they know what their students are learning and can reinforce the concepts as they weren't able to see the lesson. This is a great opportunity for differentiated instruction from both the teacher and school counselor as well!

- In schools where students have electives, such as Advancement via Individual Determination (AVID) or health, school counselors are encouraged to work with the elective teacher and/or co-instruct. Rather than duplicate content on topics such cyber-safety, anti-drugs/alcohol, study strategies, or college exploration, school counselors can collaborate to ensure that counseling lessons are not repetitive for students.
- If all else fails, consider offering to deliver lessons when there is a substitute. Although teaching a lesson when a substitute teacher is covering a class is preferable to not teaching the curriculum at all, the best scenario is when teachers and counselors are present in the classroom together.

School counselor: Sometimes teachers leave the classroom when I am teaching to make copies, prep for classes, or perform other work outside of their classroom. Is that okay?

Authors' answer: We recommend that teachers be both present and engaged during the school counseling lesson so that they will understand and reinforce concepts taught after the counselor leaves. Teacher involvement in classroom lessons assists students in their learning, such as when the teacher shares a personal example related to the topic or helps students complete an activity. Additionally, because secondary school counselors teach in grade-level classrooms only once a month or quarter, reinforcement can be supported by teachers. Although teachers may have to leave for an emergency, secondary teachers have a designated prep time, so ideally they are in the class and participating when the counselor is teaching. School counselors can include teachers in the lessons by letting them know in advance that they will ask them a question about the topic, require assistance for students with an activity, or issue a homework assignment. This strategy can be particularly effective for a teacher who hasn't previously been engaged when the counselor is leading instruction.

Core Curriculum: Ensuring Value Added

How school counselors approach entering the teacher's classroom matters. It is appropriate to be aware and respectful that any interruption of instructional learning time is indeed just that—an interruption of the students' instruction. During an age of increased accountability for student outcomes, teachers are equally concerned about student achievement and success. Thus, it would not be surprising to find that from time to time, school counselors encounter faculty or administration who appear initially resistant to the implementation of the core counseling curriculum. In addition, in districts where secondary school counseling lessons haven't been taught before, counselors may initially encounter confusion or pushback as to when, where, why, and how they will garner time for instruction from administrators and/or teachers. As the school counselor is beginning the work of franchising the curriculum, it is recommended that they meet with administrators and faculty to discuss the core curriculum as part of the comprehensive school counseling program. This should include discussion of ways in which the school counselor's curriculum will add value and contribute in a meaningful way to the instructional learning environment and student development in the three domains (academic, college/career, and social/emotional).

It may help to compare the counselor's core curriculum action plan to the teacher's use of scope and sequence and to share lesson plans and assessment tools. Finally, teachers will be less concerned about an interruption of instructional time if they can clearly see the value to their students. In the authors' experience, teachers most often complain about core curriculum lessons when they experience the lesson as a "random act of guidance" by a school counselor who has poorly prepared curriculum, appears unable to control the classroom, and does not assess student learning. School counselors do not have to be credentialed teachers, but they must know how to teach. Therefore, school counselors are encouraged to use a variety of student engagement strategies and to use strong classroom management (see Chapters 5 and 6). Confident school counselors seek feedback from the teachers at their school and engage them in the improvement process, for example, by using the Core Curriculum Lesson Feedback Tool provided in Chapter 6.

Figure 2.5 shows a school counseling core curriculum overview, modified from an action plan, in an easy-to-read format for families. This document was included on the school counseling program website and shared in various presentations about the school counseling program. What are other ways to advertise the core curriculum to families and school stakeholders?

Figure 2.5 School Counseling Core Curriculum Action Plan Overview for Staff and Families

Core Curriculum Lesson Topic	Curriculum/Materials	Dates	Subject Areas	Grade(s)
Student Expectations: Show Your Potter P.R.I.D.E.	Administration/school counselor–generated presentation including *Leader in Me*	1st week of school	P.E.	7 & 8
Respect Yourself and Cyber Awareness	School counselor–generated respect/anti-bullying/cyberbullying lesson with Safe School Ambassador materials	1st week of September	Social Studies	7 & 8
Check Grades Online/ Academic Success and 8th Grade Promotion Requirements	School counselor–generated lesson using Infinite Campus Student Information System	1st week of October (after 1st trimester progress reports)	Math	7 & 8
Red Ribbon Week: Drug-Free and Healthy Choices	School counselor–generated lesson using RedRibbon.org	Last week of October	Science	7 & 8
Student Expectations Review: Show Your Potter P.R.I.D.E.	Administration/school counselor–generated presentation including *Leader in Me* and discipline data from 1st semester	1st week after winter break	P.E.	7 & 8

(Continued)

Figure 2.5 (Continued)

Core Curriculum Lesson Topic	Curriculum/Materials	Dates	Subject Areas	Grade(s)
College and Career Readiness	School counselor–generated lesson with California Careers Resource Network and College & Career Day presentations	Mid-January Language Arts ***Schoolwide College and Career Day last Friday in January*	All classes	7 & 8
Transition to High School and 4-Year Plans	Jr. high counselor–generated 4-year plan lesson with high school course registration and high school counselor lesson	February/March	Math	8
Positive Decision-Making	School counselor–generated lesson using *7 Habits of Highly Effective Teens* materials	March/April (after Spring Break)	Social Studies	7 & 8
Transition to Jr. High School	Administration/counselor-generated presentation Future Braves Academy (half-day)	March Elementary School Visits Future Braves Academy—Mid-May	All classes	6

Franchising Family Education

Just as school counselors determine "franchisable" curriculum for students, so too should they provide family education that is preplanned, consistent, aligned with student developmental needs, and calendared, assessed, and improved each year. Some beginning school counselors prefer to loosely design their family education programs by utilizing a drop-in approach, which may consist of a monthly coffee with the counselor or an occasional family education workshop. However, secondary counselors are encouraged to design curriculum (aligning with what students are learning) that all families will receive each year from the comprehensive counseling program.

online resources ►

To determine the content of the family lessons, secondary counselors may want to conduct a needs assessment like the one in *The Use of Data in School Counseling* (Hatch, 2013, p. 114; also available on our website) or review family feedback on the school or district's climate survey to design the curriculum to address top priorities. Another option is to align the family education to core curriculum topics being taught to students so that families receive similar instruction and ideas to reinforce the concepts at home. For instance, during Red Ribbon Week, the lesson would cover drug and alcohol prevention tips for parents and would review key concepts taught to students. Like students and teachers, families should be able to know what they can count on from the school counseling program each year. Ideally, and when at all possible, seek ways to collaborate with other counselors to franchise family education from school to school within your district. To the extent that counselors design a consistent instructional family curriculum and calendar events each year, families will come to know and trust what they can expect from the school counseling program as foundational. Then, as needs arise or a crisis occurs, school counselors can add or build upon the family education as necessary.

Example of Feedback Form for District Office School Counseling Leaders

Dear School Staff and Families:

At XYZ School District, school counselors deliver classroom lessons on many topics. To assist us in meeting the needs of our students, please rank the lessons in order of your preference for your students. This information will be useful to us (along with districtwide academic and climate survey data) as we make important school counseling curriculum decisions. Thank you for your assistance!

<u>6th Grade:</u>

_____ Promotion Requirements

_____ Career Interest Inventory

_____ Study Skills/Organizational Strategies

_____ Test-Taking Skills

_____ Bullying and Bystanders

_____ Conflict Resolution Skills

_____ Friendship Skills

_____ Making Healthy Choices (Drugs, Alcohol, etc.)

_____ High School Graduation Requirements

<u>7th Grade:</u>

_____ Promotion Requirements

_____ Career Pathways

_____ Study Skills/Organizational Strategies

_____ Test-Taking Skills

_____ Sexual Harassment

_____ Conflict Resolution

_____ Making Healthy Choices (Drugs, Alcohol, etc.)

_____ Taking Responsibility for My Education

(Continued)

(Continued)

<u>8th Grade:</u>

_____ Promotion Requirements

_____ Preparing for High School

_____ College Preparation Requirements

_____ Careers of Tomorrow

_____ Study Skills/Organizational Strategies

_____ Test-Taking Skills

_____ Sexual Harassment

_____ Conflict Resolution

_____ Making Healthy Choices (Drugs, Alcohol, etc.)

Additional Comments: _____

The table that follows shares a sample from a school counselor who has pre-planned family workshops for the year to align with the core curriculum for students. Note the alignment with topics to be addressed with students according to the curriculum action plan from "A Districtwide Franchising Story" on pages 40–42. For example, 12th grade families receive instruction on filling out college applications in the fall, and 8th grade families receive instruction on the transition to high school in the spring:

Sample Calendar of School Counseling Curriculum for Parents and Families			
GRADE LEVEL	**TOPIC**	**CONTENTS**	**WHEN**
8	High School 101 for Parents & Families	Incoming high school family information, programs, resources available, and A–G requirements	Spring
9, 10, 11	Keeping Doors Open Postsecondary Family Night	Postsecondary pathways, financial aid, testing, and Naviance information for families	Fall
11	College Connection Family Information Night	Concurrent enrollment program between Shasta College and public comprehensive high schools	Winter
12	Senior Orientation and Money Matters	FAFSA, scholarships, Cal Grants, Student Aid Reports (SAR), First Year Free, decision-making tools, senior information pertaining to graduation, yearbook ads, senior merchandise, and Sober Grad Night	Early Fall

Whether you are a new or veteran school counselor, creating a family core curriculum is an essential component of a comprehensive school counseling program and contributes to the foundation of Tier 1 core curriculum and schoolwide activities within the framework of a Multi-Tiered, Multi-Domain System of Supports (MTMDSS).

BEST PRACTICES FOR SUCCESSFUL FAMILY EDUCATION PROGRAMS

Research confirms that the involvement of families in their children's education is critical to students' academic success. To ensure parent and family engagement and a successful program, follow these suggestions:

- Create a welcoming school climate for families. Depending on the time of day, offer snacks and beverages if possible, or some time for social networking. Be positive and let families know that they are valued. Consider offering transportation funding assistance and translators if needed.

- Offer attendance incentives if possible. Don't underestimate the draw of free school store supplies or spirit wear, a special parking space, or some door prizes! Seek donations from local businesses.

- Establish timely and effective school-to-home and home-to-school communication that suits the community. Whenever possible, schedule all workshops for the school year in advance of the first day of school. Distribute flyers at back-to-school events and add to the school and district websites.

- Consider creative ways to advertise upcoming family nights. Ask students to help advertise during drop-off and pickup by holding up signs several days before the event. Work with teachers to see if they'll offer extra credit or a no-homework night for students who come to the event with their families (and make sure to ask attendees to sign in!). Coordinate an automatized call and/or text reminder about the event several days beforehand and the day of. Make sure topics are relevant to families and based on strengthening knowledge and skills to support and extend their children's learning at home. Remember to validate and utilize the knowledge families have as a foundation for the information you are sharing.

- Connect students and families to community resources as much as possible. Consider providing a personal greeting and welcome packet for all families visiting the school that includes a community services directory/list, important school contact information, the annual school counseling calendar and brochure, and coupons to local businesses. Posting this information on the school website also makes it more accessible to families.

- Create a suggestion or comment box (both electronic and onsite) for families to anonymously provide their questions, concerns, and recommendations for the program.

3

Determining Core Curriculum

TRISH'S STORY

When I was hired as the coordinator of student services in Moreno Valley Unified School District years ago, the deputy superintendent shared my goal of having teachers create common curriculum scope and sequences. As a strong school counseling advocate, I suggested students deserved a scope and sequence from school counselors as well. The deputy superintendent agreed and charged me with surveying all of the 72 counselors in 32 schools to see what the current state of the state was in terms of delivering curriculum. After collecting all the lesson titles, it was clearly a collection of random acts of lessons. There were more than 200 different lessons being taught to students in no particular order. Lessons varied from PowerPoint presentations to reading off a paper with Courier New font in a purple color from either the ditto machine or the carbon paper. Some students received lessons on college and career preparation; and others didn't—it was simply random. After much discussion with counselors they agreed that all schools would provide four lessons each year per grade. The counselors set about to create the lessons because no prepackaged materials existed. Counselors dedicated their own time after school and during the summer to contribute to the goal of common lessons. So impressed was the deputy superintendent that he approved funds (the same funds teachers received) for extra duty and curriculum development.

INTRODUCING THE ART AND SCIENCE OF SCHOOL COUNSELING

Figure 3.1   The Art and Science of School Counseling

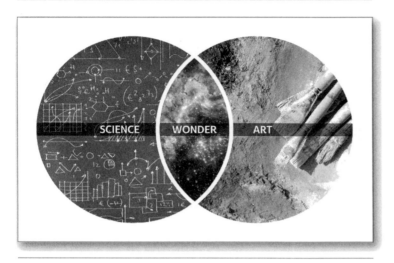

Source: Illustration by Gogis Design, http://www.gogisdesign.com.

Counseling is an art. For decades, school counselors have been providing counseling to students, staff, and families utilizing active listening skills, reflective listening, conflict resolution skills, mediation, reflective listening, and so forth. The counseling skills taught to future school counselors are truly the art of the profession. The science of school counseling, although some might think of it as new, has been present since the profession began. However, in the last two decades, school counselors have been called on to use data, report results, and implement evidence-based practices (ASCA, 2012; Dimmitt, Carey, & Hatch, 2007; Hatch, 2013; Hatch, Duarte, De Gregorio, 2018).

School counseling is increasingly becoming a beautiful combination of art *and* science in practice. The *science* of employing data to drive school counseling programs means identifying specific needs of students and providing evidence-based interventions to impact student achievement, and the *art* is found in employing counseling theories and strategies to meet the unique situation. Within this framework, the *science* of a more clinical or mental health scientific perspective is combined with the *art* of the person-centered, rapport-building practice of a practitioner (see Figure 3.1). This is reflected even in today's school counselor preparation programs. Just think—do you possess a Master of Science (MS) or a Master of Arts (MA) degree? Both are graduate programs offered by universities across the country; the main difference between an MA and MS degree is that an MA applies to arts and humanities degrees, whereas an MS applies to scientific and technical degrees. The difference can be seen through the types of courses required, the sequence of study, and possibly the culminating thesis, capstone project, and/or fieldwork requirements. The art and science of school counseling have implications when counselors plan for core curriculum in the classroom—the best lessons have a balance of both.

EVIDENCE-BASED PRACTICE AND CORE CURRICULUM

Recently there has been a strong movement toward evidence-based practice (EBP) and implementation of an evidence-based school counseling program built from research and data, but what does this really mean? The EBP movement originated in the medical field and is defined as "the integration of [the] best research evidence with clinical expertise and patient values" (Sackett, Straus, Richardson, Rosenberg, & Haynes, 2000, p. 1). The approach combines the best available research with the medical practitioner's integration of knowledge and clinical skills. EBP has been applied to nursing, counseling in psychology, and, most recently, to school counseling (Dimmitt, Carey, & Hatch, 2007; Zyromski & Mariani, 2016). Dimmit et al. (2007) propose a model of evidence-based school counseling practice that encourages school counselors' use of data to determine 1) the needs that will be addressed (the problem description), 2) which practices or interventions should be implemented (using outcome research), and 3) whether the interventions or practices utilized were effective (the evaluation of the curriculum or intervention; see Figure 3.2).

Figure 3.2   A Model of Evidence-Based School Counseling Practice

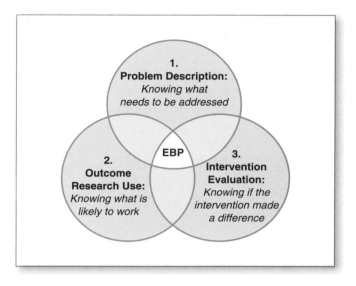

EBP and a Research-Based Curriculum

Applying EBP to school counseling curriculum delivery commonly refers to selecting a curriculum that was previously found to be effective, delivering this curriculum, and measuring its impact with the school population. Prepackaged research-based curriculum is not easily found at the secondary level. Many evidence-based programs are primarily for elementary. It is challenging to locate curriculum that is designed for secondary and has been found to enhance student outcomes in achievement and achievement-related data. Utilizing an EBP approach, however, school counselors can implement a research-based curriculum while evaluating the lesson with perception data and monitoring results to ensure positive outcomes for their particular student demographic. In some middle schools prepackaged research-based curriculum programs can be found; however, they might be quite costly and, in many cases, can have multiple lessons (typically far more than the school counselor has time to deliver alone). These program choices are often schoolwide decisions, as school counselors must partner with teachers to ensure that comprehensive delivery systems are in place.

EBP and a School Counselor–Generated Curriculum

At the secondary level, school counselors often use self-generated curriculum. In these situations, school counselors are encouraged to use data, needs assessments, and their professional wisdom (knowledge and experience) as guides to designing their own lesson development that aligns to research-based best practices. Within this approach, school counselors use their knowledge of and experience with the students they serve to generate a curriculum that meets the developmental needs of their students. They 1) research content and resources; 2) create lesson plans and actively teach the lessons using a variety of engagement strategies; 3) measure students' gains in attitudes, knowledge, and skills; 4) assess achievement-related and achievement data aligning with the lesson content; and 5) diligently evaluate their materials and lessons to make modifications as needed. Within this approach, school counselors evaluate perception data (attitude, knowledge, and skills) to determine that the learning objectives for the lessons have been met, and they use the results to make decisions regarding any changes to core curriculum they deliver and/or the school counseling program overall. School counselors who generate core curriculum employ a systematic procedure for gathering good-quality data from routine practice and align the work of the school counselor within the evidence-based model approach.

EBP and a Statewide Curriculum

Some states have created a statewide curriculum for school counselors to utilize when teaching classroom lessons. A statewide curriculum can be helpful for school counselors as they're beginning to implement their programs because it provides them with immediate resources that they can add to their curriculum action plans. The challenges may be similar to those outlined in Table 3.1 for counselor-generated curriculum. The process of creating a statewide curriculum can be comprehensive and lengthy. The following box presents comments submitted by Dr. M. René Yoesel regarding Missouri's process and experience. More information on the history of this process can be found on our website.

Missouri's Comprehensive School Counseling Program

The State of Missouri has developed the Comprehensive School Counseling Program, which includes K–12 lesson plans arranged by standard. This process has required field tests, curriculum updates, and lots of collaboration among school counselors, counselor educators, the Missouri Department of Elementary and Secondary Education (DESE), and the Missouri School Counselor Association. The authors of this book learned more about the process of creating the statewide program from Dr. Norm Gysbers, Dr. Carolyn Magnuson, Dr. Bragg Stanley, Carolyn Roof, and Linda Lueckenhoff, as submitted by Dr. M. René Yoesel.

Q: Describe the rationale/need for developing a curriculum framework for your state.

A: The rationale began with an awareness that local, state, and national educational reform efforts did not address the development of the nonacademic skills required of all students' success—the skills that school counselors emphasized in their work. To address this need, we started with a vision of what graduating students needed to know, understand, and be able to do (in addition to academic skills) to be successful. We applied basic, universal domains of human development and the factors that facilitate and block that development. From there, the curriculum framework was developed.

Q: Explain the process for developing the curriculum—who was involved, what resources you utilized, how you developed/crosswalked lessons, and how long it took.

A: The development of the actual curriculum (sample classroom lessons for each aspect of the curriculum framework) began in 2004, and the first phase was completed in 2009. However, this was preceded by many years of creating materials that led to the need to develop a resource of sample strategies for full implementation of the Missouri Comprehensive School Counseling Program components.

Prior to the creation of the writing team, a meeting was held with DESE's assistant commissioner for curriculum and instruction and the coordinator of the K–12 academic curriculum areas. The idea was introduced that the comprehensive "guidance" school counseling program *should* be a part of the department's academic curriculum efforts/materials. This was a risk, as the individuals making the pitch for the integral role of the statewide plan were not DESE employees, but the meeting was successful!

The Comprehensive Guidance (School Counseling) Program writing team members utilized the ASCA standards and the Missouri Show-Me Standards (and subsequent iterations) to crosswalk units and lessons. This process resulted in developing awareness among users that there is an interrelationship of the ASCA National Model, the Show-Me Standards, and the Missouri Comprehensive Guidance (School Counseling) Program Curriculum Framework. In turn, it gave users talking points for conversations with classroom teachers, school administrators, and school boards.

Q: How long did it take?

A: Depending on your perspective, 40+ years (or 5 years, or forever) because development is ongoing.

Q: What has been the response/utilization of the curriculum?

A: Both have been excellent! One example is the fact that on the first day the classroom curriculum was active online, the Missouri Center for Career Education server was overloaded. The national response is reflected in one beginning school counselor's unsolicited response at a national meeting—she used one of the lessons during a supervisory visit, and her supervisor said it was the best lesson she had seen. Many states have implemented the Missouri model, and the curriculum has been used internationally as well. Most important are the data gathered in a statewide study demonstrating the effectiveness of full implementation.

Q: If you could do it over again, what might you do differently, and what are the next steps?

A: We trusted the process, took risks, believed in the program, and built on available resources at each step of the way. Next steps include continuing to review, revise, and renew existing materials to ensure that they are relevant to the needs of today's school counselors. DESE continues to fund and facilitate a state writing team that ensures that materials are rigorous and relevant.

Source: R. Yoesel, personal communication, April 27, 2017.

The art and science in school counseling might also be referred to as practice informing research and research informing practice. These may be inseparable concepts. Neither element is complete on its own; they are complementary. Research-based prepackaged curricula are typically easy to use, graphically organized, clearly written, and aligned with standards. They often include extension activities, assessments, and parent/family engagement components. Well-researched and well-designed school counselor–generated lessons meet the specific needs of the school population to produce successful student outcomes. Most often, school counselors at the secondary level will design Tier 1 school counseling programs with counselor-generated lessons in academic, college/career, and social/emotional domains. With experience and time, school counselors will determine core curriculum lessons that best fit the needs of their students as they assess and modify lesson topics and contents yearly. Regardless of whether the school counselor utilizes research-based curriculum and/or school counselor–generated curriculum, collecting perception and outcome data is most important. See Chapter 10 for more on collecting and sharing program results.

Table 3.1 Research-Based Curriculum Versus School Counselor–Generated Curriculum

Research-Based Curriculum		School Counselor–Generated Curriculum (self-generated or located online—may also apply to some state curricula)	
Benefits	Challenges	Benefits	Challenges
Evidence supporting effectiveness	EBP still requires school counselors to create local measures to assess impact	Allows counselors to be creative and add the art of school counseling	School counselors must create their own lessons through trial and error and must evaluate and improve lessons regularly
Prepackaged	Costly and may become outdated, requiring expensive fees for replacement	Free	It takes time to make/revise/locate lessons—so it is not free if you add up the costs of the extra duties of creating/modifying the curriculum
Ready-made—typically easy to pick up and teach with little prep	May not culturally align with the needs of local students and may be outdated	Can create/revise curriculum to meet cultural or other needs of the student population	Requires prep time to create lessons
Proven impact through research	Many lessons are needed to implement/teach with fidelity	Counselors can collaborate to divide up lessons to create/revise	Lessons may be haphazard and not scaffolded as in prepackaged programs
Many lessons	Too many lessons for the school counselor to teach alone (requires consolidation or selecting a few)	Online lessons are easy to locate and are often well vetted by many counselors	May lend itself to personal preferences and be overly heavy in one domain versus balancing the three domains

Research-Based Curriculum		School Counselor–Generated Curriculum (self-generated or located online—may also apply to some state curricula)	
Benefits	Challenges	Benefits	Challenges
Packaged in sequential/scaffolded lessons	Not as impactful if randomly taught	Can take local developmental needs into account	Often is created in a vacuum
When teachers buy in, the whole school supports delivery	Requires teacher buy-in	Can be tech savvy, cutting edge, and engaging for students with a skilled school counselor	May be less sophisticated if a school counselor lacks tech training/tools
May have some assessment tools (typically self-reported behaviors)	May not include perception assessments (counselors may have to create their own)	Self-generated content allows pre-/post-tests to align better with attitudes, knowledge, and skills	May require assessment tools and rubrics to be created
May be scripted—easy to pick up and go	Scripted—may not be in line with the counselor's voice or may hinder creativity	May be helpful for first-year counselors who are just starting to learn by creating their own material	Risk of random acts of curriculum

School Counseling Program SMART Goals

Prior to determining what core curriculum to teach, school counselors are advised to create overarching program SMART goals that the curriculum will support. The acronym SMART is described in different ways, as seen in Figure 3.3, but for our purposes we will focus on SMART goals as **S**pecific, **M**easurable, **A**ttainable, **R**esults-Oriented, and **T**ime-Bound. SMART goals align with a Multi-Tiered, Multi-Domain System of Supports (MTMDSS) as each goal targets one area of focus within the domains of academic, college/career, or social/emotional development, with tiered levels of prevention and intervention.

When designing school counseling program SMART goals, school counselors can best prepare by collecting reference documents, such as state performance indicators, district strategic plans, and school improvement goals. Through strategically connecting the goals of school counseling programs to established state and local targets, school counselors show how they align their work to support these initiatives. In this way, the services and activities that school counselors provide are integrated into the comprehensive school system. See Table 3.2 for tips on writing a SMART goal, and see Figure 3.4 for an example of a goal-drafting process, with school counseling program activities supporting that goal. If struggling to write a goal in SMART format, school counselors can use the ASCA Template for Developing a School Counseling Program Goal in SMART Goal Format, found at http://bit.ly/ASCASMARTTEMPLATE.

Table 3.2   Tips for Writing SMART Goals

Specific What is the specific issue based on our school's data?	To be **S**PECIFIC, look up data that align to the areas of focus. School counselors want to choose an area of need, and the data help determine what is and isn't an area on which to focus. For instance, if a school goal is to increase the college enrollment rate, the school counselor can find out the percentage of graduating seniors enrolling in college from each of the last few school years (see Figure 3.4).
Measurable How will we measure the effectiveness of our interventions?	Once baseline (previous-year) data are determined, consider how to continually collect and **M**EASURE the data needed to assess progress toward the selected goal. In the example (Figure 3.4), college enrollment data are only available once per school year (in October), so the school counselor must determine which incremental data makes the most sense to monitor on a regular (monthly or bimonthly) basis. In this case, the counselor might consider measuring FAFSA completion rates, the percentage of seniors with three or more college applications, % accepted into a college, percentage completing a net price calculator, and other similar metrics.
Attainable What outcome will stretch us but is still attainable?	Determining the rate at which a success will be **A**TTAINABLE is slightly more subjective. Although you want to choose a goal that will stretch you, you don't want to be stretched to an unrealistic level. Just as when advising students who have mostly Ds and Fs to focus on getting all passing grades, rather than on getting straight As, so they won't be discouraged, school counselors also want to choose a rate that will push them in a realistic way. It is suggested that school counselors collaborate with their administrators to set realistic goals that support schoolwide and district goals. This often helps the school counselor determine a realistic goal. In the example (Figure 3.4), the school counselor chose a 5% increase in the college enrollment rate. When taking into account that they have historically improved the rate by 1% each year, a 5% increase is a stretch while still being realistic.
Results-Oriented Is the goal reported with results-oriented data (process, perception, and outcome)?	To ensure that a goal is **R**ESULTS-ORIENTED, school counselors consider process, perception, and outcome data. See Chapters 9 and 10 for more information about different types of data.
Time-Bound When will our goal be accomplished?	Considering when the goal will be accomplished makes it **T**IME-BOUND. Generally, school counseling program goals are created for the year, and periodic checks (monthly, quarterly, etc.) are important, as is tracking progress toward the goal. In the example (Figure 3.4), the school counselors are monitoring several data metrics incrementally to assess whether they are on track. By checking regularly, the school counselor is able to provide additional prevention or intervention activities as needed to help reach the goal.

Figure 3.3 SMART can mean many things!

SMART Goals

Goals should be SMART:

S specific, significant, stretching

M measurable, meaningful, motivational

A agreed upon, attainable, achievable, acceptable, action oriented

R realistic, relevant, reasonable, rewarding, results oriented

T time based, time bound, timely, tangible, trackable

Figure 3.4 Example School Counseling Program SMART Goal

XYZ High School	
Area of Focus: College Enrollment (College/Career)	
Specific Issue What is the specific issue based on our school's data?	In the 2016–2017 school year, 53% of graduating seniors were enrolled in a 2- or 4-year postsecondary institution. In the 2017–2018 school year, 54% of graduating seniors will be enrolled in a 2- or 4-year postsecondary institution.
Measurable How will we measure the effectiveness of our interventions?	College enrollment data will be collected from the National Student Clearinghouse (NSC).
Attainable What outcome would stretch us but is still attainable?	2018–2019 goal: 5% increase (59% of graduating seniors will enroll in a postsecondary institution).
Results Oriented Is the goal reported in results-oriented data (process, perception, and outcome)?	Outcome data—college enrollment
Time Bound When will our goal be accomplished?	Monitor the progress of related data monthly to assess progress. Final goal accomplished by October 2019, when we receive enrollment data from the National Student Clearinghouse.

(Continued)

Figure 3.4 (Continued)

By October 2019, there will be a 5% increase in the college enrollment rate (59% of graduating seniors enrolling).

Aligns with School District LCAP Goal 2: Improve the college-going rate of graduating seniors.

Aligns with State/Local Performance Standards:

- College and Career Readiness Outcomes
- Culture and Climate

Activities to Address the Goal

- All seniors will receive a minimum of four core curriculum lessons pertaining to the college application process, creating balanced college lists (match, reach, and safety), FAFSA completion, scholarship searches, and transition support (see annual program calendar for details).
- School counselors will be active members on the Postsecondary Leadership Team.
- School counselors will coordinate multiple college nights/events for seniors and their families (FAFSA completion workshops, Alumni Day, Scholarship Fair, college rep visits, College Decision Day).
- School counselors will assist in developing and presenting staff in-service presentations on topics including writing recommendation letters, supporting first-generation, undocumented, and underrepresented students and their families throughout the college application process.
- School counselors will support summer transition and summer activities from May to August.
- School counselors will support the development of a college and career-going culture.
- School counselors will provide intentional interventions for students who have not completed the FAFSA by October 15 (small groups).
- School counselors will monitor the data monthly to determine areas of focus as well as celebrate successes (i.e., FAFSA submission & completion; % of seniors with more than three applications to at least one match, one reach, and one safety school; % of seniors accepted to at least one college, % of seniors completing at least one net price calculator).

RESOURCES

Resources for an Evidence-Based Curriculum

How can school counselors identify evidence-based programs and products that have been proven to be effective? Since 2002, the What Works Clearinghouse (WWC), part of the U.S. Department of Education's Institute of Education Sciences, has been a central and trusted source of scientific evidence on education programs, products, practices, and policies by focusing on high-quality research to answer the question, "What works in education?" (see Figure 3.5). The WWC reviews the research to determine which studies meet rigorous standards and summarizes the findings so that educators and schools can make informed decisions to improve student outcomes. For examples, refer to the WWC's website at http://ies.ed.gov/ncee/wwc.

In their mission to help make evidence-based social and emotional learning (SEL) an integral part of education from preschool through high school, the Collaborative for Academic, Social, and Emotional Learning (CASEL) synthesizes the research of others and conducts its own original research on curriculum and programs. To address educators who want to know which programs will promote social and emotional competence in their students, CASEL develops and publishes reviews of evidence-based SEL programs, including the CASEL *Guide: Effective*

Figure 3.5　What Works Clearinghouse

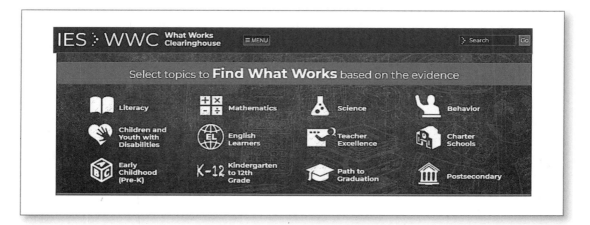

Social and Emotional Learning Programs—Middle and High School Edition (see Figure 3.6). This free, consumer-friendly guide 1) identifies and rates well-designed school-based programs that incorporate SEL practices and classroom instruction, 2) shares best-practice guidelines for district and school teams on how to select and implement SEL programs, and 3) offers recommendations for future priorities to advance SEL research and practice. The CASEL program guide will be continuously updated; contact info@casel.org to nominate new programs to be reviewed for possible inclusion in the guide. You can access the program guide at http://www.casel.org/guide.

Figure 3.6　2015 CASEL GUIDE

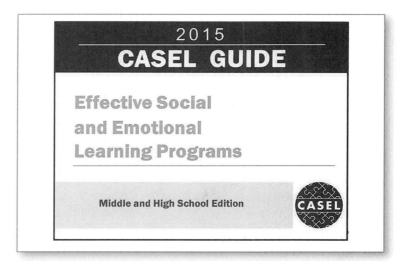

Source: Reprinted with permission from the Collaborative for Academic, Social, and Emotional Learning (®CASEL 2017) www.casel.org

WHITNEY'S STORY

The Creation of a Freshman Seminar Course

I collaborated with the freshman grade-level team at my school to develop and implement Freshman Seminar, an interdisciplinary, credit-bearing course designed uniquely for freshman students as they transition to high school. Taught by rock star teacher Jill Knopic Pammler, it integrated the themes of career and life planning into the traditional subjects

(Continued)

(Continued)

of literacy and mathematics, using the *Career Choices* textbook, AVID, and What's Next Illinois, the state-approved college and career readiness tool at that time, to frame unit themes.

Using a reality theory lens, the course centered on the questions "who am I, what do I want, and how do I get it" to engage freshmen in their own life planning and create motivated learners from day one of high school. School counselors can serve as leaders by advocating for such a course and aligning it to school counseling standards. It is also a great opportunity for school counselors to team up with teachers to facilitate school counseling core curriculum. Visit our website for the full syllabus and course unit plans and then check out Chapter 11 for best practices in teaming to create such systems.

Resources for a School Counselor–Generated Curriculum

Unlike many classroom teachers who receive textbooks with teachers' manuals, secondary school counselors typically self-create developmentally appropriate and engaging lessons for several topic areas and multiple grade levels. Therefore, quickly identifying low and no-cost resources to help school counselors get started is essential. Refer to Table 3.3 for a list of online web links to core curriculum resources that can be used as resources in creating lessons and student activities. Please note that this list is not meant to be all-inclusive of online core curriculum resources for lesson plans and activities, nor is inclusion here an endorsement by Hatching Results® or the authors of this text.

Table 3.3   Resources for School Counselor–Generated Curriculum

Website	Description of What You'll Find
Advancement Via Individual Determination (AVID) www.avid.org	A variety of lesson plans, classroom activities, engagement strategies, videos, and articles that seek to support students holistically toward college and career readiness
American Student Achievement Institute www.asainstitute.org/schoolcounseling/lessonplans.html	Free, downloadable lessons across the three domains that provide steps to implement effective practice
Anti-Defamation League https://www.adl.org/education-and-resources/resources-for-educators-parents-families	Free tools and lesson plans for promoting anti-bias and culturally responsive learning environments at all grade levels
ASCA Scene http://scene.schoolcounselor.org/home	Free to American School Counselor Association (ASCA) members; contains lesson plans contributed by practicing school counselors from across the country
Attendance Works www.attendanceworks.org/resources/teaching-attendance-curriculum	Free lesson plans and tools for teaching the importance of attendance and reducing chronic absenteeism through Grade 12

Website	Description of What You'll Find
California Career Resource Network (CalCRN) www.californiacareers.info	Free college and career readiness lesson plans for Grades 5–12; includes an educator guide, videos, and handouts in English and Spanish
California College Guidance Initiative (CCGI) http://bit.ly/CCGIoverview	Free, 6th-12th grade curriculum that supports educators in guiding students through a series of developmentally appropriate college and career planning activities
Casey Life Skills for Postsecondary Planning through NCDA http://caseylifeskills.force.com	Free; includes lessons around independent living skills such as self-advocacy, self-protection, and healthy relationships
Chicago Public Schools Advisory Curriculum https://sites.google.com/site/cpspositive-behavior/home/advisory-framework	Free, advisory lessons for Grades 6–12 on topics within the three domains such as communication, empathy, diversity, leadership development, coping skills, postsecondary planning, and academic skills
Classroom Circle Handbook www.pathseducation.com/files/docs/cps-classroom-circle-handbook.pdf	Free, 5-week curriculum that teaches life skills such as empathy, positive self-talk, problem-solving, goal setting, active listening, and being assertive
College Board https://professionals.collegeboard.org/guidance/counseling/counselor-resources	An easy-to-navigate web page of free and timely resources for teaching students how to plan, apply, and pay for college
Common Sense www.commonsense.org/education	Free, downloadable lesson plans on digital citizenship for all grade levels
ConnectEd Studios https://www.connectedstudios.org/url-zu5qkbnyIFUpWSn7jexJBg	Free, downloadable college access and college development curricula
Gay, Lesbian, and Straight Education Network (GLSEN) https://www.glsen.org/educate/resources/lesson-plans	Free, downloadable lesson plans and videos for teaching and promoting respect, empathy, and action so that students develop the skills to interact in our diverse world
Get Focused, Stay Focused http://www.getfocusedstayfocused.org	Curriculum for a semester- or year-long freshman course designed to increase high school and college completion *and* assure successful entry into the workforce with the skills required to succeed
Green 360 Career Catalyst http://green360careers.net	Free lesson plans that offer stand-alone lesson delivery, enrichment, and group activities as well as strategies for curriculum integration
iCouldBe www.icouldbe.org	Online mentoring with employers in a secure and monitored platform as well as interactive academic and career planning curriculum to enhance self-efficacy
Johns Hopkins Adolescent Depression Awareness Program (ADAP) www.hopkinsmedicine.org/psychiatry/specialty_areas/moods/ADAP/index.html	Three-session curriculum that educates students, staff, and families about the illness of depression

(Continued)

Table 3.3   (Continued)

Website	Description of What You'll Find
Missouri Department of Education's School Counseling Curriculum https://dese.mo.gov/college-career-readiness/school-counseling/curriculum	Free, downloadable lesson plans across the three domains by grade level
National Association for College Admission Counseling (NACAC) Curriculum for College Awareness and Planning www.nacacnet.org/advocacy—ethics/initiatives/steps	Free, downloadable lesson plans and PowerPoints in English and Spanish for use with both students and families
Naviance www.naviance.com	A college and career planning tool that houses lesson plans and activities for Grades 6–12
Overcoming Obstacles https://www.overcomingobstacles.org	Free, research-based life skills curriculum for middle and high school students
Share My Lesson https://sharemylesson.com	Free lesson plans for all grade levels on a wide variety of topics including career and technical education, drug prevention, mental/emotional/social health, community health, and safety
Student Success Skills http://studentsuccessskills.com	An evidence-based curriculum that helps students develop key cognitive, social, and self-management skills
Teaching Tolerance https://www.tolerance.org/classroom-resources	Hundreds of free, downloadable lesson plans that help educators teach anti-bias both in the classroom and through schoolwide activities

FACTORS TO CONSIDER IN SELECTING AND DEVELOPING CORE CURRICULUM

Fidelity of Evidence-Based Programs

The fidelity of evidence-based program implementation and the proposed effects are diminished when programs are not delivered as prescribed. Some school counselors or schools may choose to develop core curriculum by combining lessons from different evidence-based curricula because they like the topics or find them particularly useful. In addition, evidence-based programs may include so many classroom lessons that school counselors reduce the numbers of lessons within their scope and sequence. School counselors are reminded that changes in adherence to the curriculum, exposure (the number of classroom lessons taught), quality of delivery, or program differentiation (using other programs) can result in modified results. This is not to discourage the use of an evidence-based program because adjustments need to be made; rather, it is to ensure full awareness of the potential impact on outcomes.

Legal Issues and Lesson Plans

As school counselors use online classroom lessons and piece together their curriculum, they may encounter blogs and online resources such as TeachersPayTeachers and

We Are Teachers, which provide an online marketplace for teachers and counselors to sell original classroom lesson plans. However, those who sell their lesson plans online might be acting outside of copyright laws. Critics cite ethical pitfalls (plagiarism and a lack of quality) in this intellectual property and caution that there may be a chance that these "authors" don't actually own the copyright to the classroom materials they produce because this content may have been developed for their current position. District employment contracts may assign copyright ownership of materials produced for the classroom to the teacher (or school counselor), which means that educators have rights to "sell" their self-generated curriculum. However, the Copyright Act of 1976 stipulates that without any written agreement stating otherwise, materials created by teachers in the scope of their employment are deemed works for hire; therefore, the school owns them (Walker, n.d.). In sum, prior to purchasing any self-generated curriculum online, school counselors should do their best to ensure that the lessons are of high quality; also, prior to posting or selling materials themselves, school counselors are advised to read their employment contracts to prevent legal issues.

Additional Ways to Select a Curriculum

When school counselors have more curriculum to deliver than time allows (given counselor-to-student ratios or other responsibilities), it's helpful to provide teachers with a survey of the predetermined lessons and ask them to prioritize which lessons they prefer. Perhaps the English teachers are already teaching students how to create a résumé. In this case, that lesson is not one the secondary counselor needs to deliver. A sample of a counselor survey for middle school counselors is provided in Chapter 2 and is also available on our website. School counselors may want to survey their teachers regarding the extent to which they perceive their students to be exhibiting the attitudes and behaviors aligned with noncognitive factors. Based on *Teaching Adolescents to Become Learners: The Role of Noncognitive Factors in Shaping School Performance* (Farrington et al., 2012), published by the University of Chicago, the Noncognitive Needs Survey is a tool for prioritizing school counseling core curriculum. It is pictured in Figure 3.7 and is available on our website.

NOTES

Figure 3.7   Noncognitive Needs Survey: A Tool for Prioritizing Core Curriculum

Hatching Results, LLC
NONCOGNITIVE NEEDS SURVEY
A Tool for Prioritizing School Counseling Core Curriculum

TEACHER NAME: _____ CLASSROOM #: _____ DATE: _____

SUBJECT/GRADE: _____ TIME: _____

INSTRUCTIONS: To the best of your knowledge and based on your *own* observations during the current school year only, please rate your classroom's demonstration and proficiency of certain noncognitive factors and skills.

ACADEMIC BEHAVIORS

1. The majority of students in my class effectively demonstrate:	5 Always	4 Usually	3 Sometimes	2 Rarely	1 Never
a. Work completion (homework, projects, class work, etc.)	☐	☐	☐	☐	☐
b. Organizational skills (materials/desk/backpack)	☐	☐	☐	☐	☐
c. Participation skills (active listening/engaged/contribute)	☐	☐	☐	☐	☐
d. Study skills (exhibited in school and/or at home)	☐	☐	☐	☐	☐

COMMENTS:

ACADEMIC PERSEVERANCE

2. The majority of students in my class effectively demonstrate:	5 Always	4 Usually	3 Sometimes	2 Rarely	1 Never
a. Grit (staying focused on task despite obstacles)	☐	☐	☐	☐	☐
b. Tenacity (determination and resolve)	☐	☐	☐	☐	☐
c. Delayed gratification	☐	☐	☐	☐	☐
d. Self-discipline	☐	☐	☐	☐	☐
e. Self-control (forgo short-term needs for long-term goals)	☐	☐	☐	☐	☐

COMMENTS:

ACADEMIC MINDSETS

3. In my assessment, the majority of students in my class believe:	5 Always	4 Usually	3 Sometimes	2 Rarely	1 Never
a. They belong to the academic community	☐	☐	☐	☐	☐
b. Their ability and competence grow with effort	☐	☐	☐	☐	☐
c. They can succeed in their school work	☐	☐	☐	☐	☐
d. See value in their work	☐	☐	☐	☐	☐

COMMENTS:

LEARNING STRATEGIES

4. The majority of my students in my class are proficient in the following areas:	5 Always	4 Usually	3 Sometimes	2 Rarely	1 Never
a. Study skills (can identify/use)	☐	☐	☐	☐	☐
b. Metacognitive strategies (thinking about thinking)	☐	☐	☐	☐	☐
c. Self-regulated learning (ability to pause self)	☐	☐	☐	☐	☐
d. Goalsetting (ability to set goals)	☐	☐	☐	☐	☐

COMMENTS:

SOCIAL SKILLS

5. The majority of students in my class demonstrate proficiency in:	5 Always	4 Usually	3 Sometimes	2 Rarely	1 Never
a. Interpersonal skills	☐	☐	☐	☐	☐
b. Empathy	☐	☐	☐	☐	☐
c. Cooperation	☐	☐	☐	☐	☐
d. Assertion	☐	☐	☐	☐	☐
e. Responsibility	☐	☐	☐	☐	☐

COMMENTS:

Source: Hatching Results®, LLC. Based on *Teaching adolescents to become learners: The role of noncognitive factors in shaping school performance (2012),* by the University of Chicago.

Teaching Social Justice

School counselors can be change agents by using current events as teachable moments in the classroom (i.e., #MeToo, Charlottesville, Black Lives Matter, Bathroom Bill, etc.) as it not only helps students make a meaningful connection between classroom content and the real world but also encourages them to think critically about social issues and empowers them to become their own agents of change. School counselors can play a leading role in teaching students to examine how social and cultural factors impact members of our society, challenge bias and all forms of oppression, and embrace the rich diversity in their communities and world. In so doing, school counselors promote active citizenship and social justice while exponentially contributing to the elimination of systemic barriers to student success.

Reflection Activity:

- How might teaching social justice in the classroom foster a stronger climate and culture in your school?
- How might it impact grades, attendance, behavior, and other school metrics?
- How might you meet your student population where they are while encouraging them to stretch their thinking on a current event that is impacting your community?
- What do our ethical standards say about social justice and the school counselor's role?

WHITNEY'S STORY

Peer-Led Freshman Advisory

One way to engage students in core curriculum is to enlist their support in actually *delivering* the curriculum! I collaborated with the freshman grade-level team at Al Raby High School to develop and implement a peer-led freshman advisory curriculum adapted from Focus Training's Ignition program (www.ignitionmentoring.com). This peer-led sequence of relationship-building mini-lessons (15–20 minutes each) continued monthly (at times weekly) throughout the school year, allowing freshmen to build relationships with upperclassmen and engage more deeply in the curriculum (because we all know that teenagers will often take their peers more seriously than us adults, lol).

Called the Star Mentors, this group of student leaders were highly trained by the school counselor and met weekly in an after-school club to continue their training throughout the school year. The content of these mini-lessons built on the summer transition curriculum that all freshmen participated in (called Freshman Connection—learn more about this program in Chapter 8) and was aligned to the core curriculum taught by the school counselor throughout the school year. The Star Mentors not only delivered lessons but supported freshman/family orientation, accompanied freshmen on field trips as quasi-chaperones, assisted with schoolwide events, and contributed greatly to the overall culture and climate of the school. The result was a series of strongly aligned, ongoing freshman transition activities that were delivered and reinforced by several key stakeholders (school counselor, teachers, and upperclassmen) and infused throughout the freshman experience. For program samples, visit our website!

COLLEGE AND CAREER READINESS IN SECONDARY SCHOOLS

Much of the curriculum at the secondary level focuses on college and career readiness. Secondary school counselors are encouraged to align schoolwide lessons in college and career readiness with schoolwide activities, such as career fairs, college visits, FAFSA completion challenges, and job exploration activities. Following the recommendations of the National Office of School Counselor Advocacy (NOSCA), the Eight Components of College and Career Readiness, commonly referred to as the NOSCA 8 (see Figure 3.9; full text available on our website), serve as foundational considerations for curriculum, schoolwide activities, and family education within a comprehensive school counseling program. The College Board (2012) also has the free *School Counselor's Guide: NOSCA's Eight Components of College and Career Readiness Counseling* (College Board, 2012; see Figure 3.8) for both middle school and high school counselors, which are available on our website.

Figure 3.8   Eight Components of College and Career Readiness

The College Board National Office for School Counselor Advocacy
Eight Components of College and Career Readiness Counseling

The Eight Components of College and Career Readiness Counseling provide a systemic approach for school counselors to implement, across grades K–12 — elementary through high school and beyond, to ensure equity both in process and results.

1. College Aspirations

Goal: Build a college-going culture based on early college awareness by nurturing in students the confidence to aspire to college and the resilience to overcome challenges along the way. Maintain high expectations by providing adequate supports, building social capital and conveying the conviction that all students can succeed in college.

2. Academic Planning for College and Career Readiness

Goal: Advance students' planning, preparation, participation and performance in a rigorous academic program that connects to their college and career aspirations and goals.

3. Enrichment and Extracurricular Engagement

Goal: Ensure equitable exposure to a wide range of extracurricular and enrichment opportunities that build leadership, nurture talents and interests, and increase engagement with school.

4. College and Career Exploration and Selection Processes

Goal: Provide early and ongoing exposure to experiences and information necessary to make informed decisions when selecting a college or career that connects to academic preparation and future aspirations.

5. College and Career Assessments

Goal: Promote preparation, participation and performance in college and career assessments by all students.

6. College Affordability Planning

Goal: Provide students and families with comprehensive information about college costs, options for paying for college, and the financial aid and scholarship processes and eligibility requirements, so they are able to plan for and afford a college education.

7. College and Career Admission Processes

Goal: Ensure that students and families have an early and ongoing understanding of the college and career application and admission processes so they can find the postsecondary options that are the best fit with their aspirations and interests.

8. Transition from High School Graduation to College Enrollment

Goal: Connect students to school and community resources to help the students overcome barriers and ensure the successful transition from high school to college.

Equity • Leadership • Transformation   3

Source: Reprinted with permission from The College Board, 2018.

Figure 3.9   School Counseling Core Curriculum Potential Topics Aligned to the NOSCA 8 Brainstormed in One District

CORE CURRICULUM Aligned with NOSCA 8				
	9th	**10th**	**11th**	**12th**
Career Exploration	Career interest inventory assessment (4, 5)	Career exploration/ research careers (4, 5)	Career & college research (4)	Career & college selection (4, 5)
	Skill vs. ability assessment (4, 5)			
	Learning styles assessment (5)			
Social/ Emotional	Anti bullying (3)	Managing stress, anxiety and other stressors (3)	Anxiety (3)	Coping skills for adult world (8)
	Respect for peers (3)	Conflict management (3)		Anxiety (3)
	Conflict resolution (3)			
	Counseling resources (3)			
Academic Success	Study skills (2, 3)	Attendance/grades/ transcripts (2)	Grad requirements (2)	Grad requirements (2)
	Time management (2, 3)	Grad requirements (2)	Pre registration course selection (2)	
	Tutoring services (3)	Pre registration course selection (2)	Intervention resources (3)	Intervention resources (3)
	Grad requirements (2)	Intervention resources (3)	Tutoring services (3)	Tutoring services (3)
	Extra curricular activities (3)	Tutoring services (3)	Modify 4-year plan (2)	
	Intervention resources (3)	Modify 4-year plan (2)	Options for credit recovery (2)	Options for credit recovery (2)
	Pre registration course selection (2)	Extra curricular activities (3)		
	4-year plan (2)			

CORE CURRICULUM Aligned with NOSCA 8				
	9th	10th	11th	12th
Post Sec. Planning	Postsecondary options (8)	Postsecondary options (8)	Postsecondary options (8)	Postsecondary options (8)
	A–G (2, 7)	A–G (2, 7)	A–G (2, 7)	A–G (2, 7)
	College assessments (5)	College assessments (5)	College assessments (5)	College assessments (5)
	College aspirations (1)	College affordability (6)	College affordability (6)	College affordability (6)
	College affordability (6)	Scholarships (6, 8)	Scholarships (6, 8)	Scholarships (6, 8)
	Scholarships (6, 8)		Testing (5, 7)	FAFSA/Dream Act (6, 8)
			Application process deadlines (5, 7)	Applying to college (7)

Senior Seminar

Designed to help students—especially those who will be the first in their family to attend college—succeed in getting to and through college, a semester- or year-long senior-year course can support students with deadlines, financial aid, applications, and social/emotional stresses of applying, enrolling, and persisting in college. Ideally taught by a licensed individual with specialized training in postsecondary advising, school counselors are critical resources in the implementation of a successful senior seminar course. School counselors can advocate for such a course, coordinate the development of a developmentally appropriate and culturally responsive curriculum, and collaborate with the teacher of record to design and deliver content. Visit our website for a sample overview of Senior Seminar.

NOTES

_____

_____

_____

_____

CREATING A DISTRICTWIDE
EVIDENCE-BASED CURRICULUM

Just as teachers participate in curriculum development and textbook adoption, so too are school counselors charged to engage fully in this process. Designing and creating a schoolwide or districtwide curriculum is a serious investment of time, talent, and resources. The process may involve scheduling time to discuss and agree upon lesson content, research content for the lesson, design curriculum, and create PowerPoints or other methods of instruction. By using Dropbox or creating a Google Drive shared folder, it is possible to divide tasks among counselors in a school, within a district, or even countywide (see Becky Love's story in Chapter 2). School counselors can also create their action plans within a Google Doc file and hyperlink Google Slides presentations, lesson plans, and pre-/post-assessments into the file for all counselors to access and utilize.

In Hatching Results professional development (see Figure 3.10), we begin by asking school counselors at the secondary level to discuss among themselves the lessons they currently deliver and then the lessons they believe all students deserve to receive. Counselors are asked to review the ASCA Mindsets and Behaviors as well as NOSCA's Eight Components of College and Career Readiness. Then we ask school counselors to divide into groups, depending on the number of counselors per site (i.e., three grade level–specific groups: 6–8th, 9–10th, and 11–12th). After receiving their charge from the group to advocate for their lessons, counselors head to chart paper and begin the process of brainstorming what curriculum they believe *every* 9th, 10th, 11th, and 12th grader deserves to receive. Of course, too many lessons are listed, so the facilitators assist the school counselors in combining lessons and/or inquiring if this lesson is developmentally appropriate and whether it is one that every student needs. For example, although some insist a lesson on attendance is necessary, not all 9th graders need this lesson at a school with a 95% attendance rate. In this case, perhaps attendance is a single slide in a longer presentation on 9th grade success, or it is reserved for the Tier 2 interventions. Either way, it would not be a full-length lesson that would be recommended for every 9th grader, as there are other lessons that are more appropriate based on the students' needs.

Figure 3.10 Examples of Districtwide Core Curriculum Mapping

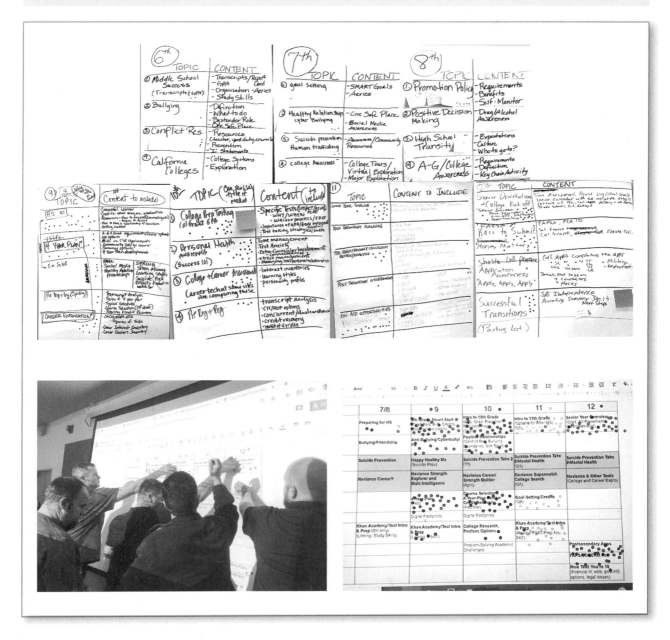

Activity 3.1

Brainstorm potential core curriculum topics and content that you would like to see in your program.

NOTES

_____

_____

_____

_____

_____

_____

_____

_____

_____

_____

_____

_____

_____

_____

_____

4

Lesson Plans

When providing professional development to school counselors, I often ask: "How many of you received instruction in your graduate program on how to plan, teach, and evaluate school counseling core curriculum classroom lessons?" Generally, less than 20% of school counselors raise their hands. When asking if counselors had an entire class on these topics, the percentage is even less. However, teaching all students through effective core curriculum classroom lessons is so essential to ensure students gain developmentally appropriate attitudes, knowledge, and skills to support their academic, college and career, and social/emotional growth. The ASCA National Model (2012) recommends that school counselors at the secondary level devote 15–35% of their time teaching core curriculum counseling lessons (formerly called guidance curriculum). However, I frequently work with school counselors, especially at high school, who haven't (yet) taught any class lessons. Teaching school counseling content within the classroom ensures all students understand essential skills such as graduation and college eligibility requirements, how to complete and submit financial aid applications, healthy ways to manage stress and other emotions, and career options and aligning postsecondary requirements.

As I began working as a school counselor at the secondary level, my district was implementing Direct Interactive Instruction (Action Learning Systems, 2012) to improve lesson design, student engagement, and assessment to positively impact student achievement. Through participating in on-site trainings and observing model teachers, I learned how to 1) write measurable objectives aligned with standards, 2) incorporate a variety of engagement strategies within my lessons, 3) improve my classroom management skills, and 4) easily assess what students had learned at the end of my lesson through multiple measures. Although some school counselors may not see the value in attending teacher trainings, these professional development opportunities have drastically improved my teaching skills and

(Continued)

(Continued)

abilities. One of my favorite compliments is when teachers are surprised that I haven't been a classroom teacher or when they tell me that I use all the same strategies that they do.

Secondary school counselors may have pushback on the time they are "taking" from teachers' instruction, so it is even more important that they demonstrate strong instructional practices when teaching counseling classroom lessons. In addition, the content taught at the secondary level is more complex; therefore, using a variety of strategic engagement strategies to help students retain and apply the information is extremely important. When teachers see school counselors teaching to standards (yes, school counselors have standards, too!), facilitating active participation throughout core curriculum classroom lessons, and assessing student learning, professional respect improves. Strong teaching and learning lead to teachers' understanding the benefit of school counseling core curriculum lessons, and when school counselors share results of their lessons, teachers are even more on board.

Chapters 4 through 6 are designed to provide the reader with the attitudes, knowledge, and skills needed to effectively teach and engage students through core curriculum classroom lessons.

LESSON PLAN DEVELOPMENT COMPONENTS

Just as teachers design lesson plans, school counselors preparing to teach content in the classroom setting do so as well (Lopez & Mason, 2018). In Chapter 2, counselors determined content for a franchisable curriculum. This chapter expands on the development of curriculum for agreed-upon topics to support school counselors' development of lesson plans. Descriptions of each lesson plan component and ways to incorporate best practices of teaching and learning within a well-developed lesson plan are included. Some sections of the lesson plan are more straightforward and shorter, whereas other sections are longer, are not typically taught in school counseling graduate programs, and include more detailed descriptions and instruction. Throughout this chapter, readers are encouraged to reference our full lesson plan example (shown in Figure 4.25, beginning on page 106).

Lesson plan development includes these components, which are expanded upon in the following text:

1. Lesson subject and title

2. Grade level of students

3. Learning objectives

4. Standards

5. Materials

6. Procedure

7. Plan for evaluation

8. Follow-up

Lesson Subject and Title

When designing a lesson, first consider the subject area (see Figure 4.1). Is the lesson focused on teaching graduation and college eligibility requirements, the risks of alcohol and drugs, or how to complete financial aid applications, for example? A general topic such as one of these would be the lesson subject. School counselors create a title that aligns with agreed-upon franchised curriculum topics (see Chapter 2) and, if possible, is also interesting. For instance, a lesson for 9th grade students about graduation and college eligibility requirements, including information about passing classes to earn credits, can be called Credits Matter. A lesson transitioning seniors into life after high school could be named Shift Happens. Although the title is written first on the lesson plan, school counselors will likely fill in this section after the lesson objectives and procedure have been completed to ensure that the title aligns with the content.

Figure 4.1 Lesson Plan: Lesson Subject, Title, and Grade Level of Students

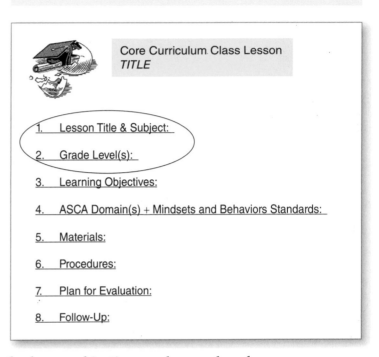

Grade Level of Students

Within the lesson plan, school counselors will indicate the grade level of students for which the lesson is designed. Considering the developmental level and specific needs for students at each grade is important to ensure the content at the secondary level is relevant. For example, while basic financial aid information is important at 9th grade, 11th and 12th grades are the years that students need the most detailed instruction on this topic. At high school, core curriculum topics generally differ per grade level as the needs of each group, Grades 9 through 12, greatly vary. The 9th grade student needs support successfully transitioning into high school, such as graduation requirements, resources on campus, getting involved, checking grades online, and basic career exploration. On the opposite end of the spectrum, 12th grade lesson topics focus on applying to college or other postsecondary options, completing financial aid applications, managing the stress of senior year, and transitioning into the "real world." Therefore, separate lessons per grade at high school are likely necessary. However, at the middle school level, content may be combined, such as all seventh and 8th graders receiving lessons on the risks of drugs and alcohol.

Figure 4.2   Lesson Plan: Learning Objectives

Core Curriculum Class Lesson
TITLE

1.   Lesson Title & Subject:

2.   Grade Level(s):

3.   Learning Objectives:

4.   ASCA Domain(s) + Mindsets and Behaviors Standards:

5.   Materials:

6.   Procedures:

7.   Plan for Evaluation:

8.   Follow-Up:

Learning Objectives

Creating measurable learning objectives is one of the most important components of lesson design and will therefore be discussed in depth (see Figure 4.2). Learning objectives are brief statements describing what students will learn during the course of a classroom lesson. Objectives are the most important learning takeaways, so they are to be determined *prior* to planning the rest of the lesson. Although some might think of classroom activities first, and frame objectives to align with what they want to teach, objectives are meant to drive the lesson content rather than the other way around. By beginning with the end in mind, school counselors plan objectives by thinking about the attitudes, knowledge, and skills they want their students to obtain by the end of the lesson.

How to Counsel (Teach) Like a Champion: The Four Ms

Doug Lemov's *Teach Like a Champion 2.0* (2015; see Figure 4.3) discusses the Four Ms for writing an effective classroom lesson objective: 1) **m**anageable, 2) **m**easurable, 3) **m**ade first, and 4) **m**ost important (see Table 4.1). These four criteria are designed to make the lesson useful and effective.

Figure 4.3   Doug Lemov's *Teach Like a Champion 2.0: 62 Techniques That Put Students on the Path to College*

Table 4.1   Teach Like a Champion: The Four Ms

Manageable	An objective should be of a size and scope that can be taught in a single lesson.
Measurable	An objective should be written so that your success in achieving it can be measured, ideally by the end of the class period.
Made first	An objective should be designed to guide the activity, not to justify how a chosen activity meets one of several viable purposes.
Most important	An objective should focus on what's most important on the path to college and nothing else.

Source: Lemov, D. (2014). *Teach Like a Champion 2.0: 62 techniques that put students on the path to college,* 2nd edition. San Francisco, CA: Josey-Bass. Reprinted with permission from Wiley.

Using the school counseling lens, the questions and descriptions that follow are framed for counselors to consider as they are planning their lesson objectives:

Manageable: Can this objective effectively be taught within the course of one school counseling lesson? School counselors' classroom time is limited. It's tempting to squeeze too much into one lesson by overplanning. However, quality is much better than quantity. When too much content is squeezed into one lesson (usually one class period at the secondary level—approximately 45 minutes to an hour), content focus is affected—and therefore so are student outcomes. School counselors are encouraged to consider the most important learning takeaway for the lesson and to focus on teaching the targeted objectives extremely well.

Measurable: How can I assess student learning of this objective? First, when writing an objective, school counselors want to consider how to measure what students have learned. Using pre- and post-tests to measure student learning is one form of assessment, yet there are other ways to do this as well. Accurately completing an activity such as a career assessment or 4-year plan, filling out a Ticket Out the Door, or even orally completing sentence frames related to the lesson objectives are all ways to measure student learning. When writing an objective, school counselors can incorporate the measures within their objective with one simple word: *by*. For example: "Students can demonstrate their understanding of high school graduation and college admission requirements *by* completing a 4-year high school plan." Although not every lesson objective must be written to be specifically measurable, best practice states that at least one objective is directly measurable.

Activity 4.1

Look at the examples that follow demonstrating how an unmeasurable learning objective was transformed into a measurable objective. Consider how you can make the additional "Not Yet Measurable" objectives measurable.

Table 4.2 Measurable Objectives

Not Yet Measurable	Measurable
Students can identify two positive ways to manage stress.	Students can identify two positive ways to manage stress by completing a Ticket Out the Door.
I understand why prioritizing is important.	I understand why prioritizing is important, and I can prioritize by using a three-step process.
Tenth grade students can describe two or more postsecondary options they are interested in for the future.	Tenth grade students can describe two or more postsecondary options they are interested in for the future by completing the What's Next Activity.
Students know the components of a SMART goal.	
Middle school students can identify test-taking strategies.	
I understand the high school graduation and college eligibility requirements.	

Made first: Why is it important to create my objective prior to the rest of my lesson plan design? As discussed previously, designing the objective to guide the activity, rather than to justify how the activity meets one of multiple outcomes, is recommended. Although it is important to review and fine-tune the objective after the lesson is created, writing the objective prior to lesson design helps better ensure that the intended goal of the lesson will be met through the delivery of content.

Most important: What is most important for students on their path to mastery of content? In *Teach Like a Champion 2.0*, Lemov (2015) discusses the importance of all curricula being focused on helping students achieve the goal of postsecondary readiness. While he is specifically addressing teachers, the message is similar for school counselors. Although the three domains of focus for school counselors are academic, career, and social/emotional development, ultimately teaching students skills in each area helps ready them to become positively contributing members of society after graduating from high school. Therefore, when considering objectives, it is important for school counselors to plan their class time wisely, ensuring that each school counseling core curriculum lesson supports student learning and students' growth on their path to becoming active members of society.

Bloom's Taxonomy

In addition to Lemov's Four Ms, school counselors are also advised to utilize Bloom's Taxonomy when creating lesson objectives. The taxonomy pyramid (see Figure 4.4) shows how remembering and understanding make up the foundation of learning, with subsequent levels promoting deeper thinking and creativity. Rather than focusing on students solely knowing or understanding concepts, creating lessons that will move students to higher levels of thinking ensures that they can apply, analyze, evaluate, and create using their base knowledge.

The first category, *remembering* knowledge, is the foundation on which the other categories are built, as depicted in the pyramid shown in Figure 4.4. Students need to first remember and recall content and then utilize this information to build their skills and abilities to the most complex level of creating. As students put information into practice, deeper levels of learning occur, and they progress from basic *understanding* to *applying* and *analyzing*, up through *evaluation* and *creation*. For example, after students can explain the graduation requirements (within the category of understanding), their ability to *compare and contrast* (analyze) different courses to meet the requirements and *create* a 4-year plan correctly incorporating the graduation requirements exhibits higher levels of thinking using their base knowledge. As school counselors create objectives and lessons, considering Bloom's Taxonomy and its accompanying verbs (see Figure 4.26) encourages critical thinking as students apply, analyze, evaluate, and create with the information they learn. Although not every lesson objective must be at the level of *apply* or above, best practice is to write at least one objective per lesson at the Bloom's Taxonomy level of *apply* or higher.

Bloom's Taxonomy

Developed under the leadership of Dr. Benjamin Bloom, Bloom's Taxonomy was created to promote higher levels of thinking within education. This framework categorizes educational goals and has been applied within the K–12 and college setting since the 1950s, and it is still relevant today. Within the framework, there are six categories: 1) remember, 2) understand, 3) apply, 4) analyze, 5) evaluate, and 6) create (Armstrong, n.d.).

Figure 4.4   Bloom's Taxonomy

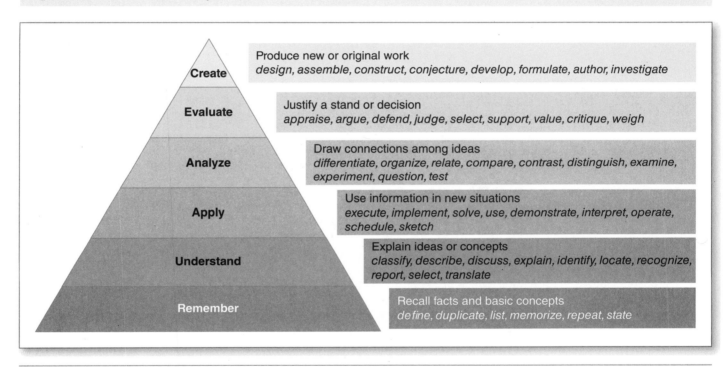

Source: Vanderbilt University Center for Teaching. Retrieved from https://www.flickr.com/photos/vandycft/29428436431 andycft/29428436431. Creative Commons Attribution license: Attribution 2.0 Generic (CC BY 2.0) https://creativecommons.org/licenses/by/2.0.

NOTES

_____

_____

_____

Activity 4.2

What follows are the objectives that were previously made to be measurable (from Activity 4.1). Now look at how these objectives have been transformed to further include the Bloom's Taxonomy levels of apply, analyze, evaluate, or create. Consider how to make the additional objectives fit into the level of "apply" or above.

Table 4.3   Incorporating Bloom's Taxonomy into Objectives

Bloom's Taxonomy Level: Remember or Understand	Bloom's Taxonomy Level: Apply, Analyze, Evaluate, or Create
Students can _identify_ two positive ways to manage stress by completing a Ticket Out the Door.	Students can _differentiate_ between positive and negative ways to manage stress by completing a Ticket Out the Door.
I _understand_ why prioritizing is important, and I can prioritize by using a three-step process.	I _can apply my knowledge of_ why prioritizing is important to prioritizing by using a three-step process.
Tenth grade students can _describe_ two or more postsecondary options they are interested in for the future by completing the "What's Next" Activity.	Tenth grade students can _compare and contrast_ two or more postsecondary options they are interested in for the future by completing the "What's Next" Activity.
Students _know_ the components of a SMART goal by completing a Guided Notes worksheet.	
Middle school students can _identify_ test-taking strategies by completing a Ticket Out the Door.	
I _understand_ the high school graduation and college eligibility requirements and can integrate them into a 4-year plan.	

Standards

In 1996, the American School Counselor Association (ASCA) created the ASCA National Standards for Students (revised in 2004), with specific competencies and indicators in the academic, career, and personal/social domains (Campbell & Dahir, 1997). Each indicator was clearly defined, for example:

A:A3.1 *Take responsibility for their actions*

C:B1.1 *Apply decision-making skills to career planning, course selection, and career transition*

PS:B1.2 *Understand consequences of decisions and choices*

In 2014, ASCA shifted to the Mindsets and Behaviors for Student Success: K–12 College- and Career-Readiness Standards for Every Student, which still incorporate the three domains of academic, career, and social/emotional development (previously personal/social) but within the broader context of two categories: mindsets and behaviors (see Figure 4.5). The Mindset Standards include six items "related to the psycho-social attitudes or beliefs one has about oneself in relation to academic work" (Sparks & ASCA, n.d., slide 1) that school counselors will encourage students to develop. The Behavior Standards fall into three categories of Learning Strategies, Self-Management Skills, and Social Skills, with nine to ten standards under each area. These behavior standards are "commonly associated with being a successful student" (Sparks & ASCA, n.d., slide 29).

Many school counselors trained in the ASCA National Standards for Students found them to be very straightforward and easy to align with each grade level. Standards were used to develop a comprehensive school counseling program, building on student learning each year. Curriculum crosswalk tools were used by school counselors to check off which standards were taught in which grades, with the goal of students' mastering all the ASCA National Standards for Students within their K–12 education.

Figure 4.5   Lesson Plan: ASCA Domain(s) and Standards

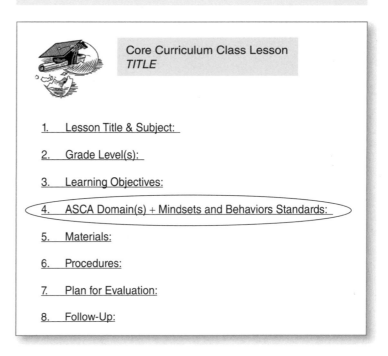

The *ASCA Mindsets and Behaviors for Student Success* are much broader, which can be helpful as well as challenging. Oftentimes school counselors teach skills that don't fit into only one domain of academic, career, or social/emotional. For instance, Mindset Standard 2 is "self-confidence in ability to succeed." School counselors can easily explain ways in which this standard can be applied to academic, career, and social/emotional domains. The *ASCA Mindsets and Behaviors for Student Success* were created based on best practices and a survey of research, including the noncognitive factors in the University of Chicago's literature review *Teaching Adolescents to Become Learners* (Farrington et al., 2012). Similar to the Common Core State Standards, the ASCA mindset and behavior standards are focused on college and career readiness within all aspects of learning. Therefore, the *ASCA Mindsets and Behaviors for Student Success* are up to date with current research and can be applied broadly within the school counselor role to best support student development.

A challenge with the mindset and behavior standards' broad and vague nature, especially for those who are familiar with the specificity of the previous standards, is that implementation and application are left up to the interpretation of school counselors. Using Mindset Standard 2 again ("self-confidence in ability to succeed"), secondary counselors can teach multiple concepts to address this standard—successfully transitioning to high school, creating postsecondary goals, maintaining a growth mindset, and more. The *ASCA Mindsets and Behaviors for Student Success* allow for flexibility in teaching content, but they are less directive for school counselors unsure of what to teach.

Figure 4.6 *ASCA Mindsets and Behaviors for Student Success*: K–12 College- and Career-Readiness Standards for Every Student

The ASCA Mindsets & Behaviors for Student Success:
K-12 College- and Career-Readiness Standards for Every Student
Each of the following standards can be applied to the academic, career and social/emotional domains.

Category 1: Mindset Standards
School counselors encourage the following mindsets for all students.

M 1. Belief in development of whole self, including a healthy balance of mental, social/emotional and physical well-being
M 2. Self-confidence in ability to succeed
M 3. Sense of belonging in the school environment
M 4. Understanding that postsecondary education and life-long learning are necessary for long-term career success
M 5. Belief in using abilities to their fullest to achieve high-quality results and outcomes
M 6. Positive attitude toward work and learning

Category 2: Behavior Standards
Students will demonstrate the following standards through classroom lessons, activities and/or individual/small-group counseling.

Learning Strategies		Self-Management Skills		Social Skills	
B-LS 1.	Demonstrate critical-thinking skills to make informed decisions	B-SMS 1.	Demonstrate ability to assume responsibility	B-SS 1.	Use effective oral and written communication skills and listening skills
B-LS 2.	Demonstrate creativity	B-SMS 2.	Demonstrate self-discipline and self-control	B-SS 2.	Create positive and supportive relationships with other students
B-LS 3.	Use time-management, organizational and study skills	B-SMS 3.	Demonstrate ability to work independently	B-SS 3.	Create relationships with adults that support success
B-LS 4.	Apply self-motivation and self-direction to learning	B-SMS 4.	Demonstrate ability to delay immediate gratification for long-term rewards	B-SS 4.	Demonstrate empathy
B-LS 5.	Apply media and technology skills	B-SMS 5.	Demonstrate perseverance to achieve long- and short-term goals	B-SS 5.	Demonstrate ethical decision-making and social responsibility
B-LS 6.	Set high standards of quality	B-SMS 6.	Demonstrate ability to overcome barriers to learning	B-SS 6.	Use effective collaboration and cooperation skills
B-LS 7.	Identify long- and short-term academic, career and social/emotional goals	B-SMS 7.	Demonstrate effective coping skills when faced with a problem	B-SS 7.	Use leadership and teamwork skills to work effectively in diverse teams
B-LS 8.	Actively engage in challenging coursework	B-SMS 8.	Demonstrate the ability to balance school, home and community activities	B-SS 8.	Demonstrate advocacy skills and ability to assert self, when necessary
B-LS 9.	Gather evidence and consider multiple perspectives to make informed decisions	B-SMS 9.	Demonstrate personal safety skills	B-SS 9.	Demonstrate social maturity and behaviors appropriate to the situation and environment
B-LS 10.	Participate in enrichment and extracurricular activities	B-SMS 10.	Demonstrate ability to manage transitions and ability to adapt to changing situations and responsibilities		

Source: American School Counselor Association (2014). *Mindsets and behaviors for student success: K–12 college- and career-readiness standards for every student.* Alexandria, VA: Author. Reprinted with permission from the American School Counselor Association, 2019.

The *ASCA Mindsets and Behaviors for Student Success* can be applied to all grade levels in a developmentally appropriate manner (see Figure 4.6). School counselors can also search for or submit suggested competencies that support specific mindsets and behaviors on the ASCA website at https://www.schoolcounselor.org/school-counselors/about-asca/mindsets-behaviors/search-or-submit-competency. For example, searching for the word "postsecondary" produced the following result submitted by Tammy Dodson: *Students will use technology, including the internet, to produce a detailed post-secondary SMART goal as part of his/her Naviance 9th grade portfolio. This goal will be updated at least once a school year* (https://www.schoolcounselor.org/standardsandmindset?itemid=58; see Figure 4.7). The competency, as shown, aligns with multiple ASCA mindsets and behaviors standards, along with several Common Core Standards.

Figure 4.7 Example Competency Supporting *ASCA Mindsets and Behavior Standards for Student Success*

Competency:	Student will use technology, including the Internet, to produce a detailed postsecondary SMART goal as part of his/her Naviance 9th grade portfolio. This goal will be updated at least once each school year.
Grade Level:	9–12

This competency aligns with:

	4.	Understanding that postsecondary education and lifelong learning …
Mindset Standards:	5.	Belief in using abilities to their fullest to achieve high-quality results and outcomes
	6.	Positive attitude toward work and learning
	1.	Demonstrate critical thinking skills to make informed decisions
Behavior Standards— Learning Strategies:	4.	Apply self-motivation and self-direction to learning
	7.	Identify long- and short-term academic, career, and social/emotional goals
Behavior Standards— Self-Management Skills:	4.	Demonstrate ability to delay immediate gratification for long-term rewards
	5.	Demonstrate perseverance to achieve long- and short-term goals
Behavior Standards— Social Skills:		
English & Language Arts Common Core Standards:	Writing Standards	
Subcategories for English Language Arts:	Standard 6	
Math Common Core Standards:	Make sense of problems and persevere in solving them	
Upload:		
Submitted by:	Tammy Dodson	

The ASCA Mindsets and Behaviors Program Planning Tool helps school counselors plan their schoolwide counseling curricula (see Figure 4.8). School counselors identify the grade level and domain (academic, career, and/or social/emotional) in which they plan to address the standards. In some districts, this tool has been used during discussions with teachers as school counselors plan their schoolwide curriculum in collaboration with faculty. Keep in mind that it is not necessary to address each standard every year.

While adapting the *ASCA Mindsets and Behaviors for Student Success* standards to meet the diverse needs of K–12 students, the variance also causes a challenge if trying to crosswalk and teach the standards across all grade levels. Teachers use their standards as a framework from which to create lesson objectives, but the ASCA mindset and behavior standards can make this more challenging because they are so broad. Therefore, school counselors may find it easier to create a strong, measurable learning objective first and then align the *ASCA Mindsets and Behaviors for Student Success* to the created objective rather than the other way around. School counselors are also encouraged to align their lesson to Common Core or other state standards, as applicable. Connecting content being taught by school counselors to state or other academic standards provides further support for the importance of the school counseling core curriculum classroom lesson. What follows is an example of state standards that could apply to core curriculum.

School Counseling Core Curriculum Objective:

Tenth grade students can compare and contrast two or more postsecondary options they are interested in for the future by completing the "What's Next" Activity.

Common Core State Standard English Language Arts—Speaking and Listening, Grades 9–10:

CCSS.ELA-LITERACY.SL.9-10.1.D

Respond thoughtfully to diverse perspectives, summarize points of agreement and disagreement, and, when warranted, qualify or justify their own views and understanding and make new connections in light of the evidence and reasoning presented.

Whether designing objectives based on standards or connecting standards to objectives, core curriculum classroom lessons must be standards based, but the process to get there is up to the individual school counselor.

Materials

List all the materials needed for the school counseling core curriculum classroom lesson (see Figure 4.9). This is especially useful for school counselors as a checklist prior to teaching to ensure they have everything required. The materials section can also include the type of curriculum to be used. If a purchased curriculum will be taught, school counselors will want to secure the purchase of the curriculum by talking to their administrator and also participate in the appropriate training, if necessary.

Activity 4.3

What follows are the objectives that were created in Activities 4.1 and 4.2. Notice how one or two *ASCA Mindsets and Behaviors for Student Success* standards were applied to several of the objectives, and state standards were added (as applicable). Consider how to add mindset and behavior standards to the additional objectives, along with any additional standards.

Table 4.4   Aligning Standards to Objectives

Learning Objective	ASCA Mindset and Behavior Standards, along with State/Other Standards That Apply to the Objective
Students can differentiate between positive and negative ways to manage stress by completing a Ticket Out the Door.	M 1. Belief in development of whole self, including a healthy balance of mental, social/emotional, and physical well-being B-SMS 7. Demonstrate effective coping skills when faced with a problem Health Education Content Standards for California Public Schools—Standard 7.1M. Manage emotions appropriately in a variety of situations
Learning Objective	ASCA Mindset and Behavior Standards, along with State/Other Standards That Apply to the Objective
I can apply my knowledge of why prioritizing is important to prioritizing by using a three-step process.	B-LS 3. Use time-management, organizational, and study skills B-SMS 2. Demonstrate self-discipline and self-control Indiana School Counseling Competencies for Students, Academic Development Competency 1, 9-12. 4. Demonstrates attitudes and behaviors related to academic skill development
Tenth grade students can compare and contrast two or more postsecondary options they are interested in for the future by completing the "What's Next" Activity.	M 4. Understanding that postsecondary education and lifelong learning are necessary for long-term career success B-LS 1. Demonstrate critical thinking skills to make informed decisions Common Core ELA Speaking and Listening, 9-10.2. Integrate multiple sources of information presented in diverse media or formats (e.g., visually, quantitatively, and orally) evaluating the credibility and accuracy of each source
Students utilize the components of a SMART goal by completing a Guided Notes worksheet.	
Middle school students can choose test-taking strategies that align with their learning style by completing a Ticket Out the Door.	
I can apply the high school graduation and college eligibility requirements by integrating them into a 4-year plan.	

Figure 4.8   ASCA Mindsets and Behaviors Program Planning Tool

ASCA MINDSETS & BEHAVIORS: PROGRAM PLANNING TOOL

AMERICAN SCHOOL COUNSELOR ASSOCIATION

This form is a tool you can use in planning your overall school counseling curriculum. Indicate the grade level in which you plan to address any standard in the cells below as well as how the standard is addressed (core curriculum-CC, small group-SG, closing-the-gap-CTG). It isn't necessary to address each standard each year.

	Grade Level/Delivery		
	Academic	Career	Social/Emotional
Mindsets	*Indicate grade level and how addressed (core curriculum-CC, small group-SG, closing the gap-CTG)*		
M 1: Belief in development of whole self, including a healthy balance of mental, social/emotional and physical well-being			
M 2: Self-confidence in ability to succeed			
M 3: Sense of belonging in the school environment			
M 4: Understanding that postsecondary education and lifelong learning are necessary for long-term career success			
M 5: Belief in using abilities to their fullest to achieve high-quality results and outcomes			
M 6: Positive attitude toward work and learning			
Behavior: Learning Strategies			
B-LS 1: Demonstrate critical-thinking skills to make informed decisions			
B-LS 2: Demonstrate creativity			
B-LS 3: Use time-management, organizational and study skills			
B-LS 4: Apply self-motivation and self-direction to learning			
B-LS 5: Apply media and technology skills			
B-LS 6: Set high standards of quality			
B-LS 7: Identify long- and short-term academic, career and social/emotional goals			
B-LS 8: Actively engage in challenging coursework			
B-LS 9: Gather evidence and consider multiple perspectives to make informed decisions			
B-LS 10: Participate in enrichment and extracurricular activities			
Behavior: Self-Management Skills			
B-SMS 1: Demonstrate ability to assume responsibility			
B-SMS 2: Demonstrate self-discipline and self-control			
B-SMS 3: Demonstrate ability to work independently			
B-SMS 4: Demonstrate ability to delay immediate gratification for long-term rewards			
B-SMS 5: Demonstrate perseverance to achieve long- and short-term goals			
B-SMS 6: Demonstrate ability to overcome barriers to learning			
B-SMS 7: Demonstrate effective coping skills when faced with a problem			
B-SMS 8: Demonstrate the ability to balance school, home and community activities			
B-SMS 9: Demonstrate personal safety skills			
B-SMS 10: Demonstrate ability to manage transitions and ability to adapt to changing situations and responsibilities			
Behavior: Social Skills			
B-SS 1: Use effective oral and written communication skills and listening skills			
B-SS 2: Create positive and supportive relationships with other students			
B-SS 3: Create relationships with adults that support success			
B-SS 4: Demonstrate empathy			
B-SS 5: Demonstrate ethical decision-making and social responsibility			
B-SS 6: Use effective collaboration and cooperation skills			
B-SS 7: Use leadership and teamwork skills to work effectively in diverse teams			
B-SS 8: Demonstrate advocacy skills and ability to assert self, when necessary			
B-SS 9: Demonstrate social maturity and behaviors appropriate to the situation and environment			

© 2003, ASCA National Model: A Framework for School Counseling Programs. American School Counselor Association

Source: American School Counselor Association. ASCA Mindsets & Behaviors: Program Planning Tool. Retrieved from https://www.schoolcounselor.org/school-counselors/asca-national-model/asca-national-model-templates. Reprinted with permission from the American School Counselor Association, 2019.

Procedure

The procedure section of the lesson plan is where detailed instructions about how to teach the content are provided. In this section, school counselors describe, step by step, how the lesson will be taught. As school counselors write their lesson plans, details to be added include explanations of key concepts, discussion questions to ask students throughout the lesson, and engagement strategies to use (refer to Chapter 5). Consider how teachers create lesson plans for a substitute teacher. Teachers must include thorough descriptions of each portion of the lesson to ensure that the content is taught in the way the teacher intended. Similarly, when completing the procedure section of a lesson plan, school counselors are encouraged to write out detailed information, so another school counselor could teach the same content solely by reading the lesson plan.

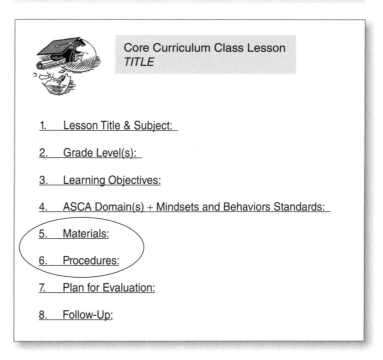

Figure 4.9 Lesson Plan: Materials and Procedure

Tips for Writing Detailed Procedures

- For lessons that include a PowerPoint or Google Slides presentation, consider writing what the school counselor will say and what the students are expected to do for each slide.
- Include student engagement strategies (discussed in Chapter 5) in the lesson plan to remind the presenter to use them.
- Add the targeted amount of time that it may take for each portion to keep the school counselor instructor on track in teaching all the content both efficiently and thoroughly.

How to Create Effective Lesson Procedures

With lesson objectives and standards already determined, creating the lesson content, or *procedures*, is the next step. The basic structure and sequence for a lesson is as follows:*

A) Welcome

B) Behavior expectations

C) Standards and objectives

D) Accessing prior knowledge

E) Input and model ("I do")

---

*Adapted from Direct Interactive Instruction (Action Learning Systems, 2012).

F) Guided and independent practice ("We do" and "You do")

G) Restate objectives, assessment, and closure

Welcome

To begin classroom lessons, school counselors introduce the lesson title (see Figure 4.10), address the students, and depending on how often school counselors visit classes, they may also restate the school counselor's role. Generally, school counselors at the secondary level do not visit classrooms weekly or every other week, so reminding students of the counselor's supportive role on campus is important. School counselors may ask students to brainstorm and share ways in which school counselors can help them, reinforcing and building on responses while also adding any important aspects that may be left unaddressed (see Figure 4.11).

Because students often say that school counselors help students "with scheduling," Danielle's school counseling team reframed the role after a student said, "School counselors make sure everyone gets the right classes." Scheduling classes is *part* of helping students create and reach postsecondary goals, but counselors also do other things like planning schoolwide events, being there to listen when students are upset, and so on. School counselors can also remind students of other supportive adults in their lives such as teachers and family members).

Describing different situations and identifying multiple adults on campus who students can lean on during difficult times helps solidify the school counselor role and helps prevent school counselors from being the person to whom students resort for everything. Additionally, if there are multiple school counselors per school or support staff who help in the school counseling department, displaying a photo of the team helps students become familiar and comfortable with everyone.

Figure 4.10 Hey, Hey, Hey . . . Let's Calculate That GPA—Slide 1: Welcome

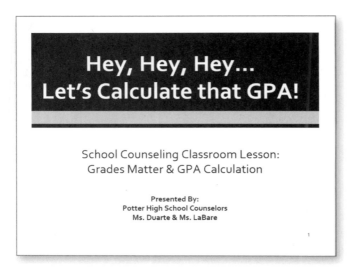

Figure 4.11 Hey, Hey, Hey . . . Let's Calculate That GPA—Slide 2: Welcome

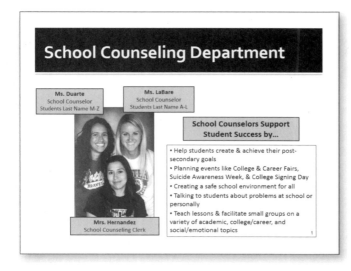

Behavior Expectations

At the beginning of the lesson, it is important to clearly state classroom behavior expectations (see Figure 4.12). Some schools have schoolwide expectations, and in that case school counselors are advised to use these same requirements in their lesson (such as Positive Behavior Interventions and Supports) while specifically relating the expectations for their presentation. For example, when reminding students to be ready, respectful, and responsible, school counselors can ask students to share examples of what that looks and sounds like while they are teaching (listening quietly, raising their hands to share, staying on topic when talking with a partner about questions asked, etc.). Another effective method is to point out students who are already modeling appropriate behavior and list specific behaviors school counselors are expecting as they are teaching:

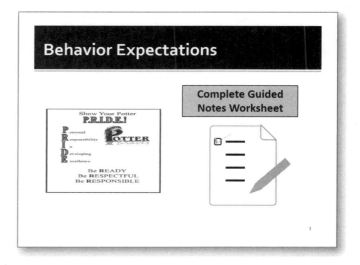

Figure 4.12   Hey, Hey, Hey . . . Let's Calculate That GPA—Slide 3: Behavior Expectations

- "I notice you all are sitting quietly while I'm talking, which is very respectful."
- "Thank you for showing you are ready by quickly clearing off your desks, James and Lupita."
- "I know you all will raise your hand when you want to share an answer, which shows respect to your classmates and me."

If the school does not have schoolwide expectations, it is recommended that school counselors create their own because remembering each different teacher's guidelines may be difficult. Because school counselors visit all classrooms, teaching students the way their school counselor expects them to behave creates universal expectations. Some teachers' strategies may be incorporated over time, such as giving class points, but starting with school counselor–specific rules and rewards is okay, too. By setting and restating clear expectations *every* time a school counselor starts a class lesson, students are reminded of appropriate behavior, which is a proactive classroom management strategy (for more on classroom management, see Chapter 6).

Standards and Objectives

Students are learning standards through the lesson objectives, which are what students are expected to believe, know, and do after the lesson. These learning takeaways are important, so school counselors want to share the objectives at both the beginning and the end of the lesson (see Figure 4.13). Sharing the objectives with students sets the focus of the lesson and gives students ownership of their learning. A recommended practice is for students to read the objectives out loud using Drop-in Reading, during which the counselor reads part of the objectives and the entire class "drops in" to read the most important

Figure 4.13   Hey, Hey, Hey . . . Let's Calculate That GPA—Slide 4: Lesson Standards and Objectives

Lesson Objectives & Standards

By the end of the lesson, we will be able to...
- Understand the importance of our grades
- Explain the required & competitive GPA for college admission and for high school athletic/extra-curricular eligibility
- Calculate our Grade Point Average (GPA)

ASCA Mindsets & Behavior Standards
- M 2. Self-confidence in ability to succeed
- B-LS 8. Actively engage in challenging coursework
- B-LS 10. Participate in enrichment and extracurricular activities

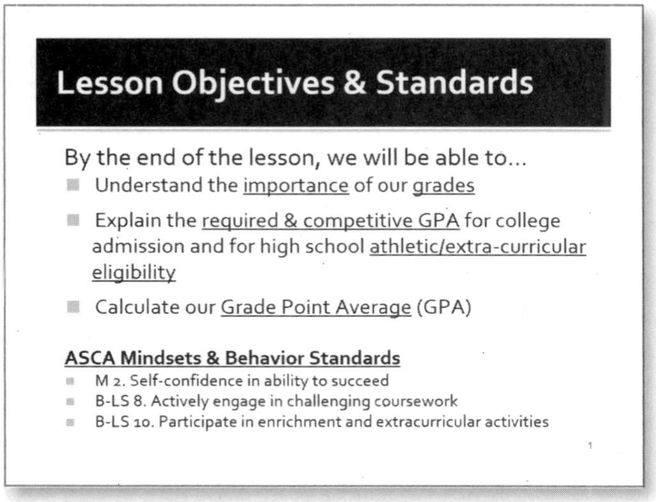

Figure 4.14   Hey, Hey, Hey . . . Let's Calculate That GPA—Slide 5: Accessing Prior Knowledge

What We Already Know about Grades...

On the index card, please write:

Your first and last name

Two or more reasons grades are important

Ms. Duarte
1.
2.

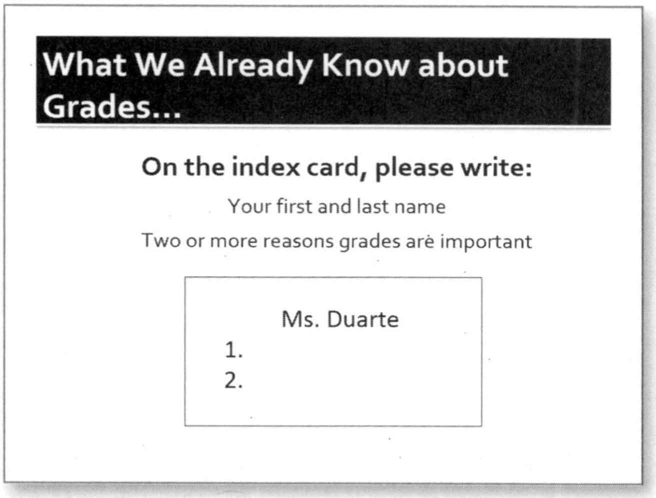

parts together (i.e., Choral Reading; see Chapter 5 for more engagement strategies). The standards that align with the lesson objectives are also shared, whether they are stated or displayed visually, to show students, teachers, administrators, and families that school counselor lessons are based on standards, just as teachers' lessons are.

Accessing Prior Knowledge

Now that the students know the school counselor, as well as the behavior expectations, standards, and objectives, the counselor can prompt students to think about and access prior information they have about the topic rather than jumping into new content (see Figures 4.14 and 4.16). This can be done by posing a discussion question and asking students to 1) share with a partner and then with the class (Think-Pair-Share) or 2) quickly write down their response and then share it with the class (Think-Ink-Pair-Share; see Chapter 5 for more details). This allows the school counselor to establish a framework for the lesson that is connected to what students already know. By bridging students' current knowledge with the new content, students can make meaningful connections to the lesson that will assist them in learning the new information presented. Additionally, accessing prior knowledge builds interest in the topic and demonstrates how the new learning can be related to other experiences in students' lives.

Benefits of Accessing Prior Knowledge

Contributed by Robin Hausheer EdD, NCC, LPC (ID),
Assistant Professor at Plymouth State University

The purpose of school counseling classroom lessons is for students to develop an understanding of new concepts, retain this information, and access and apply it later when needed.

Evidence suggests students are more likely to retain information when they can connect new concepts with already existing, relatable information (Siegler & Alibali, 2005; Willis, 2006). When developing classroom lessons, school counselors should consider how to assist students in connecting the new concepts to already-existing information. It is essential that school counselors have awareness about the level of understanding their student population already possesses about specific concepts. School counselors can build upon this knowledge by scaffolding new information within each lesson and between lesson sequences. This scaffolding process provides students the opportunity to link what they already know to the new concepts, increasing the likelihood of retaining information in long-term memory.

Initially the conceptual understanding of the new information is not developed but will mature over time as long as a student is challenged in a manner that does not cause too much frustration (Driscoll, 2005). One strategy to aid in this process is to consider each student's zone of proximal development (Vygotsky, 1978). Considering what a student can do independently in comparison to when they receive assistance can aid in the process of understanding to what extent students are learning new concepts. School counselors should challenge students to learn new concepts while providing check-in points to ensure students are acquiring the knowledge before introducing additional concepts.

Additionally, when new information is part of students' ongoing education instead of a one-time-only lesson, they are more likely to retain the concepts because they are frequently required to recall this information (Willis, 2006). This repetitive process increases the likelihood information will be stored in long-term memory.

Activity 4.4

What follows are examples of secondary school counseling lesson topics. The first three include questions to access prior knowledge; fill in the others with questions to ask students at the start of a new lesson.

Table 4.5

Lesson Topic	Suggested Question for Accessing Prior Knowledge
High School 101 (Transition to High School)	What excites you about starting high school, and why?
Postsecondary Planning	What are your college and/or career goals after high school?
R-E-S-P-E-C-T . . . Find Out What It Means to Me	Make a list with two sides—one with examples of how students can show respect to one another and one with examples of how students can be disrespectful.
Transcript Analysis & 4-Year Plan Update	
Money Matters (Financial Aid)	
Stress Management & Healthy Coping Skills	
Shift Happens—Preparing for Life after High School	

Figure 4.15   Hey, Hey, Hey . . . Let's Calculate That GPA: Slides 6–9 Input of Knowledge

Grades Matter!!!

What are reasons that grades matter?

HIGH SCHOOL
- Graduation!!!
- Sports eligibility
- Participation in clubs & other school activities

AFTER HIGH SCHOOL
- Meet requirements & be competitive for college admission & other post-secondary options
- Earn scholarships (FREE money!)

Grades Matter!!!

Study of 187,000 high school freshmen found...
- How well students performed academically in 9th grade predicted students' future success
- 9th graders with A's, B's, and C's were much more likely to graduate high school than their classmates with lower grades
- Academically strong 9th graders were more likely to attend college

US News & World Report, 2017

Grades Matter - Graduation

- Total of **220 credits** needed to graduate
  - Credits are "**points**" you receive for each class you pass with a **D** or higher
  - Passing one full year class at Potter HS = **10 credits**
  - Students generally earn **60 credits each year**
    (6 classes x 10 credits per class = 60)
- If you get an F in a required class you have to **take the class again** ☹

Grades Matter – Sports & Activities

- Student athletes must maintain a **2.0 GPA**
- No more than **1 F** on quarter progress report or final report card
- Students need 2.0 or higher to be **club leaders**, attend **college fieldtrips,** and **earn a work permit**

Input and Model ("I Do")

Now that students understand the topic, it's time for school counselors to dive into the content of the lesson, which is called *input*. By definition, *input* is "the act or process of putting in" (Input, n.d.). Within core curriculum classroom lessons, this means that school counselors share important information needed to master the objective(s) with students (see Figures 4.15 and 4.17). There are many ways to spice up the input portion of lessons with a variety of engagement strategies, which are discussed in greater detail in the next chapter. Choral or Drop-in Reading of information, using visuals, pausing for students to discuss, and sharing examples are all ways to engage students in the lesson content. In addition, having students take notes (such as by using a Guided Notes sheet) also supports engagement and retention of material.

Modeling is a way to support input through demonstrating a new skill while students watch. In the same way a fashion model on a runway demonstrates how to wear a new outfit, school counselors model, or show students how they can use the information they are learning. For example, in a lesson on checking grades online, the school counselor can include a variety of screenshots to walk students through the process of using the correct login credentials, accessing grades for the appropriate quarter, and finding missing assignments. *Non-modeling* is another way to utilize this strategy; in this case, the school counselor shows students what *not* to do and explains why. For instance, school counselors can show students previous quarter grades and explain the difference

Figure 4.16   Hey, Hey, Hey . . . Let's Calculate That GPA—Slide 10: Accessing Prior Knowledge

Figure 4.17   Hey, Hey, Hey . . . Let's Calculate That GPA—Slides 11–14: Input of Knowledge

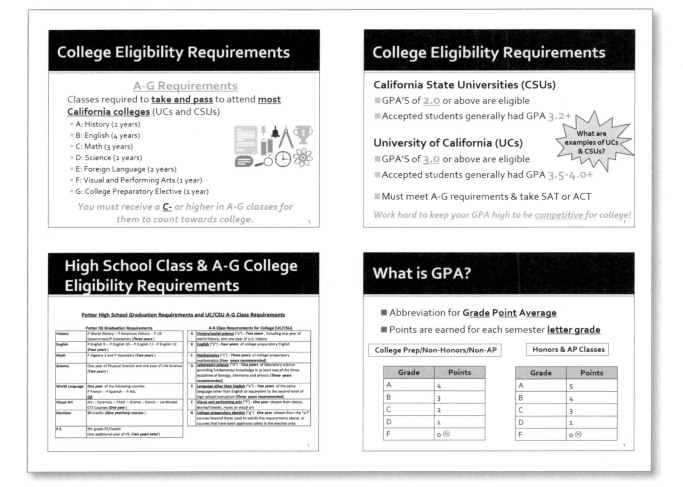

between looking at old grades compared to current ones. Using non-modeling teaches students what not to do and the reasons why the behavior is not effective. Non-modeling is especially effective when discussing a common mistake or frequent problem to help prevent student error. By modeling and non-modeling, school counselors help students remember what is being taught, feel confident in their answers, and reduce potential errors. When using technology with students, such as filling out an online survey, modeling is extremely important so that students understand what to do prior to working independently. In this case, school counselors may want to create step-by-step screenshots of ways to navigate the information. In the sample lesson, the school counselors use modeling by showing students a step-by-step example of how to calculate GPA prior to students calculating their own GPAs (see Figure 4.18).

The input and modeling portion of the lesson can also be called "I Do," which means that this is the part of the lesson during which the school counselor is directly teaching students what they need to know and showing them how to learn this through examples (Killian, 2015). During this part of the lesson, school counselors check for understanding throughout while delivering content (see Figure 4.17 and accompanying lesson plan description in Figure 4.25). Rather than solely asking students whether they understand (because they may say they do, but this may not actually be true), the strategies listed in Table 4.6 can be incorporated into teaching content during the input phase (these are discussed further in Chapter 5).

Table 4.6 Checking for Understanding

Strategy for Checking for Understanding	Suggested Question for Checking for Understanding
Thumbs-Up/Thumbs-Down	Ask students: "If you understand what was just taught, give me a thumbs-up; if not, give me a thumbs down." Then randomly call on a student with a thumbs-up to explain what they learned. If the student doesn't know, ask another student. If 25% of the class or more have their thumbs down, or the students you call on can't answer, explain the concept in a different way. Additionally, to create a safe learning environment, allow students to temporarily pass when called on, but tell them you will come back to them (and do so!).
Explain to Your Elbow Partner	At the beginning of the lesson, help students find an elbow partner sitting near them. Periodically throughout the lesson, ask students to turn to their partners, choose one of the partners to explain what was learned, and then randomly call on a student to share with the class. If students are having difficulty explaining, reteach the content.
Fist to Five	Ask students: "Using your right hand with a fist to mean you don't understand at all, five fingers to mean you could teach your neighbor what we learned, or three fingers to mean you halfway understand, show me how much you learned." Assess how many students show a four or five, and if approximately 75% of the class do have a four or five, randomly call on a student to explain what they learned. If that student doesn't know, ask another student, and if less than 75% of the class indicate a four or five, share an example or teach the material differently.

Guided and Independent Practice ("We Do" and "You Do")

Students have now been taught the content knowledge to apply to an activity. In the guided practice phase, the school counselor supports students as they use the information they have learned to compare and contrast, evaluate, organize, design, predict (or any of the level-three and beyond verbs from Bloom's Taxonomy, page 81) with their knowledge. During *guided practice*, students will often work together, and the school counselor may lead them step by step, asking questions and calling on students to share. As students answer, the school counselor praises correct responses or politely corrects answers that are off track, helping teach the rest of the group. The guided practice portion of a lesson is also referred to as "We Do." As students work together with the school counselor and their peers ("we"), they are supported in learning the steps to gain mastery of skills (see Figure 4.18).

Guided practice moves to *independent practice* when, through checking for understanding and providing group support, students appear to fully understand and can apply their learning. As students work independently, the school counselor moves

Figure 4.18   Hey, Hey, Hey . . . Let's Calculate That GPA—Slides 15–17: Modeling & Guided Practice

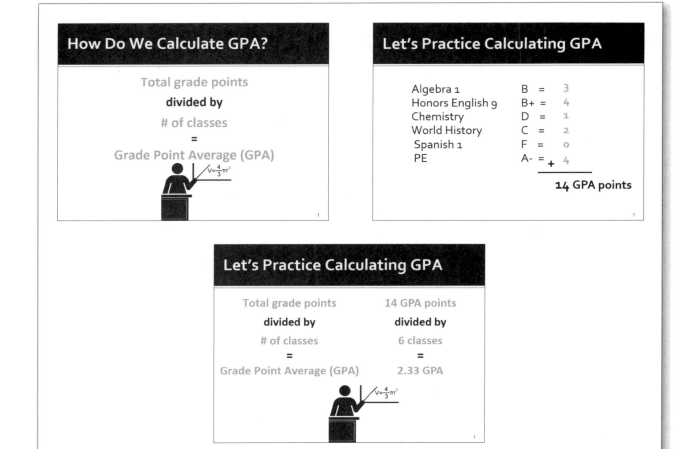

around the room, monitoring students' progress, providing feedback (praising or correcting), and observing students in their attainment of mastery. Hopefully the wonderfully engaged classroom teacher is supporting the independent practice phase as well. In addition, to support students finishing on time, the school counselor can display a timer so they can monitor their time as they work. Independent practice can also be called "You Do" as students retain what they have learned by practicing on their own (see Figure 4.19).

Examples of guided and independent practice include the following:

- After students are walked through steps to create a Naviance account and complete a career assessment (modeling), each student creates their own account, logs onto the site, and completes a career assessment, filling out an accompanying worksheet to process the results.
- Students are shown an example transcript, and the different parts are explained including grade point average, the number of credits completed, and the number of courses that align with college requirements. Then students are given their own transcripts to find this information for themselves.

Figure 4.19   Hey, Hey, Hey . . . Let's Calculate That GPA—Slides 18–20: Independent Practice

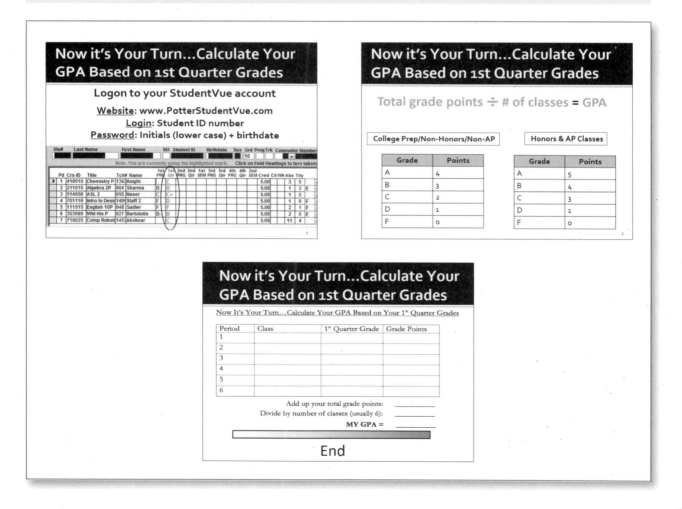

- After students are taught appropriate ways to email teachers/adults on campus (i.e., including an appropriate subject, writing in complete sentences, proofreading, signing the email, etc.), students draft an email to the school counselor.

Figure 4.20 Hey, Hey, Hey . . . Let's Calculate That GPA—Slides 21–22: Input of Knowledge

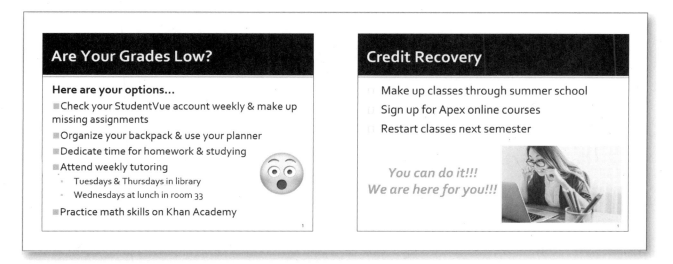

Restate Objectives, Assessment, and Closure

At the end of the lesson, the school counselor may provide some final content to help with closure (see Figure 4.20), and then it's time to refer back to the objectives stated at the beginning. One effective way to review the objectives is to take the objective statements and turn them into sentence frames, calling on students to answer. A *sentence frame* involves providing the beginning of a sentence and asking students to fill in the end, as shown in Figure 4.21. This is also a way to informally assess that students

Figure 4.21 Hey, Hey, Hey . . . Let's Calculate That GPA—Slides 23–24: Restate Objectives & Closure

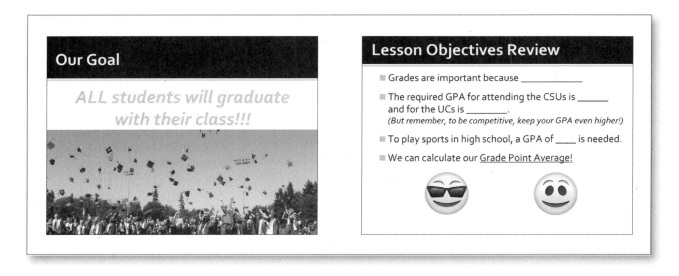

Figure 4.22 Hey, Hey, Hey . . . Let's Calculate
That GPA—Slide 25: Assessment

have learned the objectives, especially when students are called on randomly. School counselors can also review and clarify key points of the lesson as they are ending. For instance, in the lesson shown here, the school counselor will use Pull Cards to ask students to explain why grades are important, required GPA for applying to colleges, and GPA needed to participate in sports.

Through restating the lesson objectives and important information, students' knowledge is reinforced and integrated into their learning. In addition to calling on students to share what they learned, counselors can use a Ticket Out the Door as a straightforward and effective assessment strategy (which is described in greater detail in Chapter 5). School counselors can ask a question or use a sentence frame for students to complete and turn in at the end of the lesson. Additionally, if the lesson includes an activity, the correct completion of the activity can also be a means of assessing a skill. Pre- and post-tests, as discussed in *The Use of Data in School Counseling* (Hatch, 2013), also assess student learning of lesson content. See Chapter 9 for additional information on assessment strategies.

School counselors may also be assessing students more formally through a post-assessment as part of the closure. In this lesson, a GoogleForms survey was used to survey students' attitudes, knowledge, and skills about the lesson content (see Figure 4.22). More details about creating assessment and using technology tools, such as GoogleForms, Kahoot!, and Mentimeter, for administration can be found in Chapter 9.

Figure 4.23 Lesson Plan: Plan for Evaluation

Core Curriculum Class Lesson
TITLE

1. Lesson Title & Subject:

2. Grade Level(s):

3. Learning Objectives:

4. ASCA Domain(s) + Mindsets and Behaviors Standards:

5. Materials:

6. Procedures:

7. Plan for Evaluation:

8. Follow-Up:

Plan for Evaluation

In this section of the lesson plan, secondary school counselors describe how they will assess their lesson:

- *Process data:* the number of students impacted by the lesson
- *Perception data:* attitudes, knowledge, and skills gained from the lesson (through pre- and post-assessments)
- *Outcome data:* the achievement-related and achievement data

This section is important for counselors to show the impact that their lesson makes on students' attitudes, knowledge, and skills related to the lesson topic and the way in which student behaviors can be affected based on the lesson (see Figure 4.23). Although not all school counseling lessons include pre- or post-assessments or other types of measurement, including the potential perception and outcome data in the lesson plan describes the ways in which the lesson *can* be assessed.

In the accompanying lesson plan, Hey, Hey, Hey . . . Let's Calculate That GPA (see Figure 4.25), the school counselor includes the plan for evaluation in the following way:

- *Process data:* all 8th and/or 9th grade students (list the total number)
- *Perception data*
  - *Attitudes:* percentage of students who believe their grades will impact them in the future
  - *Knowledge:* percentage of students who know what GPA stands for; percentage who know the different point values for each letter grade to calculate GPA
  - *Skills:* percentage of students who can calculate GPA
- *Outcome data*: tracking the GPA for students before and after the lesson (looking for increase); tracking the percent of students on track to graduate (looking for increase)

More information about different types of assessment data is described in Chapter 9.

Figure 4.24   Lesson Plan: Follow-Up

Follow-Up

The final section of the lesson plan discusses next steps after the lesson is completed (see Figure 4.24). For example:

- After a lesson during which 8th grade students draft a 4-year plan for their high school courses, their middle school counselor will conduct short one-on-one meetings with all students to discuss their postsecondary goals and review their plans. Copies of 4-year plans will be given to each student, and a call will go out to families letting them know their child drafted a

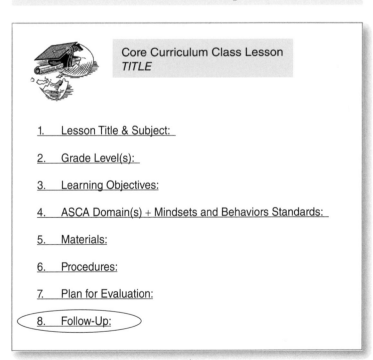

Core Curriculum Class Lesson
TITLE

1.   Lesson Title & Subject:

2.   Grade Level(s):

3.   Learning Objectives:

4.   ASCA Domain(s) + Mindsets and Behaviors Standards:

5.   Materials:

6.   Procedures:

7.   Plan for Evaluation:

8.   Follow-Up:

4-year plan. In the week following the 4-year plan meetings, high school counselors will present in all 8th grade classes and provide students with 9th grade course registration forms. The middle and high school counselors will provide a joint family presentation including information about 4-year planning, 9th grade course registration, and other tips about beginning high school. Course registration forms will be collected by the middle school counselors and sent to the high school.

- Suicide Prevention Week will coincide during the time of Suicide Awareness and Prevention core curriculum class lessons. During this week students will make end-of-day announcements about positive coping skills and reminders of resources on campus to seek out help for friends or self. All families will receive a letter explaining Suicide Prevention Week, with suggestions for developmentally appropriate discussions with their children and family resources.

- After learning about the basics of FAFSA submission through classroom lessons, school counselors will provide workshops to support students' completion. Students can attend workshops during lunch on Tuesdays and Thursdays in the College and Career Center. Additionally, three FAFSA Family Nights will be scheduled to allow students and families to work on the FAFSA with support from the school counseling team. The school counselors will also monitor which students have/have not submitted their FAFSA application and will call students out of class to see if they need additional support.

While the process of creating lesson plans is time-consuming in the beginning, school counselors who dedicate this time to making detailed plans will save themselves time in the future. Creating detailed lesson plans allows school counselors to build and franchise their comprehensive school counseling program for future consistency and program sustainability.

CULTURAL RESPONSIVENESS AND CONSIDERATIONS WHEN LESSON PLANNING

Being mindful of students' diverse cultures and including multiculturalism within school counseling lesson plans is important to ensure that students' backgrounds are both respected and celebrated during the lesson, which helps students feel connected to the topics they are learning. Culturally responsive teaching aims to improve both engagement and motivation of diverse populations, especially students of color, infusing their culture into lessons to make meaningful connections and improve student outcomes (Gay, 2010; Vavrus, 2008). It is also described as "a process that often requires educators to step out of their comfort zones and change their ways of thinking about students and how best to teach them" (Boyko, 2016, p. xxi). Learning about the diverse backgrounds of their school is important to help school counselors address the varying needs of their students, and incorporating this knowledge into core curriculum helps students feel both respected by and connected to their counselor. In some cases, the school counselor may become the student as they learn about the school population and come to understand the needs, challenges, and support that their students require socially and academically.

The book *Culturally Responsive Teaching: Theory, Research and Practice* (2010), by Dr. Geneva Gay, outlines essential elements of culturally responsive teaching, including developing a cultural diversity knowledge base. Through deepening their understanding that culture is not only about ethnicity but also encompasses values, contributions, traditions, relational patterns, and communication styles, counselors can better integrate multiculturalism into lessons (and their practices in general). Learning about and honoring the unique contributions of different ethnic groups helps all students feel seen. Cross cultural communication is another essential element; when school counselors understand characteristics of different ethnic communication styles, they will have a better context through which to communicate with diverse students "without violating the cultural value of a student's cultural communication style" (Boyko, 2016, XXXIII). Understanding differences in cross cultural communication among their students can also provide an opportunity for counselors to teach students about code-switching to help them successfully navigate different settings and audiences. As school counselors integrate and value the diverse backgrounds of their student populations into core curriculum class lessons, students will likely feel more connected to the content and the counselor.

When planning for core curriculum lessons, school counselors can incorporate cultural responsiveness in the following ways:

1. Creating a welcoming and inclusive environment that embraces diverse sharing—school counselors can explain and remind students what this looks like during their expectations at the beginning of classroom lessons. See Chapter 6 for more on creating classroom expectations.

2. Incorporating students' personal and cultural perceptions into the lesson—when school counselors activate prior knowledge before teaching content, they can be mindful in seeking out diverse ideas.

3. Embedding diverse student backgrounds and voices into lessons—for example, including examples and photos that represent diverse cultures, especially those that directly apply to students in the school community.

4. Including time for cooperative learning through group work—although this is not possible for every lesson, working in heterogeneous groups allows for diverse students to collaborate with and learn from one another.

In the sample lesson Hey, Hey, Hey . . . Let's Calculate That GPA (see Figure 4.25 for complete lesson plan), Danielle was mindful of including a variety of postsecondary options into the discussion rather than only college. She also used photos of diverse students within the PowerPoint. As Danielle presented the topic, she was mindful not to imply that college was superior to other options after high school, especially because students' family members may not have attended postsecondary education. Instead, Danielle focused on having a variety of options after high school, which students will explore individually and with their family.

Additional examples of topics for specific cultural considerations include the following:

- FAFSA/financial aid lessons
  - Depending on a student's immigration status and the state in which you live, undocumented students may not be able to apply for financial aid. School counselors are suggested to look up financial aid information and resources that support undocumented students, and include basic facts in the general presentation, to ensure undocumented students who may not have identified themselves will receive the information.
  - School counselors are suggested to title the presentation Financial Aid Options (or something more clever) rather than FAFSA because *financial aid* is a broad term that encompasses a variety of types of financial aid options.
  - During presentations about financial aid, be aware of student reactions, as this may be a stressful topic for students who are low income and/or undocumented.

- School success and study skills lessons
  - Consider the responsibilities students may have outside of school, such as babysitting younger siblings, chores, or working to support their families. Students may need to prioritize other family needs along with homework and school responsibilities; let students know you are there to support them if they need help.
  - Teaching students to advocate for their learning by reaching out to teachers may be difficult for some students based on language barriers or cultural approaches to interacting with authority or questioning adults. Consider presenting a variety of ways students can talk with teachers to help them find one that is most comfortable.
  - Based on students' home situations, studying in a quiet place or having their own desk may be unrealistic; instead, provide diverse options about how and where to study.

- English language learners
  - Incorporate pictures, use a slow cadence of speech, and provide additional opportunities to check for understanding. If possible, consider presenting some information in students' native language to ensure they fully understand important concepts.
  - Include lots of time to pair-share so that students have practice speaking and hearing others' ideas prior to sharing with the class.

- Consider modifying lesson content to address needs specific to English language learners. Modification is *not* intended to water down the content but instead to refine the information to specifically address English learner populations. For example, during a 9th grade High School 101 lesson, consider highlighting resources such as the writing center, so students can get tutoring if they are interested.

- College, career, and postsecondary exploration/planning lessons
  - Be mindful of incorporating diverse careers and vocational pathways that do not all require a 4-year degree, including the military. Consider ways to incorporate diversity of postsecondary options into events like career days.
  - Represent diverse photos of men and women from different backgrounds in a variety of roles. Also include a variety of people from different careers and cultures as guest speakers on campus.
  - When describing jobs compared to careers, be careful not to imply that one is better than the other, especially because students' family members may work in jobs; instead, focus on diverse options.
  - Recognize and honor diverse education levels (especially with populations who will be first-generation college students; use caution to avoid minimizing their parents' education levels).

- Lessons including technology
  - If technology is being discussed for at-home activities (such as using Google Calendar for homework and class assignments), include options for students who do not have access to technology at home.

What is the student population at your school? What cultural considerations do you need to make when planning your core curriculum classroom lessons? What additional professional development might you need?

Family Education Lesson Plans

As school counselors are creating lesson plans for their schoolwide curriculum, they are encouraged to also create lesson plans for their family education workshops. In this way, family education becomes consistent and predictable year to year. As you look back through this chapter, it will be helpful to utilize similar strategies for family education and workshops. What are some of the ideas in this chapter that most resonate with you to include in your family education lesson plans? How might your family education lesson plans differ from your student lesson plans?

Figure 4.25   Lesson Plan: Hey, Hey, Hey . . . Let's Calculate That GPA!

 Core Curriculum Class Lessons
Hey, Hey, Hey . . . Let's Calculate That GPA!

LESSON TITLE & SUBJECT: Hey, Hey, Hey . . . Let's Calculate That GPA! (Grades Matter & GPA Calculation)

GRADE LEVEL(S): 8 or 9

LEARNING OBJECTIVES:

By the end of the lesson, students will be able to . . .

- Understand the importance of their grades
- Explain the required & competitive GPA for college admission and high athletic/extra-curricular eligibility
- Calculate Grade Point Average (GPA)

ASCA DOMAIN + MINDSETS & BEHAVIOR STANDARDS:

- Domains: Academic & College/Career
- Mindsets & Behaviors Standards:

  - M 2: Self Confidence in ability to succeed
  - B-LS 8. Actively engage in challenging coursework
  - B-LS 10. Participate in enrichment and extra-curricular activities

MATERIALS:

- Lesson PowerPoint
- Laptop & projector
- 3x5 cards
- Copies of Guided Notes sheets for all students
- Copies of High School Class & A–G College Eligibility Requirements sheet
- Pre/post assessment (via GoogleForms)

PROCEDURES:

Slide 1: **Welcome**

  - Welcome students to the class and share the lesson title (Hey, Hey, Hey . . . Let's Calculate That GPA) and topic (importance of grades in high school and learning how to calculate Grade Point Average).

Slide 2: **School Counseling Department Introduction**

  - Remind students about the members of the school counseling department including the school counselors and any additional support staff (guidance clerks, interns, etc.).
  - Ask students to share what they know about the role of a school counselor. Depending on what students share, the counselor may also want to add that their job is to help students be successful in school by: teaching them lessons on a variety of topics including academics and well-being (like today), helping them create goals for now and the future, supporting them with any problems at school or personally, planning schoolwide events like College Signing Day, and helping everyone at school feel safe and happy.

<u>Slide 3</u>: **Behavior Expectations**

- ○ Remind students of the three Potter Rs (be ready, respectful, and responsible), and ask them to repeat them together.
- ○ Praise the class for already demonstrating the three Rs, and list specific examples (such as, "You are all showing me respect by staying quiet while I am talking." "I can see how responsible you are by having a writing utensil ready.").
- ○ Tell students that one part of being ready and responsible during today's lesson is to complete their Guided Notes worksheet during the lesson.
- ○ Ask two students to quickly and quietly pass out the Guided Notes to each student.

<u>Slide 4</u>: **Objectives**

- ○ Explain the objectives that are the focus of the presentation and what students are intended to learn. Ask students to participate in Drop-in Reading—the counselor will read the non-underlined portion of the objectives, and the students will read the underlined portion of the objectives together. By the end of the lesson, we will be able to . . .
  - • Understand the <u>importance</u> of our <u>grades</u>
  - • Explain the <u>required & competitive GPA</u> for college admission and for high school <u>athletic/extra-curricular eligibility</u>
  - • Calculate our <u>Grade Point Average</u> (GPA)
- ○ Tell the students the objectives are aligned to the school counseling standards at the bottom of the slide.

<u>Slide 5</u>: **Access Prior Knowledge**

- ○ Ask students to quietly think about the reason grades are important.
- ○ While they are thinking, ask two students to pass out a 3x5 card to each student.
- ○ Tell the students to write their first and last name on the top of the card and then write down at least two reasons grades are important. Explain the example on the PowerPoint (name and numbered items).
- ○ Walk around and observe while students are writing, noticing any specific students you'd like to call on to share and any you'd want to avoid.
- ○ After several minutes, regroup the class, call on the students you noticed, and/or ask students in general to share. As each student shares one example, ask the class to raise their hands if they wrote down something similar.
- ○ After calling on three to four students, ask all students to raise their cards up in the air and for two students to quickly and quietly collect all the cards and bring them up to the front as you proceed with the next slide.

<u>Slide 6</u>: **Grades Matter** (Input)

- ○ Explain that grades matter for a variety of reasons now and in the future, as was just discussed.
- ○ Tell students you will be specifically discussing how grades matter in high school for eligibility for sports and extra-curricular activities, along with graduation. The lesson will also talk about how grades will impact students in the future, such as for college and other postsecondary options.

<u>Slide 7</u>: **Grades Matter—Research** (Input)

- ○ Explain to students that there is research from *US News and World Report* of high school freshmen that explains the importance of getting good grades.
- ○ Use the 3x5 cards to select a student to read the first bullet point—*How well students performed academically in 9th grade predicted students' future success.*
- ○ Then ask the student sitting next to the student who just read to read the next bullet point—*Ninth graders with As, Bs, and Cs were much more likely to graduate high school than their classmates with lower grades*—and the following student to read the last bullet—*Academically strong 9th graders were more likely to attend college.*

(Continued)

Figure 4.25 (Continued)

Slide 8: **Grades Matter—Graduation** (Input)

- ○ Direct students to the Guided Notes sheet that was passed out at the beginning of the class, which they will begin filling in.

- ○ Explain that you will again use Drop-in Reading for students to read the underlined sections, and they will also fill the information in their Guided Notes.

  - • Total of **220 credits** needed to graduate
  - • Credits are "**points**" you receive for each class you pass with a **D** or higher
  - • Passing one full year class at Potter HS = **10 credits**
  - • Students generally earn **60 credits each year**
  - • If you get an F in a required class you have to **take the class again**

- ○ Walk around the room while presenting information on this slide to ensure students are filling in their Guided Notes sheet.

Slide 9: **Grades Matter—Sports & Activities** (Input)

- ○ Continue to use Drop-in Reading to explain sports and other activity eligibility while walking around the classroom to ensure students are filling in Guided Notes.

  - • Student athletes must maintain a **2.0 GPA**
  - • No more than **1 F** on quarter progress report or final report card
  - • Students need 2.0 or higher to be **club leaders**, attend **college fieldtrips,** and **earn a work permit**

Slide 10: **Access Prior Knowledge**

- ○ Explain to students that their choices now can impact them as they begin thinking about life after high school.

- ○ Ask students to think about their postsecondary goals and what they can do now to get there (and allow about 20 seconds of silent think time).

- ○ Ask students to pair with a partner to discuss their thoughts about the questions, and alert them you'll be using the 3x5 cards to call on a few students to answer.

- ○ While students are talking with their neighbors, walk around to listen to their answers and prompt students with good answers that you may call on them.

- ○ After several minutes, call on several students to share their answers with the class.

Slide 11: **College Eligibility Requirements** (Input)

- ○ Ask students to read the statement describing the A–G requirements all together—*classes required to take and pass to attend most California colleges (UCs and CSUs)*—and fill in the information on their Guided Notes sheets.

- ○ Explain that students who want to attend a University of California (UC) or California State University (CSU) need to complete the A–G requirement classes, and the grade they need in these classes to count towards college is a C-. Ask students, *"What grade do you need in A–G classes?"* so they repeat the word C-, and also remind them to fill it in on their Guided Notes sheets.

- ○ Tell students that even if students aren't sure if they want to go to college, they should still take and pass these classes so they can have all the options available to them.

Slide 12: **College Eligibility Requirements** (Input)

- ○ Discuss the difference between eligible for college and competitive, and share the difference between eligible GPA and the average GPAs for students who were admitted:

California State Universities (CSUs)

- GPAs of <u>**2.0**</u> or above are eligible
- Accepted students generally had GPA **3.2+**

University of California (UCs)

- GPAs of <u>**3.0**</u> or above are eligible
- Accepted students generally had GPAs of **3.5–4.0+**

○ Explain to students that being competitive means working hard in their classes to get higher than the minimum and also reinforcing what students said about what they can do now (like study, join clubs, etc.).

○ Remind students they will also need to take the SAT and/or ACT test, and the counselor will share more information about this in a future class lesson.

<u>Slide 13</u>: **High School Class & A–G College Eligibility Requirements** (Input)

○ Explain to freshmen that most, if not all, classes they are currently taking are likely helping them become eligible for graduation and for the A–G requirements.

○ Ask two students to pass out the Potter High School Graduation Requirements and UC/CSU A–G Requirements sheet to see how the classes compare.

○ Discuss a few examples:

- Ask students to put a finger on the number of years of history they need to graduate from high school, and then say it out loud (3 years). Then ask them to slide the finger to the right to read how many years they need to be A–G eligible (2 years).

- Ask students to move the finger down to math, and ask them how many years they need for graduation (2 years) and then how many they need for A–G (3 years, but 4 recommended). Explain how taking more than the minimum number of classes can be important to be competitive for college acceptance.

<u>Slide 14</u>: **What Is GPA?** (Input)

○ Ask students to chorally read what GPA stands for (Grade Point Average)

○ Explain that each letter grade equals a certain point value, which makes up student GPAs. GPAs are calculated at the end of each quarter, when final grades are released.

○ Ask students to fill in the number of points on their Guided Notes sheets for College Pre/Non-Honors/Non-AP as the numbers come out one by one from the PowerPoint animation.

○ Tell students that honors and AP (advanced placement) classes earn more GPA points because they are accelerated, rigorous classes.

<u>Slide 15</u>: **How Do We Calculate GPA?** (Input)

○ Explain students will now learn how to calculate their GPA, so they can understand where they stand for sports/activities eligibility and college eligibility.

○ GPA is calculated by adding up the total number of points per grade, and divide by the total number of classes. Remind students to fill in the formula on their Guided Notes sheets.

<u>Slide 16</u>: **Let's Practice Calculating GPA** (Modeling/Guided Practice)

○ Guide students through the GPA example, asking the class to chorally say how many points each grade is worth, and then add up the total GPA points together (14).

Figure 4.25 (Continued)

Slide 17: **Let's Practice Calculating GPA** (Modeling/Guided Practice)

- ○ Remind students of the formula for GPA calculation (total points, divided by the number of classes) and divide 14 by 6 (answer: 2.33).
- ○ Explain that most times the number of classes will be six, unless they take zero period or after-school classes.

Slide 18: **Now It's Your Turn to Calculate GPA** (Guided/Independent Practice)

- ○ Explain to students they will calculate their own GPAs based on their first quarter grades.
- ○ To find their grades, students will need to log on to their StudentVue account. Remind them how to do the following:
  - • Go to the Website: www.PotterStudentVue.com
  - • Login: Student ID number
  - • Password: Initials (lower case) + birthdate
- ○ *Before* setting students loose to logon, remind them their quarter grades will be in red.

Slide 19: **Now It's Your Turn to Calculate GPA** (Guided/Independent Practice)

- ○ *Before* students begin to calculate their GPAs, remind students of the GPA formula and the points for each letter, which they wrote on their Guided Notes sheets.

Slide 20: **Now It's Your Turn to Calculate GPA** (Guided/Independent Practice)

- ○ Remind students to use the Guided Notes worksheet to calculate their GPAs by writing down their class names, grades, and grade points on the form. Also remind students that grades are private.
- ○ Tell students they will have 10 minutes to go online to check their grades and calculate their GPAs. Explain that the bar on the bottom of the PowerPoint screen is a timer, and the color will start filling in as the time passes, so they can gauge their time.
- ○ As students begin logging on to their accounts and calculating their GPAs, walk around the room to answer questions, support students struggling to log on, and monitor completion time. If the class finishes before the time is up, click forward on the PowerPoint to automatically make the timer stop.

Slide 21: **Options to Improve Grades** (Input)

- ○ Use the 3x5 cards to select a student to read the first bullet point, then ask the student sitting next to the student who just read to read the next bullet point, and so on to read the options around the room:
  - • Check your StudentVue account weekly & make up missing assignments
  - • Organize your backpack & use your planner
  - • Dedicate time for homework & studying
  - • Attend weekly tutoring
    - • Tuesdays & Thursdays in library
    - • Wednesdays at lunch in Room 33
  - • Practice math skills on Khan Academy

Slide 22: **Credit Recovery Options** (Guided/Independent Practice)

- ○ Explain that students who need to make up credits, so they can be on track to graduate, will meet with school counselors. Their options are the following:
  - • Make up classes through summer school
  - • Sign up for Apex online courses
  - • Restart classes the following semester

Slide 23: **Goal—All Students Graduating!**

- ○ Tell students that your job is to support *all* students in graduating on time with their class, and you believe they can do it!

Slide 24: **Lesson Objectives Review**

- ○ Share each of the sentence frames reviewing objectives with the class one by one, and call on students using the 3x5 cards to answer:
  - • Grades are important because _____.
  - • The required GPA for attending the CSUs is _____ and for the UCs is _____. *(But remember, to be competitive, keep your GPA even higher!)*
  - • To play sports in high school, a GPA of ___ is needed.
- ○ Remind students they can all now calculate their Grade Point Averages.

PLAN FOR EVALUATION

Process Data:

- • <u>Who</u>: Eighth and/or 9th grade students (list total number)
- • <u>What</u>: Students receive a lesson on why grades matter and how to calculate their grade point average
- • <u>When</u>: Spring for 8th grade students or fall for 9th grade students
- • <u>Where</u>: Taught in English classes

Perception Data:

- • Pre-/post-assessment (pre-administered a week prior to the lesson via GoogleForms, post-assessment given immediately after the lesson, using Kahoot!)
- • Attitudes:
  % of students who believe their grades will impact them in the future
- • Knowledge:
  % of students who know what GPA stands for
  % of students who know the different point values for each letter grade to calculate GPA
- • Skill
  % of students who can calculate GPA

Outcome Data:

- • Tracking the GPA for students before and after the lesson (looking for increase)
- • Tracking the % of students on track to graduate

FOLLOW UP

The school counseling department will monitor grades for each quarter to track changes. School counselors will also identify students with failing grades, who will receive Grade Check Workshops to discuss goals for improvement and credit recovery options.

Figure 4.26 Bloom's Taxonomy Action Verbs

Action Words for Bloom's Taxonomy

Sample of 176 unique words identified for a level of Bloom by 4 or more lists in a sample of 30 published lists (f = number of lists that nominate the word for a level of Bloom).

This document reformats **Table 1**, published in Stanny, C. J. (2016). Reevaluating Bloom's Taxonomy: What Measurable Verbs Can and Cannont Say about Student Learning. *Education Sciences*, 6 (4), *37*; doi:10.3390/educsci6040037, for single-page printing. Used under CC-BY, licensed under CC-BY by Claudia J. Stanny.

Knowledge	f	Understand	f	Apply	f	Analyze	f	Evaluate	f	Create	f
arrange	6	articulate	4	act	19	analyze	24	appraise	22	arrange	22
choose	4	associate	4	adapt	4	appraise	11	argue	12	assemble	14
cite	17	characterize	4	apply	22	break	8	arrange	5	categorize	7
copy	4	cite	4	back / back up	5	break down	7	assess	17	choose	7
define	21	clarify	5	calculate	10	calculate	9	attach	4	collect	9
describe	14	classify	18	change	9	categorize	19	choose	10	combine	14
draw	5	compare	11	choose	11	classify	10	compare	18	compile	7
duplicate	7	contrast	7	classify	6	compare	24	conclude	13	compose	19
identify	20	convert	13	complete	5	conclude	6	contrast	8	construct	29
indicate	4	defend	12	compute	10	contrast	19	core	6	create	19
label	21	demonstrate	6	construct	13	correlate	5	counsel	4	design	24
list	27	describe	22	demonstrate	20	criticize	11	create	4	develop	18
locate	10	differentiate	8	develop	4	debate	8	criticize	11	devise	13
match	14	discuss	21	discover	8	deduce	6	critique	14	estimate	5
memorize	10	distinguish	12	dramatize	16	detect	7	decide	4	evaluate	4
name	22	estimate	11	employ	16	diagnose	4	defend	15	explain	8
order	5	explain	28	experiment	6	diagram	12	describe	4	facilitate	4
outline	11	express	17	explain	5	differentiate	20	design	4	formulate	18
quote	7	extend	11	generalize	5	discover	4	determine	6	generalize	7
read	4	extrapolate	5	identify	4	discriminate	11	discriminate	9	generate	11
recall	24	generalize	11	illustrate	18	dissect	6	estimate	15	hypothesize	8
recite	12	give	4	implement	4	distinguish	21	evaluate	16	improve	5
recognize	14	give examples	8	interpret	15	divide	12	explain	9	integrate	4
record	13	identify	14	interview	6	evaluate	4	grade	4	invent	10
relate	11	illustrate	9	manipulate	10	examine	18	invent	8	make	6
repeat	20	indicate	8	modify	12	experiment	9	judge	25	manage	8
reproduce	11	infer	15	operate	17	figure	4	manage	15	modify	10
review	4	interpolate	5	organize	4	group	4	mediate	9	organize	21
select	16	interpret	17	paint	4	identify	7	prepare	12	originate	9
state	23	locate	10	practice	15	illustrate	8	probe	4	plan	21
tabulate	4	match	7	predict	9	infer	14	rate	5	predict	8
tell	4	observe	5	prepare	11	inspect	8	rearrange	19	prepare	12
underline	7	organize	5	produce	13	inventory	9	reconcile	12	produce	13
write	5	paraphrase	22	relate	12	investigate	7	release	6	propose	9
		predict	12	schedule	11	order	5	rewrite	4	rate	21
		recognize	11	select	4	organize	6	select	5	rearrange	8
		relate	7	show	13	outline	10	set up	15	reconstruct	9
		report	10	simulate	5	point out	12	supervise	9	relate	8
		represent	4	sketch	17	predict	4	synthesize	16	reorganize	9
		restate	15	solve	19	prioritize	4	test	8	revise	12
		review	15	translate	5	question	12	value	7	rewrite	7
		rewrite	12	use	25	relate	17	verify	9	role-play	4
		select	7	utilize	4	select	12	weigh	5	set up	9
		summarize	20	write	5	separate	10			specify	5
		tell	7			solve	8			summarize	7
		translate	21			subdivide	10			synthesize	4
						survey	7			tell / tell why	5
						test	14			write	17

5

Student Engagement

Yessenia and Shahara are school counselors at two different high schools in the same district. They are both on the district school counseling curriculum committee and helped create a general financial aid lesson for all the school counselors in the district to implement at their sites (franchising, as discussed in Chapter 2). In addition to the lesson, all counselors agreed to administer a pre-/post-assessment to see the effectiveness of the lesson and to modify and improve for the following year.

When the counseling curriculum committee reconvened, Yessenia and Shahara had different results. Whereas Shahara had great gains in students' attitudes, knowledge, and skills, Yessenia saw only moderate improvements. Yessenia felt frustrated, and as they discussed further, she noted that students did not seem engaged in the lesson. The presentation included a lot of information, and Yessenia felt like she talked at the students the whole time. She also commented that students didn't participate, and many seemed off task while she was teaching. This lack of learning was reflected in her post-assessment data, and Yessenia was very disappointed.

On the other hand, Shahara reported great classroom participation and saw large gains on pre- and post-assessments, with students improving their attitudes, knowledge, and skills. She shared with Yessenia that she added a Guided Notes worksheet for students to complete while they were listening to the information to keep their attention focused and so they would have the information after the lesson. In addition, Shahara used other engagement strategies such as Think-Ink-Pair-Share to get students thinking and talking with one another. Students were so busy engaging in the material she was teaching that there were few disruptions, even in classes that typically experienced behavior challenges.

As Shahara shared the strategies with Yessenia and the rest of the counseling curriculum committee, they discussed the value of engagement strategies to support student learning. Shahara also told the team about research stating that people remember far more of what they say and do over what they only hear. This information further reinforced the need to incorporate active participation in lessons, and the committee brainstormed ways to incorporate a variety of engagement strategies in all future lesson plans.

ENGAGING STUDENT LEARNERS

Effectively engaging students throughout the beginning, middle, and end of classroom lessons is essential. Research supports strong connections between high levels of student engagement throughout the teaching and learning process and improved student performance (Action Learning Systems, 2012; Schunk, 2012). By utilizing a variety of student engagement techniques, school counselors assess student learning throughout the lesson, and lesson content becomes more fun.

Within the educational environment, *engagement* is defined as "a student's persistence at a task and includes cognitive, emotional, and behavioral engagement" (Action Learning Systems, 2012, p. 145). Therefore, school counselors are encouraged to help students think deeply, connect emotionally with the content, and demonstrate engagement through their actions during core curriculum lessons. There are two kinds of engagement within classroom teaching: overt and covert.

Cognitive Engagement Through Overt and Covert Engagement Strategies

To promote cognitive engagement, consider the following ways to incorporate both overt (observable) and covert (not observable) strategies within classroom lessons.

Overt	Covert
Observable	Not observable
Use when observable results are needed	Use when students need processing (thinking) time

Overt strategies are used when observable results are wanted or needed. They include students' sharing their responses to a question with a partner, writing down the answer to a prompt, or reading a passage out loud as a class. School counselors can observe students' participation in all of these examples, making them overt.

Covert strategies allow students time to mentally process. Examples are asking students to think about their answers, silently remember a past experience, or follow along while the school counselor is reading. In these examples, school counselors cannot see students' mental processes, but paired with overt strategies, students' unobservable thinking can be assessed.

For example, after students think about their answers (covert), they can pair with a partner to discuss (overt), and then several students can be called on at random to share their answers with the class (overt again). Think-Pair-Share, as this strategy is called, is a way to hold students accountable to the unobservable covert strategy because they will have to share their answers with a partner and also possibly with the class. When students know that they are being held to these standards, they are more likely to be engaged in the topic rather than thinking about what they are going to eat for lunch. Combining overt and covert strategies together allows for deeper student engagement in the lesson content.

Through utilizing both overt and covert engagement strategies during the beginning, middle, and end of core curriculum classroom lessons, school counselors engage all students throughout their teaching (see Figure 5.18 at the end of the chapter for the Hey, Hey, Hey . . . Let's Calculate That GPA lesson plan with engagement strategies highlighted throughout a section of the lesson). As students actively participate, their attention improves, their speed of learning increases, and their retention of the information is stronger (Schunk, 2012). In addition, as students are busily engaged with the lesson content, there is less time for them to be off task or disruptive. Strong instructional practices are some of the best classroom management strategies.

There are a variety of ways to incorporate different overt and covert strategies within classroom lessons. By allowing for more mental engagement through covert strategies, paired with overt teaching practices, secondary school counselors can actively engage students throughout the entire lesson and make learning more fun.

Activity 5.1: Covert or Overt?

What follows are examples of phrases school counselors can say to engage students in the lesson content as they are teaching. Read each one, and determine whether it is overt or covert and why:

Example 1: "Think about a college or career goal you have."

- **Covert:** Although school counselors hope that students are thinking about the topic, they cannot observe what each student is actually thinking.

Example 2: "Everybody repeat the number of credits to graduate."

- **Overt:** School counselors can both hear and watch the mouths of students as they say a phrase together.

1. "Be prepared to answer the question."

2. "Write down what you would do in the following scenario."

3. "Give me a thumbs-up if you agree or a thumbs-down if you disagree."

4. "Remember to follow along in your head as I read."

5. "I'm going to pull a card with a student's name on it to answer the next question."

6. "Think about _____. Give me a thumbs-up when you have it."

Answers

1. "Be prepared to answer the question."
   - **Covert:** School counselors cannot observe whether students are preparing to answer the question in their minds, but they hope so!

2. "Write down what you would do in the following scenario."
   - **Overt:** School counselors can observe students writing and can later read what they wrote to determine whether students are on track.

(Continued)

(Continued)

3. "Give me a thumbs-up if you agree or a thumbs-down if you disagree."

   * ***Overt:*** Watching students' thumbs allows the school counselor to observe participation and assess students' thoughts about the question. Tip 1: Wait until all thumbs are observed, allowing for processing time and setting the expectation of full class participation. Tip 2: Ask a student with a thumbs-up to explain their thought process, and then ask a student with a thumbs-down to do the same. Compare and contrast the two answers.

4. "Remember to follow along in your head as I read."

   * ***Covert:*** School counselors cannot observe whether students are following along, but the following tips can help: This strategy can become overt if the counselor asks students to follow along with their fingers on the book or paper (so that the counselor can observe their actions) or if the counselor stops periodically and calls on a student at random to pick up reading where the counselor left off.

5. "I'm going to pull a card with a student's name on it to answer the next question."

   * ***Overt*** and ***covert:*** As the counselor pulls a card, students are (hopefully!) thinking about their responses, which is covert. Once the called-upon student answers the question, the strategy becomes overt.

6. "Think about _____. Give me a thumbs-up when you have it."

   * ***Overt*** and ***covert:*** School counselors cannot observe what students are thinking, but students are held accountable by showing that they are ready through a thumbs-up. Tip: Remember to call on students at random to share their answers to ensure that they do "have it."

Sometimes school counselors at the secondary level feel that using strategies such as Pull Cards or Drop-in Reading (both described later in the chapter) seems elementary. They worry that students (or teachers) will think they are being cheesy and won't participate. However, children and adults alike benefit from not only seeing and hearing new information but by *speaking* and applying their knowledge (*doing*). Brain research tells us that students (or adults) are more engaged when they are actively participating in firsthand experiences rather than traditional lectures. Additionally, as school counselors help students connect the content presented to their own lives, they will develop meaningful conceptual links and better retain the information (Wesson, 2018). Therefore, activities like Think-Pair-Share that allow students to process what they have heard and apply the information to their own experiences provide opportunities for deeper learning. As school counselors are designing classroom lesson content, taking into account students' attention spans and processing speeds are important considerations. For presentations that are very content heavy, such as on financial aid or graduation requirements, breaking up the information into digestible chunks allows students to take in all the details. Strategies such as Guided Notes or Echo/Repeat Response also call students' attention to the most important content. In Sharon Bowman's *Presenting with Pizzazz* (1997), she suggests not to talk longer than the average age of the group. Therefore, secondary counselors will want to break up their presentation in some way every 12 to 18 minutes (at minimum). Even something simple such as asking students to repeat an important phrase (Echo/Repeat Response) or asking students to reflect on a question and give a thumbs-up if they agree provides opportunities for students to participate more fully and therefore better retain the information. Although applying these new engagement strategies may feel uncomfortable at first, remember that practice makes perfect! In addition, your confidence implementing the strategies will help students engage, as they will respond to your cues; when you act excited and hold them accountable to participate, they will likely rise to the challenge.

STUDENT ENGAGEMENT STRATEGIES

As school counselors plan their core curriculum class lessons, consideration is given to include different types of strategies, depending on the intended results. Do school counselors want students to 1) think deeply about a concept and share ideas with a partner, 2) learn and apply new information, and/or 3) stay focused on the content being taught? There's a strategy for that! Following are descriptions of the authors' favorite overt (observable) strategies, which may also include covert (unobservable) think time as well. The explanations help school counselors decide which strategy to use, with tips and reminders for effectiveness. The section is organized by go-to strategies suggested for use in nearly every lesson to strategies that may not be included every lesson and include more processing. The strategies are also listed in Table 5.1 to help school counselors choose strategies based on the intended student outcome. As you are reading, first review the steps in the figure boxes, and then read the description and tips.

Pull Cards

How and When to Use

Calling on students randomly throughout a class lesson, rather than relying solely on raised hands, sets the expectation that all students will participate in the lesson. Some teachers may have seating charts or cards with student names for school counselors to borrow, but rather than risk it, counselors can add a quick activity to create Pull Cards to their lesson (see Figure 5.1). Students are distributed cards when they come into the classroom and are asked to write their names on the cards. Additionally, by asking the student to respond to a question that aligns with the lesson topic, the school counselor can activate prior knowledge (see Chapter 4) or quickly

Figure 5.1   Pull Cards

Pull Cards

1. Give each student a 3x5 index card as they come into the classroom and ask them to write their name on the card.
2. You can also ask them to write other information that aligns with the lesson topic (like how often they write in their planner every week before a lesson on organization) or answer questions (such as a pre-test question).
3. Collect cards and use to randomly choose students to participate during the lesson.

Table 5.1   List of Student Engagement Strategies and Ways They Support Student Learning (Alphabetized)

Engagement Strategies	Figure Number	Suggested for Use in Most Lessons	Improves Student Learning in the Following Areas:					Supports English Learners and/or Students with IEPs
			Collaboration	Communication Skills	Knowledge Building	Processing Information	Remembering Content	
Drop-in Reading	5.2	★					★	★
Echo/Repeat Responses	5.4	★					★	★
Fist to Five	5.8					★		
Four Corners	5.13			★		★		★
Give One, Get One	5.15		★	★	★	★	★	★
Guided Notes	5.5	★			★		★	★
K-W-L-A Chart	5.10				★	★		★
Pull Cards	5.1	★		★		★		
Lines of Communication	5.17		★	★		★		
Numbered Cards	5.9		★	★				
Jigsaw	5.12		★	★	★	★	★	★
Ticket Out the Door	5.7	★				★	★	
Think-Pair-Share	5.3	★	★	★		★		★

pre-assess the class before teaching content. Once Pull Cards are created, school counselors collect the cards and call on students to read parts of the lesson or to answer questions after they have discussed their answers with a partner.

Why to Use

The average school counselor-to-student ratio is 464:1 (ASCA, n.d.), which can make it difficult for counselors to remember student names. Rather than calling only on known students or saying, "The student in the red shirt," Pull Cards allow for counselors to address the whole class. As mentioned previously, using Pull Cards engages the entire class of students in the lesson because they don't know who will be chosen, and it sets the expectation that all students will be participating.

Tips and Reminders

Remind students to write legibly, and if there are two students with the same name in the class, ask them to write their last names on the cards as well. To save instructional time, the school counselor can ask a student or two to politely help collect the cards as they move on to the next part of the lesson. School counselors can also use apps such as Stick Pick to create electronic lists of their students.

Drop-in Reading

How and When to Use

The strategy of Drop-in Reading can be incorporated into classroom lessons when the school counselor wants the entire class to read a phrase or passage together (see Figure 5.2). Within the visual presentation the counselor creates (with PowerPoint, Google Slides, etc.), key words or phrases are underlined. These are the words or phrases that the whole class will read together. Prior to use, the school counselor can teach Drop-in Reading by saying something like, "We are going to read this sentence together—I am going to read the sections that are not underlined, and you will read the underlined sections all together at the same time." The counselor may want to change their tone of voice prior to the underlined section to cue the students to drop in and read. The practice of Drop-in Reading is particularly useful for bringing classroom focus to an important concept, such as the lesson objective or new terminology. For example, Drop-in Reading can be used for the objective "We will learn steps to complete a Free Application for Federal Student Aid (FAFSA)" because this phrase is likely new to students.

Figure 5.2   Drop-in Reading

Drop-in Reading

1. Within a visual presentation (PowerPoint, Google Slides, etc.) underline key words or phrases.
2. Explain to students that they will be "dropping in" by reading these underlined portions together as a class.

- This strategy is especially useful for new and/or important information.

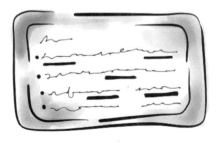

Why to Use

The strategy of reading out loud helps students form both visual and auditory links in memory pathways. In addition, students (and adults) remember more of what they say, as opposed to only 20% of what they hear. Therefore, asking all students to read an important word or phrase together improves learning. Students who are less confident readers also benefit from practicing within a safe group setting, where their voice will blend in.

Tips and Reminders

Teach or remind students *how* to read together, prior to prompting for Drop-in Reading, to gain desired results. Ensure that the sentence or phrase students are reading is not too long, otherwise students might have trouble reading it together. Once taught, school counselors can use this strategy throughout their entire lesson, either through underlining or making certain words or phrases a specific color and prompting students to read out loud each time a word is in the desired color. This can help hold students' attention and engage their participation throughout the entire lesson as they are looking for the words or phrases. Additionally, if the majority of students do not read out loud or together, ask the class to try again until the entire class participates appropriately. By maintaining and following through with high expectations, the school counselor both engages students in the lesson and applies strong classroom management techniques.

Think-Pair-Share

How and When to Use

When posing a question to students, first give them time to *think* to themselves about the answer (several seconds). Then, ask them to find a partner to *pair* with and discuss their ideas. Finally, call on partners to *share* their ideas with the class (see Figure 5.3). When using Think-Pair-Share, school counselors can also discuss the importance of stopping and thinking prior to answering a question (e.g., by allowing the class to think more deeply about their answers and giving time for students who think at different speeds).

Ideas of when to use this strategy include the following:

- At the beginning of the lesson, when asking a question to access prior knowledge:
  - *"What are reasons to check your grades online once a week?"*

- In the middle of lesson to break up teaching content:
  - *"What strategies have you used to help you manage stress?"*

Figure 5.3 Think-Pair-Share

Think -Pair-Share

1. Identify point of discussion.
2. Allow students time to think individually.
3. Have students face partner to share ideas.
4. Pair/student contributes to whole group.

- At the end of the lesson, when reviewing the objectives:
  - *"Share two or more resources that can help support you at our high school."*

Think-Pair-Share can easily be turned into Think-*Ink*-Pair-Share by asking students to write down their ideas on a paper or card prior to sharing with a partner.

Why to Use

This strategy can and should be built into every school counseling core curriculum classroom lesson. Rather than having full-class discussions with only a few students participating, or calling on students who raise their hand, Think-Pair-Share allows the entire class to engage in the content. By allowing students to consider their own answers first, talk with a partner, and then share and/or listen to answers from the class, Think-Pair-Share provides an opportunity for all students to be engaged.

Tips and Reminders

School counselors may want to pair up students for Think-Pair-Share, for example, by asking rows to face one another and discuss, or by telling students to talk with the student in the desk facing theirs. Directing students on how to find partners decreases confusion and gets them talking without wasting time. When using Think-Pair-Share, remember to call on students randomly to share their answers with the class. By selecting random students to respond, rather than taking volunteers, the school counselor sets the expectation that all students must be prepared to share their answers, which keeps them further engaged during independent think time and their partner discussions. Additionally, while students are talking with their partners, the school counselor can listen to a group and, upon hearing a strong answer, praise the student and tell them to be ready to share with the class. This builds confidence and is especially effective with students who may be less sure of their answers or need extra support (such as dual language learners, quiet students, or children with Individualized Education Plans [IEPs]).

Echo/Repeat Responses

How and When to Use

Similar to Drop-in Reading, the Echo/Repeat Responses strategy involves all students saying a word or phrase together. The difference is that the school counselor will say a word or phrase first, and the students will then repeat the word with prompting (see Figure 5.4). For example, a school counselor presenting new financial aid terminology may include "FAFSA" and "expected family contribution." The school counselor can say these new words

Figure 5.4   Echo/Repeat Responses

Echo/Repeat Responses

1. Students "echo" the word, phrase, etc. school counselor states.

- Appropriate for school counselor to use with whole group, and/or with individual students.
- A useful way of ensuring that students practice the target vocabulary being taught.

to students and then ask them to repeat the words as a group. In addition, key terms such as the numbers of credits needed to graduate or specific dates are other important words to have students repeat (when we say things out loud we are 80% likely to remember them).

Why to Use

Students (and adults) remember more when they are engaged in the learning, and asking them to repeat a key word or phrase helps ingrain the information into long-term memory. Therefore, the Echo/Repeat Responses technique is extremely effective when emphasizing important points within a lesson. The secondary school counselor will say the word or phrase first for effect, and then students can repeat together. This strategy also supports dual language learners and students with IEPs as the school counselor models saying the word prior to students needing to pronounce it on their own.

Tips and Reminders

As with all whole-class engagement strategies, set and reinforce the expectation that all students will participate in Echo/Repeat Responses. If the whole class does not echo the words, ask them to try again. Additionally, school counselors can ask the students to repeat words or phrases multiple times throughout the lesson to ensure they will remember.

Figure 5.5   Guided Notes

Guided Notes

1. Create a set of notes with fill in the blank information about the lesson you are teaching (ex: A-G requirements are _____; A growth mindset is _____).
2. Provide guided notes handout to students to fill in as you are presenting the lesson content and allow time to fill in the blanks.

Guided Notes

How and When to Use

Guided Notes are an extremely useful addition to classroom lessons that include a lot of knowledge for students to learn, which is typical at the secondary level. Rather than solely presenting information to students, creating a Guided Notes sheet for students to fill in while the school counselor speaks helps draw student attention to the most important content (see Figure 5.5). To create a Guided Notes page, school counselors design a worksheet that aligns their lesson content with some words missing that students will fill in (see the example in Figure 5.6).

Why to Use

Guided Notes engage students because they are looking for missing information to add to their note sheet provided by the school counselor. Additionally, creating a Guided Notes page for students allows them to organize and save the information they are learning.

Figure 5.6   Hey, Hey, Hey . . . Let's Calculate That GPA Guided Notes Worksheet

Potter High School Core Curriculum Counseling Classroom Lesson:
Hey, Hey, Hey . . . **Let's Calculate That GPA!**

Name: _____

Lesson Objectives: By the end of the lesson, we will be able to . . .

- Understand the importance of our grades
- Explain the required & competitive GPA for college admission and for high school athletic/extracurricular eligibility
- Calculate our Grade Point Average (GPA)

American School Counselor Association Mindsets & Behaviors Standards

- M 2: Self-Confidence in ability to succeed
- B-LS 8. Actively engage in challenging coursework
- B-LS 10. Participate in enrichment and extracurricular activities

----

Grades Matter—Graduation

- A total of _____ credits needed to graduate
- Credits are _____ you receive for each class you pass with a _____ or higher
- Passing 1 full-year class at Potter HS = _____ credits
- Students generally earn _____ credits each year
- If you get an _____ in a required class you have to _____

Grades Matter—Sports & Activities

- Student athletes must maintain a _____ GPA
- No more than _____ on quarter progress report or final report card
- Students need _____ or higher to be club leaders, attend college field trips, and earn a work permit

College Eligibility Requirements

The A–G requirements are _____ required to take and pass to

_____.

You must receive a _____ or higher in A–G classes for them to count toward college.

(Continued)

Figure 5.6 (Continued)

What Is GPA?

G _____ P _____ A _____

College Prep/Non-Honors/Non-AP	
Grade	Points
A	
B	
C	
D	
F	

Honors/AP	
Grade	Points
A	
B	
C	
D	
F	

How Do We Calculate GPA?

_____ ÷ _____ = GPA

Let's Practice Calculating GPA

Period	Class	1st Quarter Grade	Grade Points
1	Algebra 1	B	
2	Honors English 9	B+	
3	Chemistry	D	
4	World History	C	
5	Spanish 1	F	
6	PE	A–	

Add up total grade points: _____

Divide by number of classes (usually 6): _____

GPA = _____

Now It's Your Turn . . . Calculate Your GPA Based on Your 1st Quarter Grades

Period	Class	1st Quarter Grade	Grade Points
1			
2			
3			
4			
5			
6			

Add up your total grade points: _____

Divide by number of classes (usually 6): _____

MY GPA = _____

Secondary school counselors can also monitor student engagement by walking around the room while students are filling out their Guided Notes and quietly reminding students to fill in the blank spaces if they are not paying attention. In addition, Guided Notes support students in learning to organize and take notes on their own, which is an essential academic skill for students to learn.

Tips and Reminders

While carefully crafted Guided Notes worksheets help students focus on the lesson, creating too many blank spaces can actually take away from students' ability to pay attention, as they'll be searching for words rather than listening. Therefore, be sure to make blank spaces only for the most important content (such as information from the pre- or post-assessments), and also pause as you are speaking to allow time for students to fill in the blanks. Boldface and/or underline the words on the PowerPoint or Google Slides presentation that fit into the blank spaces, and also refer students to their Guided Notes worksheet to help alert them to write down the content. Using Drop-in Reading or Echo/Repeat Responses (described previously), the class can read or repeat the words that fit into their Guided Notes. School counselors may also want to title and/or number the sections for students to fill in so that it is easier for them to follow along.

Activity 5.2

Compare the Hey, Hey, Hey . . . Let's Calculate That GPA Guided Notes worksheet to the lesson slides and lesson plan in Chapter 4. Consider which areas of the lesson the counselor added to the Guided Notes sheet and the specific components where students filled in information. Now refer back to a content-heavy lesson you taught or are going to teach and create a Guided Notes worksheet for your students.

Ticket Out the Door

How and When to Use

Assessing what students have learned and how they are applying the lesson content may come in the form of a Ticket Out the Door (see Figure 5.7). One way to apply this concept is to ask students a question and/or provide a sentence frame to complete at the end of the lesson, based on the content taught. Students can write their responses (preferable), or if time is limited, the counselor can choose one or two students at random to share their

Figure 5.7   Ticket Out the Door

Ticket Out the Door

1. At the end of the lesson, give an index card or piece of blank paper to each student.
2. Pose a question or sentence starter that relates to lesson objective.
3. Have each student write their answer and as they exit they are to turn in their index card or slip of paper containing their answer.
4. School counselor can use student responses to gauge student leaning (and even as a brief post-assessment).

Ticket Out the Door Examples:

1. Career Exploration Lesson

   One career I would like to explore further is _____. A next step I will take to begin exploring is _____.

2. Goal-Setting Lesson

   My academic goal for 9th grade is _____.

   Three actions I can take to achieve my goal are the following:

   1. _____

   2. _____

   3. _____

3. Respect and Anti-Bullying Lesson

   Showing respect on campus is important because _____. I commit to showing respect by _____.

4. Growth Mindset Lesson

   The difference between a fixed and a growth mindset is _____ _____.

5. College Knowledge Lesson

   What are two (or more) steps needed when applying for college?

answers out loud. The Ticket Out the Door can also be the completion of an assignment or activity given during the lesson.

Activity 5.3

Consider an upcoming classroom lesson you will teach. What type of Ticket Out the Door can you create to align with your lesson?

Why to Use

A Ticket Out the Door is a means of assessment, helping school counselors understand what students learned from the lesson. Although school counselors are advised to more formally assess one or two classroom lessons with pre- and post-tests, a Ticket Out the Door is a less formal way to evaluate the attitudes, knowledge, and/or skills gained from the lesson content. Although the school counselor does not have comparison (pre-test) data, results can still be reported, which is discussed further in Chapter 9.

Tips and Reminders

When writing the Ticket Out the Door question or sentence frame, be specific. Rather than asking students, "What did you learn from the lesson?" ask a detailed question aligned with the most important concepts. If students are completing an assignment or activity, school counselors can either briefly check for completion (if the students should keep the information) or collect the tickets. Completion of a Ticket Out the Door can also be an incentive to stay on task and work efficiently if the tickets are to be turned in prior to lunch or end-of-the-day dismissal.

Fist to Five

How and When to Use

Strategies like Fist to Five or Thumbs-Up/ Thumbs-Down (described in Table 4.6, on page 96) allow school counselors to quickly assess the entire class for participation and to see how many students are on the right track (see Figure 5.8). Counselors can ask students to rate, on a scale of fist (zero) to five, how much they understand a concept or how much they agree or disagree with a statement.

Figure 5.8   Fist to Five

Fist to Five

1. Ask students to rate, on a scale of fist to five, with a fist meaning they don't know at all and a five meaning they could teach someone else, the answer to the following question, or whether or not they agree with a statement.
2. Pose the question to the students.
3. Observe the range (or lack of range) within the room and randomly call on students to explain their number.

Fist to Five for Understanding. By scanning the room, a school counselor can instantly observe the number of students who report they understand at a high (four or five) level. If 30% or more students are reporting ones or twos, the school counselor can reteach or ask students who are displaying fours and fives to explain to the group in their own words. If a strong majority of the class report that they understand, the counselor is still advised to ask several students to explain to deter students from mimicking the answer of their classmates when they really may not know.

Prompting students to display numbered fingers can also be used for classroom responses to a multiple-choice question. The school counselor can post a question related to the lesson topic, asking students to show their answers on their fingers. Again, the counselor is advised to call on students to share their rationales for their answers to further evaluate students' knowledge.

Fist to Five for Agree/Disagree. When using this strategy to assess students' attitudes, the school counselor can ask students with different levels of agreement to share their opinions. The school counselor can facilitate a discussion with the diverse thoughts and ideas shared.

Why to Use

Fist to Five is a quick way to observe the range (or lack of range) within the class. Following up by calling on students to explain their rationales for their responses supports deeper reflection and allows the school counselor to check for understanding.

Figure 5.9   Numbered Cards

Numbered Cards

1. Using a stack of index cards, label each card with a number, so you have two cards with the same number (For example – two cards with the number 1, two cards with the number 2, etc.). Create enough cards for each student to end up in pairs.
2. Shuffle cards and distribute to students.
3. Post a question or a writing prompt.
4. Have students write their answer on their index card.
5. After a designated amount of time, ask students to get up, find the matching numbered card, and share their response.
6. Then choose several numbers randomly to share with the whole class.

Tips and Reminders

Wait until all students have their hands up, allowing for students at all levels to have enough processing time and setting the expectation that everyone in class will participate.

Numbered Cards

How and When to Use

Another way to pair up students for a partner activity is through Numbered Cards (see Figure 5.9). Prior to the lesson school counselors write a number on each 3x5 card, so there are two cards with the same number (i.e., two cards with the number 1, two cards with the number 2, etc.). Make enough cards so each student will end up in pairs, and shuffle prior to distributing. Provide each student with a numbered card, and pose a question to students, allowing them time to write down their answers on the back of the card (non-numbered side). Then direct students to stand up and find the partner with the corresponding number from their card to share. After students share, call on different group numbers randomly to contribute to the whole class discussion.

Why to Use

Using an activity like Numbered Cards to partner students allows them to get up and talk with someone from the other side of the classroom. It also helps them create connections with someone new in a creative way.

Tips and Reminders

Prior to releasing students to find their partners, remind the class of behavior expectations, such as using indoor voices, and the signal to finish sharing. School counselors may suggest that students hold up their cards so they can more easily find their partner. If groups larger than two are desired, the counselor can modify by writing each number on three or four cards. This modification can be helpful to break students into different groups for an activity later in the lesson. In addition, an effective way to stop the partner share is by using an attention getter, such as "If you hear me, clap once. If you hear me, clap twice." (Additional attention getters are discussed further in Chapter 6.) The cards can also be collected and used as Pull Cards (see Figure 5.1, on page 117).

Along with Numbered Cards, there are other ways to pair up students. Each student can be given a shape, image, or color, and students need to find someone with the same one they were given to be their partner. The school counselor can laminate these and use them repeatedly. Students can also be told to find someone with similar shoes to theirs, in any way they define similar, to be their "Sole Mate." The pairings can also be related to the lesson topic such as by using key words and definitions. Each student can be given a different word or definition, and students have to find the person with the accompanying word/definition that matches their own. For example, in a lesson on financial aid, the word *scholarship* can be used, along with what scholarship means. One student would be given the word, and a different student would be given the definition, and when the class breaks, they need to find one another and are then partners. When using matching to group students, remember to print with a somewhat large font so students can find their partners more easily.

K-W-L-A CHART

How and When to Use

K-W-L-A stands for **K**now, **W**ant to Know, **L**earned, and **A**pply (see Figure 5.10). Creating a K-W-L-A Chart is a great way to activate prior knowledge (see Chapter 4, page 92) before starting a lesson. The lesson topic is provided, and students write down what they already *know* and what they *want to know* about the topic. For instance, prior to teaching an Apply to College lesson, students can write down what they already know and what they want to know about the college application process. Their thoughts can be captured by creating their own K-W-L-A Chart (see the example in Figure 5.11) or writing down their ideas on different sticky notes (one idea per sticky note). Once they have captured their own ideas, students will pair up with another student or several students to discuss what they wrote that they *know* and *want to know*, looking for common themes. As their partners or group members share, ask students to put check marks by items they have on their list. Then have students choose two or three common themes for K and W. These can either be shared with the class verbally or added to a whole class chart (on chart paper or electronically, such as through Google Docs). Secondary counselors will debrief with the class about what they, as a whole, *know*, emphasizing their collective strengths as a group and highlighting items they *want to know* that will be covered in the lesson.

After the lesson is taught, the counselor will go back to the K-W-L-A Chart and ask students to reflect on what they *learned*, which can be visually moved from the W column to the L column with sticky notes or on an electronic chart. Then, students

Figure 5.10   K-W-L-A Chart

K-W-L-A Chart

1. Create a chart with four columns – K (**K**now), W (**W**ant to know), L (**L**earned), and A (**A**pply).
2. Share the lesson topic and ask students to reflect on what they already *know* and what they *want to know* about the lesson topic. Students can write this down on their own K-W-L-A Chart or on post-it notes.
3. Students then share their K and W with a partner or small group, looking for commonalities.
4. Then conduct a whole group discussion about what the class already knows and what they want to learn, emphasizing which parts will be taught in the lesson.
5. After the content is taught, refer back to the K-W-L-W Chart to see which items can be moved from W to L (learned) and discuss how students can apply the information (such as, having *learned* how to study with note cards and will *apply* the strategy before the next vocabulary test).

can be asked how they will *apply* this information. For example, during the same Apply to College lesson, students may have wanted to know how to sign up for the SAT. Hopefully they *learned* the process and important dates, which would fit into the L column. They can also *apply* this information by committing to sign up by the deadline, which can be noted in the A column.

Why to Use

A K-W-L-A Chart helps school counselors tailor the teaching of the lesson toward what students want to learn. They can spend less time on topics students indicate they know and more time on areas in which students want additional information. Students are engaged because they are thinking about what they already bring to the lesson (activating prior knowledge) and what they want to know further. It also validates students in the process, as their current knowledge and additional questions are acknowledged by the counselor. Additionally, by circling back to what they learned and how they will apply the knowledge, students can see their growth from just one lesson.

Tips and Reminders

Creating a K-W-L-A Chart takes additional time at the beginning and end of a lesson, so allowing students only a few minutes for each section is advised to ensure content can be taught in between. Although school counselors should take into account what students say they already know, remember to still teach important content you want to ensure all students learn (such as graduation requirements, important deadlines, etc.). Not all students may know the information, and students who *think* they know may not actually know. Additionally, even if counselors don't have all the content ready that the students want to learn about, they can find additional ways to provide the information in the future. Additional class lessons,

Figure 5.11   K-W-L-A Chart Example

KWLA

- List everything you already **KNOW** about the college application process.

- List three things you **WANT TO KNOW** about submitting a college application during our lesson.

- Share your ideas with your neighbor.

- At the end of class we will return back to the chart to see what we **LEARNED** and how we can APPLY the information to apply to college!

Know	Want to Know	Learned	Apply

lunch workshops, and/or including the information on the school website are all ways of providing more content to students if it cannot all be covered in one lesson.

Jigsaw

How and When to Use

Jigsaw is a strategy used to break up a large amount of lesson content, while having students investigate and become experts in different topics, and then sharing with their peers (see Figure 5.12). The school counselor will separate students into groups, and each group will receive a specific topic or a portion of the information. Jigsawing can also be used when students start responding to or acting out different scenarios based on the lesson content. Students form groups and work together based on the school counselor's directions. Examples include the following:

Figure 5.12   Jigsaw

Jigsaw

1. Each student receives a portion of the materials to be introduced.
2. Students leave their "home" groups and meet in "expert" groups.
3. Expert groups discuss the material and brainstorm ways in which to present their understandings to the other members of their "home" group.
4. The experts return to their "home" groups to teach their portion of the materials and to learn from other members of their "home" group.
5. Students can use a graphic organizer to write down notes as experts talk.

- The school counselor gives each group pamphlets from different types of colleges. Teams also receive a handout with information to fill in, such as where the school is located, the cost of tuition, location, and so forth.
- Teams are provided packets of information about the risks of using tobacco, alcohol, and marijuana during a Red Ribbon Week lesson. Groups investigate the facts, write down risks they discover, and then share their results with the class.
- Each group is given a scenario with different situations in which bullying or mistreatment has occurred. Using the strategies the school counselor has taught, teams brainstorm what to do and act out the scenario to the class.
- After learning about creating an effective résumé, groups are each given different examples of résumés. Teams compare and contrast the résumés and share with the class strengths and areas for growth among the résumés they viewed.

While groups are working, the school counselor (and hopefully the teacher) walks around the room to answer questions and monitor group progress. At the end of the given time, the school counselor will ask each group to share their expert knowledge with the entire class. The class can take notes or fill in an additional portion of the handout (if one is provided) while their classmates present. If a role-play or other activity is showcased in which students apply the information learned from the lesson, the school counselor can reiterate what was taught after each group shares or presents.

Why to Use

Using Jigsaw is a way to help students learn experientially, and it also breaks up a large amount of content. By working collaboratively, students own their learning and also learn from one another.

Tips and Reminders

School counselors may want to consider different ways to group students prior to beginning the lesson, such as by current table groups, numbering off into random groups, or using Numbered Cards (see Figure 5.9). Consider the number of students in the group and how this impacts group dynamics. Typically, forming groups of three to five students is ideal. If students must move to find their team members, remember to consider ways to reduce transition times, such as all students being in their new groups as the school counselor counts backward from 10 (for more on transitions, see Chapter 6).

Prior to starting group work, school counselors may want to set group protocols, such as one group member is the timer, another is the recorder, a third is the presenter, and so on. Regardless of students' roles, remind them that they will all participate in the discussion. Also remind students about using an inside voice during teamwork so that all groups can hear as they are working. Prior to beginning, tell students how much time they will have to complete the work and consider setting a timer (a timer they can see while they are working is particularly helpful; see Chapter 6, page 153).

The school counselor is also advised to assess whether groups are on track to finish by walking around, and they may need to adjust the time as necessary. Providing several countdown warnings also helps groups finish up on time. As student "expert" groups are sharing with their peers, remind students of expectations as they are listening and advise presenters to use loud voices. The school counselor may want to repeat the most important information shared to ensure that all students gain the necessary content.

Figure 5.13 ·Four Corners

Four Corners

1. Read a statement to the class related to lesson topic and allow them to think of whether they strongly agree/agree/ disagree strongly disagree.
2. Hang signs in the four corners of the classroom with the four choices and ask students to move to the corner that applies to them.
3. When at their corner, give them 1–2 minutes to discuss the reason for their choice with other members of the group and be prepared to share with the entire class.
4. Discuss as a group.

Four Corners

How and When to Use

During lessons that include more discussion time, an activity like Four Corners may be appropriate (see Figure 5.13). The school counselor will set up by hanging signs with different responses in the four corners of the classroom. Statements will be read to the class related to the lesson topic, and students will be given a short amount of time to consider their reactions and then move to the corner of the room that applies to them. When at their corner, the counselor will give students one to two minutes to share the reason for their choice with others at that corner and to be prepared to share their answers with the entire class. The school counselor will facilitate a short discussion based on the different perspectives. Then a new prompt will be read, and the process will start over again.

Titles for the different corners can be strongly agree, agree, disagree, strongly disagree, or more specific based on the lesson topic. See Figure 5.14. for an example. During the activity, observe students as they move to different corners, as some may continually choose to travel with their friends or to the most populated corner. Encourage students to think independently and honor the voices of the entire class, even when their corner is less represented.

Why to Use

Four Corners is a great strategy to allow students to express their opinions and listen to the thoughts and ideas of others. Through providing a format that both demonstrates and celebrates diversity, students can consider the perspectives of others.

Tips and Reminders

Consider how to structure the lesson delivery and classroom setting to promote success. Because this engagement strategy involves students expressing different opinions, creating a safe space for participating respectfully is essential to ensure students feel comfortable sharing. Consider the maturity of the grade level to help decide whether or not the class will be receptive and benefit from an activity like Four Corners. Setting ground rules prior to participating in Four Corners is advised, such as listening with an open mind. The physical space may also need to be considered—do desks or tables need to be moved to allow for students to get up and move around the room safely? Remember to discuss with the classroom teacher beforehand if you would like to rearrange the room. Finally, remember to teach students an "Attention Getter" (Chapter 6, page 152) so they will quickly quiet down after moving and sharing.

Figure 5.14   Four Corners in a Respect and Anti-Bullying Lesson

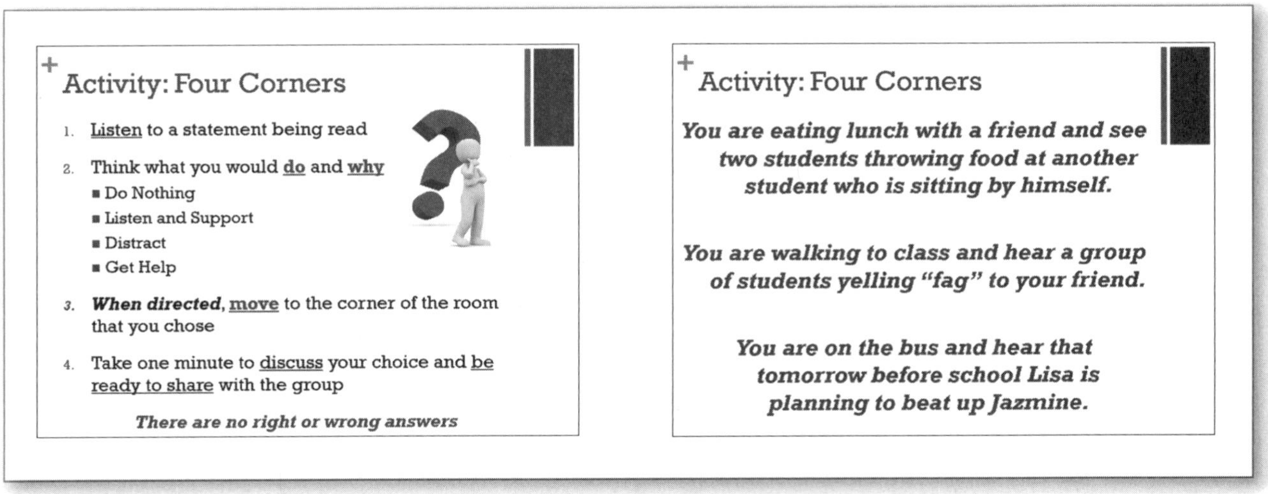

Activity: Four Corners

1. <u>Listen</u> to a statement being read

2. Think what you would <u>do</u> and <u>why</u>
   - Do Nothing
   - Listen and Support
   - Distract
   - Get Help

3. **When directed**, <u>move</u> to the corner of the room that you chose

4. Take one minute to <u>discuss</u> your choice and <u>be ready to share</u> with the group

   There are no right or wrong answers

Activity: Four Corners

You are eating lunch with a friend and see two students throwing food at another student who is sitting by himself.

You are walking to class and hear a group of students yelling "fag" to your friend.

You are on the bus and hear that tomorrow before school Lisa is planning to beat up Jazmine.

Figure 5.15   Give One, Get One

Give One, Get One

1. Using a structured template, have students write a list of facts or ideas learned.
2. Have students begin with a partner assigned by you.
3. Instruct them to collect one new and different fact or idea from their partner.
4. Then they are to give one new and different fact or idea.
5. If neither has a new and different idea, tell them to brainstorm and try to create one.
6. Have students go from person to person until they generate several ideas on the subject.
7. Compile a group list of ideas generated.

Give One, Get One

How and When to Use

Give One, Get One is an effective strategy to use after students are taught content to help them more deeply process the information (see Figure 5.15). Using a structured template (see the example that follows), ask students to write a list of information they learned. Once they are finished the school counselor assigns students their beginning partner (such as through counting off, "Sole Mates," etc.). Instruct students to collect one new fact or idea from their partner and then give one new or different idea to their partner. If neither student has a different idea, tell them to brainstorm and create one. After their first partner, students will go from person to person until they have several new ideas on the same subject. After the designated amount of time, come back together as a class, and compile a group list of ideas generated.

Why to Use

Providing time for students to recall and process the information shared will help with remembering. Give One, Get One also allows students time to collaborate with and learn from other members of their class. By completing the Give One, Get One activity, students will also have tangible information they can keep and refer back to based on what they learned from the lesson.

Tips and Reminders

Similar to other engagement strategies during which students will be out of their seats collaborating with their peers, set ground rules for their interactions with one another and how to come back together as a class. Observe the group as they are interacting with one another, and help pair up any students who are struggling to find partners. Also use the observation time to gauge how much more time is needed based on the progress students are making. All students might not complete every section of their Give One, Get One worksheet, but you can likely finish when most students have completed the activity and others have interacted with multiple partners.

Creating a structured template for the Give One, Get One activity can be as simple as asking students to fold a blank paper into four squares or a more detailed worksheet with different sections (see Figure 5.16). Also consider the Give One, Get One prompt you are providing to students; how specific do you want their answers to be? For instance, "Write down a study strategy and how you will apply it" is advised over "Write down one thing you learned from the lesson." The more clearly you describe the prompt, the richer student responses will be.

Figure 5.16   Give One, Get One

Give One, Get One

In ONE BOX, write down one studying strategy you learned and how you can use the strategy.

When you are finished, find a partner and share your idea (they will write it down in a new box on their paper) and listen to their idea (you will write it down in a new box on your paper). If you both wrote down the same idea, try to think of a new one.

Find a new partner and do the same. Repeat until all your boxes are filled.

Lines of Communication

How and When to Use

Another way to facilitate a discussion among different students is by Lines of Communication. Have students form two lines facing one another (see Figure 5.17). Provide students with a talking prompt, and decide which side of the line will begin the conversation. Give each partner one minute or less to speak, and then switch to the other partner. After both sides of the line have shared, ask one or two students from the end of one line to walk to the other end of the same line, while all the students in that line shift down to a new partner. Hence, one line is moving and one line is staying in place, and each student now has a new partner. After the switch, provide a new talking prompt and continue for several rounds, as appropriate to the lesson. School counselors may want to consider using Lines of Communication for topics such as discussing career interests, study strategies, ways students cope with stress, or sharing feelings of excitement and nervousness about life after high school.

Figure 5.17   Lines of Communication

Lines of Communication

1. Have students form two lines facing each other.
2. Provide students with a talking prompt.
3. Decide which side of the line begins the conversation.
4. Give about 1–2 minutes for students to communicate.
5. Have one end person from one line go to end of the line and have students from same line slide down.
6. Give same prompt or different talking point.

Why to Use

Effective communication is an essential academic and life skill. Therefore, providing opportunities within school counseling core curriculum classroom lessons for students to discuss with a variety of classmates helps them develop and improve verbal communication. Lines of Communication also provides a state change—an opportunity for students to move from the state of sitting to standing. Taking into account how long students have been sitting and incorporating movement can help students refocus on the lesson content.

Tips and Reminders

When creating the two lines, it may be helpful to have students count off (such as 1, 2, 1, 2 . . .); ask the 1s to line up first and then the 2s to stand across from a partner. The school counselor may want to use a timer with a buzzer for students to hear to cue them when to switch partners and when to rotate.

Using Engagement Strategies Within Family Workshops

School counselors can also use a variety of the engagement strategies listed previously when presenting to families; adult learners need engagement, too! Imagine the parent or guardian who has been up since 5:30 a.m. to get ready for work and get their children dressed, fed, and ready for school, and then dropped off their kids, worked all day, and is now at a family meeting at 6:00 p.m. That parent or guardian is tired and needs an engaging presentation just as much as the students did earlier in the day! In addition, connecting families to one another and incorporating their knowledge into the presentation are essential to validate their knowledge and engage them into the workshop content.

The Parent Institute for Quality Education (PIQE) recommends building community within the first 20 minutes of a family workshop by authentically engaging families at two levels—love and fear. One way to do this is by asking families to meet someone new and respond to questions such as: *"What is the dream you have for your child, and what obstacles can get in their way?" "What types of challenges are young people (our children) facing different from the ones we faced?"* (Mayer, 2017, slide 14). Questions like these can be posed to families using strategies such as Think-Pair-Share or Lines of Communication. Consider how you can incorporate engagement strategies into future presentations for families, and some suggestions follow:

- *Think-Pair-Share:* Incorporate reflection questions pertaining to the topic into the presentation, and ask parents or guardians to introduce themselves to a neighbor as they pair and exchange ideas, and then share some with the larger group.
- *Thumbs-Up/Thumbs-Down or Fist to Five:* Both of these strategies are great ways to assess the audience, for example, by asking how much knowledge they have on the topic (from zero to five) or to observe how much participants agree or disagree with statements (using a thumbs-up or down or a fist [not at all] to open hand [strongly agree]).
- *Guided Notes:* Topics with a lot of information, such as Successful Transitioning to High School and Completing a FAFSA, can offer a good opportunity to include Guided Notes. Rather than passing out a handout with all the information in a traditional manner, school counselors can create Guided Notes for participants to fill out while they are listening to keep parents and guardians engaged as they fill in the information. However, consider your family population, and keep some filled-in Guided Notes sheets on hand for any parents or guardians who may have difficulty writing.
- *"Sole Mates":* Incorporating "Sole Mates" into the family workshop provides participants with a chance to stand up and meet someone new as they share their thoughts.

- *Jigsaw:* Depending on the topic, school counselors may want to include a Jigsaw, for example, by having parents and guardians split into groups to discuss different topics or respond to scenarios. This strategy is especially impactful for multisession family workshops, as participants can dive deeper into workshop content and connect with one another.
- *Give One, Get One:* After presenting new content, ask participants to get up and meet new people to share a takeaway they have with several different partners. Allowing families to get up and meet one another, while also sharing, helps them meet new people and learn from one another.
- *Ticket Out the Door:* Asking parents and guardians to respond to a question as they leave is a great way for them to reflect on the topic they learned and for the school counselor to see what parts of the family workshop were most impactful and/or what questions still remain.

Incorporating a variety of classroom engagement strategies throughout the beginning, middle, and end of school counseling core curriculum classroom lessons involves students in the learning, which becomes interactive and fun. School counselors can include different strategies in their lessons, trying out a variety of techniques to see which work best for various situations. Through using these techniques, school counselors engage all students in the lesson, deepening their learning to create a greater impact on their attitude, knowledge, skills, and future behaviors.

NOTES

_____

_____

_____

_____

_____

_____

_____

_____

Figure 5.18   Portion of Lesson Plan: Hey, Hey, Hey . . . Let's Calculate That GPA, With Engagement Strategies Highlighted

Core Curriculum Class Lessons

Hey, Hey, Hey . . . Let's Calculate That GPA!

PROCEDURES:

Slide 1: **Welcome**

- ○ Welcome students to the class and share the lesson title (Hey, Hey, Hey . . . Let's Calculate That GPA) and topic (importance of grades in high school and learning how to calculate grade point average).

Slide 2: **School Counseling Department Introduction**

- Remind students about the members of the school counseling department including the school counselors and any additional support staff (counseling clerks, interns, etc.).
- <u>Ask students to share what they know about the role of a school counselor.</u> Depending on what students share, the counselor may also want to add that their job is to make students be successful in school by: teaching them lessons on a variety of topics including academics and well-being (like today), helping them create goals for now and the future, supporting them with any problems at school or personally, planning schoolwide events like College Signing Day, and helping everyone at school feel safe and happy.

Whole Group Sharing

Slide 3: **Behavior Expectations**

- Remind students of the three Potter R's (be ready, respectful, and responsible) and <u>ask them to repeat them together.</u>
- Praise the class for already demonstrating the three R's and list specific examples (such as, "You are all showing me respect by staying quiet while I am talking." "I can see how responsible you are by having a writing utensil ready.").
- Tell students that one part of being ready and responsible during today's lesson is to complete their guided notes worksheet during the lesson.
- Ask two students to quickly and quietly pass out the guided notes to each student.

Choral Reading

Slide 4: **Objectives**

Drop-in Reading

- Explain the objectives that are the focus of the presentation and what students are intended to learn. Ask students to participate in <u>"Drop in Reading" – the counselor will read the non-underlined portion of the objectives and the students will read the underlined portion of the objectives</u> together. By the end of the lesson, we will be able to . . .
  - ○ Understand the <u>importance</u> of our <u>grades</u>
  - ○ Explain the <u>required & competitive GPA</u> for college admission and for high school <u>athletic/ extra-curricular eligibility</u>
  - ○ Calculate our <u>Grade Point Average</u> (GPA)
- Tell the students the objectives are aligned to the school counseling standards at the bottom of the slide.

<u>Slide 5</u>: **Access Prior Knowledge**

Think-Ink-Pair-Share

- <u>Ask students to quietly think about the reason grades are important.</u>
- While they are thinking, ask two students to pass out a 3x5 card to each student.
- Tell the students to write their first and last name on the top of the card, and then <u>write down at least two reasons grades are important.</u> Explain the example on the PowerPoint (name and numbered items).

Connecting Student Answers

- Walk around and observe while students are writing, noticing any specific students you'd like to call on to share and any you'd want to avoid.
- After several minutes, regroup the class and call on the students you noticed and/or ask students in general to share. <u>As each student shares one example, ask the class to raise their hand if they wrote down something similar.</u>
- After calling on three to four students, ask all students to raise their cards up in the air and for two students to quickly and quietly collect all the cards and bring them up to the front as you proceed with the next slide.

<u>Slide 6</u>: **Grades Matter** (Input)

- Explain that grades matter for a variety of reasons now and in the future, as was just discussed.
- Tell students you will be specifically discussing how grades matter in high school for eligibility for sports and extra-curricular activities, along with graduation. The lesson will also talk about how grades will impact students in the future, such as for college and other post-secondary options.

<u>Slide 7</u>: **Grades Matter – Research** (Input)

Pull Cards

- Explain to students that there is research from *U.S. News & World Report of* high school freshmen that explains the importance of getting good grades.
- <u>Use the 3x5 cards to select student to read the first bullet-point</u> - *How well students performed academically in 9th grade predicted students' future success.*

Read Around the Room

- <u>Then ask the student sitting next to the student who just read to read the next bullet point</u> <u>-</u> *9th graders with A's, B's, and C's were much more likely to graduate high school than their classmates with lower grades; and the following student to read the last bullet - Academically strong 9th graders were more likely to attend college.*

Guided Notes

<u>Slide 8</u>: **Grades Matter – Graduation** (Input)

- Direct students to the <u>Guided Notes sheet</u> that was passed out at the beginning of the class, that they will begin filling in.
- Explain that you will again use "drop in reading" for students to read the underlined sections, and they will also fill the information in on their guided notes.
  - Total of **220 credits** needed to graduate
  - Credits are "**points**" you receive for each class you pass with a **D** or higher
  - Passing one full year class at Potter HS = **10 credits**

Drop-in Reading

  - Students generally earn **60 credits each year**
    If you get an F in a required class you have to **take the class again** ☹
- Walk around the room while presenting information on this slide to ensure students are filling in their guided notes sheet.

(Continued)

Figure 5.18 (Continued)

Slide 9: **Grades Matter – Sports & Activities** (Input)

More Drop-in Reading

- Continue to use "Drop-in Reading" to explain sports and other activity eligibility, while walking around the classroom to ensure students are filling in guided notes.
  - Student athletes must maintain a **2.0 GPA**
  - No more than **1 F** on quarter progress report or final report card
  - Students need 2.0 or higher to be **club leaders**, attend **college fieldtrips,** and **earn a work permit**

Slide 10: **Access Prior Knowledge**

Think-Pair-Share

- Explain to students that their choices now can impact them as they begin thinking about life after high school.
- Ask students to think about their post-secondary goals and what they can do now to get there (and allow about 20 seconds of silent think time).
- Ask students to pair with a partner to discuss their thought to the questions, and alert them you'll be using the 3x5 cards to call on a few students to answer.
- While students are talking with their neighbor, walk around to listen to their answers and prompt students with good answers that you may call on them.
- After several minutes, call on several students to share their answers with the class.

Slide 11: **College Eligibility Requirements** (Input)

Choral Reading

- Ask students to read the statement describing the A-G requirements all together – *classes required to take and pass to attend most California colleges (UC's and CSU's)* – and fill in the information on their guided notes sheet.
- Explain that students who want to attend a University of California (UC) or California State University (CSU) need to complete the A-G requirement classes, and the grade they need in these classes to count towards college is a C-. Ask students, *"What grade do you need in A-G classes?"* so they repeat the word C-, and also remind them to fill it into their guided notes sheet.

Guided Notes

- Tell students that even if students aren't sure if they want to go to college they should still take and pass these classes so they can have all the options available to them.

Slide 12: **College Eligibility Requirements** (Input)

Drop-in Reading & Guided Notes

- Discuss the difference between eligible for college and competitive, and share the difference between eligible GPA's and the average GPA's for students who were admitted:

California State Universities (CSUs)

- GPA'S of **2.0** or above are eligible
- Accepted students generally had GPA **3.2+**

University of California (UCs)

- GPA'S of **3.0** or above are eligible
- Accepted students generally had GPA **3.5-4.0+**
  - Explain to students that being competitive means working hard in their classes to get higher than the minimum and also reinforcing what students said about what they can do now (like study, join clubs, etc.)

- ○ Remind students they will also need to take the SAT and/or ACT test, and the counselor will share more information about this in a future class lesson.

Slide 13: **High School Class & A-G College Eligibility Requirements** (Input)

- Explain to freshmen that most, if not all, classes they are currently taking are likely helping them become eligible for graduation and for the A-G requirements.
- Ask two students to pass out the Potter High School Graduation Requirements and UC/CSU A-G Requirements sheet to see how the classes compare.
- Discuss a few examples:
  - ○ Ask students to put their finger on the number of years of history they need to graduate from high school, and then say it out loud (3 years). Then ask them to slide their finger to the right to read how many years they need to be A-G eligible (2 years).
  - ○ Ask students to move their finger down to math and ask them how many years they need for graduation (2 years), and then how many they need for A-G (3 years, but 4 recommended). Explain how taking more than the minimum number of classes can be important to be competitive for college acceptance.

Slide 14: **What is GPA?** (Input)

- Ask students to chorally read what GPA stands for (Grade Point Average)
- Explain that each letter grade equals a certain point value, which makes up student GPAs. GPAs are calculated at the end of each quarter, when final grades are released.
- Ask students to fill in the number of points on their guided notes sheets for College Pre/Non-Honors/ Non-AP as the numbers come out one by one from the PowerPoint animation.
- Tell students that honors and AP (advanced placement) classes earn more GPA points because they are accelerated, rigorous classes.

Kinesthetic Engagement

Echo/ Repeat Response

Choral Reading

Guided Notes

6

Classroom Management

> *Mariko did not receive training in classroom management during her school counseling graduate program. Although she has spent time planning an engaging beginning-of-the-year lesson, she worries that students won't pay attention. "What will I do?" wonders Mariko. She is hoping all students listen and participate but isn't sure how to respond if they don't. Mariko also worries that she will lose credibility with teachers if she reacts inappropriately to student misbehavior. Several teachers have asked Mariko for advice about ways to work with difficult students, but she doesn't feel skilled enough to give them feedback.*
>
> *Mariko is not alone. According to a survey by the American School Counselor Association (ASCA), 74% of school counselors reported that they did not receive training in classroom management, and only 11% definitively stated that they did receive such training (see Figure 6.1; "Classroom Management Skills," 2016). However, while the large majority have not received instruction in classroom management strategies, 82% report that teachers have asked them for help in this area ("Classroom Management Skills," 2016). This mismatch highlights the need for school counselors to be effectively trained in classroom management techniques for their own implementation of classroom lessons and to support others.*

MANAGING CLASSROOMS

Teaching core curriculum classroom lessons provides school counselors with the opportunity to impact a large number of students simultaneously. Therefore, utilizing classroom time effectively and efficiently is extremely important to maximize student learning. Proactive classroom management skills are correlated with positive school climate, improved student–teacher relationships, and high levels of achievement (Gettinger & Kohler, 2006; Mitchell & Bradshaw, 2013; Simonsen,

Figure 6.1   ASCA School Counselor Classroom Management Survey

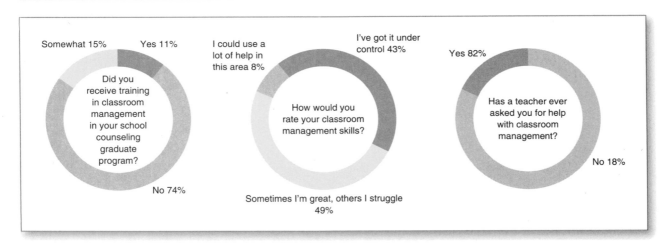

Source: ASCA School Counselor (2016). *Classroom management skills: From chaos to calm, from inattentive to inspired 53(6),* Reprinted with permission from the American School Counselor Association, 2019.

Fairbanks, Briesch, Myers, & Sugai, 2008). Because school counselors don't have a consistent group of students for each lesson, they must be skilled in employing effective strategies to keep students focused and participating appropriately. To support the varying structures of different classes, school counselors will use flexibility within their management styles to adapt to the needs of the class, while consistently maintaining high expectations for all students. Students at middle and high school exhibit a varying developmental range, which requires that school counselors learn and apply different management techniques across the varying grade and developmental levels to effectively support student success.

The classroom management strategies presented in this chapter are primarily focused on prevention, the key to effectiveness. Explicitly teaching and practicing behavior expectations during class lessons is an essential component of impeding off-task and other problem behaviors. The engagement strategies presented in the previous chapter support a well-managed classroom. Students who are involved in the learning during the entire lesson are less likely to demonstrate off-task behavior. Paired together, engaging lesson content and strong classroom management result in the ideal combination to produce a well-executed core curriculum lesson. Later in the chapter, strategies for ways to address minor, recurrent, or extreme problem behaviors are presented. Approaches are also provided that school counselors can apply to appropriately and swiftly redirect and/or provide consequences to students.

PROACTIVE CLASSROOM MANAGEMENT

Explicitly Teach Expectations

Ensuring that all students understand and can perform to the school counselor's expectations is essential for successfully teaching core curriculum classroom lessons. When students are attending and participating appropriately, deeper learning occurs (Evertson & Weinstein, 2013). Therefore, school counselors are advised to spend a fair amount of time explaining, practicing, and reinforcing procedures and routines during their first few classroom visits. The extra time spent initially will save time in the long run as students will know what is expected when the school counselor is teaching.

Ideally, universal behavior expectations are already in place schoolwide. Common expectations at the secondary level, aligning with schoolwide programs such as Positive Behavior Intervention and Supports (PBIS), may include three to four of the following:

- Be ready
- Respect yourself and others
- Always do your best
- Be responsible
- Demonstrate integrity

When working at a school with universal behavior expectations, school counselors are advised to clearly explain what each expectation means in the context of their teaching. For instance, one example of being responsible might be turning in homework; however, if school counselors don't give homework, what does being responsible look like during a school counseling lesson? Students can brainstorm what the school counselor will see and hear when following each expectation, sharing specific examples with the class. Helping students process each of the expectations together, in a developmentally appropriate way, increases their understanding and therefore increases their compliance with the expectations.

Activity 6.1

Look at the behavior expectations in the column on the left side of this table. Notice the sections on the right that are filled in with explicit examples of what the school counselor will see and hear when students are following directions. In the first category, the three examples on the right side of the table explicitly detail how to be ready. Complete the table by filling in additional ideas for how school counselors can prompt students to provide specific examples of expectations for core curriculum lessons.

Table 6.1

Behavior Expectation	What Will School Counselors See and Hear During Class Lessons?
Be ready	- Actively participate in the lesson - Raise your hand when you want to share an answer - Follow directions the first time they are given
Respect yourself and others	- Quietly listen to the school counselor and other students when they are sharing - Use positive words and body language - Seek first to understand, then to be understood

(Continued)

Table 6.1   (Continued)

Always do your best	•
	•
	•
Be responsible	•
	•
	•
Demonstrate integrity	•
	•
	•

Figure 6.2   SLANT

Sit up
Listen
Ask and answer questions
Nod your head
Track the speaker

Good Listeners SLANT

If a school does not have universal expectations, secondary counselors generally have two options: 1) to create consistent expectations that the school counselor always uses with every class, or 2) to incorporate each teacher's expectations when visiting different classes. The first choice is recommended because learning the variety of rules and procedures for each classroom is a lot to remember. Even if the school counselor's expectations are slightly different from a teacher's, students at the secondary level are generally able to code shift, especially when expectations are taught well and reinforced. School counselors may want to adopt three to four of the expectations listed previously as their universal school counseling expectations, or SLANT (discussed in the box that follows).

In addition, school counselors can still use components of teachers' classroom management systems. For example, if a teacher gives out "Scholar Dollars" for participating students or table points when groups are following directions, the school counselor can do the same when students are participating in ways that align with counselor expectations. If school counselors decide to incorporate each teacher's classroom rules (option two), they will want to work with teachers before the school year to clearly understand the expectations and consider how they will fit with core curriculum. This option is advised only for school counselors with smaller caseloads and/or who visit classrooms frequently (weekly or every other week).

SLANT

The SLANT classroom management strategy (see Figure 6.2) has been shared by multiple educational leaders, including by Doug Lemov in *Teach Like a Champion 2.0* (2015; discussed in Chapter 4).

S: Sit up straight

L: Listen

A: Ask and answer questions

N: Nod your head

T: Track the speaker

Slightly different variations for each letter are available, but the intent of SLANT is the same—focusing students on learning. As is advised for all behavior expectations, explicitly teach students what each letter means. "Track the speaker" is likely a new phrase for students, so more depth may be needed when describing this expectation. Tracking the speaker means that students are looking at the speaker, whether it is the school counselor or a student called on to answer a question. As the counselor moves around the room, which is advised (see the section on circulating later in the chapter), students' heads follow as the counselor walks. When a student is sharing a response with the class, the other students' heads turn to the student speaker. Once these ideas are taught, school counselors can use this one word—SLANT—to remind students of all five behavior expectations.

Review Expectations Each Visit

Reminding students of the school counselor's classroom expectations at the beginning of each visit is a preventative strategy that helps set the tone for the lesson. Readers will recall that this was mentioned when discussing lesson plans in Chapter 4. Although students may remember the expectations from the last visit, reviewing them up front is much better than having to stop mid-lesson to attempt to redirect behavior after students are not following directions. After explicitly teaching and reviewing classroom norms during the first two visits, there are a variety of ways to quickly review procedures and expectations during subsequent visits:

- Provide a short opportunity for students to discuss what the counselor will hear when the class expectations are being followed, such as through Think-Pair-Share.
- Ask all students to read the expectations together out loud, then call on students randomly to share examples of each expectation.
- Remind students of the expectations, then positively praise students or the class as a whole for demonstrating the expectations (e.g., "Our classroom expectation is to be respectful, and your entire class is showing me respect by listening quietly while I'm talking," or "Remember that we track the speaker, and I see Malik and Juana doing just that as they are keeping their eyes on me while I walk around the room").

Positive reinforcement increases the likelihood that students will follow directions, so school counselors are encouraged to recognize students or the class as a whole.

Reinforce Appropriate Behavior

Acknowledging students who are on task and following directions is an effective strategy to maintain a positive classroom environment (Canter, 2010). Educational research suggests a ratio of five positive interactions (thanking students for staying on task, providing nonverbal acknowledgment for following directions, praising a correct answer, etc.) for every one negative interaction (redirecting misbehavior, disciplining a student, etc.) within the classroom. By maintaining a 5:1 ratio, school counselors develop positive relationships with their students, encouraging better behavior and decreasing classroom disruption.

Outward recognition of students who are following the school counselor's expectations signals to the class that the counselor is monitoring everyone's behavior and motivates students to follow directions and stay on task. Reinforcing appropriate behavior often corrects the behavior of students who are not following directions as well. This strategy is useful to incorporate throughout the lesson to maintain positive energy and high expectations. Suggestions on how to reinforce behavior include the following:

- Positively acknowledge the behavior immediately after it takes place.
- Specifically state the behavior you are acknowledging.
- Use a positive, sincere tone of voice.
- Acknowledge effort and improved behaviors.
- Vary the positive reinforcement provided to individual students and the class.

In some cases, school counselors may want to use incentives to reinforce positive behavior. Counselors can build on what teachers are already doing, such as assigning group or class points. School counselors can also create their own special incentives, such as creating class raffles, giving stickers to students with exemplary behavior (even high school students still enjoy stickers—try it!), or giving students one minute of free time at the end of the lesson.

The School Counselor's Role in Discipline

Adapted from Hatch (2013, pp. 213–215)

As school counselors collaborate with members of the school community to create a positive culture, climate, and behavior expectations, as well as to deliver classroom lessons, school counselors (and other school staff) sometimes wonder about the school counselor's role in discipline. For example, as providers of professional development to school counselors, we often hear school counselors pushing back with administrators that they "don't do discipline." Although we support the counselor's role in *not* meting out discipline, school counselors absolutely *do* have a vital role in discipline, including supporting a positive culture and climate; contributing to the establishment of positive schoolwide behavioral expectations; and addressing discipline prevention, intervention, and post-suspension follow-up.

It's important to note that school administrators possess a license or credential providing them authority to mete out student discipline. They take classes in due process and law and are employed to provide discipline as part of their expected responsibilities. The school counselor's role is fundamentally different, because their credentials do *not* provide them the authority to suspend students. Rather, the school counselor's role in discipline is to support the collaborative schoolwide system that works to ensure that students possess the knowledge, attitudes, and skills necessary to prevent and reduce the number of referrals requiring discipline.

ASCA's 2013 position statement on "The School Counselor and Discipline" supports this perspective:

> The school counselor is **not a disciplinarian** but should be a resource for school personnel as they develop individual and schoolwide discipline procedures. The school counselor collaborates with school personnel and other stakeholders to establish policies encouraging appropriate behavior and maintaining safe schools where effective teaching and learning can take place. . . . It is **not the role of the school counselor to mete out punishment** but instead to help create effective behavior change focused on positive, healthy behaviors. (Bold added for emphasis; read the full statement here: https://www.schoolcounselor.org/asca/media/asca/PositionStatements/PS_Discipline.pdf.)

Additionally, there are several related ethical standards (ASCA, 2016):

- "School counselors . . . **defer to administration for all discipline issues** for this or any other federal, state or school board violation" (A.11.a.).
- "School counselors . . . avoid dual relationships beyond the professional level with school personnel, parents/guardians and students' other family members when these relationships might infringe on the integrity of the school counselor/student relationship. Inappropriate dual relationships include, but are not limited to, **providing direct discipline**, teaching courses that involve grading students and/ or **accepting administrative duties in the absence of an administrator**." (A.5.c.)
- "School counselors . . . work responsibly through the correct channels to **try and remedy work conditions that do not reflect the ethics of the profession**." (B.2.s.)

School counselors are addressing *discipline prevention* when they do the following:

- Use data to locate trends in student behavior (e.g., referrals, suspensions, Youth Behavior Risk Surveys, or climate surveys) and present this important information to staff.
- Advocate for evidence-based curriculum to be delivered in classrooms schoolwide to address data-driven needs.

(Continued)

(Continued)

- Coordinate, design, oversee, and evaluate the impact of conflict resolution, peer mediation, and peer helper and restorative practices programs and services for students.
- Participate in leadership conversations regarding schoolwide discipline issues.
- Provide training for staff, students, and parents about conflict resolution, restorative practices, violence prevention, and early warning signs of violence.
- Ensure systems are in place that allow anonymous referrals from concerned persons.
- Participate in PBIS.
- Advocate for classroom, school, and district consistency in discipline policies, practices, and procedures.
- Promote accurate and consistent collection of discipline data.

School counselors are addressing *discipline intervention* needs when they do the following:

- Query student discipline data records to determine which students need counseling interventions for frequent offenses (e.g., five or more referrals = anger management group).
- Ensure students who are identified by data (or referral) are provided with appropriate interventions (group/individual counseling).
- Refer students requiring more intensive intervention than is appropriate to provide in school to outside agencies (ASCA, 2010, pp. 22, 50).
- Participate in meetings to create Student Success Teams (SSTs), 504 plans, and Individualized Education Plans (IEPs) and to develop behavior contracts as appropriate and necessary.
- Provide parent, teacher, and administrator consultation and collaboration.
- Follow up with feedback after receiving a referral from faculty member or administrator.

School counselors are addressing *discipline post-suspension* needs when they do the following:

- Collaborate with administrators to ensure timely notification when students on their caseload have been suspended.
- Provide a scheduled appointment following a suspension (upon return to school) to review and discuss the following:
  - What happened
  - What the student did to get the suspension
  - What the student could have done differently
  - What the student can do next time
  - Referrals as appropriate to group counseling, peer mediation, or outside counseling

Some school counselors state they are comfortable with the investigation portion of the discipline process so long as they don't actually mete out discipline. The concern with the school counselor providing even this part of the discipline process is the idea that the counselor is available to provide such assistance. As mentioned earlier, "professional" school counselors are not sitting in their offices waiting to investigate discipline problems or resolve minor he-said-she-said conflicts. Rather, they are busy implementing their programs, providing direct and indirect services such as classroom curriculum, group counseling, consultation, individual planning meetings, and so on. If the school counselor has the time to investigate discipline-related issues, one might wonder why that is the case. The school counseling office is not an emergency room where trained counselors wait around to provide services to those who drop by in need. Rather, the school counselor's calendar should be filled with the activities previously mentioned to prevent, intervene in, and remediate issues leading to behaviors warranting a discipline referral.

That having been said, if one day the administrator directs the school counselor to perform a discipline-related investigation or to provide a first-level discipline consequence (not suspension), it is not in the best interest of the school counselor to refuse or to enlarge and laminate this page and paste it to the administrator's door, at least not as the first action, anyway. It is recommended instead that the counselor follow the directive and then schedule a meeting to discuss the counselor's appropriate role in supporting the reduction of the need for discipline and the creation of a safe climate for learning. Prior to the meeting, it might be a good idea for school counselors to familiarize themselves with their contracts and with relevant portions of state education code, so they can show the administrator what the law allows.

For example, California Education Code 48900 reads: "A pupil shall not be suspended from school or recommended for expulsion, unless the superintendent or the principal of the school in which the pupil is enrolled determines that the pupil has committed an act as defined pursuant to any of subdivisions" (see https://leginfo.legislature.ca.gov/faces/codes_display Text.xhtml?lawCode=EDC&division=4.&title=2.&part=27.&chapter=10.&article=).

Next, the counselor should get busy collecting, disaggregating, and reviewing discipline and other youth behavior data. The idea is to educate the administrator about the prevention, intervention, and post-suspension activities the school counselor is providing or will provide and show how those align with the counselor's professional training, relevant education code, and counseling professional organizations' recommendations.

Reviewing the data and sharing the plan will go a long way toward helping the administrator learn the value of the school counselor's appropriate role in reducing the need for discipline. Start by collecting data on the impact of the interventions with students identified as 1) not attending, 2) not behaving, and 3) not achieving. Then share the results and the difference the school counseling program is making!

Effectively Manage Transitions

Effectively and efficiently coordinating the shift from one activity to another takes practice and well-honed skills. Although secondary school counselors generally teach for one 45- to 60-minute class period, transitions within lessons still occur, such as shifting from partner sharing to whole group discussion, taking out Chromebooks to complete a career assessment, or getting supplies for a group activity. Minimizing transition time reduces disruption and increases the efficiency of classroom lesson instruction.

Providing clear, explicit, step-by-step directions for transitions before they take place ensures that students understand what is expected. If the directions are multistep, ask students to repeat them out loud: "First we will _____," and "Then we will _____." Remember to give only a few steps at a time to ensure students will remember everything, and/or add the steps to the visual presentation so students can refer back if they forget. The school counselor may also want to model what the students will be doing to show an example of what is expected (see the section on modeling in Chapter 4, page 95).

Attention Getters

School counselors skilled in effective transitioning are able to quickly regain students' attention at the beginning of a lesson or when regrouping the class. *Attention getters* are strategies often used to refocus all students in a fun and impactful manner. School counselors call out a word or phrase, allowing the students to respond with a different phrase and to stop talking. Although school counselors at the secondary level may initially find using attention getters with older students uncomfortable, they are an effective strategy to regroup students (and adults!). Remember to practice and remind students how they will be called back together *before* starting an activity or partner discussion. See the examples that follow of call-and-response attention getters suggested for the secondary level:

School Counselor:	I say *bulldogs* [insert school mascot here]; you say *rock!* Bulldogs!
Students:	Rock!
School Counselor:	Bulldogs!
Students:	Rock!

School Counselor:	Ready, set?
Students:	You bet!

School Counselor:	Ready to rock?
Students:	Ready to roll!

School Counselor:	Flat tire!
Students:	Shhhhhh.

School Counselor:	Class, class!
Students:	Yes, yes!

The school counselor can also instruct students to quiet down without a verbal response by using the following prompts:

School Counselor:	Finish up in 5, 4, 3, 2, 1.

School Counselor:	If you can hear me, clap once.
Students:	[Clap]
School Counselor:	If you can hear me, clap twice.
Students:	[Clap, clap]
School Counselor:	If you can hear me, clap three times.
Students:	[Clap, clap, clap]

School Counselor:	[Silently raises hand into the air]
Students:	[As they see the counselor's hand, students stop talking and raise their own hands]

Countdown Timer

Displaying a *countdown timer* is another way to manage transitions by preparing the class for the transition to come. When students are working in groups or participating in an activity, countdown timers can be included in PowerPoint presentations (you can google "countdown timer" to find step-by-step instructions on how to do this), displayed through YouTube (check this out on YouTube.com), and Google itself offers a timer. School counselors can also give several verbal warnings to cue students, such as warnings at 5 minutes, 2 minutes, 30 seconds, and so on.

School counselors are encouraged to positively reinforce the class after all students quickly refocus their attention. If all students do not respond, practice again until you receive full-class participation. This holds students to high expectations and also sets the tone for full-class compliance next time. Positive reinforcement for all transitions is suggested to recognize and appreciate the class for following directions. Remember to be specific in praise—for example, "Thank you for quickly and quietly getting out your Chromebooks," or "I appreciate how you all just stopped what you were doing and turned your attention toward me."

Differentiating Instruction

Differentiating instruction is another strategy that ensures that students at various developmental levels and with different learning abilities can access the curriculum based on their needs. Additionally, differentiating the curriculum also provides students with activities to keep them engaged and to prevent unstructured time for those who finish faster than others (which can lead to misbehavior). Whether students are taking a pre- or post-test, working on an activity, or completing a Ticket Out the Door, they are likely to finish at different rates. School counselors can anticipate and plan for this with the following strategies:

- After students finish a pre-test, ask them to write down their thoughts to a prompt about the lesson topic (which is also activating prior knowledge; see Chapter 4, page 92).
- Between activities, ask students to begin thinking about a question related to the lesson.

- If some students have finished a response to a question ahead of others, ask them to add additional answers or examples.
- When students finish an activity, ask them to help a neighbor or share their activity with another student who has finished.
- As students are completing a Ticket Out the Door, ask several who have finished first to pick up the tickets of others.

Proactive Classroom Management in Action

Mr. Bacerra was teaching a lesson on college exploration, and student groups were researching different types of colleges including the location, admission requirements, majors, and clubs/activities on campus. Prior to breaking into the activity, Mr. Bacerra informed the students that they had 20 minutes to research each section and to be ready to share the information with the class. He also displayed a 20-minute timer for everyone to see while they were working. While students were looking up information, Mr. Bacerra circulated the classroom to answer questions, provide suggestions, and ensure that groups were on task. When one group finished early, he asked them to look up typical careers for college alumni. When the 20 minutes up, Mr. Bacerra used an attention getter to refocus the group. Because the class was in Ohio, the students were trained to respond to "O-H" by saying "I-O." Mr. Bacerra yelled "O-H" at the end of the activity, and all the students responded with "I-O" before becoming quiet. After the class quieted down, signaling to Mr. Bacerra that he had their attention, he thanked them for staying on task during the group time and reminded the class to listen carefully and take notes while groups presented about different colleges.

Student Leaders

Incorporating *student leaders* is another strategy for efficient transitioning. A school counselor can spend several minutes passing out papers, which is a loss of those instructional minutes. Instead, ask students to perform the task while the school counselor proceeds with the lesson content. Multiple students helping can also get the job completed faster. In addition, school counselors can be strategic about utilizing students who may benefit from movement and/or from being helpful.

School counselors can also intentionally minimize their own time spent transitioning between one activity and another, reducing unstructured time for students (which thereby can reduce misbehavior). Here are a few examples:

- The school counselor can come into the classroom before first period to set up for the lesson so that the counselor is ready to begin when the school day starts.
- Rather than allowing 30 seconds of silence while loading a video on the computer, the school counselor can fill that time by asking students to silently think about a question and/or tell a partner what they know about the topic being discussed.
- The counselor can ask a student to pass out materials for an activity rather than stopping instruction to give out the items.
- School counselors can begin setting up for the next activity or discussion while students are finishing up their current activity.

Seating Arrangements

Although school counselors don't structure class seating, understanding seating arrangements is helpful for effectively teaching different types of lessons. For some lessons, students will need to work in pairs or groups; other times students will need to be out of their seat to participate in an activity like Four Corners (see Chapter 5, page 132). Considering the classroom structure prior to entering the class, and communicating the desired formation with the teacher in advance, can reduce the time needed to make these changes to maximize success. If a major room change is needed, such as for a group activity, the school counselor will likely want to discuss this with the teacher beforehand and arrive at the classroom early.

As school counselors learn the personalities and dynamics of individual students and groups, they may want to make modifications to seating during counseling lessons, for instance, as follows:

- A 7th grade teacher seats a talkative student alone while other students are in groups; however, Think-Pair-Share is incorporated into the counselor lesson. The school counselor finds a suitable partner for the solo student to sit with during the counseling lesson, with the agreement that the student will appropriately participate in the lesson.
- Students choose their own seats as they walk into the computer lab for the counseling core curriculum lesson. As the counselor is presenting, several boys in the back are talking to each other and laughing. During a partner discussion, the counselor walks to the back and politely asks two of the boys to move up front.
- During the last several classroom lessons, the school counselor has noticed that two students are off topic during partner activities. Before the lesson starts, the counselor quietly asks one of the off-task students and another student who is generally on topic to switch seats.

Seating Arrangements in Action

As a school counseling trainee, Ashley Hansen from Ohio State University asked the class to make name tags prior to beginning teaching. During the classroom lesson, she observed which students worked well together and who would benefit from sitting apart. In the following class lesson, Ashley placed their name tags strategically so that the students had to sit where their name tags were placed. This created an environment for students to sit by new students and not by their peers who would be distracting. Overall, Ashley found the seat changes allowed for a better classroom lesson, and the students were active participants the whole time.

Circulate the Classroom

Moving around the classroom while teaching is an effective strategy for keeping students focused because proximity stresses accountability. Students are more likely to be on task when they think their teacher—or, in this case, their school counselor— is watching them (Lemov, 2015). Therefore, circulating while teaching both holds students' attention and refocuses the beginning of off-task behaviors. While moving around the room, the school counselor can subtly redirect students while still leading instruction by pointing to a Guided Notes sheet that isn't filled in, putting a hand on the shoulder of a student who is talking to a neighbor, or making eye contact with an off-task student and quickly shaking his or her head. Counselors should remember to teach students to follow the counselor with their gaze as the counselor moves around the room (which is called "tracking the speaker"; see the SLANT box earlier in the chapter).

Tip: School counselors who frequently use PowerPoint or Google Slides presentations can invest in a clicker to advance their slides. This allows school counselors the flexibility to walk around the room rather than be tethered to a computer. School counselors can also ask a student to be the technology leader by helping move from one slide to the next. The student can sit by the computer and advance slides when cued. This is a great strategy for a student who sometimes loses focus, as this role alerts their attention to what is coming next.

Culturally Responsive Classroom Management

As school counselors incorporate classroom management strategies while teaching core curriculum lessons, understanding and appropriately responding to diverse student behaviors is important. General school expectations in the United States incorporate Western, White, middle-class practices (Weinstein, Curran, & Tomlinson-Clarke, 2003), which may or may not reflect students' cultural norms. The high proportion of disciplinary action received by Latino and African American boys in school (U.S. Department of Education Office for Civil Rights, 2014) is one example of why school counselors should be mindful of their own unintentional biases and learn about students' cultural backgrounds, which may impact their behavior. Understanding the student population where counselors work allows them to recognize and modify classroom management strategies to fit diverse student populations.

Adapted from Weinstein, Curran, and Tomlinson-Clarke's article "Culturally Responsive Classroom Management: Awareness into Action" (2003), the following strategies help integrate culturally responsive practices into classroom management during core curriculum counseling lessons:

- *Creating caring, inclusive classrooms:* Regardless of the cultural makeup of the classroom, a goal of school counselors when teaching core curriculum lessons is to create a safe and supportive learning environment. This is especially essential for counseling lessons because the topics may address sensitive items, such as students sharing hopes and dreams for the future, discussing drugs or alcohol, or sharing about how bullying has affected them. Setting expectations for both respect and inclusion, while also incorporating diversity into classroom lessons, helps all students feel safe, welcome, and valued. By incorporating multicultural examples and diverse content into lessons, as well as acknowledging and praising differences (such as positively validating English language learners for speaking two languages), school counselors help all students feel valued.

- *Establishing clear behavior expectations:* Clearly defined and consistently reinforced behavior expectations ensure that all students understand what is expected, which is particularly important in diverse classrooms. Different cultures view and value behaviors differently—in some cultures, students engage more interactively, such as by calling out answers without raising their hands; in other cultures, students show respect to teachers by not making eye contact. Both of these examples could be unintentionally viewed as incorrect participation, so explicitly teaching and explaining the purpose behind expectations provides clarity and prevents confusion. Additionally, understanding, respecting, and accommodating for variations in student behavior based on culture is also important.
- *Communicating with students in culturally consistent ways:* Addressing students' multicultural needs includes understanding and responding to a variety of ways in which communication is expressed and understood in different cultures. For instance, in some cultures, asking questions to authority figures is a sign of disrespect; in other cultures, straightforward directives are more clearly understood than passive strategies (e.g., "Please sit down" versus "Can you sit down for me?"). In addition, cultural differences apply to tone of voice and body language. Therefore, school counselors' understanding of their school population and adapting their communication styles to meet diverse student needs can impact student behaviors.
- *Applying multicultural awareness when addressing misbehavior:* To approach classroom management from a culturally responsive framework, school counselors are advised to reflect on the types of behaviors they interpret as off task or problematic, considering how students' diverse backgrounds may play a role. Providing an example, Weinstein et al. (2003) explained that Black children may be more likely than White children to jump into activities without waiting their turn or to challenge school authority figures, which may be interpreted as disruptive or rude. However, if these behaviors can be reframed as signaling excitement and passion, school counselors can identify students' strengths and focus them appropriately within the classroom setting prior to implementing punishment. School counselors can appropriately modify their expectations to meet the diverse needs of the classroom while also helping students understand the school system and act accordingly. Additionally, considering race, ethnicity, and gender within the framework of disciplinary actions can reduce inequities in the numbers of students who receive punishment.

HOW TO HANDLE STUDENTS WHO ARE OFF TASK OR MISBEHAVING

Although school counselors can implement all the strategies previously listed and incorporate active participation into their lessons, they still might encounter an off-task or misbehaving student. Not to be confused with school counselors administering discipline, effectively addressing problem behavior in the class is essential to facilitating a successful lesson in which students participate appropriately. Mastering strategies to apply when swift intervention is needed, in an effective and respectful way, is an essential component of being a successful school counselor.

Managing problem student behaviors can generate fight-or-flight reactions in any educator, including school counselors, and parents, too (Gesek, n.d.). In *fight* mode, a counselor might want to argue or yell at a student, and in *flight* mode, the counselor may escape the problem by ignoring it. Although both responses stem from basic instincts, neither is an effective strategy for addressing and changing the problem. The following sections present multiple strategies for the secondary school counselor to consider using while remaining calm and positive. As a reminder, if several students are off task or misbehaving during a lesson, school counselors are encouraged to revisit and practice expectations with the entire class.

Proximity

Just as circulating the classroom can prevent off-task behavior, moving into close proximity to the off-task student often corrects the behavior. The school counselor can continue teaching while also putting their hand on the student's desk or shoulder or shaking their head, which generally redirects the behavior. If needed, the school counselor can quietly remind the student of the expectations, which is less obstructive than saying the same thing loudly across the room.

Quickly and Positively Redirecting Misbehavior Early On

Many types of off-task behaviors quickly change when they are immediately and effectively addressed. Predictable and consistent redirection, before the off-task behavior escalates, prevents the need for further discipline. School counselors are advised to remain calm, use a positive tone of voice, and talk to the student privately if possible. The school counselor may incorporate an engagement strategy into the lesson, such as Think-Pair-Share, or ask the class to think silently about a question while the counselor addresses the student who is misbehaving.

Students may tune out when long directions are given, so brevity and specificity are recommended. Consider using sentence starters such as "Please ____" and "I need you to ____," followed by the specific direction:

- "Please start working on the activity."
- "I need you to stop talking to your neighbor."
- "Remember to raise your hand before answering."

After the direction, allow the student a minute to self-correct, then demonstrate follow-through. When the student modifies the behavior, the school counselor can positively reinforce the change with a nod or smile toward the student, or quietly say, "Thank you," to show that the counselor has noticed the change. This simple acknowledgment recognizes the student for the correction but does not distract from the lesson. If the student continues with the behavior, provide another specific reminder and watch for follow-through before taking further action (such as assigning consequences or having problem-solving conversations, as explained in the next two sections).

Assigning Appropriate Consequences Within the Classroom Setting

If consequences are necessary, make them short and to the point:

- Ask a student to apologize to their classmate after roughly grabbing a notebook out of their hand.
- Walk over to a student who is using a phone, after having been warned twice, and put your hand out to signal that you will take and hold onto the phone until the end of the day.
- Politely and quickly ask a student who is continually talking to a neighbor after multiple warnings to move their seat next to you.

Remember not to argue with students but instead wait patiently until they follow through with your directions. Generally, when students are given time to calm down, they adhere to any consequences given. If school counselors are struggling with a particularly difficult student, they can also seek out the classroom teacher for support.

Individual (or Small Group) Problem-Solving Conversations

If a student (or two) is continually misbehaving during a classroom lesson, the school counselor is advised to talk with the student about the observed actions after the lesson concludes. Remaining positive and supportive, the school counselor can ask the student about the observed behaviors and problem solve ways to improve next time. By brainstorming alternatives to the inappropriate behaviors, school counselors reteach students what is expected (see the following box for an example). Additionally, because school counselors teach in classrooms only periodically, prior to the start of the next lesson, the counselor may want to privately and encouragingly remind the student who was off task during the last lesson about the previously made agreement to be on task.

A Problem-Solving Conversation in Action

Ms. Tang was presenting High School 101 lessons in all 9th grade math classes to ensure students knew graduation requirements, activities on campus, and school resources. During one of the lessons a student, Lily, was talking to her neighbor and not completing her Guided Notes worksheet. The school counselor first redirected Lily's attention by asking her to read out loud the next section that would be filled onto the Guided Notes sheet. The counselor reminded the whole class to write down what Lily wrote onto section four. When Lily was talking again, the counselor moved in Lily's direction while continuing to present, and quietly put their finger next to the Guided Notes section for Lily to complete. The counselor also stayed in Lily's area of the room for several minutes while continuing to present.

(Continued)

(Continued)

After the lesson, the school counselor asked to speak with Lily:

School Counselor:	Hi, Lily! I'm glad we're getting to talk today, because I really like coming into the 9th grade classes to speak with you and your classmates. I want to make sure you all are prepared to be successful in high school but noticed that you were distracted. Can you tell me what I saw?
Lily:	I kept talking to Malik.
School Counselor:	I did see you talking to Malik. What else did I see?
Lily:	I wasn't filling in my worksheet.
School Counselor:	You're right. Thank you for reflecting. Do you know the reason why I was asking you to complete the Guided Notes worksheet?
Lily:	You want me to learn.
School Counselor:	I do want you to learn, and we were talking about requirements for high school graduation, ways to get involved on campus, and resources if you need help. As your school counselor I am one of those resources, and I want you to have a great high school experience. I'm worried that by talking and not completing your work, it will be harder for you to get your work done, not just when I'm in your class but with your teachers as well. Was there something going on with you this afternoon?
Lily:	I was distracted because Malik is my friend.
School Counselor:	That happens to me sometimes too—even as an adult. When I sit by my friends if I'm at a meeting, I want to talk with them, so sometimes I purposely sit somewhere else so I can focus. What would help you be more successful in your math class, not just when I'm in there, but all the time? Would sitting in a different seat help?
Lily:	I don't want to move my seat away from Malik, but I really will try not to talk.
School Counselor:	I believe you will try! What will help you be successful?
Lily:	I'll tell Malik I can't talk until after class. And I'll pay more attention. Usually I listen more.
School Counselor:	Okay! I believe you will do your best. Is there anything your teacher or I can do to help you?
Lily:	I don't think so.
School Counselor:	How about I check in with you next week to see how things are going?
Lily:	Am I in trouble?

School Counselor:	You're not in trouble, and I don't want you to be in trouble. My job is to help you be successful at school, and I'll check in to see if you've been able to finish more of your work and not talk with Malik. If you need help in any of those areas, we can talk about it so you *don't* get into trouble but instead have a great year.
Lily:	Okay.
School Counselor:	I'm really glad we were able to talk about this problem, and I appreciate that you reflected on your actions and have a plan for what to do next. I look forward to talking with you next week and seeing how it's going.
Lily:	Thanks, Ms. Tang.

Employing effective classroom management skills ensures that the entire class is engaged and on task during core curriculum lessons. Although many school counselors do not have training in this area, through practicing the strategies discussed in this chapter, they will likely see improved classroom behavior as students are following directions and staying on task. Through a strong preventative approach, coupled with swiftly and effectively managing off-task behaviors, school counselors will foster engaged and efficient classrooms during their lessons.

School Counseling Core Curriculum Lesson Feedback Tool

The last three chapters described how secondary school counselors plan core curriculum lessons, teach using effective engagement and classroom management strategies (see Figure 6.3), and evaluate what students learned from the lesson. Putting all of these areas together, the School Counseling Core Curriculum Lesson Feedback Tool shown in Figure 6.4 was designed to help counselors assess and increase their skills in teaching as they self-evaluate and/or ask others for feedback to improve their practices. Not to be confused with an official evaluation, counselors can instead use this tool to reflect on areas within core curriculum where they feel strong and others where they want to grow. School counselors can review the feedback tool prior to teaching to ensure their lesson incorporates all the listed components as well as reflect back after teaching the lesson to consider their strengths and areas for improvement. Additionally, counselors can ask a school counseling colleague or teacher they trust to provide them feedback. Utilizing their growth mindset, counselors can learn from the external feedback given as they focus on improving in the suggested areas.

Depending on the evaluation system set up in their district, counselors may want to provide the Core Curriculum Feedback Tool to administrators as a supplement for their

(Continued)

(Continued)

evaluation process. Unfortunately, many school counselors are given district evaluations using teacher rubrics rather than one set up specifically for the counselor role. If this is the case, the Core Curriculum Feedback Tool can support administrators' knowledge of how counseling core curriculum is planned and implemented, which also helps administrators better understand the school counselor role. In a district without a school counselor–specific evaluation system, counselors are advised to work with the district office officials and their union, if applicable, to create an evaluation that aligns with the ASCA National Model and includes core curriculum.

Figure 6.3   Chapter 4 Lesson Plan Highlighting Classroom Management Strategies

Core Curriculum Class Lessons

Hey, Hey, Hey . . . Let's Calculate That GPA!

PROCEDURES:

Slide 1: **Welcome**

- o Welcome students to the class, and share the lesson title (Hey, Hey, Hey . . . Let's Calculate That GPA) and topic (importance of grades in high school and learning how to calculate Grade Point Average).

Slide 2: **School Counseling Department Introduction**

- o Remind students about the members of the school counseling department including the school counselors and any additional support staff (counseling clerks, interns, etc.).

- o Ask students to share what they know about the role of a school counselor. Depending on what students share, the counselor may also want to add that that their job is to help students be successful in school by: teaching them lessons on a variety of topics including academics and well-being (like today), helping them create goals for now and the future, supporting them with any problems at school or personally, planning schoolwide events like College Signing Day, and helping everyone at school feel safe and happy.

Teaching clear expectations

Slide 3: **Behavior Expectations**

- o Remind students of the three Potter Rs (be ready, respectful, and responsible), and ask them to repeat them together.

- o Praise the class for already demonstrating the three Rs, and list specific examples (such as, "You are all showing me respect by staying quiet while I am talking." "I can see how responsible you are by having a writing utensil ready.").

Praising appropriate behavior

- o Tell students that one part of being ready and responsible during today's lesson is to complete their Guided Notes worksheet during the lesson.

- o Ask two students to quickly and quietly pass out the Guided Notes to each student.

Utilizing student volunteers

<u>Slide 4</u>: **Objectives**

- ○ Explain the objectives that are the focus of the presentation and what students are intended to learn. Ask students to participate in Drop-in Reading—the counselor will read the non-underlined portion of the objectives, and the students will read the underlined portion of the objectives together. By the end of the lesson, we will be able to . . .
  - Understand the <u>importance</u> of our <u>grades</u>
  - Explain the <u>required & competitive GPA</u> for college admission and for high school <u>athletic/extracurricular eligibility</u>
  - Calculate our <u>Grade Point Average</u> (GPA)
- ○ Tell the students the objectives are aligned to the school counseling standards at the bottom of the slide.

<u>Slide 5</u>: **Access Prior Knowledge**

- ○ Ask students to quietly think about the reasons grades are important.
- ○ While they are thinking, <u>ask two students to pass out a 3x5 card to each student.</u>
- ○ Tell the students to write their first and last names on the tops of the cards and then write down at least two reasons grades are important. Explain the example on the PowerPoint (name and numbered items).
- ○ <u>Walk around and observe while students are writing,</u> noticing any specific students you'd like to call on to share and any you'd want to avoid.
- ○ After several minutes, <u>regroup the class</u> and call on the students you noticed and/or ask students in general to share. As each student shares one example, ask the class to raise their hands if they wrote down something similar.
- ○ After calling on three to four students, ask all students to raise their cards up in the air and <u>for two students to quickly and quietly collect all the cards and bring them up to the front as you proceed with the next slide.</u>

<u>Slide 6</u>: **Grades Matter** (Input)

- ○ Explain that grades matter for a variety of reasons now and in the future, as was just discussed.
- ○ Tell students you will be specifically discussing how grades matter in high school for eligibility for sports and extracurricular activities, along with graduation. The lesson will also talk about how grades will impact students in the future, such as for college and other postsecondary options.

<u>Slide 7</u>: **Grades Matter—Research** (Input)

- ○ Explain to students that there is research from *U.S. News & World Report* of high school freshmen that explains the importance of getting good grades.
- ○ <u>Use the 3x5 cards to select a student to read the first bullet point</u>—*How well students performed academically in 9th grade predicted students' future success.*
- ○ Then ask the student sitting next to the student who just read to read the next bullet point—*9th graders with As, Bs, and Cs were much more likely to graduate high school than their classmates with lower grades*—and the following student to read the last bullet—*Academically strong 9th graders were more likely to attend college.*

Utilizing student volunteers

Circulate the classroom

Reground the class with Attention Getters

Utilizing student volunteers

Using a variety of engagement strategies prevents off-task behavior

(Continued)

Figure 6.4 Continued

<u>Slide 8</u>: **Grades Matter—Graduation** (Input)

- ○ Direct students to the <u>Guided Notes sheet</u> that was passed out at the beginning of the class that they will begin filling in.
- ○ Explain that you will again use <u>Drop-in Reading</u> for students to read the underlined sections, and they will also fill the information in on their Guided Notes.
  - Total of **220 credits** needed to graduate
  - Credits are "**points**" you receive for each class you pass with a **D** or higher
  - Passing one full-year class at Potter HS = **10 credits**
  - Students generally earn **60 credits each year**
  - If you get an F in a required class, you have to **take the class again** ☹
- ○ Walk around the room while presenting information on this slide to ensure students are filling in their Guided Notes sheets.

> Circulate the classroom

<u>Slide 9</u>: **Grades Matter—Sports & Activities** (Input)

- ○ Continue to use Drop-in Reading to explain sports and other activity eligibility while <u>walking around the classroom to ensure students are filling in Guided Notes.</u>
  - Student athletes must maintain a **2.0 GPA**
  - No more than **1 F** on quarter progress report or final report card
  - Students need 2.0 or higher to be **club leaders**, attend **college field trips**, and **earn a work permit**

> Letting students know they may be called on after a discussion helps keep them on topic during pair-share

<u>Slide 10</u>: **Access Prior Knowledge**

- ○ Explain to students that their choices now can impact them as they begin thinking about life after high school.
- ○ Ask students to think about their postsecondary goals and what they can do now to get there (and allow about 20 seconds of silent think time).
- ○ Ask students to pair with a partner to discuss their thoughts to the questions, and <u>alert them you'll be using the 3x5 cards to call on a few students to answer.</u>

NOTES

_____

_____

_____

_____

_____

Figure 6.4   School Counseling Core Curriculum Lesson Feedback Tool

School Counseling Core Curriculum Lesson Feedback Tool

One aspect of school counseling program delivery is teaching core curriculum classroom lessons. School counselors can use this feedback tool to help them evaluate their teaching strategies. You can use this tool for self-reflection and/or to receive feedback from a teacher, fellow–school counselor, or administrator. The intention is to learn and improve your teaching practices. Please note that perfection is not necessary and also not likely . . . everyone is learning and improving! Responses reflecting future growth are highly encouraged.

Name: _____   Date: _____

Lesson topic: _____   Grade level: _____

Standards and Objectives

Standards/lesson objectives are clearly explained to students, referenced throughout the lesson, and referred back to at the end of the lesson.

5	4	3	2	1
Outstanding		Adequate		Weak

REASONS:

Lesson topic is relevant and meaningful, connecting with students' academic, college and career, and/or social/emotional needs, interests, and concerns.

5	4	3	2	1
Outstanding		Adequate		Weak

REASONS:

Standard(s) addressed in lesson are developmentally appropriate and are reasonable to learn within the classroom presentation time (not too few, not too many).

5	4	3	2	1
Outstanding		Adequate		Weak

REASONS:

(Continued)

Figure 6.4 (Continued)

Lesson Structure & Sequence

Lesson is organized and proceeds in a sequential, logical order.

5	4	3	2	1
Outstanding		Adequate		Weak

REASONS:

Prior knowledge is accessed and built upon during the lesson.

5	4	3	2	1
Outstanding		Adequate		Weak

REASONS:

School counselor checks for understanding throughout the lesson.

5	4	3	2	1
Outstanding		Adequate		Weak

REASONS:

Students demonstrate their learning at the end of the lesson.

5	4	3	2	1
Outstanding		Adequate		Weak

REASONS:

Delivery & Student Engagement

School counselor engages the entire class in the lesson through discussions and activities.

5	4	3	2	1
Outstanding		Adequate		Weak

REASONS:

School counselor appropriately incorporates a variety of interaction strategies throughout the lesson, both covert and overt (such as think-ink-pair-share, choral reading, random response cards, anticipatory sets of questions, choral response, etc.).

5	4	3	2	1
Outstanding		Adequate		Weak

REASONS:

Lesson delivery is clear, as the school counselor speaks audibly, maintains positivity, makes eye contact with students, etc.

5	**4**	**3**	**2**	**1**
Outstanding		Adequate		Weak

REASONS:

Proactive Classroom Management

Behavior expectations are clearly explained and routines to maximize learning time are established.

5	**4**	**3**	**2**	**1**
Outstanding		Adequate		Weak

REASONS:

School counselor quickly and positively refocuses off-task behavior with minimal disruption to the entire class.

5	**4**	**3**	**2**	**1**
Outstanding		Adequate		Weak

REASONS:

Lesson maintains momentum as the school counselor moves around the room, alerts students for what will happen next, and smoothly transitions from one activity to another.

5	**4**	**3**	**2**	**1**
Outstanding		Adequate		Weak

REASONS:

Additional Sections (As Appropriate)

Lesson was developed based on developmental standards and/or data-driven need.

5	**4**	**3**	**2**	**1**
Outstanding		Adequate		Weak

REASONS:

Pre/post-assessment is clearly written and effectively administered.

5	**4**	**3**	**2**	**1**
Outstanding		Adequate		Weak

REASONS:

Technology facilitates active participation and engagement practices (if available).

5	**4**	**3**	**2**	**1**
Outstanding		Adequate		Weak

REASONS:

7

Individual Student Plans

Figure 7.1   MTMDSS—Individual Student Planning

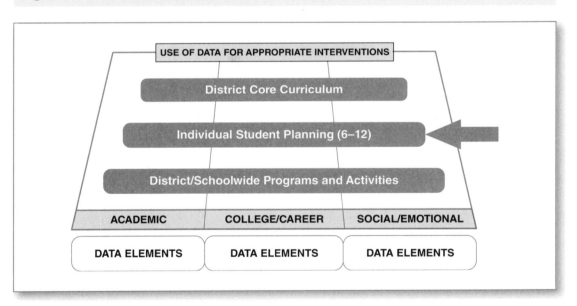

When we (Vanessa, Trish, and Whitney) were brainstorming ideas for this chapter, we were sitting together having a passionate conversation about our personal and professional experiences with Individual Student Planning (ISP) and Individual Learning Plans (ILP). We discussed why they are important and how confusing it is because these terminologies are

(Continued)

(Continued)

used in different ways by different entities and professional organizations. We all agreed on how critical it is for our students to have an ISP and an ILP. Trish talked about her own experiences with her sons; she has three sons, and each one had a different experience in spite of attending the same school. She described the best experience was when she and her son met with the school counselor in 9th grade and laid out her son's ILP (called a 4-year plan) based on his postsecondary plans. Vanessa talked about her experience as a school counselor working with ILPs and how versions of ILPs have changed during her 23-year career. She shared how she had heard the plan referred to as a 4-year plan, 7-year plan, and 10-year plan. Then Whitney began to talk about the important role that the ILP plays in Chicago Public Schools. We asked her, "What does your plan look like?" and she explained it is not one particular plan or document but a comprehensive approach of ILP tasks and support strategies that plays a significant role in the comprehensive school counseling program. In addition, we shared how the ASCA National Model refers to it as "Individual Student Planning." At that moment, we realized that each of us had a different understanding of Individual Learning Plans. In our combined 70 years of experience, we were astounded by the fact that we each had different impressions of what ISP and ILPs are and realized that, depending on the state you live in, school counselors across the United States may very well have different impressions and definitions too. Therefore, in this chapter, we will use our varied experiences and expertise to define and discuss ISP and ILPs as Tier 1 activities and the school counselor's role in ensuring that all students complete these important plans (see Figure 7.1).

Tier 1 initiatives led by school counselors for all students at the secondary level include delivery of core curriculum classroom lessons, individual student and/or learning plans, and schoolwide programs and activities. Chapters 2 through 6 provided extensive conversations on designing and teaching core curriculum. This chapter is intended to address the important, complex, and often underutilized process of ensuring that *all* students have a plan for graduation and postsecondary education that all students deserve to receive.

ISP OR ILP?

If you google "Individual Student Planning," you'll find ASCA refers to ISP as follows: "School counselors coordinate ongoing systemic activities designed to assist students in establishing personal goals and developing future plans" (ASCA, 2017).

If you google "Individual Learning Plan," you will find this definition from Wikipedia (Individual Learning Plans, 2018): "Individual Learning Plan or ILP is a specific program or strategy of education or learning that takes into consideration the student's strengths and weaknesses." Other definitions describe the ILP as a tool that students in Grades 6 through 12 can use to prepare themselves for their futures or as a tool to help students understand their pathways based on their postsecondary goals.

Depending on the state and/or district where you work, there are a variety of names:

- *Individual Learning Plans*
- *Individual Graduation Plans*
- *Individual College and Academic Plans (ICAPs)*
- *Education and Career Action Plans*
- *Academic and Career Plan*
- *Individual Career/Academic Plans*
- *4-year plan, 7-year plan, or 10-year plan*

The concept of ISP is not new to school counseling. One of the most helpful documents you'll ever find on the history of ISP is an article written by our beloved father of school counseling, Dr. Norm Gysbers, called "Individual Student Planning in the United States: Rationale, Practices, and Results." Gysbers (2008) describes "the Individual Student Planning (ISP) as a program component designed to assist all students with educational/career planning, educational transitioning, and self-appraisal for decision making." Gysbers posits that ISP is not a stand-alone activity; instead, it is a component of a comprehensive school counseling program and essential for students' success. "The point of the activities is to have students focus on their current and future goals by developing life career plans (personal plans of study) drawing on the strengths-based content embedded in the guidance curriculum" (Gysbers, 2008, p. 122).

According to Gysbers, ISP is implemented in the program through *individual appraisal, individual advisement*, and *transition planning* as an integral part of a comprehensive guidance and counseling program. The guidance (now called "core") curriculum provides students with the disposition, knowledge, and skills they need to plan their futures personally, educationally, and occupationally. ISP activities assist students by helping them organize and focus their knowledge, skills, and dispositions as they plan their futures. In the Gyspers model, core curriculum and ISP components support each other (Gysbers, 2008).

Alignment With the ASCA National Model

As a school counselor in the 21st century, it is essential to look to our professional associations to see their positions on matters related to school counseling. In the American School Counselor Association (ASCA) *Position Statement on Individual Student Planning for Postsecondary Preparation*, they recognize the important role that school counselors have in collaborating with students, families, and educational staff to ensure all students develop an academic and career plan reflecting their interests, abilities, and goals including rigorous, relevant coursework and experiences appropriate for the student (ASCA, 2017). A comprehensive school counseling program includes career and educational planning for *all* students. School counselors assist students in making informed decisions about how they can reach their education and career goals.

According to ASCA, the focus of academic and career planning falls into three areas including 1) helping students acquire the skills to achieve academic success, 2) assisting students in connecting life and school experiences, and 3) assisting students in acquiring the knowledge and skills to be college and career ready (ASCA, 2017).

One may wonder how a school counselor accomplishes this task. The school counselor is in a unique position of understanding local, state, and national guidelines and requirements for students' postsecondary opportunities, whether that be attending a university, community college, trade school, apprenticeships, or public service program; entering the military; or obtaining full-time employment with a family-supporting wage.

The ASCA (2017) position statement indicates that school counselors can assist all students with ISP by doing the following:

- helping students connect coursework to their career and life experiences
- assisting students in making course selections allowing students to choose from a wide range of postsecondary options
- assisting students in exploring interests and abilities in relation to the knowledge of self and the work world
- identifying and applying strategies to achieve future academic and career success, and to demonstrate the skills for successful goal setting and attainment
- developing a portfolio that highlights strengths and interests

According to the ASCA (2016) Ethical Standards, school counselors are leaders, collaborators, consultants, and advocates who create systemic change by providing equitable educational access to all students. Additionally, the ASCA Ethical Standards indicate that the ethical school counselor believes all students have the right to receive information on postsecondary options, including timely information on college and career, while ensuring that our students understand the magnitude and meaning of how college and career readiness can impact their future opportunities. We can also look to ASCA Ethical Standard A.4(b), which states that school counselors provide and advocate for individual students' PreK–postsecondary college and career awareness, exploration, and postsecondary planning, which supports the students' right to choose from a wide array of options.

By ensuring that each of our students has an ISP, we promote equity and access by ensuring that *all* students are aware of *all* postsecondary options, career pathways, and requirements. Implementing comprehensive ILPs with all of our students also ensures that we adhere to our ethical standards.

Call to Action:

- Be aware of your state guidelines and recommendations related to ILPs.
- Make sure school counselors in your state have a voice in terms of recommendations and processes for developing and implementing ILPs.
- If your state does not have legislation related to ILPs, advocate by getting involved with your state school counselor association and state leadership.

Laws Related to ISPs and ILPs

According to the Office of Disability Employment Policy, 34 states across the United States have mandated ILP policies within schools, and an additional 10 states use ILPs, but they are not mandated by the state. To see what your state requires and to view ILP resources for each state, visit the United States Department of Labor at https://www.dol.gov/odep/ilp/map/. Each state is listed in a table form that describes the state's purpose of the ILP as well as the specific documents and tools that are used to create the ILP. This is a great resource for school counselors who do not live in a state that requires ILP and are seeking to look at samples of ILP and lessons.

Figure 7.2   Individualized Learning Plans Across the United States

New Mexico's Next Step Plan (NSP) is mandated by the state. It includes all students, 8th–12th grade.

States with mandated ILP in use | No ILP in use | States with ILP in use, but no mandate

Source: United States Department of Labor.

Missouri

The Missouri School Counselors and Educators (2015) describe ISP as a component in a comprehensive school counseling program that is designed to assist *all* students with educational and career planning. In 2015 Missouri developed a comprehensive Individual Student Planning Guide: see https://dese.mo.gov/college-career-readiness/school-counseling/individual-student-planning. This extensive document details planning rubrics, guides, and documents to assist in developing the process for implementing ISPs.

In 2016 Senate Bill 6238 resulted in new legislation for Missouri that now calls for each and *every student in 9th grade* to develop a personal plan with the (guidance)

school counselor. This new plan is called the Individual Career and Academic Plan (ICAP). According to the Missouri Department of Elementary and Secondary Education, the following elements should be included in the student's ICAP checklist:

- ❏ Student name
- ❏ Graduation year
- ❏ Career path/career cluster identified
- ❏ Postsecondary plans identified
- ❏ High school courses to be taken each year
- ❏ Career technical education courses/program offerings
- ❏ District high school graduation requirements
- ❏ Additional learning opportunities (community service, volunteer, or work experiences)
- ❏ Assessment/certification
- ❏ Annual review/revision signatures

(Retrieved from https://dese.mo.gov/sites/default/files/MCSCP%20Individual%20Student%20Planning%20Voice%20Draft.pptx)

Kentucky

Recently Kentucky went through a large change shift in how school counselors will provide ILPs. Although they previously used Career Cruising, they are discontinuing that program. An ILP in Kentucky means "a comprehensive framework for advising students in grades six (6) through twelve (12) to engage in coursework and activities that will best prepare them to both realize college and career success and become contributing members of their communities" (Kentucky Department of Education, 2018).

District Requirements:

- Implement an advising and guidance process from Grades 6 through 12 to provide support for the development and implementation of an ILP for *each student*.
- Develop a method to evaluate the effectiveness and results of the ILP process, which includes: indicators related to the status of the student in the 12 months following the date of graduation and input from students, parents, and school staff.

ISP Requirements:

- Be readily available to the student and parents, and have the ISP be reviewed and approved at least annually by the student, parents, and school officials.
- Set learning goals for the student based on academic and career interests (beginning with the student's 8th grade year).
- Identify required academic courses, electives, and extracurricular opportunities aligned to the student's postsecondary goals.
- Begin by the end of the 6th grade year.

- Focus on career exploration and related postsecondary education and training needs.
- Include information about financial planning for postsecondary education.

School Requirements:

- Work cooperatively with feeder schools to ensure that each student and parent receives information and advising regarding the relationship between education and career opportunities to maintain each student's ILP (paper or electronic format).
- Use information from the ILPs about student needs for academic and elective courses to plan academic and elective offerings.

Washington

The connection between the guidance (core) curriculum and ISP is demonstrated by the five key elements of the state of Washington's Navigation 101 program. The five key elements include: personalizing—guidance (core) curriculum content; planning—developing and using portfolios; demonstrating—student-led conferences with parents, teachers, and school counselors; empowering—student-driven scheduling; evaluating—helping students understand what they are accomplishing (State of Washington, Office of Superintendent of Public Instruction, n.d.).

Iowa

Senate File (SF) 2216 requires Iowa schools to help 8th grade students develop a plan that includes the goal of completing the Iowa Core Curriculum and the Iowa minimum graduation requirements (4 years of English language arts, 3 years of mathematics, 3 years of science, and 3 years of social studies). The plan needs to include career options and coursework needed in Grades 9 through 12 to achieve students' college and career goals. For more information about the 4-year plans and the Iowa Core Curriculum, visit www.educateiowa.gov and select the A to Z Index and then 8th Grade Plans from the menu.

Wisconsin

Wisconsin's Academic and Career Plan (ACP) is an example of a comprehensive plan and includes an implementation guide that covers the four stages to successful academic and career planning. The four stages include: know, explore, plan, and go. Through the ACP process students are guided through the self-awareness stage of identifying who they are, including their interests, strengths, and skills. Next they conduct career exploration and identify where they want to go; students explore career pathways and educational opportunities. During the career planning stage, students examine how they get there as well as create a plan, set goals, choose courses, join clubs and activities, obtain financing, fill out applications, and write résumés. In the final stage students focus on career management and execute their plans as well as update their plans, recalculating as needed. The implementation guide provides a visual description of the difference between a 4-year plan and the ACP. Compared to a typical 4-year plan, Wisconsin's ILP is a process that acts like a navigation tool for students, and career development is the responsibility of the whole school, not just the school counselor. In this case a 4-year plan is created as part of the ACP process and serves as a plan for courses with high school graduation being the end point.

How to Decide?

One of the dilemmas that school counselors face is the fact that the definition of an ILP and its varying names make it difficult for school counselors to have the same understanding of what an ILP is. The National Collaborative on Workforce and Disability (NCWD) describes ILPs as a *process* and not just a document. It is critical that each school counseling program determines what definition it will use, taking into consideration district and state policies when developing the counseling program plan for ILP implementation.

Examining research can help guide our work of creating a comprehensive ILP. Solberg, Willis, Redmond, and Skaff (2014) found that when students are more competent in self-exploration, career exploration, and career planning and management, they are more motivated and confident learners. These students actively set goals and have better academic outcomes, resulting in entering college with a purpose, and therefore are less at risk for leaving college prior to completing their degree.

After examining a wide range of ILPs, some of the common elements include ensuring that the plan is individualized to meet the goals of the student and focusing on academic, career, and postsecondary plans. Many ILPs include coursework as well as career pathways, goal setting, graduation planning, and postsecondary planning. It is the belief of the authors that effective ILPs should be a *process* and not just the development of one document such as a 4-year plan or only one classroom lesson on ILPs. **In fact, the comprehensive ILP *could very well be* your Tier 1 core curriculum for the college and career domain.**

As co-authors, we like the definition created by the NCWD (Solberg et al., 2016):

> An Individualized Learning Plan is a document/portfolio consisting of an individual's (a) course taking and postsecondary plans aligned to career goals; and (b) documentation of the range of college and career readiness skills he/she has developed including out-of-school learning experiences. ILPs provide individuals with personalized career development opportunities focused on developing their self-exploration, career exploration, and career planning and management skills that enables them to become aware of the relevance of academic preparation, work-based and other learning opportunities and the importance of completing a two- or four-year postsecondary credential, program or degree. (p. 2)

[NOTE: Moving forward within the text, then, we will attempt to refer to these as ILPs (even though we recognize that ISP is synonymous for many organizations).]

> **Tips for Developing Individual Learning Plans**
>
> - Always follow your local and state mandates. See the U.S. Department of Labor for listings of state mandates at https://www.dol.gov/odep/ilp/map/.
> - Ensure that each student has an ILP that connects their career interests and postsecondary goals to coursework and extracurricular activities.
> - Create a plan for reviewing ILPs annually.
> - To ensure that your school counseling program is equitable and accessible to all students, ensure that *all* students and parents or guardians are knowledgeable about every postsecondary option and requirement and are aware of all pathway options available at your site.
> - Connect the ILP process to your course selection process.
> - Remember, you can help students create ILPs in a small group or classroom lesson, but it is important to determine how you will individually follow up and how often.

Alignment With MTMDSS

As previously mentioned in Chapter 1, the Multi-Tiered, Multi-Domain System of Supports (MTMDSS) can be utilized to organize a continuum of core instruction and interventions to meet students' needs (see Figure 7.3). On a Tier 1, universal level, we can ensure that all students receive developmentally appropriate core curriculum instruction focused on helping students create an ILP. By involving all stakeholders (students, parents, teachers, and community members) in the development of an ILP, we can contribute to the creation of a comprehensive college and career culture on our school campuses. Many school counselors implement components of ILP, but unless you live in a state that mandates ILPs, various components of student planning may be implemented but lacking a comprehensive approach. Districts are strongly encouraged to use the 80/20 model outlined in Chapter 2 to franchise approximately 80% of the ILP across the district, whereas approximately 20% may be reserved for site-specific components.

ILPs can vary school to school, district to district, and state to state. When beginning this process, it's important to think developmentally. A comprehensive approach can begin in elementary or middle school and utilize online resources and standardized documents created by a state and/or district that develops into a portfolio that is completed in 12th grade. Less comprehensive approaches may be as simple as a paper 4-year plan that is completed in high school based on the student's postsecondary plan. To implement a comprehensive Tier 1 school counseling program within the college and career domain, the authors *recommend a thoughtful and fully comprehensive approach to ISP.*

Promoting Quality Individualized Learning Plans throughout the Lifespan: A Revised and Updated "ILP How to Guide 2.0" (see http://www.ncwd-youth.info/wp-content/uploads/2018/03/Promoting-Quality-ILPs-Throughout-the-Lifespan-WEB.pdf) is an excellent online document highlighting a comprehensive model that demonstrates the ILP as a process and not a document. This is an excellent tool for school counselors who are seeking to align their college/career core curriculum to the development of a comprehensive ILP that is based on research. Solberg et al.'s (2014) ILP Theory of Change (see Figure 7.4) states that when students have life and career goals, these goals become the change mechanism that leads to improved academic outcomes and postsecondary completion rates. Based on their theory, if an engaging

Figure 7.3 Multi-Tiered, Multi-Domain System of Support (MTMDSS)

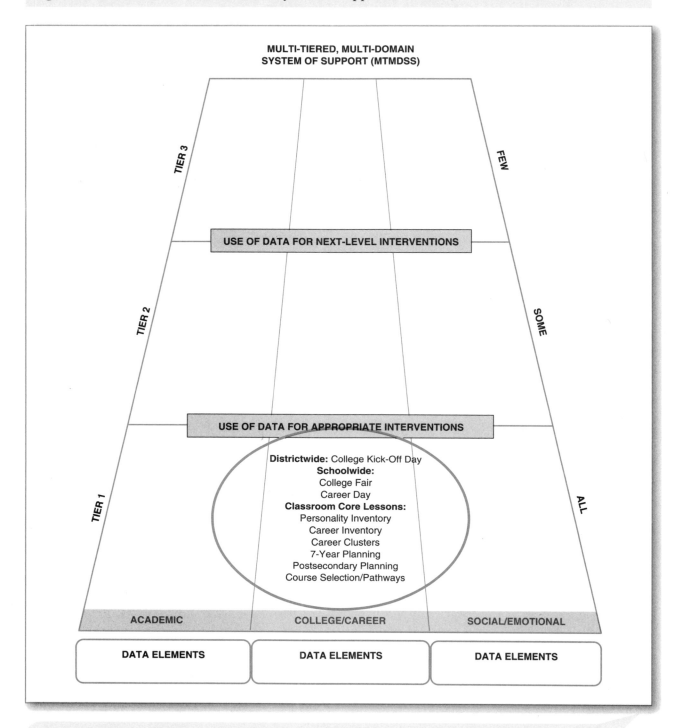

As professional development specialists, we often see many secondary lessons in the college and career domain that are connected piecemeal together, with little scope, sequence, or unity. A best practice for school counselors at the secondary level is to use the ILP as a road map for the school counseling core curriculum, whereby each lesson centers on an ILP task. By aligning the components of the ILP with core curriculum lessons, students develop a stronger ILP with the context that supports them in connecting the importance of that plan with their goals for the future.

and quality ILP is developed with the help of an encouraging adult, students can create career and life goals that can help them perceive their education as more meaningful and ultimately help them reach their set goals. This will enable students to pursue rigorous education and college/career opportunities, which could ultimately increase academic potential and postsecondary completion rates. The bottom line is that we, as school counselors, want our students to feel connected to school and believe their coursework is helping them achieve their current and future goals. The ILP is an excellent Tier 1 activity that helps school counselors support students!

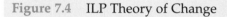

Figure 7.4   ILP Theory of Change

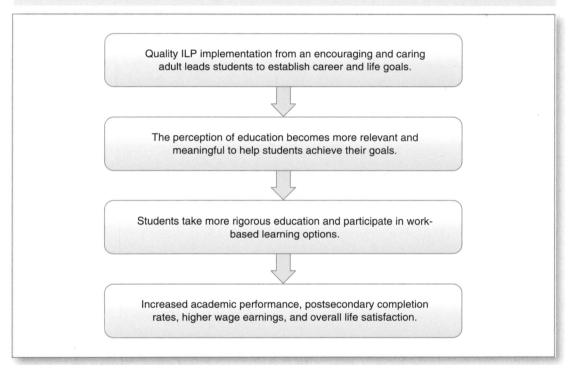

Quality ILP implementation from an encouraging and caring adult leads students to establish career and life goals.

The perception of education becomes more relevant and meaningful to help students achieve their goals.

Students take more rigorous education and participate in work-based learning options.

Increased academic performance, postsecondary completion rates, higher wage earnings, and overall life satisfaction.

Many school counselors provide Tier 1 college/career development activities that promote self- and career exploration, postsecondary options and planning, and exploration of course pathways needed to reach students' goals. Secondary school counselors understand that when students can see the connection between their current education and their postsecondary goals, they are more likely to be successful in reaching their goals. A critical component of the ILP is the plan of study that is connected to postsecondary goals that can be adjusted yearly. When looking at types of ILPs, counselors can compare the differences between a comprehensive ILP to a traditional ILP, often referred to as a 4-year plan.

FROM VANESSA'S DESK: ONE DISTRICT'S STORY

When I began working in San Jacinto Unified School District, I was tasked with redesigning the school counseling program and implementing the ASCA National Model. Part of our

(Continued)

(Continued)

school counseling core curriculum was to implement Tier 1 college and career classroom lessons. One of the lessons helped students design 4-year plans based on their postsecondary goals. As part of the lesson we were able to utilize Naviance, a product that is an online one-stop shop for college and career readiness. We created a wonderful lesson that was engaging, and the students seemed to love it. Having an electronic 4-year plan that students and families could access regularly was great. I had experience with implementing 4-year plans in the past, but they were on paper, making it difficult for students and parents to access. You can imagine how excited I was to utilize a state-of-the-art 4-year plan system that students and parents could refer to after the lesson. Students were able to create their plans based on their postsecondary options, and they looked beautiful.

Our school counseling team was able to pull data indicating how many students had a 4-year plan, and we had annual follow-up classroom lessons to review the 4-year plan and revisit our students' postsecondary plans. During course selection we would encourage our students to review their 4-year plans as they were selecting courses for the following year. As a team we thought we had the 4-year plan system dialed in. After all, we had data to prove that the plans were created. Not only did we have data to show that each student had a plan, but our college preparatory course pathway (in California we call it A–G requirements) had been increasing yearly.

Then one day I attended a district collaborative meeting where there were community members, educators, and some of our students. The superintendent was sharing college and career data and mentioned how every high school student had a 4-year plan discussing the advantages of having an ILP. Then she asked the high school student next to me, "What do you think about your 4-year plan?" The student responded, "I don't know because I don't have one." I was shocked by that answer. I quickly grabbed my electronic device and pulled up the program we used to see if she had a 4-year plan. Sure enough, she had a 4-year plan. I showed her the plan, and I said, "You have a 4-year plan, and here it is." With embarrassment the student responded that she had forgotten that was the 4-year plan.

After the meeting my superintendent and I spoke about how the student had a 4-year plan but had forgotten about it. It was then that we both realized that although we had created systems for students to create and update 4-year plans, they were not meaningful for most students. I took this information back to our counseling team; we had a discussion about the purpose of a 4-year plan and created an implementation plan to make it more meaningful and not just a once-a-year lesson. Part of that plan included changing the name to a 7-year plan. As a district we realized that we needed t o start the ILP when students entered 6th grade. In terms of equity and access we realized we needed to ensure that all of our 5th grade students and parents/guardians were aware of all of the pathways available in middle school and make sure that students saw the connection with course selection and their postsecondary plan.

It was through the implementation plan that we began to interweave all of our college and career Tier 1 activities into connecting with our Individual Learning Plans (7-year plans; see Figure 7.5). This facilitated the beginning of the Individual Learning Plan becoming something that is much more meaningful. Just this year the information systems that we used rolled out an Individual Academic Plan, and the high school counselors transitioned the students to using this Individual Learning Plan. The great thing about this I.A.P. is that it is connected to course selection. Course requests are pulled from the Individual Academic Plans. This has saved the high school counselors time and has made the plans even more meaningful because it is directly connected to their college/career pathway and the courses that students sign up for. This has also made it easier for students to understand which classes to take in order to complete a college/career pathway.

Figure 7.5   7-Year Plan–Implementation Plan for Middle School

Grade	Action Item	Objectives
5th Grade (conducted by middle school counselor)	Transition Lesson 1: Preparing for middle school (Fall—November)	• Importance of good grades • Differences between middle school and elementary school • Middle school success strategies
5th Grade (conducted by middle school counselor)	Transition Lesson 2: Course selection and introduction to postsecondary plan and 7-year plan (Spring—February)	• Purpose of middle school to prepare for high school • Review of course pathways • Introduction of postsecondary plan and options after high school • Preparing for college and career starts now • Course selection • 3-year plan provided to students
6th Grade	Academic success lesson (Fall)	• Postsecondary options reviewed • A–G* requirement reviewed • Connecting your postsecondary goal to your success here • Strategies for academic success • Resources available to help you be successful • Passing courses linked to your postsecondary plan
6th Grade	Introduction to Naviance and Strengths Finder (Fall)	• Provide students with an overview of the resources available via Naviance • Have students take the Strengths Finder and start career exploration • Explain how this connects to their 7-year plans
6th Grade	Course selection, 3-year plan review, postsecondary plan review (Spring—February)	• Review of course plan • Review postsecondary options and plans • Connect course selections to postsecondary plans • Review A–G • Course selection • Review 3-year plan
7th Grade	Academic success lesson (Fall)	• Postsecondary options reviewed • A–G requirement reviewed • Connecting your postsecondary goal to your success here • Strategies for academic success • Resources available to help you be successful • Passing courses linked to your postsecondary plan • Review 3-year plan
7th Grade	Naviance Lesson: Finding your career (Fall)	• Students complete the career inventory • Students research one career • Students complete postsecondary plan sheet • Connect how middle school and high school prepare them for careers • Explain the connection to 3-year plan

(Continued)

Figure 7.5   (Continued)

Grade	Action Item	Objectives
7th Grade	Course selection, 3-year plan review, and postsecondary plan review (Spring)	• Review of course plan • Review postsecondary options and plans • Connect course selections to postsecondary plans • Review A–G • Course selection • Review 3-year plan
7th Grade	Individual review (Spring)	• Transcript review • Course selection review • Postsecondary/3-year plan check
8th Grade	Academic success lesson (Fall)	• Postsecondary options reviewed • A–G requirement reviewed • Connecting your postsecondary goal to your success here • Strategies for academic success • Resources available to help you be successful • Passing courses linked to your postsecondary plan • Preparing for high school • Review 3-year plan
8th Grade	Naviance Lesson: College super match and transcript review (Fall)	• Review postsecondary goals • A–G requirement reviewed • Teach students how to read their transcripts and how to earn credits in high school • High school graduation requirements • Researching colleges • Connect how this is part of their 3-year plans
8th Grade (done by SJHS school counselors)	Course selection and postsecondary plan (January)	• Review course pathways • Review A–G • Review postsecondary options and plans • Create/review 4-year planning document • Course selection
8th Grade (done by SJHS school counselors)	Individual review of course selection, 4-year plan, and postsecondary plan reviewed (February)	• Transcript review • Postsecondary plan and 4-year plan review • Summer school review
8th Grade	8th Grade visit to SJHS (Spring)	• Campus tour • Club sign-up • Strategies to be successful in high school • Importance of passing all classes • Remember your postsecondary plan

*A–G refers to the minimum course requirements for admission to state college or university.

Developing Concrete Postsecondary Plans

Concrete postsecondary plans are an extension of the ILP. As seniors prepare to graduate from high school, it is important that they have plans for what they intend to do after graduation. Even further, it is important to ensure that they have equitable access to resources and supports to successfully realize and fulfill those plans.

In Chicago Public Schools, this process is called a "concrete postsecondary plan" and requires that students produce evidence of steps taken toward matriculating to the postsecondary pathway of their choice, as outlined in Figure 7.6.

Figure 7.6 Postsecondary Plan Options and Required Evidence ("Learn.Plan.Succeed.")

LEARN.PLAN.SUCCEED.
Post secondary Plan Options and Required Evidence

COLLEGE	MILITARY	WORK	TRADE/ APPRENTICESHIP PROGRAM	JOB PROGRAM	GAP YEAR PROGRAM	OTHER**
Acceptance and Financial Aid Award Letter	Enlistment Letter	Offer Letter	Acceptance Letter	Admission Letter	Admission Letter	Counselor/Coach Verified Option

* Evidence will be audited by the OSCPA office and internal audit for fidelity.

** Ultimately, college and career specialists and network chiefs will ultimately confirm options that do not fall under the expanded definition.

Source: Chicago Public Schools, Office of College Career Success.

This process has even been formalized in recent years in the form of a graduation requirement, an initiative called Learn.Plan.Succeed., designed to better support all graduating seniors while reducing the number of out-of-school, out-of-work youth in Chicago. When a report from the Great Cities Institute was published in 2016, it was clear that once students leave Chicago Public Schools, many struggle to enter college or find work, creating a class of "jobless youth" (Córdova & Wilson, 2016). According to the report, as of 2016, there were approximately 58,000 out-of-school, out-of-work young adults in the Chicago area. This highlighted the reality that Chicago's "college for all" approach was neither serving all students effectively nor equitably, and they began developing strategies for improving the postsecondary advising, resources, and supports that students and families receive from their public schools.

ILPs are at the core of this initiative. By starting conversations and exploration as early as possible, students will be prepared to make postsecondary decisions during their senior year. Elementary, middle, and high school counselors play vital roles in ensuring ILPs are developed for each student from Grades 6 through 12. Usage of the ILP tool (Naviance) and completion of the ILPs at all grade levels, 6 through 12, are monitored on a monthly basis as a district key performance indicator, with reports being sent to network chiefs, principals, and school

(Continued)

(Continued)

counselors. Senior year, students upload their own evidence as outlined in Figure 7.7, and then the evidence collected is used to compute the related School Quality Rating Policy metric.

Figure 7.7   Learn.Plan.Succeed. Flyer

Source: **Chicago Public Schools, Office of College Career Success.**

School counselors serve as equity leaders by ensuring that all students and families are advised around multiple postsecondary pathways, not just the broader college and career. School counselors are options brokers, providing a wealth of information on apprenticeships, college options, gap year and public service programs, trade and jobs programs, military, and full-time employment with a family-supporting wage, to the end that students have primary, secondary, and tertiary plans. The goal is that 100% of graduating seniors successfully matriculate to and persist in their chosen postsecondary pathway.

MAKING DECISIONS ON YOUR ILP, IMPLEMENTATION, AND BEST PRACTICES

Decision-Making Tool for ILPs

For school counselors who are just getting started on implementing ILPs, we have created a decision-making tool for ILPs to facilitate the process (see Figure 7.8). One of our first recommendations is to determine what your state and district

Figure 7.8 Decision-Making Tool for ILPs

Individual Learning Plan Worksheet

Who Completes It?	What Tool Will You Use?	When?	Method of Delivery?	Content Covered	How Do Families Provide Input?	Corresponding Schoolwide Activity	What Outcome Is This Related To?
☐ All students ☐ Grade level(s): ☐ Multiple grade level(s):_,_,_	☐ District-developed tool ☐ Commercial tool (i.e., Career Cruising, Naviance) ☐ Electronic ☐ Paper	☐ What month ☐ What quarter	☐ Classroom instruction ☐ Small group meeting ☐ Individual meeting	☐ Course selection and . . . list below	☐ In-person large group or small group meeting ☐ In-person individual meeting ☐ Google Hangouts, Skype, etc. ☐ Phone call ☐ Email ☐ Other____	☐ Orientation ☐ Parent night ☐ Career day ☐ College day ☐ Advisory ☐ College tours ☐ Transition events ☐ FAFSA workshops	☐ College enrollment ☐ College persistence ☐ Graduation rate ☐ Scholarship dollars/financial aid dollars earned
6th Grade							
7th Grade							
8th Grade							
9th Grade							
10th Grade							
11th Grade							
12th Grade							

requires. We also recommend that you collaborate with stakeholders, such as administrators; lead teachers, parents, and students to create a culture around students having comprehensive ILPs.

1) First, looking at the Individual Learning Plan (see Figure 7.8), determine *which students will complete* the ILP, and determine what grade levels might benefit during this phase from planning with school counselors from multiple levels. By having input from elementary, middle, and high school counselors, you can ensure that the plans are developmental in design, and this will help design Tier 1 college/career lessons or help integrate existing lessons that are in place. Sometimes when school counselors are piloting a new tool, it is helpful to start at one grade level and build from it if you are not on a tight implementation schedule.

2) The next step of determining *what ILP tool* you will use may require research if your state or district does not have a common ILP tool. In that case you would determine what resources do you have available and then determine if the district or state has a tool you can use. Perhaps your district or site has purchased a commercial tool such as Naviance or Career Cruising, or some states have ILP tools they have created.

3) *When* will you have meetings? Will it be in the summer? Or during the school year? If so, what month or semester? It's best to calendar these activities in advance so everyone (parents, students, administrators, etc.) knows what to count on.

4) Now it's time for your team to determine the *method of delivery* for the ILPs. Often school counselors assume the most effective way to deliver an ILP is via a one-on-one meeting. However, the issue that many school counselors have is that it is often difficult and time-consuming to meet with each student (and family member if that's the plan) individually, especially if you have a large caseload. ILPs can be individualized and delivered effectively in a classroom lesson or a small group. You can review the ILPs when students do course selection, which provides an individual contact.

5) Once your team decides on the method of delivery, you can determine the *content to be covered* as well as determine if you choose to make the ILP more comprehensive by tying career and college exploration to the ILP. If that is the case, then you can assess what lessons or activities you are already doing related to college and career exploration and determine how you can connect the ILP to these activities. Perhaps your school has a senior project during which the ILP portfolio can be developed every year, and the final senior project is a compilation of all of the college/career activities. If you have never implemented an ILP, it may feel daunting to examine all of these steps, but remember, if you break it down by one grade level at a time, it is more manageable. Maybe in 9th grade you do a lesson on career exploration and describing what an ILP is, explaining that future lessons will add and build onto the ILP. The second lesson could be on postsecondary options and requirements (a common lesson that most high school counselors give), and the third lesson could be on developing an ILP based on the student's postsecondary plan. Implementing those three lessons with all 9th graders can be an excellent plan to get started on to develop a comprehensive ILP.

6) Determining how parents/guardians and *families will have input* into the development of an ILP is the next step. Family input can be done via workshops, video lessons, or small groups. If possible, it is always helpful to provide families the same lesson you provide to students so they have clear understanding of what the Tier 1 lessons are that school counselors provide. Family engagement is an issue that some school counselors struggle with, so we have to get creative. Perhaps you can video record the family workshops that you provide and post them on your school counselor web page so all parents have access.

7) Once you go through these steps, you can further determine how to *connect the ILP to the core curriculum or schoolwide activities*. For example, maybe you are a middle school counselor and you organize a career fair; you could create a classroom lesson that connects the students' ILPs to the career fair and ask the English teachers to teach it.

8) To prevent an ILP from being an activity that you just check off the list and is a one-shot lesson, think about ways you can have students *follow up* with their ILPs. The way that one high school did this was through advisory time. The school counselors provided the lesson to the teachers, and the teachers implemented it. It became a schoolwide document that was at the center of creating a college and career culture.

9) Last, determine what *outcomes* you want to see and how you will measure your success. Outcomes could include graduation rates, scholarships earned, financial aid applications submitted, number of students meeting the college preparatory requirements, military enlistments, acceptances to postsecondary institutions, and college enrollment, persistence, and degree attainment rates.

Activity 7.1

Figure 7.9 is a list of the ILP agreements in Chicago Public Schools. In what way is this helpful to counselors and stakeholders? In what way might it be improved?

Figure 7.9   Chicago Public Schools' ILP in Naviance

Grade Level	Task	Suggested Quarter of Completion	Estimated Time (minutes)
Grade 6	Complete the Academic Success Survey	Quarter 1	30
	Create a Goal for 6th Grade	Quarter 1	15
	Complete Career Cluster Finder	Quarter 1	30
	Complete the Academic Goal Midyear Reflection	Quarter 3	15
	Complete the Academic Goal End-of-Year Reflection	Quarter 4	15

(Continued)

Figure 7.9 (Continued)

Grade Level	Task	Suggested Quarter of Completion	Estimated Time (minutes)
Grade 7	Create a Goal for 7th Grade	Quarter 1	15
	Complete Career Cluster Finder	Quarter 1	30
	Add at Least Three Career Clusters to Favorite Career Cluster List	Quarter 1	10
	Complete the Academic Goal Midyear Reflection	Quarter 3	15
	Complete the High School Planning and Research Survey	Quarter 4	45
	Attend a GoCPS Information Workshop	Quarter 4	10
	Complete the Academic Goal End-of-Year Reflection	Quarter 4	15
Grade 8	Create a Goal for 8th Grade	Quarter 1	15
	Complete Your Roadtrip Nation Reflection	Quarter 1	30
	Add Three Careers to My List	Quarter 1	10
	Complete Your High School Planning Checklist—Part 1	December	20
	Complete the Academic Goal Midyear Reflection	Quarter 3	15
	Complete Your High School Planning Checklist—Part 2	Quarter 4	20
	Complete the Academic Goal End-of-Year Reflection	Quarter 4	15
Grade 9	Create a Postsecondary Goal for 9th Grade	Quarter 1	15
	Complete Career Cluster Finder	Quarter 1	30
	Add at Least Three Careers to My List	Quarter 1	10
	Complete StrengthsExplorer	Quarter 2	30
	Complete the Postsecondary Goal Midyear Reflection	Quarter 2	15
	Attend a Postsecondary Options Workshop	Quarter 4	10
	Complete the Postsecondary Goal End-of-Year Reflection	Quarter 4	10
Grade 10	Complete Career Interest Profiler	Quarter 1	30
	Add at Least Three Careers to My List	Quarter 1	10
	Complete Postsecondary Game Plan	Quarter 2	15
	Attend 1 College/Career Fair/or Career Shadow Day	Quarter 4	10
Grade 11	Complete Postsecondary Game Plan	Quarter 1	15
	Complete the Expected Family Contribution (EFC) Survey	Quarter 3	15
	Build a Résumé *or* Upload Your Résumé	Quarter 3	30
	SuperMatch College Search	Quarter 4	30

Grade Level	Task	Suggested Quarter of Completion	Estimated Time (minutes)
	Add at Least Three Colleges to My Prospective List	Quarter 4	15
	Upload Your Draft Personal Statement	Quarter 4	15
Grade 12	Apply to at Least Three Colleges	Quarter 2	10
	Complete the Net Price Calculator Survey	Quarter 2	30
	Upload Evidence That You Applied for a Scholarship	Quarter 3	10
	Award Letter Review Meeting with Staff Member	Quarter 4	30
	Senior Transition Survey	Quarter 4	25
Grade 12 Evidence of a Concrete Postsecondary Plan	If College Going: - Upload Your College Acceptance Letter - Upload Your Financial Aid Award Letter	Quarter 4	15
	If Career Prep/Apprenticeship Going: - Upload Evidence of Career, Apprenticeship, Job Program Acceptance, or Offer Letter	Quarter 4	15
	If Employment Going: - Upload Evidence of Employment Verification and/or Offer Letter	Quarter 4	15
	If Gap Year Going: - Upload Evidence of Deferment or Gap Year Program Acceptance	Quarter 4	15
	If Military Going: - Upload Evidence of Military Enlistment	Quarter 4	15
SURVEYS:	Extracurricular Activities Survey 9th–12th	Yearly	15
	Brag Sheet Survey	Yearly	30

Source: Chicago Public Schools, Office of College Career Success.

Additional Tools

Fortunately there are many tools and resources that school counselors can use to help students develop a comprehensive ILP. Some of the tools are free, and others cost money.

State or District Designed Tools: Many tools are electronically enabling students, parents, and school counselors to access ILP materials regularly. A common practice is having an online portfolio that can be comprised of items such as course pathways that list courses students would take each year in secondary school, career inventories, career exploration items, and postsecondary plans.

Some states have created a specialized website or portal that students can access to create and have access to ILP materials. One example is the California College Guidance Initiative (CCGI), which recognizes that improving college and career readiness and transition improves postsecondary success. CCGI is designed to ensure that all Grade 6 through 12 students in California have access to guidance and support as they plan and prepare for postsecondary education and training. Partnering with school districts, school counselors, and parents, they provide technological tools that help guide this work.

Contracted Tools: There are several companies that have developed electronic one-stop shops that districts contract with to assist with ISP. Examples of these programs include: Hobson's Naviance, Career Cruising, and Choices Planner. Many of the contracted programs provide all of the resources to connect students to career exploration, career inventories, personality inventories, résumé building, college exploration, 4-year planning tools, and postsecondary planning. One company is Hobson's Naviance, which offers a 4-year course planner, along with career inventories, classroom lessons, and a college matching system. Many school counseling programs will develop classroom lessons developmental in design to ensure that components of the ILP are complete. For example, in San Jacinto Unified School District school counselors' core classroom action plans address the components of the ILP, which they call the 7-year plan.

What is Naviance?

Hobson's Naviance provides a one-stop shop for a comprehensive approach to college and career readiness. Students are able to create their ILPs, which include a 4-year plan, career clusters, and career and personality inventories that enable students to make career plans; students are also able to create journal entries, which can be assigned by a teacher or school counselor. Other features of Naviance include an in-depth college search tool called SuperMatch College Search, with which students can narrow the college search by type of college, major, location, and so on. Students are also able to use Naviance to create a résumé and much more. Many high schools utilize programs like Naviance to help create a college and career culture within schools.

School Counselor–Generated Tools: In many districts counselors create their own tools to use during ISP through the use of Google Docs, Microsoft Word, and so on. In what follows Jeff Ream shares what he created (see Figures 7.10 and 7.11).

Jeff Ream, a.k.a. "The Counseling Geek," Shares His Tools

I created several documents to use with our 10th grade students (see online appendix) during our advisory periods in the time frame leading up to course requests. Students use these during a series of core curriculum lessons over 2 weeks that help them review their transcripts for college and graduation requirements as well as have them start thinking about which courses they would like to pursue the following year. Students then use these tools as a guide when they go online to our Student Information System (SIS) and request courses online. They access their online transcripts with the same SIS during these lessons.

Creating these documents required a little bit of technical know-how but could be reproduced in online programs like Canva or even within PowerPoint. The course planning document was created in Adobe Illustrator with use of stock icons from Envato Elements. There are many places to find free stock icons and images like Vecteezy.com. The credit tracking sheet was created in LucidChart—a flow chart, diagram, and mind-mapping tool. It can be very useful for making checklists for students.

Although most of these tools cost some money, there are free ways to get to useful forms if you are enterprising and willing to try something new. YouTube has some great tutorials, and you can also feel free to contact me directly via email with questions: thegeek@the counselinggeek.com.

Figure 7.10 NTHS A–G Progress Check

Figure 7.11 NTHS Graduation Credit Check

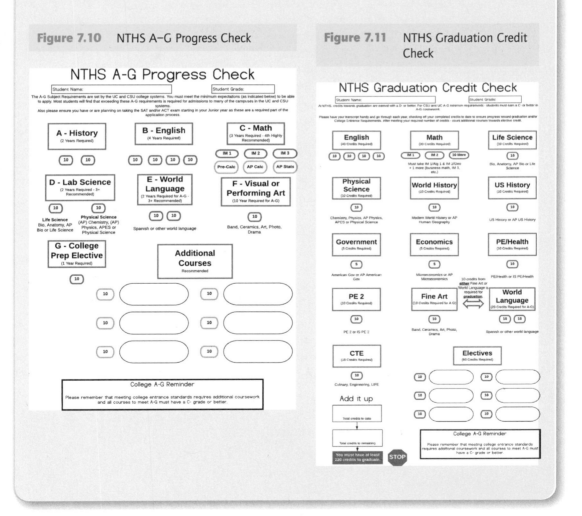

OVERCOMING BARRIERS TO IMPLEMENTATION

Potential Barriers to ILP Implementation	Possible Solutions! :)
School counselors are not part of the ILP planning.	Ensure that school counselors work with district and state leaders in creating a plan for ILP implementation. At the school level, this can often be resolved through a conversation with the administrator.
Lack of buy-in from administrators, teachers, students, and parents.	Involve all stakeholder voices in the planning and decision-making of ILPs. Help stakeholders understand why ILPs are important and how they connect to postsecondary success.
Responsibilities of implementing ILPs fall solely on school counselors. School counselors are mandated to meet with each student individually for a certain length of time, causing most of the year being spent providing individual services. This ultimately impacts other Tier 1 activities.	It is essential that school counselors work with district and state leaders to understand the role of the school counselor and what a comprehensive school counseling program looks like. Help leaders recognize that ILPs can be reviewed in multiple settings, such as small groups and classroom lessons.
Your school or district cannot afford to pay for tools needed to implement ILPs.	Research free and cost-effective tools. Work with your technology department to modify documents used in other districts. Work with your district and state leaders in the implementation planning to ensure that funds are dedicated to ILPs.
You do not have a clear plan on how ILPs will be implemented, or ILPs are stand-alone activities that have no meaning to students.	Create a multidisciplinary task force team made up of all stakeholders (including students) and complete the Individual Learning Plan Worksheet (see Figure 7.8).

Any time a school system is implementing a new project, there will likely be barriers. Systems are designed to get the results they get, good or bad, and excellent planning often yields excellent results. Although there could be barriers to implementing ILPs, we know that a strong team can overcome any barrier. The good news is if school counselors use components of ILPs to meet their college/career objectives, then the ILPs become a driving force to ensure that *all* students are college and career ready.

Schoolwide Programs and Activities

Figure 8.1   MTMDSS—Schoolwide Programs and Activities

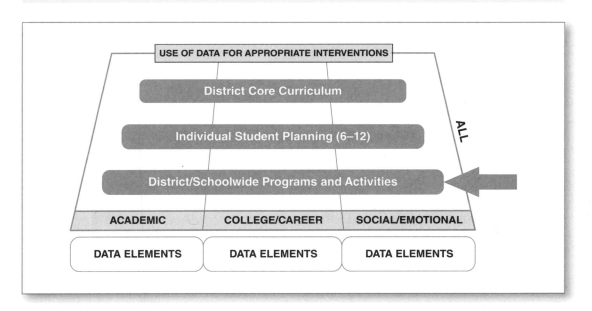

Abla, a district school counseling lead, was always ahead of the curve and set up expectations and systems districtwide for her school counselors to deliver schoolwide programs and activities long before it became "a thing." However, after learning about the new MTMDSS and the concept of providing consistent programs and activities among her six high schools,

(Continued)

(Continued)

she realized that the schools in her district were implementing "random acts of school counseling programs and activities." For example, one of her high schools had three family events in the fall, whereas another held a family conference in the spring, and a third encouraged families to make appointments as needed.

Abla believed in the concept of ensuring equity and access for all families, and she found it increasingly difficult to justify inconsistent family education. How could she guarantee that all students and families had the knowledge and skills they needed to be college and career ready? She returned home to her district and initiated a steering team to begin aligning those programs and activities to a franchised school counseling core curriculum for greater student impact throughout the district.

Tier 1 initiatives led by school counselors for all students at the secondary level include delivery of core curriculum classroom lessons (Chapters 2–6), individual student and/or learning plans (Chapter 7), and schoolwide programs and activities (see Figure 8.1). In this chapter, we will discuss the school counselor's role in schoolwide programs and activities and how, when appropriate, to align them to core curriculum and family education.

WHAT ARE SCHOOLWIDE PROGRAMS AND ACTIVITIES?

Although core curriculum classroom lessons and individual student planning are large components within Tier 1 services, school counselors also play roles in implementing schoolwide programs and activities aligned with the three school counseling domains—academic, college/career, and social/emotional—within MTMDSS. Note how in the MTMDSS pyramid shown in Figure 8.2, schoolwide/districtwide activities are indicated in *all* domain areas within Tier 1. Figure 8.3 displays the MTMDSS pyramid with some examples of activities a secondary school counselor may participate in or lead at their site within each domain area and the additional tiers, although those are not all covered in this chapter. Table 8.1 provides additional examples. Throughout this chapter, multiple examples will be shared—some briefly and others in greater detail. Extensive support materials are also provided on our website.

online resources

Schoolwide Programs and Activities Defined

Within this chapter, the samples and examples presented align with the three school counseling domains. Some are schoolwide *programs*, whereas others are *activities*. Programs tend to be ongoing throughout the school year and more systemic in nature (e.g., schoolwide behavior expectations, restorative practices, and

Figure 8.2   Multi-Tiered, Multi-Domain System of Supports (MTMDSS)

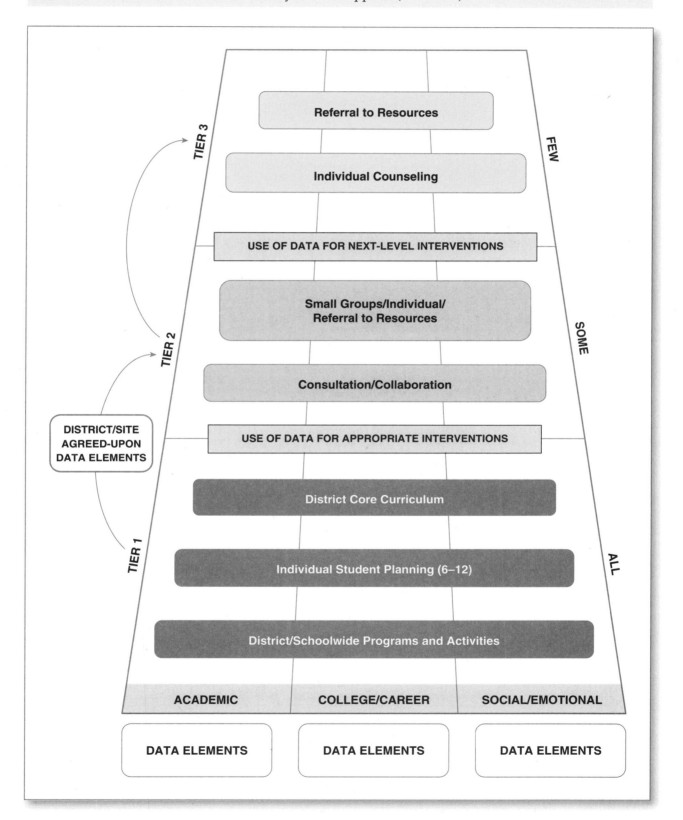

Figure 8.3 Sample MTMDSS at the Secondary Level

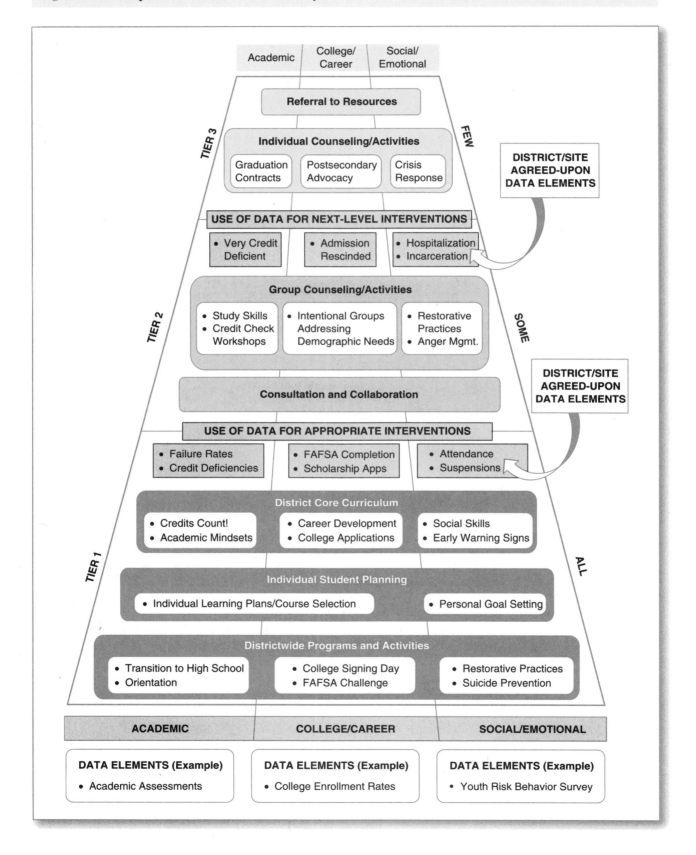

Table 8.1   Examples of District/Schoolwide Programs and Activities by Domain

Academic	College/Career	Social/Emotional

• Transition programs:
  ○ Elementary school to middle school
  ○ 8th to 9th grade
  ○ 12th grade to postsecondary
• Orientations
• Attendance programs
• New student welcome programs
	• College Signing Day
	• College tours and rep visits
	• Summer melt counseling
	• Scholarship and FAFSA initiatives
	• College Kick-Off Day
		• Bully prevention
		• Mix It Up Day
		• Restorative practices
		• Day of Silence
		• Suicide Prevention Week
		• Mentorship programs
		• Red Ribbon Week (Drug/Alcohol Free)
		• World Kindness Day

scholarship dissemination), whereas activities are confined to a period of time, such as a specific month, week, or day (i.e., Red Ribbon Week and College Signing Day). Depending on factors such as how much an activity appropriately aligns with the role of the school counselors, the ratio or caseload of students, areas of expertise, and the amount of support provided for serving in a leadership capacity, the school counselor's role may vary from directing the entire *activity*, such as College Signing Day, to being an integral part of a schoolwide *program*, such as restorative practices.

When coordinating and supporting schoolwide programs and activities, the school counselor is advised to consider the amount of time spent in this area to ensure that it doesn't take away from other Tier 1 services or inhibit delivery of Tier 2 or 3 supports. Additionally, school counselors want to align schoolwide activities with their comprehensive core curriculum action plans to supplement learning rather than planning random acts of schoolwide activities. There is no schoolwide prescription or recipe other than for school counselors to pay attention to their roles within schoolwide programs and activities and to balance services provided across the three domains. Districts are also strongly encouraged to use the 80/20 model outlined in Chapter 2 to franchise approximately 80% of the school counseling schoolwide programs and activities across the district, whereas approximately 20% may be reserved for site-specific programs and activities. Figure 8.4 presents an example of a 9th grade core curriculum and its accompanying schoolwide activities.

Alignment With the ASCA National Model

The purpose of this text is to provide thorough instruction on the activities that secondary school counselors provide within Tier 1, including core curriculum, individual student planning, and schoolwide programs and activities. Rather than conducting random acts of schoolwide programs and activities, school counselors assess the developmental and data-driven needs of the school and create schoolwide action plans within the three ASCA domains and aligned to school and district goals.

Figure 8.4   Example of Alignment Between Schoolwide Activities and Core Curriculum Action Plan

9th Grade Orientation	**9th Grade**	Welcome to 9th Grade: Credits Count!	M3, B-LS 7, B-SMS 10	School counselor–generated transition lesson	September
Mix It Up Day		Relationships Matter	M3, B-SS 2, B-SS 5	School counselor–generated lesson on inclusion and unity	September–October
SADD Grim Reaper Day		Red Ribbon Week	B-LS 1, B-SMS 9, B-SS 9	School counselor–generated anti-alcohol and drug lesson	October
		Introduction to Naviance	M4, B-LS 4, B-LS 7	Prepackaged Naviance lesson plan	January–February
College Fair		Course Planning	M6, B-LS 7, B-LS 9	School counselor–generated lesson on course selection	March
Alumni Day		Postsecondary Exploration and Self-Assessment	M4, B-LS 4, B-LS 7	Prepackaged Naviance lesson plan	April–May

The ASCA National Model, 3rd edition (2012), states that "school counselors conduct planned activities outside the classroom to promote academic, career, or personal/social development, such as college and career fairs, postsecondary site visits, student team building/leadership workshops, community/business tours" (p. 85). These schoolwide programs and activities support students in mastering the student standards (i.e., ASCA Mindsets and Behaviors) and often reinforce the core curriculum content taught in the classroom by the school counselor.

ACADEMIC DOMAIN PROGRAMS AND ACTIVITIES

The secondary school counselor implements strategies and activities to support and maximize each student's ability to learn. At the Tier 1 level, these may include support for student transitions (e.g., High School Investigation Day and grade-level orientations), schoolwide attendance improvement incentives, and new student welcome programs (if offered as part of schoolwide expectations programs or in an effort to familiarize all new students who may have missed new school year orientation events or curriculum). Please note that support for the high school to postsecondary transition will be discussed in the college/career domain section of this chapter.

Middle School Transition Programs and Activities

Secondary school counselors at the middle school level are involved in supporting elementary school students' transition to middle school. The move from a traditional elementary setting where many students have only one or two teachers to a comprehensive middle school with class changes, multiple teachers, lockers, and heightened academic expectations can be overwhelming for students. Nationwide, 88% of students in public schools transition from elementary to middle school (Association for Middle Level Education, n.d.), which can be a stressful time for students and their parents. In addition to the academic change, students beginning middle school are maturing physically, developing more autonomy, beginning to take more risks, and starting to define their identities outside of their families. To ease students' fears and set them up for success, school counselors can coordinate orientations for students and families, campus tours, and summer bridge programs. Well-designed transition plans help students feel a sense of belonging as they enter a larger school campus and set them up for success academically and socially (Association for Middle Level Education, n.d.).

DANIELLE'S STORY

At my last middle school we began the elementary to middle school transition in February by first presenting to all students in 6th grade at their individual elementary school sites. The other school counselor and I worked with our principal and several middle school students to create and present on the following topics:

- Normalizing the diverse feelings students may be experiencing with the impending school change
- Sharing the school behavior expectations and describing campus culture
- Providing details such as typical class schedules, times for breaks and lunch, and information about lockers and dress-out physical education
- Informing students about the different clubs, sports, and activities on campus (current middle school presenters shared about the activities in which they were involved)
- Discussing elective class options (again, current middle school presenters talked about which electives they chose and why)
- Answering elementary student questions

The week after students received their presentation, families from all five feeder elementary schools were invited to our campus for a presentation with similar information. For the family presentation, we added specific information about the developmental changes students experience during adolescence and ways to support students in middle school. We encouraged

(Continued)

(Continued)

families to attend our middle school open house in early May to learn more about the clubs, activities, and elective classes and to meet the teachers on campus. For any families who were not able to attend the February presentation, we gave a repeat performance before open house.

In addition to visiting elementary sites, our school counseling team coordinated a half-day Future Braves Academy during which elementary students toured campus on a scavenger hunt, participated in team-building activities with students from other schools, and met teachers and other campus staff. We trained our middle school students to lead the variety of activities with the incoming students and also showcased the band, choir, and drama programs. Families were welcome to attend as well, and before leaving, each student received a school T-shirt.

Through providing students and their families multiple opportunities to visit the middle school campus, meet a variety of school staff, and ask questions, we felt proud of our work to make the transition to a new school successful. Our school counseling team also worked with elementary school teachers and counselors to discuss any specific student issues that may need future follow-up. The transition program received positive feedback from students (both incoming students and middle school students who were able to participate in helping transition new students), elementary school teachers, families, and middle school staff, and we were grateful to have district and administrative support as well.

Eighth to Ninth Grade Transition Programs and Activities

School counselors support students in successfully transitioning to middle school, high school, and beyond. By collaborating with families, school staff, and community members, school counselors can help students gain the attitudes, knowledge, and skills needed to reduce their anxiety and improve their self-efficacy when moving on to whatever comes next. This section will focus on schoolwide programs and activities that school counselors can implement as direct services to students that support a successful transition to high school.

Research on the Eighth to Ninth Grade Transition

As school counselors have long known, the eighth to 9th grade transition is critical to student success in high school and beyond. Recently, new research has confirmed the importance of the 9th grade year. Allensworth and Easton (2005) noted that 9th grade can be a make-or-break year for students. "Given the right set of positive experiences during the freshman year, students with relatively weak elementary school records can turn around, do well in high school, and go on to graduate. At the same time, students who enter high school with strong track records in the middle grades can falter and end up doing poorly, even dropping out" (Easton, Johnson, & Sartain, 2017).

In addition to being a strong predictor of 11th grade GPA, "freshman GPA also predicts high school graduation, college enrollment, and one-year college retention, and in fact, is a much better predictor of these important milestones than test scores"

(Easton et al., 2017). Additionally, implementing targeted strategies aimed at helping students successfully transition to 9th grade results in substantial increases in the graduation rate (Roderick, Kelley-Kemple, Johnson, & Beechum, 2014).

To address both of these issues, some districts have adopted a freshman on-track metric to help them monitor and target students at risk of falling off track during the freshman year (Allensworth & Easton, 2005). In these instances, districts monitor students' progress every grade reporting period and calculate their projected on-track rate. School counselors ideally have access to these data and use them to flag and "fishnet" students for Tier 2 supports every 5 weeks in addition to their Tier 1 supports for all students.

Both middle school and high school counselors have critical roles in facilitating a successful 9th-grade transition for students. Students earn better grades and have higher attendance rates in schools with strong teacher–student relationships and where students see high school as preparing them for their future (Allensworth & Easton, 2007). Similarly, the school counselor relationship contributes to a successful transition experience. Freshman transition events that take place *prior to the first day of school* and are focused on relationship building, and challenging academics can be crucial to freshman year success, which in turn is highly predictive of high school graduation (Allensworth & Easton, 2005).

School counselors serve as leaders by coordinating comprehensive, evidence-based, Tier 1 systems of support at both the middle and high school sites to ensure that all incoming 9th graders gain the attitudes, knowledge, and skills that they need for a successful freshman year. What follows are specific examples of schoolwide programs and activities that school counselors can implement to support the high school transition:

- High School Investigation Day (8th grade)
- Freshman Connection (summer between 8th and 9th)
- Freshman Orientation (summer between 8th and 9th)
- Family Orientation to High School (summer between 8th and 9th)
- Peer Mentorship Program (9th grade)
- Freshman Seminar Course (9th grade)

High School Investigation Day (Eighth Grade Year)

This 1-day event, typically taking place during May or June, provides 8th grade students with the opportunity to explore their intended high school and begin building relationships. High schools showcase their sports teams, extracurricular activities, dynamic teaching staff, course offerings, and much more to their incoming freshman class. At the end of the day, the goal is for students to leave feeling more excited and less apprehensive about attending high school. High School Investigation Day (HSI Day) is a unique opportunity for high school counselors and their major feeder school counselors to collaborate to support student transition.

Guiding Principles of HSI Day

- *Student-Led*: Student leaders are a driving force on HSI Day. Current high school students help personalize the high school experience by guiding incoming freshmen through a series of fun, positive activities designed to help the students get to know one another as well as learn important school information. It is imperative that the student leaders are included in the planning of the day's events as well as leading the day's activities.

- *Relationships*: All students will be known, valued, and inspired and have at least one involved, caring adult who knows them well.
- *Safe and Welcoming Environment*: All students will attend, adjust, and achieve in an environment of high expectations and strategies of support.
- *Rigor*: All students will complete a preliminary, individual 4-year academic plan, which includes an awareness of opportunities to take rigorous coursework, such as Advanced Placement (AP), dual credit/dual enrollment, International Baccalaureate (IB), Advancement Via Individual Determination (AVID), and college-level coursework while in high school. Students will understand the steps to college and postsecondary pathways and understand that they can choose their future and that college is possible.
- *Relevance*: All students will be connected to their school through extracurricular activities and service learning projects and will see the connections between their class work and their personal lives.
- *Student Support*: All students will be assessed and provided early interventions to meet individual student needs.

Expected Outcomes

Incoming freshmen will:

- Feel welcome and supported in their transition to high school.
- Develop a sense of belonging in their new school.
- Engage as active participants in their transition to high school.
- Develop relationships with upperclassmen and at least one caring adult who will help them through the transition process.
- Understand the high expectations for a successful freshman year.
- Be excited about starting high school!

Suggested Activities:

- Fun, positive, student-led activities that evoke discussion and thought about the responsibilities and challenges of high school
- Large group activities that allow students to get to know one another, student leaders, and key staff
- Scavenger hunts, classroom visits, and a tour of the building
- Distribution of a school spirit/swag bag including items such as pencils, stickers, book bag swag, button, school T-shirt, spirit flag, and so on
- Student-led question and answer panels and faculty/staff question and answer panels
- Distribution of information on summer activities (e.g., orientation, Freshman Connection, extracurricular activities, and enrichment)

HSI Day Planning Considerations

Collaboration and delegation are key to implementing a successful HSI Day. Although school counselors are ideally suited to coordinate such an event, participation from all major stakeholders groups is important (i.e., administrators, teachers, paraprofessionals, lunchroom staff, security, bus drivers, upperclassman student leaders, sports teams, student club/organization leaders). Participation from all groups results in an event that is truly part of the fabric and culture of the school.

Obtaining buy-in from administration is a necessary first step. School counselors might consider putting together a proposal that addresses how such an event would support a school in meeting its freshman data goals (i.e., grades, attendance, and behavior). Also include monies, staffing, and other resources needed, as well as a possible rough outline of the day's activities. Once buy-in is obtained, high school and middle school counselors can begin the planning process by convening a meeting to discuss the following logistics:

- Who should be involved in planning
- Budget
- Transportation
- Chaperones needed
- Attendance record keeping
- Communication to the high school(s)
- Field trip permission procedures
- Breakfast and lunch
- Communication to students and parents (letters, emails, classroom visits, etc.)
- Accessibility for students with special needs
- Determining a plan for students who are staying behind the day of the trip (supervision, activities, etc.)
- How best to prepare students for HSI Day (expectations, behavior, logistics, clues to be successful in high school, how to get the most out of high school, partner with a high school to have student leaders visit your school to lead these discussions, etc.)
- How best to help students process their experience after HSI Day
- Planning to communicate the results of the event to key stakeholders

Please visit our website for HSI Day program implementation suggestions!

Freshman Connection (Summer Between Eighth and Ninth Grade Year)

Originating in Chicago Public Schools (CPS), Freshman Connection (FC) is a summer transition program designed to help incoming freshmen make a successful transition to high school. Most often coordinated by the high school counselor, most FC programs run for 2 to 4 weeks, although schools can easily condense or expand the length of the program to fit the needs of their student populations.

Mornings consist of a class rotation in which students take math and reading enrichment classes and a school counseling class, led by the school counselor, which centers around the attitudes, skills, and knowledge that incoming 9th graders need to thrive during freshman year. Afternoons consist of team building, cultural, and sports activities. Fridays consist of service learning projects and field trips.

FC Program Objectives:

- Promote a successful transition experience for all incoming 9th graders
- Reduce "summer slide" and pre–high school student dropout

- Promote healthy interactions among incoming 9th graders, their teachers, upperclassmen, and peers
- Decrease anxieties among freshman students entering high school
- Reinforce expectations about academic performance, positive behavior, post-secondary readiness, and goal setting

The school counseling class is a hallmark of the FC program and covers key content such as differences between middle school and high school, high school expectations and lingo, school culture, what "freshman on track" means, credits, selecting extracurriculars, talking to teachers, making and keeping friends, self-advocacy, and much more.

Upperclassman FC youth leaders play key roles throughout the program in providing tutoring support during the academic classes, leading interactive team-building activities, chaperoning cultural enrichment and sports activities, and generally building relationships with the incoming freshman class.

 Visit our website for a full FC implementation manual, sample course outlines and class rotation schedules, and full lesson plans.

Freshman Orientation (Summer Between Eighth and Ninth Grade Year)

Most high schools implement some type of freshmen orientation to welcome their 9th graders to the school community. Although orientation is a great opportunity to take care of necessary housekeeping items such as completing forms, paying fees, and getting student schedules, the authors recommend also using it to build relationships between the school counselor and the incoming students. Being highly visible, helpful, and approachable during freshman orientation helps the school counselor begin building rapport and legitimacy in the eyes of incoming students and their families.

As a second-year school counselor, co-author Whitney obtained a grant to bring Focus Training's Ignition program (www.ignitionmentoring.com) to her school. As part of that grant, she collaborated with the freshman grade-level team to implement a 2-day, comprehensive freshman orientation kick-off event for students and families (see Figure 8.5), which continued throughout the school year in the form of peer and near-peer mentoring, team-building activities, core curriculum, family education, and eventually a full, yearlong freshman seminar transition course required for all 9th graders.

Sample Freshman Orientation Activities and Topics

- Staff introductions (including the role of the school counselor and other staff in supporting students)
- Tour of building
- Team building (especially when led by upperclassmen)
- How to unlock a locker
- What to expect in terms of homework/study load
- Behavior expectations
- Attendance expectations
- Important paperwork to complete
- Saving for college

- Bell schedule
- School calendar and important events
- School culture and climate
- Academic support services (i.e., tutoring and credit recovery)
- Extracurricular opportunities

How to Get Them to Show Up

- Feed them
- Send automated phone calls home, email blasts, text blasts
- Provide T-shirts
- Post announcements on a scrolling marquee outside of school
- Post on website
- Organize a neighborhood walk (i.e., either door-to-door visits or a back-to-school parade; see the Bud Billiken Parade at www.budbillikenparade.org/about)
- Visit feeder schools to announce Freshman Orientation dates and drum up excitement
- Make it a fun weekend event (e.g., music, water games, ice cream social, picnic, bus to kick-off football game, or movie on the lawn)
- Have a competition with area rival high schools to see who can get the biggest percentage of their freshmen there (creates school spirit and pride)
- Tell them it's mandatory
- Offer incentives: raffles, prizes, gift cards, uniform-free or dress-down/up days for those who attend

Family Orientation to High School (Summer Between Eighth and Ninth Grade Year)

Don't forget about families during freshman orientation! The transition to high school can also be a confusing and anxiety-inducing experience for parents, guardians, and other caring adults in the lives of rising 9th graders. Ensuring that they feel welcome in the school building and have early, positive interactions with school staff go a long way toward fostering a strong family–school relationship throughout high school. The school counselor is uniquely qualified to educate families about the developmental needs of adolescents and ways that the school and families can work together to support their students throughout freshman year. See Figure 8.6, a sample agenda of a family orientation that co-author Whitney used to facilitate to orient families to a rigorous high school environment. Visit the online appendix for her slide presentations.

Peer-Led Freshman Mentorship Program (Ninth Grade Year)

Intentional transition supports must continue after orientation. It is helpful to view freshman transition as a process rather than a single event. Many schools implement near-peer mentorship programs to continue support throughout freshman year. Introduced in Chapter 3, co-author Whitney collaborated with the freshman grade-level team at her school to develop and implement a peer-led freshman advisory curriculum. Those same student leaders also served as peer mentors, providing an extra layer of

Figure 8.5   Sample Freshman Orientation Schedule

Freshman Orientation Day
Saturday, August 4
12pm – 9pm

"Ropes course set-up pizza party" Friday night after school dismissal.

Time	Activity
10:30am	Set-up/staff arrive
11:50am-12:20pm	Student sign-in & report to homeroom to receive color group and sign trip slips

12:20-2:00pm
 	
Rotations:
12:20 – 12:40pm
12:45 – 1:05pm
1:10 – 1:30pm
1:35 – 1:55pm
	Rotations
	1. Welcome to Raby Lesson (led by youth leaders in homeroom)
	   a. (5 min) Circle up, go around the circle, and do names, elementary school, one reason you're excited about attending ARHS
	   b. (10 min) Connection Chain Activity
	   c. Human Knot (only if there is remaining time)
	2. School tour
	3. Decorate Locker
	4. Visit Lunchroom Fair:
	   a. Paperwork booth (complete needs assessment, emergency contact form, electronics policy, photo consent form, computer usage form, lunch form, school supply list, receive student program, medical/physical form, social security card, birth certificate)
	   b. Fees booth (student fees, buy gym uniform)
	   c. Take ID picture/pick it up
	   d. Parent info booth
	   e. Extracurricular sign-ups booth
	Sign the welcome banner

2:00-2:15pm	Snack Break
2:15-4:45pm	**Ropes Course** • Mentors lead student groups to each station • Supervisors to pick up snacks from the lunchroom for the mentors and bring them to the ropes course at 2pm. Also bring bag for trash.
4:45-5:30pm	Pizza!
5:30-9pm	Ride the Spirit Bus to ARHS Football Game at Hanson Stadium

Ropes Course Set-Up

of students anticipated = 100
Time allotted = 135 min.
2 sets of 6 ropes stations

As students arrive to Raby, they will be assigned a color – either red or black. When it is time for the ropes course, all students of one color will go to that ropes course, then break up into groups of no more than 10 students. One mentor will be assigned to each group of 10. Mentors can choose where they want their group to begin.

Groups will have 20 minutes at each station (including the intro, activity, and debrief). When 5 minutes are remaining, the whistle will sound. When it is time to move stations, the air horn will sound. After completing a station, each group will move to the next station, as indicated on the chart below.

Intro – 20 min. (Kung Fu Intros, Team Cheer)
   Station #1 – 20 min.
   Station #2 – 20 min.
H$_2$0 break – 5 min.
   Station #3 – 20 min.
   Station #4 – 20 min.
H$_2$0 Break – 5 min.
   Station #5 – 20 min.
   Station #6 – 20 min.

Hear the whistle? = 5-minute warning. Begin debriefing if you haven't already.
Hear the air horn? = time to move to the next station!

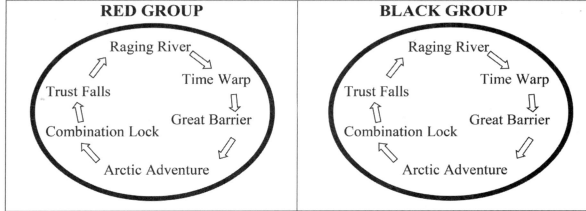

Ropes course activities part of Focus Training's Ignition program

Timekeeper will be responsible for signaling the whistle when 5 minutes are remaining in each rotation and the air horn when it is time to rotate to the next station.

✚ Each group will have a first aid kit with antiseptic wipes, band aids, and tissues.

Figure 8.6   Sample Family Orientation Invitation

You are cordially invited to attend an information session for parents of new students and incoming freshmen at Pine Lake Preparatory's Upper School!

Supporting Your Child's Transition to Upper School

When: **Thursday, April 25th from 6:30 p.m. – 8:15 p.m.**

Where: PLP Upper School

Who: All parents of new PLP Upper School students, including incoming freshmen and transfer-in students

Sessions will be specifically geared toward parents and will be facilitated by PLP Upper School academic partners. Topics to be discussed:

- General **policies/procedures** such as attendance, checking your child in/out, **counseling services** available, service learning and PE X requirements, general strategies for supporting your upper schooler

- Your child's new academic responsibilities; **workload expectations**; assessing your child's **readiness** for upper school and devising a plan to "meet them where they are" in order to "get them where they need to be"; myths and facts about the **importance of grades** freshman year; how to encourage effective **study habits** and **organizational strategies**

- Key differences between 8th and 9th grade

- How parent–school **communication** changes in upper school: maintaining effective communication with your teenager and with the school; walking the line between encouraging your child to handle their problems on their own versus knowing when to step in and assist; **troubleshooting problems** that may arise; **how to get help** and who to go to for help; knowing when an IEP or 504 plan may be helpful

support to freshmen in their "adopted" homerooms, seeking out those who were sitting by themselves in the lunchroom, meeting with those whose grades were slipping, and providing encouragement to those who were having a more challenging transition. When properly trained and supervised, peer mentors can be incredibly helpful in transforming the climate and culture of a school.

Other Freshman Transition Strategies:

- Freshman-only first day of school: allows 9th graders the opportunity to experience their first day apart from upperclassmen
- Upperclassmen decorate the school and line up outside and in the main lobby to welcome 9th graders as they enter the building on their first day (e.g., banners, posters, balloons, high-fives, and clapping)
- Match each freshman with an upperclassman mentor to leave them notes of encouragement, answer questions, tutor, and so on
- Freshman midyear lock-in focused on building relationships, breaking up cliques, strengthening the "team" of the freshman class

Additional Resources:

- **Freshman On Track Toolkit:** https://ncs.uchicago.edu/freshman-on-track-toolkit
- **The Freshman Transition Network:** http://freshmantransition.ning.com
- **Freshman Guide Book:** https://bit.ly/2Ev0jLr
- **On-Track for Success: The Use of Early Warning Indicator and Intervention Systems to Build a Grad Nation:** bit.ly/OnTrackGradNation

Test Prep Events

School counselors are important resource brokers and supports for students as they prepare for standardized tests. In fact, ASCA's (2018c) position statement on "The School Counselor and Test Preparation Programs" states:

School counselors understand the impact of testing and test scores on college admissions, industry credentialing and other areas pertaining to students' postsecondary plans and goals. School counselors assist students in preparing for standardized tests by promoting opportunities designed to increase knowledge and improve test-taking skills. School counselors help students and their families become knowledgeable about test preparation programs and assist them as they decide which programs best meet their needs.

Some schools have implemented full- or half-day events that assist students in preparing to do their best on standardized tests. Secondary school counselor Nicole Cannon developed Boost Day, in which juniors spent the entire day rotating through workshops and activities that prepared them for their statewide standardized test. Topics included the purpose and importance of the exam, test-taking strategies, time usage, overcoming anxiety, interpreting scores, and retest options.

Attendance Programs

Students who attend school regularly do better than students who do not (Bruce, Bridgeland, Fox, & Balfanz, 2011; Easton & Engelhard, 1982). Therefore, school counselors are served well to be involved in schoolwide attendance improvement efforts. Involvement doesn't mean performing clerical and administrative responsibilities. Rather, it is recommended that school counselors support schoolwide attendance and intervention programs, facilitate parent workshops, and intervene with students. School counselors can provide a variety of schoolwide supports to improve attendance. For resources, research, and ideas, visit www.attendanceworks.org.

New Student Welcome Programs

School counselors can support the success of students who transfer from other schools by creating new student welcome programs. Whether the new students transfer at the beginning of a school year or midway through, familiarizing them with the school, teaching them about expectations, and linking them with their peers can help them feel welcome and connected. For counselors working in schools with a high new student enrollment at the beginning of each school year, such as in communities with military connections, international students, or other high-transient populations, planning an activity for new students within the first few days of the school year can help connect students to one another.

One example is hosting a new student ice cream social, while also inviting some current students and teachers, and facilitating a team builder during the event to help students meet each other. For students who may transition midyear, developing structure to help them learn the school expectations, tour the campus, and meet their peers can help facilitate their transition. Figure 8.7 is an example of one school's "New Student Welcome Program" that connected new students to a peer mentor with specific meeting locations and suggested activities such as asking about interests and introducing the new students to other peers. See the online appendix for additional welcome templates, checklists, and resources.

WHITNEY'S STORY

Equity and Access for New Students

Beginning at a new school is hard. From Kindergarten through high school graduation, I attended eight different schools. Whether in 1st grade, 11th, or any in between, each new start brought its own challenges. Some schools had great new student programs, and others not so much, but I remember that going on a tour, finding my classroom, and especially meeting a friendly face went a long way to helping me feel not only welcome but that I *belonged*.

We know from research that students who feel connected to an adult at school are more likely to be successful. Because of their unique skill set and understanding of students' developmental needs, school counselors are ideally suited to coordinate or contribute to new student welcome programs. Many students are new to our school communities at one time or another, and school counselors with effective systems for connecting new students and their families can mean the difference between a rocky start and a smooth start. This is one way that school counselors can work toward ensuring equity and access for *all* students.

Figure 8.7   New Student Welcome Program

New Student Welcome

New Student Name: _____   Grade: _____

Leadership Students Selected:

_____ & _____

- Day 1:
  - ☐ Meet the student at the school counseling office at 16-minute passing.
  - ☐ Introduce the student to three or more new people.
  - ☐ Find out what three things the new student likes to do for fun, and share two things you like to do for fun.
  - ☐ Show the student around the different areas—the quad, the tables, the field, and the cafeteria areas.
  - ☐ Plan where to meet the student during lunch that day and help them get an ID card.

- Day 2
  - ☐ Meet the student during 16-minute passing.
  - ☐ Introduce the student to three or more new people.
  - ☐ Find out what the new student's favorite food is, and share what your favorite food is.
  - ☐ Tell the student about one fun place to go in Fallbrook.
  - ☐ Plan where to meet the student during 16-minute passing or lunch the next day.

- Day 3
  - ☐ Meet the student during 16-minute passing or lunch.
  - ☐ Re-introduce the student to some of the people they have already met.
  - ☐ Ask the student about some things they like about their new school.
  - ☐ Ask the student who their teachers are and tell them about your favorite teachers.
  - ☐ Tell the student you enjoyed meeting them and decide if you want to meet with them again in the future.

COLLEGE/CAREER DOMAIN PROGRAMS AND ACTIVITIES

School counselors recognize that each student, regardless of background, possesses unique interests, abilities, and goals, which will lead to future opportunities. Collaborating with students, families, educational staff, and the community, the school counselor works to ensure all students select a postsecondary path to productive citizenry (e.g., military, career, technical certificate or 2-/4-year degree program) appropriate for the student, (ASCA, 2017b, p. 1).

College and career development activities correlate to students' understanding the connection between school and the world of work. As students gain knowledge and skills in this area, they can plan for and make a successful transition to postsecondary education and/or the workplace and experience self-fulfillment across the life span. At the Tier 1 level, this should manifest through the development of a schoolwide college- and career-going culture, which can include activities such as college tours, career fairs, College Signing Day, College Kick-Off, summer melt supports, scholarship and FAFSA initiatives, concrete postsecondary plans, Senior Seminar, and much more.

Research on the Transition From High School to Postsecondary

School counselors are critical levers in the high school to postsecondary transition. Seniors who meet with a school counselor about their future plans are 6.8 times more likely to complete a FAFSA, 3.2 times more likely to attend college, and two times more likely to attend a bachelor's degree program (Velez, 2017). School counselors are so impactful that an additional high school counselor in a school has been shown to cause an increase in the 4-year college enrollment rates by a staggering 10 percentage points (Hurwitz & Howell, 2013). "Poised to lead, school counselors can and should play an essential role in ensuring that our nation's secondary schools prepare all students—especially those most often underserved—for a productive future" (Education Trust, 2011).

Additionally, students who attend high schools with strong college-going cultures "where a school leader has established college attainment as a clear and shared goal for students, where teachers are well versed on the most important factors for college admission and success, and where teachers and counselors are involved in supporting students in completing their college applications" are significantly more likely to apply to and enroll in a four-year college. (Roderick, Nagaoka, Coca, & Moeller, 2008)

Indeed, school counselors are key leaders in helping students and families to explore, decide on, plan for, and matriculate to their postsecondary pathway of choice.

School counselors serve as leaders by coordinating a comprehensive, evidence-based, Tier 1 system of supports to ensure that all seniors gain the attitudes, knowledge, and skills they need for a successful transition to whatever comes next in life. What follows are specific examples of schoolwide programs and activities that school counselors can implement to support the post-graduation transition:

- College Tours
- Scholarship/Financial Aid Events
- College Signing/Decision Day
- Summer Melt Strategies
- College Persistence Strategies

School counselors are "change agents for equity" (Mason, Ockerman, & Chen-Hayes, 2013; Ockerman et al., 2013). They are uniquely trained and perfectly positioned to *use data to identify inequities*; put in place supports that *close opportunity, achievement, and attainment gaps* among students of different groups; *empower* students and families from historically oppressed populations; and *advocate for the elimination of systemic barriers* that prevent equitable access to a high-quality education. School counselors are the drivers of **a culturally responsive school climate**, serving their school communities as change agents. *An integral part of this is establishing a solid foundation in Tier 1.* What types of schoolwide programs and activities might you put in place to promote equity in your building across the three domains? What support can you enlist from stakeholders? How might you be a change agent for equity?

College Tours

Campus visits are important to the college decision-making process as they help prospective students to determine "fit," or whether an institution meets the student's social, cultural, academic, and financial needs. Fit can also be described as a feeling of belonging on campus that encompasses factors such as size, location, majors, weather, support services, cultural/social factors, distance from home, and other similar factors. Students are more likely to complete college when it is a good fit (Bowen, Chingos, & McPherson, 2009). Visiting a class, checking out the dorms, and seeing the cafeteria all help students determine whether they can picture themselves on campus and whether the institution will meet their needs. Campus visits can also benefit students by allowing them an opportunity to demonstrate interest in the institution—a factor that has been shown to give students an edge in the admission process (Dearden, Li, Meyerhoefer, & Yang, 2017).

School counselors ensure equity in the college exploration process by providing opportunities for *all* students to visit college campuses. They reject the notion that only certain students are deserving of college visits, such as those who meet test score benchmarks or those with certain grade point averages, and advocate for the removal of such policies.

School counselors serve as leaders by organizing college and other postsecondary site visits—both daytime and overnight trips—as well as help students prep for the trip through core curriculum classroom lessons. School counselors also advocate for funding to offset the costs for college trips—especially for students from underrepresented and impoverished populations. When in-person college visits are not an option, school counselors help students access campuses through virtual tours (e.g., www.collegeweeklive.com, www.campustours.com, and www.ecampustours.com), Skype interviews with faculty and students, videos, and print materials to provide all students with opportunities to assess institutions for fit.

Resources

- **College Board's Campus Visit Guide:** https://bigfuture.collegeboard.org/find-colleges/campus-visit-guide
- **Collegewise's College Visit Guide:** https://collegewise.com/docs/CollegewiseCollegeVisitGuide.pdf

Scholarship/Financial Aid Programs and Activities

Contributor: Michele Howard, Scholarship Manager, Chicago Public Schools

Financial aid is a critical component in the college application process. School counselors serve as equity champions by learning about the types of scholarships and financial aid available for a variety of postsecondary pathways and funneling that information to all students and families. To ensure equity and access, and to help eligible and deserving students succeed, scholarships must be part of the school counselor's Tier 1 strategy within the college/career domain, not only through core curriculum but also schoolwide programs and activities.

One way that school counselors ensure equity and access is by providing *all* students with information about scholarships and financial aid, regardless of each student's postsecondary intentions. Financial aid is not just available for traditional 2- and 4-year colleges; students can access financial assistance for trades, pre-apprenticeships, public service, or even gap year programs. For example, students can access individual training accounts that will pay up to $8,000 of tuition at an approved Workforce Innovation and Opportunity Act (WIOA) training vendor. School counselors can ensure that this information is included in Tier 1 activities such as scholarship fairs and drives.

Another way that school counselors serve as equity champions is by advocating for the establishment of a districtwide, franchised scholarship access program. This ensures that students and families have access to the same scholarship information across school sites within a district. A solid scholarship access program is comprised of three components, of which school counselors are integral:

1) An *advocate* who builds relationships with local, regional, and national scholarship providers to compile the information for students and families—this is ideally a district or regional scholarship manager rather than a school-level coordinator as it helps ensure equity and access across school sites.

2) A *tool/system* to organize the scholarship information (e.g., Blackbaud or scholarshipplus.com)—as the saying goes, "You have to spend money to make money." There must be an investment in a tool or system to ensure legitimate scholarship information is organized in one place. There are a number of education organizations that offer scholarship management platforms. As the world of college access is expanding, a centralized, searchable hub on which to post a wide variety of scholarship opportunities helps ensure access to the widest audience.

3) *School-level scholarship coordination*, that is "boots on the ground," accomplishes the following:
   - Drive student usage of the tool/system that houses scholarship information and query usage to determine which students might need Tier 2 supports for scholarship applications.
   - Disseminate biweekly or monthly reminders of scholarship, financial aid, and enrichment program deadlines. This is essential to keeping students and families engaged around the importance of scholarship acquisition. Many families, especially those from low-income and undocumented populations, do not realize the costs associated with college until they are reviewing award letters senior year. Sharing scholarship alerts directly

with students and families will help encourage early engagement and application completion.

- Drive scholarship reporting. Knowing the amount that students are offered and awarded in scholarships can easily provide school counselors with strategic scholarship goals. Compiling this information shares a number of data points that are helpful for schools to establish strategies for each graduating class (i.e., the number of scholarship applications completed by each student, the amount of scholarships offered versus awarded to each student, merit-based aid that is specific to a college/university versus scholarships that can be applied at any university, etc.).

FAFSA Completion

The Free Application for Federal Student Aid (FAFSA) can be a game changer regarding financing postsecondary options. It makes sense that students who complete the FAFSA are more likely to enroll in college (Reeves & Guyot, 2018). According to the National College Access Network (NCAN), "90% of high school seniors who complete the FAFSA proceed directly to college, versus only 55% who don't complete the FAFSA" (U.S. Department of Education, 2002). According to another study, "Students who reported completing a FAFSA by May and had been accepted into a four-year college were more than 50 percent more likely to enroll than students who had not completed a FAFSA," even when controlling for factors such as differences in students' qualifications, family background and neighborhood characteristics, and support from teachers, counselors, and parents (Roderick et al., 2008). Particularly for students from impoverished backgrounds, the FAFSA can be a game changer with regards to postsecondary options. "The very fear about cost and debt stops millions of students from even pursuing and finishing the education they need" (Duncan, 2015).

Indeed, if school counselors are concerned about the college enrollment rates of their populations, FAFSA completion is a primary strategy for improving that rate. Students and families, particularly those who are the first in their family to go to college, need direct guidance on FAFSA including early awareness of the process (i.e., freshman year or earlier), financial aid opportunities, requirements, reminders, and Tier 2/3 support as needed (queried by the school counselor through a review of the FAFSA completion data from the federal government). Although schools had to internally track completions in the past, the federal government now provides this data to schools for ease of tracking (for more information, please visit http://bit.ly/FAFSAdatainfo).What follows are a few examples of how school counselors can be leaders and equity champions by collaborating with key stakeholders to implement Tier 1 schoolwide programs and activities that promote FAFSA completion.

In 2015, First Lady Michelle Obama launched the FAFSA Completion Challenge as part of her #ReachHigher campaign to encourage more high school seniors to complete the FAFSA. Schools can use these videos or create their own to raise awareness about FAFSA within their schools. See a few sample videos:

- **Mock episode of hit TV show *Scandal* (King College Prep, Illinois, the national winner of the contest):** http://bit.ly/2BKwwVH
- **"Blank Space" parody (Steinmetz College Prep, Illinois; song starts at 0:52):** http://bit.ly/2MBGCdy

- **"All About That Aid" parody (North Iredell High School, North Carolina):** http://bit.ly/2wqaj6B
- **"Latch" parody:** http://bit.ly/2MRF4Mg
- **"My FAFSA Story" (Clemente Community Academy, Illinois):** http://bit.ly/2PbderP
- **"Thrift Shop" parody (University of Washington):** http://bit.ly/2MvP7qK
- **FAFSA PSA (Shasta County Office of Education):** http://bit.ly/2PFUf9S

Getting a Head Start: Junior Postsecondary Prep Day

School counselor Valerie Franklin has implemented a structured day during which juniors gain a head start on senior year postsecondary expectations (see Figure 8.8). Students are introduced to their Individual Learning Plan (ILP) tasks in Naviance for the upcoming year, complete their FSA ID, learn about the common application, hear tips on writing a strong college essay from a real college admissions representative, and dive into the types of schools they are eligible to apply to based on their current selectivity level. The structured day results in a positive impact on student beliefs and attitudes about college and increases their skills in completing college application-related tasks before senior year even begins!

Figure 8.8 Rotation Schedule for Junior Postsecondary Prep Day

	5th Period	6th Period	7th Period	8th Period
Group A	Room 202/204—Common Application (40) Groups A & B	Library—FSA ID Group A	Room 202/204—Essay Writing (40) Groups A & B	Room 205—Naviance Group A
Group B	Room 202/204—Common Application (40) Groups A & B	Room 205—Naviance Group B	Room 202/204—Essay Writing (40) Groups A & B	Library—FSA ID Group B
Group C	Room 205—Naviance Group C	Room 202/204—Common Application (40) Groups C & D	Library—FSA ID Group C	Room 202/204—Essay Writing (40) Groups C & D
Group D	Library—FSA ID Group D	Room 202/204—Common Application (40) Groups C & D	Room 205—Naviance Group D	Room 202/204—Essay Writing(40) Groups C & D

Incentive Programs

Some schools implement incentive programs to encourage students to complete the FAFSA:

• Free prom tickets • Extra tickets for graduation • First semester of books paid	• Detention erasure • Dress down/up days • Gift cards	• Pizza party • College housing bill payment • Plane or train ticket to campus

Districts, cities, or even states such as California have even created a Race to Submit initiative or event, fostering friendly competition among the local high schools (https://www.csac.ca.gov/race-submit).

Getting the Word Out About Scholarships and Financial Aid

Disseminating information can be challenging, but a multifaceted approach is key. Establishing a series of direct engagement activities in which information can be shared helps ensure that families have ample opportunity to participate (i.e., senior/family scholarship information night, FAFSA completion workshops, scholarship and essay writing workshops, and school-level presentations during which scholarship providers are invited to share with students and families directly). These events are ideally coordinated by school counselors and supported by school staff, postsecondary partners, and community volunteers.

Other methods for disseminating scholarship/financial aid information in a Tier 1 manner include the following:

- Standards-based, developmentally appropriate lessons on financial aid for students
- Workshops for parents and families
- Newsletter (either printed and disseminated or emailed directly to the student)
- Social media, such as a Twitter or Instagram account just for scholarships or financial aid information (i.e., @CPSScholarships)
- Direct text messages (i.e., UPNEXT)
- Poster/print material campaign
- Establishing an email account specifically for scholarship information (i.e., "CollegeScholarships@abcschooldistrict.edu")

Additional resources to help school counselors implement a comprehensive scholarship strategy include the following:

- **U.S. Department of Education Financial Aid Toolkit** (https://financialaid toolkit.ed.gov/tk): Designed with school counselors in mind, this tool kit includes all the basics about FAFSA, types of aid and eligibility, loan repayment, and more!

- **On-Demand Webinars** https://mappingyourfuture.org/services/web inararchive.cfm
- **Information on Scholarship Scams** bit.ly/2w4TjCG
- **RaiseMe (www.raise.me):** This is an opportunity for students to earn micro-scholarships from colleges for their achievements as early as 9th grade.

Chicago Public Schools (CPS) has a unique approach to ensuring students have access to funds that can assist with college costs. Boasting of over $1.3 billion in scholarship offers to students in the class of 2017, CPS has created a formula that works for their population. The full-time district scholarship manager works directly with strategic scholarship providers, which are organizations, companies, institutions, foundations, and individuals who target CPS students for scholarship opportunities. All of the scholarship information is then compiled and housed in a web-based scholarship application, completion, and management tool called Blackbaud (formerly Academic Works). Moving to an electronic system allowed for a targeted approach to connect eligible students to scholarships, gauge student application progress, and monitor access to scholarship providers.

School counselors are an integral component of ensuring students are accessing the Blackbaud system to review and apply to eligible opportunities throughout the school year. They are also key collaborators when providing feedback on system usage, strategies for completion, and support. For example, school counselors shared that the electronic tool was more efficient; however, it was difficult to navigate, and students needed access to the system as soon as the school year began. Overall, this feedback pushed the district to make the system available in early September as well as establish the Scholarship Alert Workbook, which mirrors the content in the Blackbaud system but allows for easier navigation within a Google workbook.

College Signing/Decision Day

Similar to National Signing Day for NCAA athletes, May 1 of each year is the nationally accepted standard day by which many seniors tell colleges that they intend to enroll. Although it does not necessarily apply to everyone (i.e., students applying to schools with rolling admission and students selecting full-time employment, military, apprenticeships, or gap year programs), College Signing Day is a great opportunity for school counselors to build the college-going culture in their building and drum up excitement for what comes after high school. Some schools have even chosen to expand College Signing Day into Postsecondary Signing Day to be more inclusive of students matriculating to other types of postsecondary pathways. Visit the tool kits that follow for ideas for developing a College Signing Day event at your school:

- **Michelle Obama's Better Make Room Campaign College Signing Day Toolkit:** https://www.bettermakeroom.org/collegesigningday/
- **Tennessee's College Signing Day Toolkit:** bit.ly/TNCollegeSigningDay
- **Michigan's College Decision Day Resource Manual:** bit.ly/MichiganDecision Day
- **Florida's College Decision Day Resources:** http://floridacollegeaccess.org/ initiatives/florida-college-decision-day/

Massac County's College Signing Day Festivities

Contributed by School Counselor Leslie Goines

In Massac County, College Signing Day is an event for celebrating seniors' commitments to their postsecondary plans (see Figure 8.9). Our school district uses the word "college" as an umbrella term that refers to one of the following postsecondary pathways: college/university, community college, vocational/technical program, armed forces, or work-training program. For the past several years, Massac County High School has had 98% to 100% of our graduating classes commit to one of these postsecondary pathways and be recognized at College Signing Day. Taking place during the school day in May of every year, the community is invited to attend, and there is *always* media coverage. Colleges and universities are even invited to take part in this special event, which in turn greatly contributes to our college- and career-going culture.

Figure 8.9   Massac County College Signing Day

Summer Melt Strategies

Summer melt is "when seemingly college-intending students fail to enroll at all in the fall after high school graduation" (Castleman, Page, & Snowden, 2013, p. 6) and often disproportionately affects low-income and first-generation students. Summer melt happens even after students apply to and are accepted to college, submit the FAFSA, and complete other college enrollment steps (Castleman & Page, 2014).

School counselors can play critical roles in freezing summer melt through the following strategies:

- Ensuring they know which students are college intending and helping them do the following:
    o Make sense of and pay the housing deposit and first tuition bill
    o Identify and budget for expenses like transportation to campus and additional college incidentals like health insurance and course textbooks
    o Complete loan paperwork and master promissory notes
    o Secure additional funds to cover gaps between the cost of attendance and the financial aid package received
    o Access, digest, and respond to considerable correspondence from the institution over the summer
    o Register for courses, attend orientation, take placement tests, enroll in possible summer enrichment course(s), and complete housing forms
    o Get connected to support services at the institution before graduation

- Creating partnerships between the school and feeder institutions
- Providing FAFSA and Student Aid Report workshops for all students and their families in their primary language
- Advocating for students to have access to summer transition support from a high school counselor over the summer to aid in students' transitions to college and other postsecondary pathways (whether at their own high school or at "pop-up centers" within the district)
- Advocating for access to National Student Clearinghouse data (www .studentclearinghouse.org) so that school counselors are able to track the effectiveness of their activities in supporting students in matriculating to and persisting in college
- Participating in ongoing professional development to stay up to date about the FAFSA/financial aid award process, enrollment procedures, and other college advising components

School counselors can also reduce summer melt by monitoring relevant data, such as the following:

- Number who apply to at least three institutions (safety, match, and reach)
- Number who have been accepted to at least one college
- Number with evidence of military enlistment
- Number who complete a personal statement
- Number of seniors who complete an expected family contribution (EFC) calculator
- Number of juniors who complete an EFC calculator
- Number of seniors who complete a net price calculator (for any school)
- Number who apply to at least three scholarships
- Number who submit the FAFSA
- Number who complete the FAFSA
- Number who receive a Student Aid Report
- Number who receive a financial aid award letter
- Number who meet with a school counselor to review the Student Aid Report

- Number who meet with a school counselor to review the financial aid award letter
- Number who complete a senior exit survey
- Number of summer student/parent contacts for graduated seniors
- Number of credit recovery plans developed for "summer seniors"
- Number of final transcripts sent for all graduated seniors attending college
- Number of job placements confirmed for students joining workforce
- Number of Individualized Education Plan (IEP) transition plans completed for graduating diverse learners
- Number of postsecondary plan completions for graduating seniors without a plan

Match Madness Event for Seniors

Contributed by School Counselor Suzie Kwan

Based on a similar event at Washington High School in Chicago, the school counselors at Von Steuben Metropolitan Science Center facilitate a Match Madness event each March to support seniors in completing crucial admissions, financial aid, and postsecondary planning steps (see Figure 8.10). Established to encourage seniors to match up and matriculate to institutions for which they are academic matches (i.e., their academic profiles fall within the middle 50% of freshmen who enroll in a particular institution), these small group, faculty-led, school counselor–coordinated/supervised meetings provide time for *every* senior to talk through their decision-making process and air concerns, worries, and excitement about their postsecondary plans. The event also greatly contributes to the college and career-going culture of the school and serves to educate and engage school staff in the postsecondary planning process (staff members are trained by the school counselors to lead the conversations). This event doesn't replace student time with the school counselors but complements it by wrapping another layer of adult and peer support around students, which has been shown to have a huge positive impact on increasing college enrollment, persistence, and degree attainment rates. Learn more about the Match Madness event by visiting the online appendix (includes an overview, discussion protocol, and planning document).

Figure 8.10 Match Madness Theme

Find additional tips for addressing and preventing summer melt here:

- ASCA Schoolcounselor. **"Prevent Summer Melt"**: https://www.schoolcounselor .org/magazine/blogs/november-december-2014/prevent-summer-melt
- **"Prevent Summer Melt"**: www.schoolcounselor.org/asca/media/asca/ ASCAU/College-Admissions-Specialist/SummerMelt.pdf
- **Summer Melt Handbook: A Guide to Investigating and Responding to Summer Melt** (Harvard University Center for Education Policy Research): http://sdp.cepr .harvard.edu/files/cepr-sdp/files/sdp-summer-melt-handbook.pdf
- Owen, L., & Winter, L. (2016). **Summer: A critical point on the path to college.** *LINK for Counselors 1*(2), 16–20.
- Castleman, B., Owen, L., & Page, L. (2016). **Stay late or start early? Experimental evidence on the benefits of college matriculation support from high schools versus colleges.** *Economics of Education Review, Special Edition.* http://dx.doi:10.1016/j.econedurev.2016.03.011
- Arnold, K., Fleming, S., DeAnda, M., Castleman, B., & LynkWartman, K. (2009, Fall). **The summer flood: The invisible gap among low-income students.** *Thought and Action*, pp. 23–34.
- Castleman, B. L., & Page, L. C. (2014). **A trickle or a torrent? Understanding the extent of summer "melt" among college-intending high school graduates.** *Social Science Quarterly, 95*(1), 202–220. http://dx.doi.org/10.1111/ssqu.12032
- Castleman, B. L., Page, L. C., & Schooley, K. (2014). **The forgotten summer: Mitigating summer attrition among college-intending, low-income high school graduates.** *Journal of Policy Analysis and Management, 33*(2), 320–344. http://dx.doi.org/10.1002/pam.21743

College Persistence Strategies

Thank you to Chicago Public Schools' Office of College and Career Success for contributing much of the following content through their College Persistence Toolkit.

College persistence is defined as the percentage of high school graduates who enrolled in a 2- or 4-year postsecondary education program the fall after high school graduation who remain enrolled 1 year later.

Postsecondary institutions and high schools must work in partnership to support students' persistence and degree attainment as outlined in the formula in Figure 8.11:

Figure 8.11 Persistence Equation Graphic

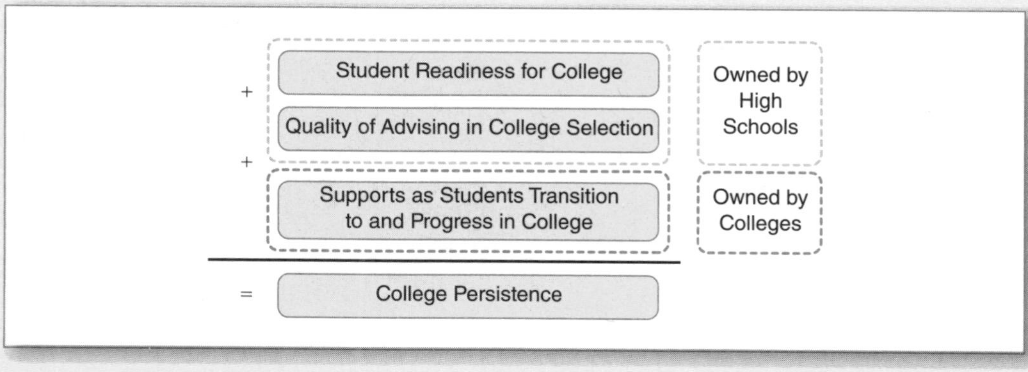

Source: **Chicago Public Schools, Office of College Career Success.**

School counselors play a critical role in leading college persistence efforts, coordinating the implementation of evidence-based strategies that have been shown to impact college persistence, including the following:

1) Establishing and coordinating a postsecondary leadership team (PLT), a group of school-based staff that drives postsecondary success by implementing student-centered, data-informed systems of support (more on this in Chapter 13)

2) Evaluating the current state and recent trends of college enrollment, persistence, degree attainment, and other key postsecondary metrics and available resources

3) Creating a college-going culture:

   a) Entire staff championing college on a daily basis (e.g., wearing college "bling" and "ask me how I did it" buttons or listing their college and degree by classroom doors)

   b) Announcements, bulletin boards, and so on that celebrate students' acceptances to college and scholarships awarded

   c) Alumni regularly returning to high school for panels, mentorship programs, events, College Decision Day, and so on

   d) College fairs and tours

   e) Hosting college application months, weeks, or days and coordinating a College Decision Day

   f) College admission reps visiting the school as much as possible to answer questions and provide face-to-face time with students and families

4) Helping students and families consider the best college options, taking into consideration match, fit, financial affordability, and graduation rates for similar populations at those institutions

5) Systematizing processes and procedures for ensuring *all* graduating seniors apply to match, reach, and safety schools as well as the FAFSA, scholarships, and other forms of financial aid

   a) Delivering core curriculum lessons to students and families, both in person and distance, such as webinars, slide presentations, and print materials

   b) Distributing (and frequently redistributing) lists of relevant scholarships to students and families at the end of junior year and beginning of senior year

   c) Sending frequent reminders to students before major deadlines for college applications, FAFSA, state aid, institutional aid for major feeder schools, and scholarships (i.e., 1 month before, 1 week before, and 1 day before)

   d) Balancing passive engagement (i.e., email, Twitter, and Facebook) with proactive follow-up (phone calls, texts, and face-to-face conversations, especially with underrepresented populations)

   e) Organizing events for alumni to return to their high school to complete key steps with current seniors (i.e., FAFSA party over Labor Day or October fall break)

(Continued)

(Continued)

    f) Leveraging external college access partners in your area

    g) Offering school-based systems such as a senior seminar or AVID program

6) Preparing students to thrive in college via the following:

    a) The delivery of a comprehensive school counseling core curriculum that includes the academic, social/emotional, and career-related aspects of matriculating to college

    b) Encouraging *all* students to take the most rigorous courses available to them in high school

    c) Supporting school staff in teaching and reinforcing key noncognitive skills that impact the likelihood of persistence, such as grit, growth mindset, perseverance, delayed gratification, tenacity, interpersonal skills, and so on

7) Supporting recent graduates who matriculate to college through summer transition counseling and other summer melt initiatives

    a) Distributing a senior exit questionnaire to obtain feedback from students about the senior year supports and gathering summer contact information for exiting students (access a sample senior exit questionnaire on our website).

Additional College/Career Resources:

- Busting Myths About What Matters for High School and College Success: https://toandthrough.uchicago.edu/mythbusters
- Teaching Adolescents to Become Learners, University of Chicago Consortium on Chicago School Research (2012): bit.ly/2Mi6o6o
- MDRC, Make Me a Match—2012: bit.ly/2Mb0F2K

SOCIAL/EMOTIONAL DOMAIN PROGRAMS AND ACTIVITIES

Social/emotional domain programs and activities improve school culture and climate and support academic success (Greenberg et al., 2003). At the secondary level, Tier 1 schoolwide social/emotional programs and activities may include assemblies, participation in national awareness/pride celebrations and campaigns, mentorship, conflict resolution, peer mediation, and other restorative practices. Although the school counselor may not lead or oversee all of these events, deciding what role the school counselor will have is important.

Research on School Culture and Climate

Although school culture and climate are often used interchangeably, they are unique:

School *climate* refers to the school's effects on students, including teaching practices; diversity; and the relationships among administrators, teachers, parents, and students. School *culture* refers to the way teachers and other staff members work together and the set of beliefs, values, and assumptions they share. (ASCD, 2019)

School culture and climate go hand in hand and can either promote or inhibit student learning. Studies show that a positive school climate is recognized as an important target for school reform and for improving behavioral, academic, and mental health outcomes for students, as schools with positive climates tend to have reduced exposure to risk factors for students, fewer student absences, and higher student academic motivation and engagement, leading to improvements in academic achievement across grade levels. When students feel socially, emotionally, and physically safe, the results include reduced bullying, increased student engagement, and enhanced student outcomes (Wilson, 2004; Durlak et al., 2011). In fact, "the extent to which students feel attached to at least one caring and responsible adult at school . . . is a powerful predictor of adolescent health and academic outcomes, violence prevention and is a protective factor against risky sexual, violence, and drug-use behaviors" (Pickeral, Evans, Hughes, & Hutchison, 2009).

A positive school climate also has benefits for teachers and education support professionals. When educators feel supported by their administration, they report higher levels of commitment and more collegiality (O'Brennan & Bradshaw, 2013). For example, see Figure 8.12, a real email from a principal to her school staff sent Sunday night so her staff would receive it on Monday morning. What does this email communicate about the culture of the school? How does such an email impact the staff culture and climate? How would you feel if this was one of the first emails you read on a Monday morning?

Figure 8.12   Email From Principal That Captures Culture and Climate for Staff

From: Principal
Date: September 9, 2018 at 8:45:08 PM PDT
To: School staff

SPARK CREATIVITY

Every one of us is a creative being, and we all have the capacity to create. Many of us buy into the false belief that we don't have a creative bone in our bodies. Let's disagree with that belief. Maybe you don't feel like you can dance, paint, draw, sing, or sculpt, but that doesn't mean you aren't creative. Every one of us creates things all the time. You create friends, ideas, and ways to give back to your community. You create a life for yourself and possibly even help those around you do the very same thing. You solve problems and create solutions that work—and when they don't, you create a new solution. It's time to SPARK CREATIVITY. What do you do to inspire your creative process? Do you put on some vibey music and burn incense or a candle? When it comes to creating your life and being clear what matters most to you, do you sit down and talk it through with trusted friends or family members? Or, do you create a vision board or set goals? What would you like to be more creative in? Remember, no one is getting a grade for this, so pick what excites you the most. This week is all about maximizing the opportunities to maximize our creativity, and sometimes all we need is a spark. Sparking creativity matters. #youmatter

Email was adapted and sent by a principal from a Facebook post (Every Monday Matters), retrieved September 3, 2018, from https://www.facebook.com/pg/EveryMondayMatters/posts/?ref=page_internal.

Although often driven by the administrators, school culture and climate are responsibilities of all stakeholders in a school community, especially school counselors. Further, school counselors have an ethical responsibility to contribute to the development of a positive school culture and climate. For example, Standard B.2, Responsibilities to the School, states:

> School counselors: (a) Develop and maintain professional relationships and systems of communication with faculty, staff and administrators to support students. . . . (d) Provide leadership to create systemic change to enhance the school. . . . (j) Strive to use translators who have been vetted or reviewed and bilingual/multilingual school counseling program materials representing languages used by families in the school community. . . . (m) Promote cultural competence to help create a safer, more inclusive school environment. (ASCA, 2014)

This poses unique leadership opportunities for school counselors. Utilizing the latest research, school counselors can develop a holistic understanding of the impact of school culture and climate on individual experiences, equitable social and academic opportunities for all students, risk prevention and health promotion, academic achievement, teacher retention, and overall school improvement. School counselors can then collaborate with key stakeholders to design schoolwide programs and activities that address areas of need in an effort to improve school culture and climate.

Universal Behavior Expectations, PBIS, and Incentive Programs

One of the most foundational ways to support a healthy culture and climate is through establishing universal behavior expectations for all students—a Tier 1 schoolwide program. A well-researched and widely adopted strategy to support clarity of school rules for all students, staff, and families, universal behavior expectations (such as positive Behavioral Intervention, and Supports [PBIS]) are a proactive and systemwide approach for an entire school or district. The primary goal is to teach behavioral expectations in the same manner that any core curriculum subject would be taught. Behavioral expectations are then reinforced by all members of the school staff.

Typically, a team of approximately 10 representative members of the school (administrators, school counselors, teachers, and staff) attend 2 to 3 days of professional development provided by skilled trainers. The school team (often the MTSS team) develops three to five behavioral expectations that are positively stated and easy to remember. A matrix is then built to show what each of the expectations looks like, sounds like, and feels like in all areas, including non-classroom spaces. Key in the process is focusing on preferred behaviors rather than telling students what not to do. These expectations may include setting voice level norms for different physical areas of the school, clean and organized classrooms, use of bulletin boards and wall space, use of encouraging quotes and posters, and others. The MTSS team then determines how the universal behavioral expectations will be taught in classroom and non-classroom settings with guided opportunities for both the students and adults to practice. Plans to review and reteach expected behavior throughout the year are also included, along with modifying the office discipline referral form and data collection process.

As universal behavior expectations are being rolled out on campus, the school counselor should align the core curriculum classroom lessons and refer to the schoolwide behavior expectations often during lessons. It is recommended that school counselors participate on the MTSS team or other teams that make decisions about universal behavior expectations, PBIS, or other social/emotional-related curriculum not only to provide input but also to ensure that the core curriculum is strongly aligned.

Another element of PBIS is the incentive program. Although most agree that intrinsic motivation is more meaningful than incentives, many schools incorporate some level of extrinsic reward system as one piece of a comprehensive universal behavior expectation program. Some prefer a combination of social praise and tangible incentives either infrequently, randomly, or at decreased frequency over time as positive behavior becomes the norm, thus raising the bar. Reinforcing a behavior increases the likelihood that the behavior will occur again and become a habit. School counselors who know their student population can select rewards that will be meaningful and age-appropriate. If unsure, school counselors can go straight to the source by asking the students! Forming a focus group, creating a survey, or meeting with student leaders allows students to weigh in with their suggestions on what would be most valuable to them. Ideas include the following:

- Spirit dollars: Students earn "dollars" that they can redeem at the school store for spirit wear, school supplies, and so on.
- Homeroom, class, or grade-level competition: Classes/grade levels earn points that are calculated once per month. The class/grade with the highest number of points gets to win some class/grade level reward, such as a dress down/up day, privilege of decorating a hallway to their liking, choosing the music that plays over the loudspeaker during class changes, and so on.
- Attendance incentives: Students can earn out-of-uniform days for reaching attendance benchmarks, donuts or treats, raffle tickets, and so on.

Restorative Practices

Restorative practices empower students to repair harm over assigning punishment. They help hold students (and adults, for that matter) personally accountable for wrongdoing, encouraging them not only to repair the relationship but take an active role in their own justice. Although most restorative practice interventions fall into Tiers 2 and 3, school counselors are integral in supporting Tier 1 by participating in (or perhaps serving in a leadership role in) staff development and family education as well as promoting proactive, systemic schoolwide norms, an inclusive culture, and a positive climate. Talking circles, use of affective "I" statements, empathy, and understanding are common Tier 1 approaches within restorative practices. Talking circles in particular are incredibly useful schoolwide-processing and community-building activities. When used by all staff on a consistent basis, these Tier 1 approaches can transform the culture and climate of the school community.

Learn more:

- https://blog.cps.edu/wp-content/uploads/2017/08/CPS_RP_Booklet.pdf
- http://schottfoundation.org/restorative-practices
- http://www.ascd.org/research-a-topic/school-culture-and-climate-resources.aspx
- http://teachingwithteachers.com/restorative-practice/
- https://www.edutopia.org/blog/restorative-justice-resources-matt-davis

NATIONAL AWARENESS/PRIDE CELEBRATIONS AND CAMPAIGNS

Awareness/pride celebrations and campaigns are specific days, weeks, or months, usually set by a major organization or the government, to commemorate an important public health, education, or ethical cause at a greater level (e.g., Mental Health Awareness Week, Mix It Up Day, Ally Week, Black History Month, National School Counseling Week, Screen Free Week, or Indigenous Peoples' Day). What's particularly useful about nationwide awareness/pride efforts is that they typically include free tool kits and downloadable resources containing curriculum for educators, flyers and informational sheets, videos, and ideas for student-led activities. They also lend themselves to a sense of increased positivity and community due to the element of fun and novel interest they add to the school year.

Why Awareness/Pride Celebrations and Campaigns?

- Evoke school spirit
- Build a sense of community
- Draw attention to initiatives and movements
- Generate student action
- Facilitate mastery of the ASCA Mindsets and Behaviors

- Inspire dialogue
- Promote inclusion and unity
- Nurture a deeper understanding
- Foster civic engagement
- Encourage commitment to positive life choices (e.g., living a drug-free lifestyle)

School counselors play an important role in the coordination and implementation of awareness/pride celebrations and events as Tier 1 schoolwide programs and activities. For example, October is National Bullying Prevention Month, so school counselors may consider making bullying/cyberbullying the focus of their lessons that month. Perhaps the first day is kicked off through a Chalk the Walk, in which the Art Club or student volunteers transform the walkways into the school with "No Bullying" graffiti. The school counselor can make weekly announcements during the month that discuss current statistics on bullying or quote celebrities' stories about their personal bullying experiences. The school counselor also can call on all staff and students to participate in Stand Up to Bullying Day by dressing in school colors to show their commitment to having a bully-free climate in school. Additionally, just as teachers may infuse awareness campaigns into their general curriculum (e.g., the Hour of Code for math), school counselors can do the same with their core curriculum classroom lessons for that month.

Selecting Awareness/Pride Celebrations and Campaigns

There are hundreds of awareness campaigns available that align with school counseling programs—how does a school counselor choose? To keep from feeling overwhelmed, start from a place of intentionality and prioritize what is most important to your student population and school community based on your school's data, vision and mission, and goals. Follow these recommendations to conduct a successful schoolwide campaign:

1) Conduct a needs/satisfaction survey of weeklong events or campaigns you've done in the past. Ask staff for their feedback to decide whether an existing program just needs to be enhanced or what is being done already is satisfactory. Don't take for granted that staff know what each event is—be sure to include dates and a clear, brief description.

2) Review data to assess whether a new program needs to be developed. If so, consider taking the lead to ensure that it happens.

3) Review the annual calendar of school counseling events to look at the level of balance each month in your time and delivery of the three counseling domains. Are there certain months that are already so heavy that they may not be a good time to offer additional activities? If so, consider conducting the campaign on a totally different day or week. What really matters is that the students get the information and activities, regardless of when an event happens.

4) Work with a team! Solicit stakeholders to help coordinate plans, make decisions, and disseminate information. Discuss this during a school counseling advisory council meeting, or collaborate to form a committee by recruiting faculty, students, parents, or community organizations/leaders who share your concerns and interests about establishing schoolwide awareness programs to help determine the curriculum and activities. If there is only one school counselor in your building, consider developing lesson plans or clear activities for classroom teachers to conduct with their students, if possible. This may require greater preparation and communication through a brief in-service training or meeting with teachers.

5) Talk with your school administration to explore the current program and opportunities for classroom education, rallies, assemblies, parent and student education events, poster and T-shirt or video contests, and so forth. Seek permission for these options if necessary.

6) Engage parent/teacher organizations or the school board to support your planned events, possibly by requesting their involvement or presence.

7) Include students who are on student leadership teams or in community service–oriented clubs, such as Student Council or Key Club. They can plan to participate to heighten awareness or provide valuable feedback and validation of your ideas.

See Figure 8.13 for a table listing online resources (with brief descriptions) for potential awareness campaigns relevant to secondary school counseling. This table is by no means all-inclusive but serves as a resource to begin your planning. A more extensive list is available on our website. ASCA also provides its own online awareness dates calendar on its homepage at the beginning of each school year (www.schoolcounselor.org).

Figure 8.13   National Awareness Campaigns

Raising Awareness:
National Campaigns throughout the Year

AUGUST

August	Description	Website and Applicable Resources
National Immunization Month	National Immunization Awareness is an annual observance held in August to emphasize the importance of vaccination. It was established to encourage people of all ages to ensure they are up to date on all recommended vaccines.	www.cdc.gov/vaccines/events/niam.html healthfinder.gov/nho/PDFs/AugustNHOtoolkit.pdf www.nphic.org/niam www.nphic.org/niam-resources
Women's Equality Day	Founded in 1971 to commemorate the passage of the 19th Amendment and to call attention to women's continuing efforts toward full equality. It also calls for women to be commended and supported in their organization and activities.	www.nwhp.org/resources/commemorations/womens-equality-day www.nwhm.org/blog/celebrate-equality-day shop.nwhp.org/womens-rights-and-womens-equality-day-resources-c198.aspx www.nwhp.org/resources/commemorations/womens-equality-day/10-ideas-for-womens-equality-day

SEPTEMBER

September	Description	Website and Applicable Resources
Attendance Awareness Month	A nationwide event, it recognizes the connection between school attendance and academic achievement.	awareness.attendanceworks.org www.educationworld.com/attendance-awareness-month-resources-making-attendance-priority
Hispanic Heritage Month *Sept. 15–Oct. 15*	Observation began in 1968, which celebrates the histories, cultures, and contributions of American citizens whose ancestors came from Spain, Mexico, the Caribbean, and Central and South America.	www.hispanicheritagemonth.gov/about www.smithsonianeducation.org/educators/resource_library/hispanic_resources.html www.nea.org/tools/lessons/hispanic-heritage-month.html
National Suicide Prevention Week *Monday through Sunday surrounding World Suicide Prevention Day*	This is a weeklong campaign to inform and engage health professionals and the public about suicide prevention and warning signs of suicide.	www.suicidology.org/about-aas/national-suicide-prevention-week https://suicidepreventionlifeline.org/] & www.sprc.org https://afsp.org/our-work/education/after-a-suicide-a-toolkit-for-schools/
Hunger Action Month	This month people all over America stand together with Feeding America and the nationwide network of food banks to take action on the hunger crisis and dedicate ourselves to a solution.	http://bit.ly/SeptemberHungerActionMonth https://www.moveforhunger.org/hunger-action-month

OCTOBER

October	Description	Website and Applicable Resources
Bullying Prevention Month	Founded in 2006 by PACER's National Bullying Prevention Center, the campaign unites communities nationwide to educate and raise awareness of bullying prevention.	www.pacer.org/bullying/nbpm stompoutbullying.org/index.php/campaigns/national-bullying-prevention-awareness-month https://www.schoolcounselor.org/school-counselors/professional-development/asca-u-specialist-trainings/bullying-prevention-specialist-en
LGBT History Month	Founded in 1994, the event celebrates the achievements of 31 lesbian, gay, bisexual, or transgender icons.	http://lgbthistorymonth.com https://gsanetwork.org/lgbthistorymonth www.schoolcounselor.org/asca/media/asca/PositionStatements/PS_LGBTQ.pdf
National Depression and Mental Health Screening Month	This event was designed to raise awareness of behavioral and mental health issues and working to reduce the stigma.	https://mentalhealthscreening.org/programs/initiatives https://nacchovoice.naccho.org/2015/10/08/national-depression-and-mental-health-screening-month-provides-opportunities-for-local-health-departments/
World Mental Health Day	This is a day for global health education, awareness, and advocacy against social stigma.	http://www.who.int/mental_health/world-mental-health-day/en/ https://www.schoolcounselor.org/asca/media/asca/PositionStatements/PS_StudentMentalHealth.pdf
America's Safe School Week *Third Full Week of October*	Established by the National School Safety Center in 1984, this event motivates key education and law enforcement policymakers, students, parents, and community residents to advocate for school safety.	http://www.schoolsafety.us/safe-schools-week http://www.schoolsafety.us/safe-schools-week http://www.nea.org/tools/lessons/56917.htm http://www.dare.org/school-safety/
Character Counts Week *Third Week of October*	This event is about the universal values we share despite differences in political or religious affiliation.	https://charactercounts.org/cc-week/ https://charactercounts.org/cc-week/ https://resources.charactercounts.org/free-resources/cc-week-resources/
Mix It Up at Lunch Day *Last Tuesday of October*	This event seeks to break down barriers between students, improve intergroup relations, and help schools create inclusive communities by sitting with different students.	www.tolerance.org/mix-it-up/what-is-mix educationforjustice.org/events/mix-it-lunch-day-1
Red Ribbon Week *Last Week of October*	Established by National Family Partnership, this event leads and supports our nation's families and communities in nurturing the full potential of healthy, drug-free youth.	redribbon.org

(Continued)

Figure 8.13 (Continued)

NOVEMBER

November	Description	Website and Applicable Resources
Military Family Appreciation Month	This celebration honors the commitment and sacrifices made by the families of the nation's service members.	www.military.com/military-family-appreciation-month
National Career Development Month	Created by the National Career Development Association, this event promotes career awareness and development.	ncda.org/aws/NCDA/pt/sp/OLD_ncdmonth
Native American Heritage Month	This is a time to celebrate rich and diverse cultures, traditions, and histories, and to acknowledge the important contributions of Native Americans.	nativeamericanheritagemonth.gov www.ncai.org/initiatives/native-american-heritage-month

DECEMBER

December	Description	Website and Applicable Resources
Special Education Day	This marks the anniversary of the nation's first federal special educational law (IDEA) signed into law on December 2, 1975. It is a day to reflect and reform.	specialeducationday.com tpcjournal.nbcc.org/the-school-counselor-and-special-education-aligning-training-with-practice
Human Rights Day	The date honors the United Nations General Assembly's adoption and proclamation in 1948 of the Universal Declaration of Human Rights.	http://www.ohchr.org/EN/AboutUs/Pages/HumanRightsDay.aspx
Impaired Driving Prevention Month	Invites families, educators, health care providers, and community leaders to promote responsible decision-making and encourage young people to live free of drugs and alcohol.	https://youth.gov/feature-article/december-national-impaired-driving-prevention-month

JANUARY

January	Description	Website and Applicable Resources
Get Organized Month	This event is dedicated to raising awareness of the benefits of getting organized.	www.napo.net/page/NAPOGOMonth
National Mentoring Month	This event focuses national attention on the need for mentors and celebrates the positive effect that mentoring can have on young lives.	https://www.mentoring.org/our-work/campaigns/national-mentoring-month/
Human Trafficking Awareness Day	This event is dedicated to raising awareness of sexual slavery and human trafficking worldwide.	https://nationaldaycalendar.com/national-human-trafficking-awareness-day-january-11/ https://www.compassion.com/world-days/human-trafficking-awareness-day.htm https://humantraffickinghotline.org/

FEBRUARY

February	Description	Website and Applicable Resources
African American History Month	This is a time to pay tribute to the generations of African Americans who struggled with adversity and their many accomplishments throughout American history.	www.africanamericanhistorymonth.gov http://www.smithsonianeducation.org/educators/resource_library/african_american_resources.html www.nea.org/tools/lessons/black-history-month.htm
Career and Technical Educational Month	This is a campaign to celebrate the value of career and technical education and the achievements and accomplishments from programs across the country.	acteonline.org/ctemonth/#.WNw5tdEzVnk khake.com www2.ed.gov/about/offices/list/ovae/pi/cte/index.html
National School Counseling Week! *First Full Week of February*	This event highlights the tremendous impact school counselors can have in helping students achieve school success and plan for a career.	www.schoolcounselor.org/school-counselors-members/about-asca-(1)/national-school-counseling-week
Teen Dating Violence Awareness Month	This event raises awareness about dating violence, highlights promising practices, and encourages communities to get involved.	https://nrcdv.org/dvam/tdvam http://www.breakthecycle.org https://vawnet.org/sc/preventing-and-responding-teen-dating-violence
Random Acts of Kindness Week *Second Full Week of February*	This is an opportunity to unite through kindness, make a difference, and bring smiles to the community.	www.randomactsofkindness.org info.character.org/blog/bid/204198/Get-Ready-for-Random-Acts-of-Kindness-Week

MARCH

March	Description	Website and Applicable Resources
Read Across America Day *School Day Closest to March 2*	This is a reading motivation and awareness program that calls for every child in every community to celebrate reading on March 2, the birthday of Dr. Seuss.	www.nea.org/grants/read-across-background.html http://www.readacrossamerica.org www.readingrockets.org/calendar/readacross
National School Breakfast Week *Second Week of March*	This is a celebration of the school breakfast program and a time to bring attention to your breakfast program.	schoolnutrition.org/Meetings/Events/NSBW/2017
International Women's Day	This is a day to celebrate the social, economic, cultural, and political achievements of women and to support a more inclusive, gender-equal world.	www.internationalwomensday.com
Kick Butts Day	This is a day of activism that empowers youth to stand out, speak up, and seize control against Big Tobacco.	https://www.kickbuttsday.org
National Youth Violence Prevention Week	This event raises awareness and educates youth and communities on effective strategies to prevent youth violence before it happens.	http://nationalsave.org/NYVPW/

(Continued)

Figure 8.13 (Continued)

APRIL

April	Description	Website and Applicable Resources
Child Abuse Prevention Month	This event recognizes the importance of families and communities working together to prevent child abuse and neglect and promote the social and emotional well-being of children and families.	https://www.childwelfare.gov/topics/preventing/preventionmonth/ http://preventchildabuse.org/latest-activity/announcing-child-abuse-prevention-month-2018/
Community Service Month	This event emphasizes the importance of volunteering in the community.	www.nationalservice.gov
Day of Silence	This is a student-led national event during which people take a vow of silence to highlight the silencing and erasure of LGBTQ people at school.	https://www.glsen.org/day-silence
National Autism Awareness Month	This is a campaign to increase understanding and acceptance of autism spectrum disorder, promote inclusions and self-determination, and support opportunity for highest possible quality of life.	www.autism-society.org/get-involved/national-autism-awareness-month www.autismspeaks.org
World Health Day	This event marks the anniversary of the founding of the World Health Organization and provides opportunities for individuals to get involved in activities that lead to better health.	www.who.int/campaigns/world-health-day/2017/event/en www.paho.org/world-health-day
Earth Day	This consists of events held worldwide to demonstrate support for environmental protection.	www.earthday.org www.epa.gov/earthday www.nea.org/tools/lessons/earth-day-curriculum.html

MAY

May	Description	Website and Applicable Resources
Asian-Pacific Heritage Month	This is a day to pay tribute to the generation of Asian and Pacific Islanders who enriched America's history and are instrumental in its future success.	asianpacificheritage.gov www.teachervision.com/holidays/asian-pacific-american-heritage-month
Children's Mental Health Awareness Day	This event focuses national attention on the mental health needs of children and teens.	https://www.samhsa.gov/children/awareness-day
Global Youth Traffic Safety Month	This event highlights road safety in an effort to raise awareness and inspire individual action that can change the tragic statistics.	https://noys.org/global-youth-traffic-safety-month
Military Appreciation Month	This event exists to publicly show appreciation for the service and sacrifice of troops and their families past and present.	https://www.military.com/military-appreciation-month
PTA Teacher Appreciation Week *One Week in May*	This is a time to celebrate teachers and other educators, expressing gratitude for their support of students.	www.pta.org/parents/content.cfm?ItemNumber=3270 www.nea.org/grants/teacherday.html
Screen Free Week (TV Turnoff Week) *First Week of May*	During this event children, families, schools, and communities are encouraged to turn off screens and "turn on life."	www.screenfree.org www.commercialfreechildhood.org/resource/screen-free-week-organizers-kit
Teen Pregnancy Prevention Month	This event highlights the historic declines in the rates of teen births in the United States.	https://www.hhs.gov/ash/oah/news/teen-pregnancy-prevention-month/index.html

JUNE

June	Description	Website and Applicable Resources
International Children's Day	This is a global celebration of the rights and well-being of children around the world, which exists to appreciate the role children play in the future of our communities.	www.nationalchildrensday.us
LGBTQ Pride Month	This event recognizes the impact that lesbian, gay, bisexual, and transgender individuals have had on history locally, nationally, and internationally.	https://www.adl.org/resources/tools-and-strategies/lgbtq-pride-month https://www.glsen.org/educate/resources/curriculum https://www.weteachnyc.org/resources/collection/june-lgbt-pride-month
National Safety Month	This event focuses on reducing leading causes of injury and death at work, on the roads, and in our homes and communities.	www.nsc.org/act/events/Pages/national-safety-month.aspx safetycenter.org/top-5-free-resources-for-national-safety-month healthfinder.gov/NHO/PDFs/June2NHOToolkit.pdf

NOTES

_____

_____

_____

_____

_____

_____

_____

_____

_____

_____

SELECTING AND ALIGNING YOUR SCHOOLWIDE PROGRAMS AND ACTIVITIES

Franchising Schoolwide Programs, Activities, and Family Education

When selecting schoolwide programs and activities, school counselors are encouraged to use a franchising approach similar to that used in Chapter 2 when designing districtwide core curriculum lessons. In this way, rather than delivering random acts of schoolwide programs and activities, all secondary schools in a district agree upon a minimum number of consistent programs and activities that stakeholders can count on year to year and school to school. Based on the information presented in this chapter, consider the following questions, and fill in the charts that follow.

1) For each school counseling domain, what schoolwide programs and activities do you currently implement? Are there additional programs and activities you would like to include in the future? Look at your school/district calendar to see if there are any events to add from there as well.

Academic	College/Career	Social/Emotional
• *Example: Orientations*	• *Example: FAFSA Night*	• *Example: Day of Silence*
•	•	•
•	•	•

2) How does each of the schoolwide programs and activities align with the core curriculum classroom lessons you will be teaching?

Schoolwide Programs/Activities	Alignment to Core Curriculum
•	•
•	•
•	•

3) For each schoolwide program and/or activity, how might you engage families or provide accompanying education for them?

Schoolwide Programs/Activities	Aligned Family Engagement Components
•	•
•	•
•	•

4) As a school counselor, what will your role be in each activity? Who will lead? Who will support?

Schoolwide Programs/Activities	School Counselor's Role
• • •	• • •

Franchising Schoolwide Programs and Activities

Now that you've completed the previous brainstorming activity, use the following tool to outline your schoolwide programs and activities that would be consistent school to school throughout your district and aligned to your school counseling program goals.

Schoolwide Programs and Activities Action Plan							
Grade Level	Activity Topic	Aligned with Which Student Core Curriculum Lesson/Unit	Month/ Date	Process Data	Perception Data	Outcome Data Achievement-Related (AR); Achievement (A)	Contact Person
Example: 9th Grade	Freshman Summer Orientation	High School 101	August	150 freshmen	% who are nervous about starting HS % who know what time school starts % who can open their lockers	Freshman-On-Track rate (A)	Counselor Triplett
Example: 11th/12th Grade	FAFSA Night	Money Matters (12th Grade)	October	200 parents	% who believe completing the FAFSA is important % who know when the FAFSA is due % who can locate the FAFSA online	FAFSA completion rate (AR) College enrollment rate (A)	Counselor Gomez

9

Pre- and Post-Tests and Assessments

At a recent professional development, school counselors were asked how many of them had been teachers before and whether or not they used to assess students when teaching curriculum. Sergio, a former math teacher, shared how he regularly assessed student learning through a variety of informal and formal assessments throughout the year. He knew each student's mastery of math standards and would help them individually achieve proficiency based on the areas in which they were struggling. However, when he became a high school counselor, Sergio stopped assessing students before and after his school counseling lessons. When questioned about his decision to not assess his students, Sergio stated that he simply hadn't thought of doing so and that he got out of the habit of assessing students when he switched roles. Now realizing the importance of collecting data, Sergio has set a goal to create, administer, and review the results of one core curriculum lesson for 9th grade students during the next school year.

Creating pre- and post-assessments is a well-developed skill that requires an understanding of the purpose of the assessment and the differences among assessments designed to measure attitudes, knowledge, skills, and behaviors. This chapter supports school counselors as they obtain the knowledge and skills needed to assess activities delivered to all students in Tier 1 core instruction, individual student planning, schoolwide programs and activities, and family education. Teachers assess the impact of their instruction on their students, and as active members of the educational community, school counselors do, too. School counselors deliver material and core content in the same way teachers do. Assessing students' progress provides valuable and immediate feedback on the effectiveness of the instruction and the likelihood that the attitude, knowledge, and skills gained will lead to behavior change.

REVISITING THE ART, SCIENCE, AND WONDER OF SCHOOL COUNSELING

Did you receive a Master of Arts (MA) or a Master of Science (MS) degree? Generally, the main method of teaching within an MA degree (focused on humanities and liberal arts) is via seminars with discussion heavily based on subject matter. MS degree programs tend to have a stronger focus on the research and the science behind the brain and behavior, and students are often involved in lab work, research, analysis, and evaluation. Within school counseling, both MA and MS programs (leading to licensing and/or credentialing, depending on the state) cover counseling as a subject, but in very different ways. Additionally, the amount of coursework devoted specifically to school counseling varies greatly from program to program. It is not surprising, therefore, that many practicing school counselors receive little or no training within their graduate programs on evaluation methodologies, the use of data to drive evidence-based interventions, and how to evaluate activity or program results.

Regardless of whether a school counselor receives an MA or MS degree, the professional field has shifted to balance the art and science of counseling—particularly as this relates to delivering evidence-based programs and practices in schools. ASCA (2012) calls for school counselors to evaluate the impact of their lessons by measuring and analyzing results. School counselors are all taught the art of counseling (e.g., listening, empathy, respect, genuineness, unconditional positive regard, self-disclosure, interpretation, open-ended questions, etc.) and the skills to utilize them (solution-focused counseling, etc.). In today's educational world, however, counselors must also become proficient in the science of evaluating their program activities and their impact on the students they serve.

Figure 9.1   The Art, Science, and Wonder of School Counseling

Source: Illustration by Gogis Design, http://www.gogisdesign.com.

The Wonder of School Counseling

You might ask: How much of the work of a school counselor each day is focused on the art of counseling as opposed to the science (see Figure 9.1)? When counselors focus exclusively on the art and ignore the science, they might be left wondering what difference they make every day. Part of the wonder of mixing the art and science of school counseling is the ability to take out the wondering by measuring the impact of the activities. When this occurs, school counselors often realize that the true wonder of the profession is the difference that counselors make in the lives of the students they serve each day.

Conceptual Diagram for Secondary School Counseling Curriculum

The conceptual diagram for a school counseling curriculum (see Figure 9.2) provides a practical model that secondary school counselors can use to guide their assessment of data in alignment with school counseling core curriculum. Adapted from the Hatching Results Conceptual Diagram (Hatch, 2013) for core curriculum at the secondary level, this visually outlines the relationships among the types of data (standards and competency, achievement-related, and achievement) and the ways to evaluate the data (process, perception, and outcome; Dimmitt et al., 2007; Hatch, 2005, 2013).

The diagram in Figure 9.2 reads left to right, representing an action framework connecting what the secondary school counselor is teaching (measured with process data) to the attainment of specific student standards and competencies (measured with perception data) and behavior change, leading to an improvement in student outcomes, which is reflected in achievement-related data and subsequently in achievement data. For example, when the school counselor teaches a classroom lesson to 9th graders, the process data constitute the recipe (the who, what, when, and how often) that explains how the curriculum was delivered (see Figure 9.3).

Figure 9.2 Hatching Results Conceptual Diagram—Secondary Level

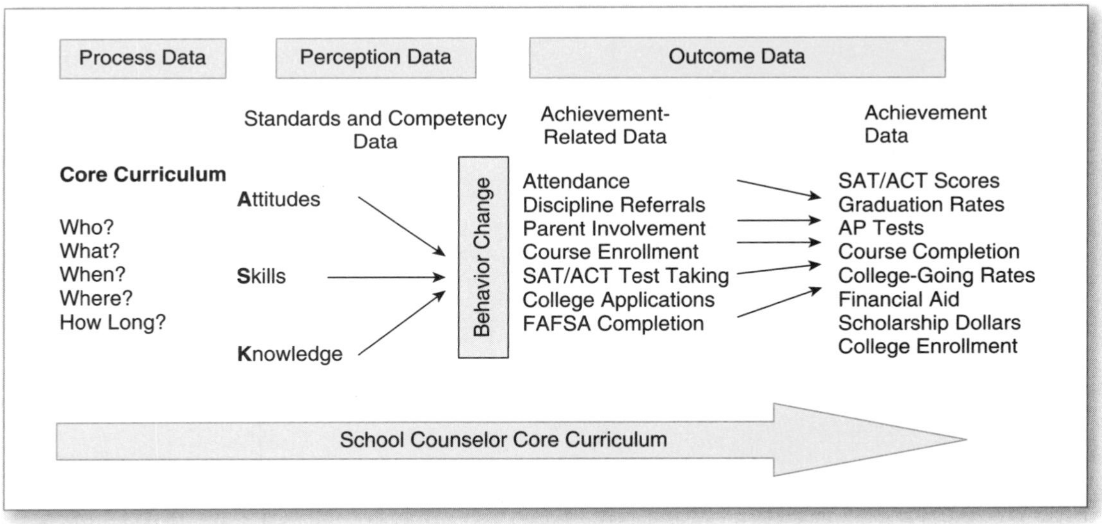

Source: Hatch, T. (2018).

Process Data for Hey, Hey, Hey . . .
Let's Calculate That GPA Core Curriculum Lesson

- 9th grade students
- October
- One lesson in each 9th grade English class on the following:
  - Understanding the importance of grades and credits
  - Gaining knowledge in required and competitive grade point averages (GPAs) for college admissions and extracurricular activities
  - Calculating GPAs

Next, the school counselor collects perception data on the lesson to assess whether students acquire the following:

1) The attitude that it is important to monitor their GPA

2) The knowledge of required and competitive GPA

3) The skill of calculating a GPA

When school counselors teach the curriculum in the classroom or provide skills-based group counseling sessions, it is also appropriate for them to assess whether students have learned what was taught. Collecting pre- and post-assessment data helps answer the following questions:

- Was this a good use of instructional learning time?
- Was this a valuable use of school counselor time?
- Did students learn what was taught?
- In which areas are students competent?
- Is more instruction needed?

Finally, the school counselor looks to connect the lesson content to measurable student outcomes—particularly in terms of achievement-related data. In this

Figure 9.3 Sample Hatching Results Conceptual Diagram—"Credits and Calculating GPA"

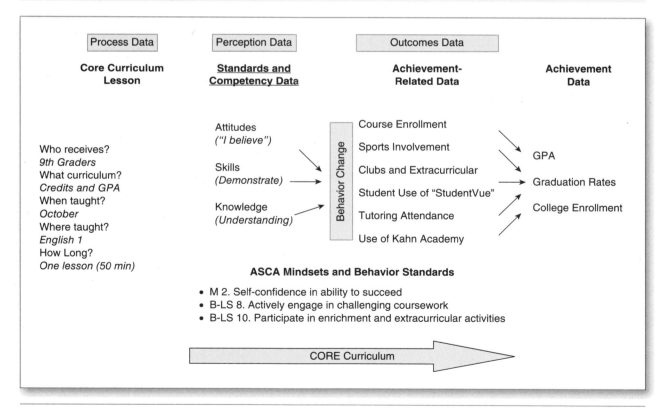

Source: Hatch, T. (2018).

scenario, the goal of the lesson would be to improve student grades on progress reports, improve attendance, increase eligibility to participate in extracurricular activities, and utilize resources (tutoring, study groups, etc.). Improvements in these achievement-related outcomes lead to increased numbers of freshmen on target (not credit deficient), students' GPAs, and reducing the number of Ds and Fs.

Activity 9.1

Refer to the "Hey, Hey, Hey . . . Let's Calculate That GPA" lesson plan from Chapter 4 (pages 106–111). Review the process, perception, and outcome data for this lesson, utilizing the information presented in the lesson plan and your understanding of the Hatching Results Conceptual Diagram.

CREATING PRE- AND POST-ASSESSMENTS

ASK Students What They Learned

As professional educators, it is appropriate for secondary school counselors to assess the impact of their teaching in much the same way teachers do. One way to do this is through assessments provided prior to and following the lesson/unit. When developing pre- and post-tests, school counselors are encouraged to assess student mastery of the ASCA Mindsets and Behavior standards, using the ASK acronym. ASK is a reminder that when the school counselor is finished teaching a lesson, they should *ASK* the students what they learned (Hatch, 2013). *ASK* stands for **A**ttitudes, **S**kills, and **K**nowledge. Although this acronym reminds us to measure all three areas, arranging questions in the order of attitudes, knowledge, and *then* skills is suggested when constructing the actual pre- and post-tests (see Figure 9.4).

Figure 9.4   Measuring ASK

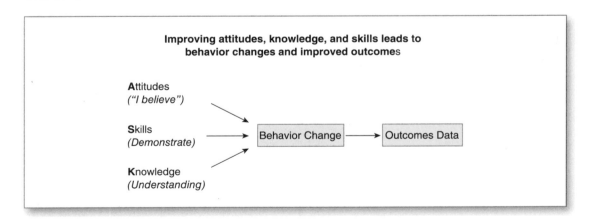

To develop an assessment, consider the following:

- What do you want students to *believe* that you don't already think they believe?
- What do you want students to *know* that you don't already think they know?
- What *skill* do you want students to demonstrate that you don't already think they possess?

Attitude Questions

Attitude questions measure the students' beliefs or opinions. The Likert (pronounced *lick-ert*) scale is most commonly used when creating surveys to assess opinions. When students answer these items, they are stating the degree to which they agree or disagree with the statement. Typically, a five-point item is written, measuring a bipolar positive or negative response to the item:

1) Strongly agree

2) Agree

3) Neither agree nor disagree

4) Disagree

5) Strongly disagree

Although this scale includes a middle value representing a neutral or undecided position, it is also possible to use a forced-choice scale by removing that option. In this way, the respondents are forced to decide whether to lean more toward the agree or disagree end of the spectrum. This can be helpful if there is concern that students may not take the survey seriously and choose to opt out via the middle ground rather than commit to an opinion. For younger students, it may be more helpful to use the terminology "not sure" instead of "neither agree nor disagree."

Questions to assess attitudes can be scaled in different ways, depending on what is being assessed. The University of Connecticut has created the chart shown in Table 9.1 with the most common Likert questions in the areas of agreement, frequency, importance, quality, and likelihood (Siegle, 2010).

Table 9.1 Likert-Type Scale Sample Ratings

Agreement		
Strongly disagree	Disagree	Completely disagree
Disagree	Neither agree nor disagree	Mostly disagree
Neither agree nor disagree	Agree	Slightly disagree
Agree		Slightly agree
Strongly agree		Mostly agree
		Completely agree

Occurrences		
Very rarely	Never	Not at all
Rarely	Seldom	Little
Occasionally	About half the time	Occasionally
Frequently	Usually	Often
Very frequently	Always	All the time
Not really	Never	Never
Somewhat	Rarely	Seldom
Quite a bit	Sometimes	Sometimes
	Often	Often
	Always	
Not much	A little	Not much
Some	Some	Little
A great deal	A lot	Somewhat
		Much
		A great deal

Importance		
Not important	Unimportant	Unimportant
Moderately important	Of little importance	Of little importance
Very important	Important	Moderately important
	Very important	Important
		Very important

Quality		
Poor	Very poor	Extremely poor
Fair	Not good	Below average
Average	All right	Average
Good	Good	Above average
Excellent	Excellent	Excellent

Content		
Too elementary	Too fast	Poor
Okay	Just right	Not good
Too technical	Too slow	Good
		Excellent
Did not understand	No help at all	Quite unsuccessful
Understood a little	Slightly helpful	Somewhat unsuccessful
Understood most of it	Fairly helpful	Somewhat successful
Understood very well	Very helpful	Quite successful

(Continued)

Table 9.1 (Continued)

Implementation		
Definitely will not Probably will not Probably will Definitely will	Absolutely no Mostly no Neither yes nor no Mostly yes Absolutely yes	Never true Sometimes true Often true
Not at all Very little Somewhat To a great extent	Not at all true Slightly true True about half the time Mostly true Completely true	Probably not Maybe Quite likely Definitely

Overall Impression	
Very dissatisfied Somewhat dissatisfied Neither satisfied nor dissatisfied Somewhat satisfied Very satisfied	Not at all satisfied Slightly satisfied Somewhat satisfied Very much satisfied
Didn't get what I wanted Got a little of what I wanted Got a lot of what I wanted Got everything I wanted	Very uncomfortable Uncomfortable Comfortable Very comfortable

Source: Used with permission from University of Wisconsin–Extension, Cooperative Extension, Program Development and Evaluation, *Building capacity in evaluating outcomes, 2009,* modified and adapted by Julie Pigott Dillard, UF IFAS Washington County Extension, 2013, http://templatelab.com/likert-scale.

In secondary schools, it is particularly important that students understand how to respond to measures of attitudes and beliefs. It will be helpful to model and practice with them prior to administering the assessment.

Juan and Elizabeth are school counselors in the same district who often collaborate on implementing school counseling lessons. They are both unsure whether their 7th graders really know the difference between agree and strongly agree and also understand that students who report that they strongly agree as opposed to agree are more likely to perform the behaviors. Additionally, both school counselors are looking for additional ways to assess their newcomer English language learners and some students with Individualized Education Plans. Therefore, Juan decides to use emoticons, and Elizabeth opts to use thumbs-up/thumbs-down

Table 9.2 Ways to Describe a Likert Scale at the Secondary Level

Sample Meanings	Strongly Agree	Agree	Unsure	Disagree	Strongly Disagree
Likert Responses (Emoticons)					
Likert Responses (Thumbs Up/ Down)					
Using Social Media	LOVE IT! I use it several times per day and wish I could be on it more!	I like it but only check it about once or twice a day.	I could live with it or without it.	Dislike it. I have an account but rarely check it.	HATE IT! I don't have an account and never will!
Pizza	LOVE IT! I eat it every day and ask for it on my birthday!	I eat it and enjoy it but not every day.	Eh . . . no opinion—I take it or leave it.	Dislike it. I don't want to eat it, or I try not to eat it.	HATE IT! It makes me want to throw up!
Earth Science	LOVE IT! It's the very best part of the day!	I like it, but I like other subjects more.	What is Earth science?	I don't like it and prefer not to do it.	HATE IT! It's my worst subject.
Field Hockey	LOVE IT! I can't wait for practice!	I like it, but I like other sports better.	I don't have any opinion because I've never played.	I don't like it and prefer not to play it.	HATE IT! I never want to play field hockey again!

Icon Source: iStock.com/MonikaBeitlova

to assess students. To explain the differences, the school counselors ask students to share which picture represents how much they like each thing listed in Table 9.2.

Both Juan and Elizabeth make sure to explain to students that there is no right or wrong answer; rather, people just have different opinions and preferences. For example, whereas some people like pizza and answer with a smiley face or a thumbs-up (agree), others may dislike this food and answer with a frown face or a thumbs-down (disagree). Juan and Elizabeth share examples from Table 9.2 with their students. Once students understand the differences among all response options, the school counselors are ready to provide the pre-test with confidence.

Knowledge Questions

Knowledge questions measure what students know about a lesson topic both before and after the lesson is delivered. Knowledge items check the accuracy of the factual content learned by students during the lesson and are either correct or incorrect. Knowledge questions are best provided in a multiple-choice format, as opposed to true/false (T/F) format, which has a 50% guessing factor, compared to 33% for three multiple-choice responses (a, b, and c). Additional response items reduce the likelihood of guessing even further (see Table 9.3). The goal is to reduce student guessing and to assist in measuring actual learning, not chance. With five multiple-choice items, the baseline correct response is much lower than true or false. It is important to consider the developmental level of students when determining multiple-choice responses, as middle school students may be more likely to be overwhelmed by a higher number of choices than high schoolers. Additionally, secondary school counselors may need to make adaptations to pre- and post-assessments for special populations such as newcomers with less English proficiency or students who have disabilities.

Table 9.3 Guessing Percentages for Pre- and Post-Assessments

Type of Question	Guessing Factor	Pre-Test Sample Correct %	Post-Test Sample Correct %	% Increase*
True/False	50%	50%	90%	60%
3-Item MC	33%	33%	90%	142%
4-Item MC	25%	25%	80%	220%
5-Item MC	20%	20%	80%	300%

*Learn how to calculate percentage increase and change in Chapter 10, page 280.

Note: MC = multiple choice.

Hassan, a school counselor, was teaching 8th graders a lesson on the dangers of smoking and how to respond to peer pressure. He wanted to assess his students to see if they knew the dangers of using cigarettes and that cigarette smoking is responsible for killing more than 480,000 people every year. He decided to use a true/false test in classroom 1. Here is the question he asked, along with the student responses he received:

True/False: *Cigarette smoking is responsible for killing about 480,000 people every year.*

60% responded True (correct)

40% responded False

He then gave students in classroom 2 a five-point multiple-choice questionnaire:

Cigarette smoking is responsible for killing about ____ people every year:
a. 200,000
b. 350,000
c. 430,000
d. 480,000
e. 550,000

Responses were as follows:

a. 12%
b. 18%
c. 22%
d. 25% (correct)
e. 23%

Essentially, his students were guessing. They didn't *know* the actual number—how could they? They had not been taught the lesson! After completing the lesson, Hassan gave students in classroom 1 a true/false assessment again and provided a multiple-choice assessment to classroom 2.

Table 9.4 Example Pre- and Post-Assessment Chart Using True/False Questions Compared to Multiple Choice

Type of Question	Pre-Test Sample Correct %	Post-Test Sample Correct %	% Increase
True/False	60%	95%	58.3%
5-item MC	25%	95%	280%

Note: MC = multiple choice.

By using multiple choice instead of a true/false question, Hassan was better able to see what students really had learned and measure the growth of their knowledge more accurately. This illustrates why we recommend using multiple-choice questions rather than true/false.

Skills Questions

The next step is to determine whether students have learned the skills taught during the lesson. Creating skills questions can be more complex than creating knowledge questions because it requires the application, or utilizing the knowledge that has been gained (Bloom, Englehart, Furst, Hill, & Krathwohl, 1956). Students think about what they learned, identify the knowledge, and apply the knowledge to a new situation or scenario (Dimmitt et al., 2007).

One way to differentiate a knowledge from a skill question is to compare it to math. In math, 2 + 2 = 4, which is knowledge. However, if a word problem asks, "If Jade has two apples and Maureen gives her two more, how many apples does she have now?" then the student must extract the equation from the word problem and apply his or her knowledge to solve it. In the same way, a scenario that asks students what comes next or what step a student missed in conflict resolution is the application of knowledge—a skill.

The following are sample ways in which school counselors can assess student *skills*:

- Provide a sample scenario within the pre- or post-assessment questions (see the following section for more details)
- Complete a career interest inventory
- Analyze a transcript
- Complete a 4-year plan aligned with the high school graduation and college entrance requirements
- Organize an assignment planner
- Complete a college application
- Complete a FAFSA
- Use a Ticket Out the Door (see Chapter 5, page 125)

Writing Effective Pre- and Post-Questions

Teach what you assess; assess what you teach. To begin creating your own questions, look closely at the curriculum you plan to teach. What is the core knowledge the curriculum wants the students to know? What is the core belief in the messaging? What skills are being taught within the lesson? Remember that no matter how valid the question is, students must know what is expected of them, so be sure to always include clear instructions, too. What follows are sample slides from the lesson presented in Chapter 4 *(Hey, Hey, Hey . . . Let's Calculate That GPA)* to demonstrate the formation of good pre- and post-assessment questions.

Figures 9.5 through 9.7 show sample slides from the *Hey, Hey, Hey . . . Let's Calculate That GPA* lesson from Chapter 4. Notice that the questions are created directly from the content presented on the slide. Additionally, the skill learned in this lesson is assessed through students calculating their GPAs, which demonstrates application of their knowledge. It would be helpful for the reader to review Chapter 4 on lesson plans prior to reading further.

Hey, Hey, Hey . . . Let's Calculate That GPA—Pre- and Post-Assessment

The speech bubbles shown extending from the *Hey, Hey, Hey . . . Let's Calculate That GPA* slides shown in Figures 9.5 through 9.7 are provided to assist in understanding how the pre- and post-assessment questions were created. Notice how the pre/post questions carefully align with the content on the slides. This is a vital skill for the school counselor to learn for creating assessments. The question must directly align to the lesson content presented. Although some school counselors may state that they will say the content when they deliver the lesson, experience teaches us that we can't control or predict whether we will remember to say what is needed to ensure that students learn the material. Additionally, students remember more of what they hear *and* see. Therefore, it is essential for school counselors to align the questions with the visual content from the lesson. In the figures that follow, the left includes information provided in the lesson, and on the right is the pre- and post-question drawn from the content.

Figure 9.5 Knowledge and Attitude Questions—Grades Matter

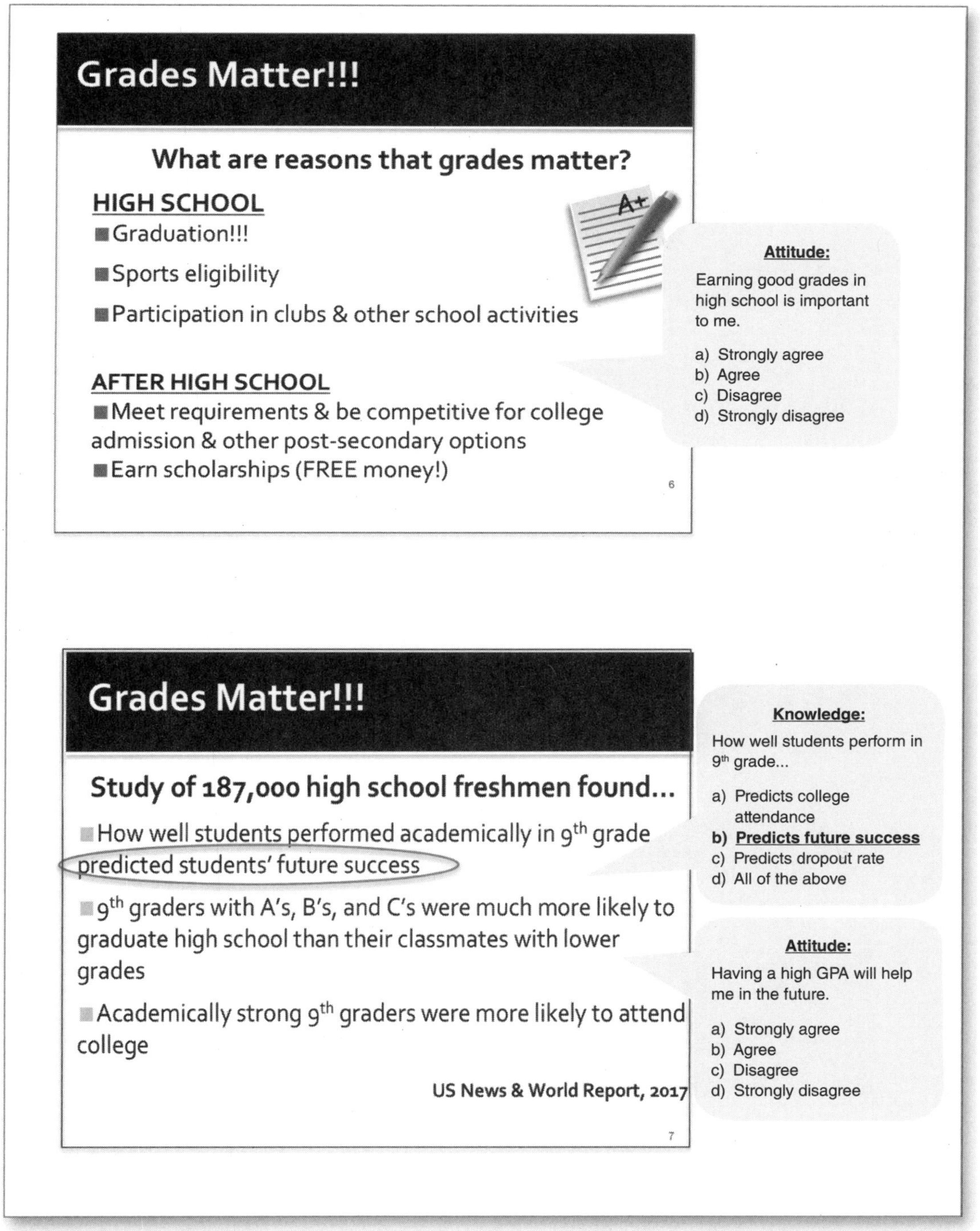

Grades Matter!!!

What are reasons that grades matter?

HIGH SCHOOL
- Graduation!!!
- Sports eligibility
- Participation in clubs & other school activities

AFTER HIGH SCHOOL
- Meet requirements & be competitive for college admission & other post-secondary options
- Earn scholarships (FREE money!)

Attitude:
Earning good grades in high school is important to me.

a) Strongly agree
b) Agree
c) Disagree
d) Strongly disagree

6

Grades Matter!!!

Study of 187,000 high school freshmen found...

- How well students performed academically in 9th grade predicted students' future success
- 9th graders with A's, B's, and C's were much more likely to graduate high school than their classmates with lower grades
- Academically strong 9th graders were more likely to attend college

US News & World Report, 2017

Knowledge:
How well students perform in 9th grade...

a) Predicts college attendance
b) Predicts future success
c) Predicts dropout rate
d) All of the above

Attitude:
Having a high GPA will help me in the future.

a) Strongly agree
b) Agree
c) Disagree
d) Strongly disagree

7

Figure 9.6 Knowledge Questions—Sports & Activities and Graduation

Grades Matter - Graduation

- Total of 220 credits needed to graduate
  - Credits are "**points**" you receive for each class you pass with a **D** or higher
  - Passing one full year class at Potter HS = **10 credits**
  - Students generally earn **60 credits each year**
    (6 classes x 10 credits per class = 60)

- If you get an F in a required class you have to **take the class again** ☹

8

Knowledge:

How many credits are needed to graduate?

a) 200
b) 210
c) 220
d) 230
e) 240

Knowledge:

Students generally earn _____ credits each year.

a) 30
b) 40
c) 50
d) 60
e) 70

Grades Matter – Sports & Activities

- Student athletes must maintain a **2.0 GPA**

- No more than **1 F** on quarter progress report or final report card

- Students need 2.0 or higher to be **club leaders**, attend **college fieldtrips**, and **earn a work permit**

9

Knowledge:

What GPA is needed to participate in high school sports?

a) 1.0
b) 1.5
c) 2.0
d) 2.5
e) 3.0

Knowledge:

What GPA is needed for a work permit?

a) 1.0
b) 1.5
c) 2.0
d) 2.5
e) 3.0

Figure 9.7   Knowledge and Skills Questions—College Eligibility Requirements and Calculating GPA

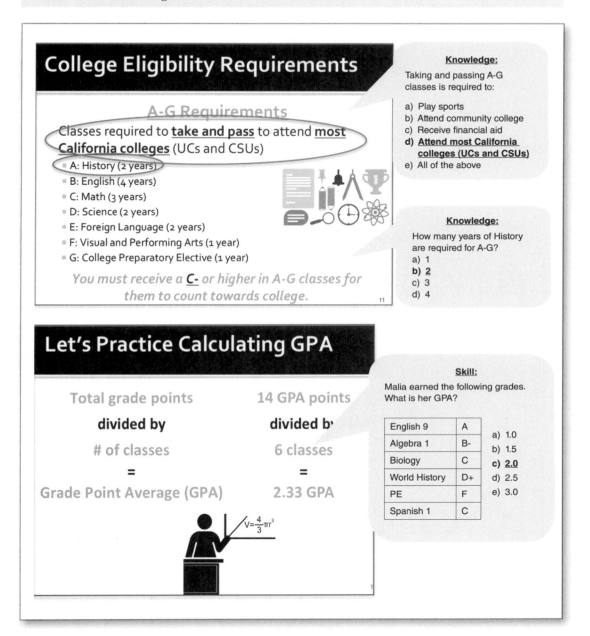

Activity 9.2

Refer to the Hey, Hey, Hey . . . Let's Calculate That GPA lesson slides (Chapter 4, pages 90–100) and aligning Guided Notes (Chapter 5, page 122). What other types of attitude, knowledge, and/or skills questions could be created from the information presented on the slides and the Guided Notes sheet? Use the information to create the pre- and post-assessment questions. The entire lesson and pre- and post-test can be found on our website.

Using Technology Tools Such as Google Forms and Kahoot! to Support Pre- and Post-Assessments

Finding an efficient way to measure students' attitudes, knowledge, and skills is extremely important for busy secondary school counselors. Gone are the days of hand scoring pre- and post-tests because of the many technology tools available to easily collect and analyze data. Google Forms and Kahoot! are two tools for administering pre- and post-assessments to students and can also be used for needs assessments and other surveys. Additionally, both are user-friendly and free. See the following descriptions for more details.

Google Forms

Google Forms is a free technology tool that allows school counselors to make an assessment or survey to collect results in an easy, streamlined fashion. After students fill out an assessment through Google Forms, their information is collected in an online spreadsheet within the creator's Google Drive folder. As Google Forms automatically creates simple charts and graphs of the data, further analysis can be completed by using the raw data in the spreadsheet. School counselors can also easily share the form with others as they are creating the questions and/or analyzing the results, making collaboration easy—so much so that many districts are using Google for their email and storage platforms. School counselors working in districts without Google can create a free Gmail account to access Google Forms. Within Google Forms, school counselors can create questions with a variety of response styles, including multiple choice, scaling, and short answer. Students access the assessment in Google Forms via a website link that is generated once the form is complete; they can fill out the survey on a computer, tablet, or any other device with Internet access. Also remember that although Google Forms automatically creates pie charts with multiple-choice and scaling question data, the best way to present pre- and post-assessment results is through side-by-side bar graphs. (See Perception Data Gone Wrong, Figure 10.17 on page 290.) School counselors are encouraged to create their own graphs using the data that Google Forms collects in a spreadsheet.

Kahoot!

Kahoot! is another online technology tool than can be used to collect pre- and post-assessment data in a fun and engaging manner (see Figure 9.8). The school counselor can sign up for a free account at create.kahoot.it and set up the assessment. When the school counselor is ready to facilitate the assessment, a unique code will be generated, and students will use a laptop, cell phone, tablet, or desktop computer to begin the assessment. Kahoot! is set up like a game in which students have a certain amount of time to answer each question (determined by the school counselor), and they can play the game as individuals or on different teams. Like Google Forms, the school counselor can access the results at any time and can view the responses either individually or holistically.

Tips

- Consider using for pre- and not for post-tests so students don't rush through their answers when it counts.
- Be mindful of including skills questions in Kahoot!, such as GPA calculation, as students may just guess rather than trying to solve the problem in the limited time.

- Think about how students may react to seeing attitude responses from their peers. (One school counselor expressed that students were trying to get reactions out of other classmates by reporting in crazy ways.)

Figure 9.8 Kahoot! Example—Hey, Hey, Hey . . . Let's Calculate That GPA

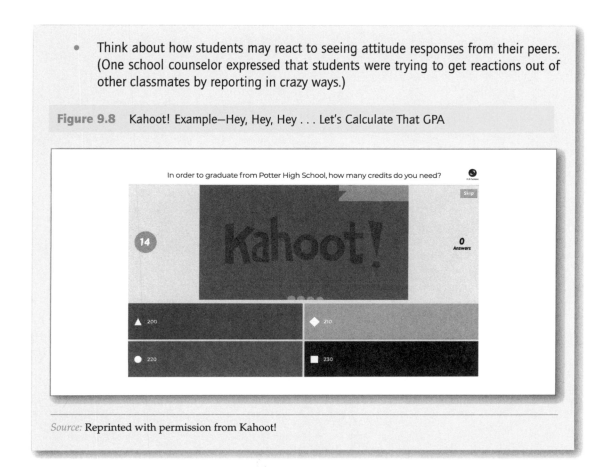

Source: Reprinted with permission from Kahoot!

Whether you've delivered hundreds of lessons, or are preparing your first one, don't let pre-post-tests intimidate you. They are designed to help us both *prove* (that your lesson made a difference) and *IMprove* (i.e., guide us to improve both teaching and assessment). Remember, teachers regularly create assessments for their students, so don't hesitate to ask a teacher you trust for feedback if needed. We challenge you to make *one* pre and post each semester and to allow yourself opportunities for growth and improvement as you learn this new skill. By learning from the results of their assessments, whether their students have gained the knowledge and skills needed for success, school counselors improve their craft and practice. This wisdom is at the center of the art and the science of school counseling.

Activity 9.3

Refer back to Chapter 2, p. 32–35, and locate the Tier 1 Core Curriculum Action Plan Agreements for Shasta County. Take a look at the perception data column and answer these questions:

- Do the ASKs align well with the intended lessons? How might you improve them?
- Practice creating pre- and post-test questions for the ASKs listed.

10

Sharing School Counseling Program Results and Marketing Your Program

VANESSA'S STORY

I was president of the California Association of School Counselors, Inc., during the recession, when school counseling positions were being cut left and right. In some districts, school counselors were being eliminated altogether. It was a difficult time for school counselors, and counselors throughout the state were inquiring about how to save school counseling positions. One trend that I noticed was school counseling programs that had a history of sharing their results with stakeholders, especially school board members, were less likely to have cuts in school counseling positions. As a result of that crisis, many school counselors who did not have a data-driven program began to implement comprehensive programs and collect school counseling program results. Fast-forward to today, when it is essential that school counselors collect program results. In California schools are monitored based on the California Accountability Dashboard; many of the items monitored are areas that school counseling programs can directly impact, such as behavior (suspensions), attendance, and college and career readiness indicators. As a result, many school districts in California have seen the value of school counselors and have increased the number of positions; California has gone from a student-to-counselor ratio of 1,016:1 to 708:1, a 30 percent improvement over 3 years (ASCA, n.d.). We still have a long way to go in reducing ratios, but California is heading in the right direction.

Secondary school counselors are vital members of the school team who help ensure the success of all students. Through developing and evaluating a data-driven school counseling program, school counselors create and continually improve school counseling lessons and activities based on school and community needs, and they share these successes with stakeholders. Data analysis helps school counselors determine what has worked and what hasn't and clarifies what needs to be changed or improved. Through showcasing process, perception, and outcome data, school counselors demonstrate how students have benefited from school counseling services. Sharing the results of your school counseling program is also an effective strategy to garner buy-in from administrators and staff. Evaluation allows for analysis of effectiveness and helps inform decisions related to program improvement while guiding future planning. Ultimately, evaluation of the impact of school counseling Tier 1 activities, as well as strengths and areas for improvement, drives updates to counseling program SMART goals and future program implementation to achieve the desired results.

There are many ways to showcase school counseling program results, whether through presentations using different technology tools or by highlighting successes more informally. Regardless of the style, sharing is important to increase understanding about the school counselor's role and to build program sustainability. This chapter walks school counselors through a variety of ways to share results and marketing their school counseling program.

RESULTS REPORTS

The American School Counselor Association (ASCA) provides Results Report templates—the School Counseling Core Curriculum Results Report (see Figure 10.1) is appropriate for Tier 1 lessons. Results Reports serve as documentation tools for ensuring that the counseling program was carried out as planned, that every student was served, and that developmentally appropriate standards were addressed. In addition, Results Reports share process, perception, and outcome data; reflections on curriculum activities' effectiveness and impact; and ideas for improving the activity or program. Although the ASCA document includes many rows for core curriculum results, the authors suggest beginning with measuring one lesson and measuring a few more each year. This tool is particularly useful for keeping track of core curriculum data throughout the year and for sharing information with administrators, teachers, and families either throughout or at the end of the year. See Figure 10.2 for a Results Report template that provides prompts to enable you to create your own report. Figure 10.3 is an example of a completed Results Report.

FLASHLIGHT RESULTS PRESENTATIONS

A Flashlight Presentation shines a light on *one* thing that the school counseling program has measured well through a simple PowerPoint or another visual presentation software (Hatch, 2013). School counselors are encouraged to present a brief Flashlight Presentation of 6 to 10 minutes to stakeholders, post the presentation to a school website, and/or share it at a district level with other counselors as a way to

Figure 10.1 School Counseling Core Curriculum Results Report Template

RESULTS REPORT
SCHOOL COUNSELING CORE CURRICULUM

Grade Level	Lesson Topic	ASCA Domain and Mindsets & Behaviors Standard(s)	Projected Start/End	Process Data (Number of students affected)	Perception Data (Data from surveys/ assessments)	Outcome Data (Achievement, attendance, and/or behavior data)	Implications

Source: Reprinted with permission from the American School Counselor Association, 2019.

Figure 10.2 How to Write a Results Report

[DISTRICT NAME] & [YEAR]
School Counselor Core Curriculum
Results Report – [LESSON TITLE]

Grade Level	Lesson Topic	ASCA Domain & Standards	Curriculum and Materials	Start/End Date	Process Data (Number of students affected)	Perception Data: Pre/post-assessments (What students learned, believe, think, or can demonstrate)	Outcome Data: How did students' behavior change because of the lesson? (Improved achievement, attendance and/or behavior)	Limitations, Implications, & Next Steps (So, what does the data tell you?)
What grade level(s) did you service?	What was the content of your core curriculum lesson? Describe the topics covered.	What domain(s) were addressed? (Academic, career, social/ emotional)	What materials did you use? Were they prepackaged or counselor generated?	When did you begin and end the lesson?	How many students received the lesson(s)?	Results of Pre/Post-Test (Pick a few relevant samples and attach the rest of the results to the report) **Attitude:** Prior to counseling lesson ___% believed _XYZ__. Afterward ___% indicated they believe XYZ. **Skills:** Prior to counseling lesson ___% demonstrated XYZ. Afterward ___% demonstrated XYZ. **Knowledge:** Prior to counseling lesson ___% knew XYZ. Afterward ___% know XYZ.	**Achievement-Related Data** Report any achievement-related data you collected or are monitoring for improvement (this will vary depending on activity). e.g., *Homework rates? Attendance? Discipline?* **Achievement Data** Report any academic achievement data you collected or are monitoring for improvement (this will vary depending on activity). e.g., *Test scores (At or above grade level on achievement test, etc.)*	What worked? What didn't? What will you do differently next time? Were there limitations to your results? What recommendations do you have for improvement?

Figure 10.3   Example Results Report

Grade Level	Lesson Topic	ASCA Domain and Mindsets & Behaviors Standard(s)	Projected Start/End	Process Data (Number of students affected)	Perception Data (Data from surveys/assessments)	Outcome Data (Achievement, attendance, and/or behavior data)	Implications
9th	Academic Success in High School	Academic: M2, M5, B-LS3, B-LS4	Month of October	171	**Attitude** 93.2% of freshmen now believe having a SMART academic goal in place is important (previously 59.5%). **Knowledge** 94.3% of freshmen now know the number of credits required to graduate (previously 55.6%). 97% of freshmen can now define a quarter grade vs. a semester grade (previously 74%). 97.7% of freshmen can now define weighted and unweighted GPA (previously 57.2%). **Skill** 99.2% of freshmen can now correctly calculate their GPAs (previously 34%).	**% of the freshman class with a 3.0 or better GPA** Significant increase from last year's freshman class: SY16 = 30% of freshmen SY17 = 54% of freshmen **Attendance rate** Slight increase in the overall freshman class rate: SY16 = 93.4% SY17 = 93.8%	The increase in GPA data as well as perception data shows that we should offer this lesson again next year, especially considering that research from the University of Chicago Consortium on School Research has found that students with a 3.0 or better are more likely to enroll and persist in college.
10th	Credit Review	Academic: M6, B-LS6	Month of February (after 1st semester grades are available)	168	**Attitude** 92.6% now believe that it is important to review their transcripts and credits earned at the end of each semester (previously 45.1%). **Knowledge** 98.2% now know what components class rank is based on (previously 41%). 100% can now identify 3 reasons that class rank is important (previously 79%). **Skill** 97.8% can now download a copy of their unofficial transcripts from their student portal (previously 0%).	**% with 1+ Ds/Fs** Significant decrease: 1st semester = 64% of sophomores 2nd semester = 41% of sophomores **Attendance rate** Slight increase in the overall sophomore class rate: 1st semester = 92.2% 2nd semester = 92.9%	The decrease in the number of sophomores earning 1 or more Ds/Fs significantly decreased, indicating that we should offer the lesson again (and perhaps sooner than sophomore year). We also saw a slight increase in attendance, but we still have a lot of work to do with credits earned!

RESULTS REPORT
MLA School Counseling Program Core Curriculum
(9th & 10th Grade Academic Success)

AMERICAN SCHOOL COUNSELOR ASSOCIATION

Source: Adapted from Marine Leadership Academy.

communicate the school counseling program's activities and impact. The Flashlight Presentation is a tool that accomplishes the following:

- shares the school counseling program's effectiveness and impact
- educates others about school counseling and the school counselor's role as a valuable educator
- shares the positive outcomes of an activity (in this case, core curriculum classroom lessons)
- reflects on the successes of the school counseling program and areas for growth
- advocates for the work of a school counselor in the school building
- gauges readiness for ASCA's Recognized American School Counselor Association Model Program (RAMP) recognition
- can be used as a possible artifact/evidence for the school counselor's performance evaluation

To create a Flashlight Presentation, select a visual presentation software. For most people, information transmitted visually makes a greater impression than text alone, so the likelihood of stakeholders' remembering information presented is greater with the use of visuals. A time-saving Flashlight PowerPoint Presentation template for core curriculum is provided in Figure 10.4, which includes the essential elements of an effective Flashlight Presentation; each slide in the template is juxtaposed to a completed sample slide to show how the template can be used. School counselors can modify and adapt the template to enter details about their schools, activities, and data; they can also add or delete slides as needed. The full downloadable template, which includes slide notes that give helpful guidance on editing and creating presentations, is available on our website.

online resources

Figure 10.4   Flashlight PowerPoint Template for Core Curriculum and Example Flashlight Results Presentation

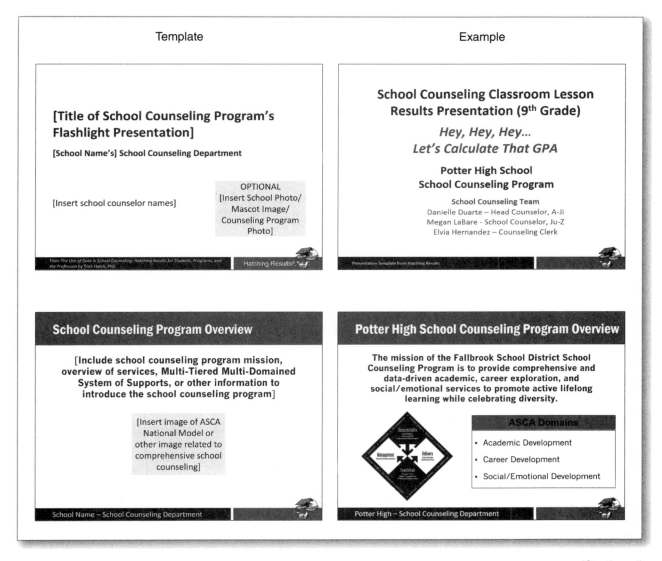

(Continued)

Note: The ASCA National Model diamond used on this page represents the ASCA National Model, third edition. Readers are advised that the American School Counselor Association is revising the ASCA National Model, to be released June 2019, and are strongly encouraged to research and utilize the new version. The ASCA National Model is trademarked by the American School Counselor Association and reprinted with permission.

Figure 10.4   (Continued)

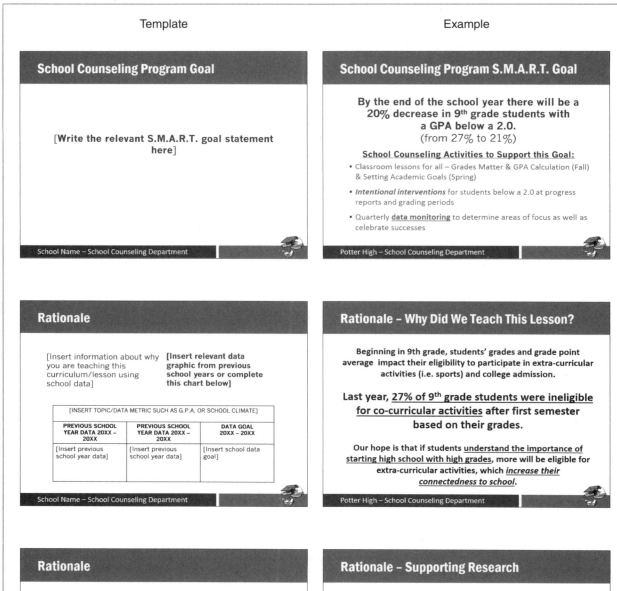
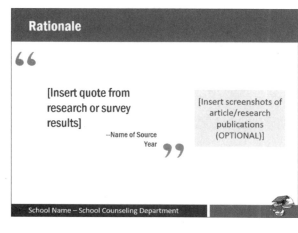

Template	Example

Student Standards:
ASCA Domain + Mindsets & Behaviors

ASCA DOMAIN
[Insert ASCA Domain – academic, college/career, and/or social/emotional]

ASCA MINDSET & BEHAVIOR STANDARDS
[Insert multiple ASCA Mindset and/or Behavior Standard(s) in format such as:
- Mindset 3. Sense of belonging in school environment
- Behavior Self Management Skill 7: Demonstrate effective coping skills when faced with a problem]

School Name – School Counseling Department

Student Standards:
ASCA Domain + Mindsets & Behaviors

ASCA DOMAIN
ACADEMIC & COLLEGE/CAREER

ASCA MINDSET & BEHAVIOR STANDARDS
- Mindset 2: Self confidence in ability to succeed
- Behavior Learning Strategies 8: Actively engage in challenging coursework
- Behavior Learning Strategies 10: Participate in enrichment and extracurricular activities

Potter High – School Counseling Department

Other Standards, School Initiative, District Strategic Plan, or State Goals Aligned with Lesson (OPTIONAL)

[INSERT NAME OF STATE/LOCAL STANDARD]
[Insert identified standard(s)]

OR

[INSERT INITIATIVE/STRATEGIC PLAN/GOAL]
[Include information about how the lesson aligns to or supports these goals]

School Name – School Counseling Department

Supporting District Goals

District LCAP Goal 2:
Increase the percentage of students who are on track to graduate college and career ready.

School Counseling Program Alignment to Goal:
The school counseling department believes that ensuring 9th grade students understand the importance of getting good grades, along with understanding how to calculate their GPA, will help more students be motivated to graduate and be eligible for post-secondary options.

Potter High – School Counseling Department

Process Data

[IDENTIFY STUDENT GRADE LEVEL OR GROUP]
Insert bulleted list with details about how
- [Insert text: When? Days/months]
- [Insert text: What frequency/how often?]
- [Insert text: Lesson topics?]
- [Insert text: Where? Which class?]
- [Insert text: How many students impacted?]

[Insert Graphic/ Image of Curriculum/ Photo, etc. (OPTIONAL)]

School Name – School Counseling Department

Process Data

9th Grade Students
- Lessons delivered in Early October
- All 265 9th graders received the lesson
- Topics –
  - Credits for graduation
  - Sports/extra-curricular eligibility
  - College eligibility requirements
  - Logging onto online grades and calculating GPA

Hey, Hey, Hey...
Let's Calculate That GPA!

School Counseling Classroom Lesson:
Grades Matter & GPA Calculation

Presented By:
Potter High School Counselors
Ms. Duarte & Ms. LaBore

Potter High – School Counseling Department

(Continued)

Figure 10.4 (Continued)

Template	Example

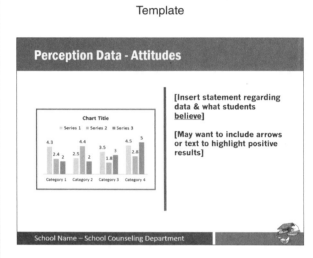

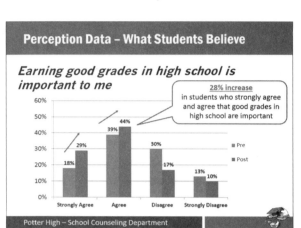

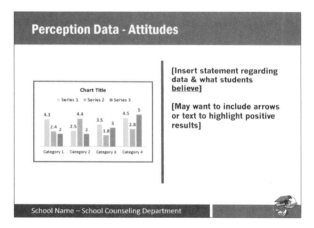

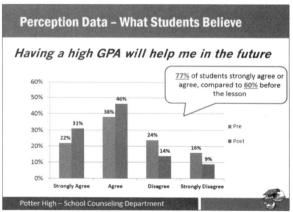

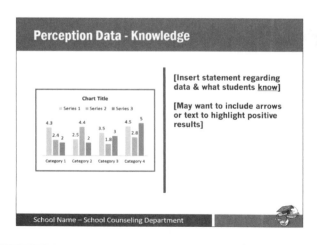

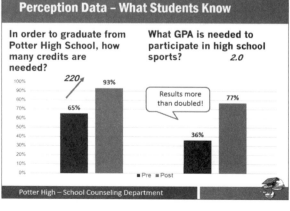

Template

Example

Perception Data - Skill

[Insert statement regarding data & what students **students can do/what skill they learned**]

[May want to include arrows or text to highlight positive results]

School Name – School Counseling Department

Perception Data – What Students Can Do (Skill)

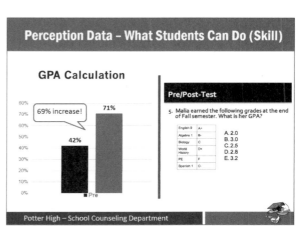

Potter High – School Counseling Department

Outcome Data

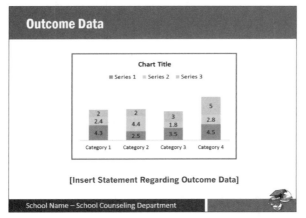

[Insert Statement Regarding Outcome Data]

School Name – School Counseling Department

Outcome Data – GPA & Grades Above 2.0

QUARTER 1 & QUARTER 2 GPA COMPARISON -

Slight improvement in overall 9th grade GPA

26% reduction in 9th graders with GPA below 2.0 after 1st semester

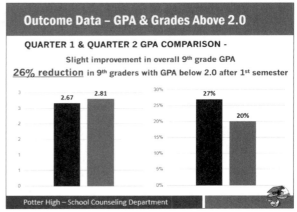

Potter High – School Counseling Department

Summary and Implications

- [Insert summary bulleted list of your results and the overall impact of your curriculum]
- Cont.
- Cont.
- Cont.

School Name – School Counseling Department

Summary and Implications

- All <u>265 9th grade students</u> received valuable information about graduation requirements, extracurricular activity participation, college eligibility, and how to calculate GPA.

- Students showed *growth* in attitudes, knowledge, and skills related to the lesson.

- The *Hey, Hey, Hey…Let's Calculate That GPA* lesson supports the increase in 9th grade GPA between quarter 1 and final grades, and <u>26% reduction in students with GPA less than 2.0</u>.

Potter High – School Counseling Department

(Continued)

Figure 10.4 (Continued)

Template

Example

Limitations, Lessons Learned, & Next Steps

- [Insert bulleted list of challenges encountered]
- Cont.
- Cont.
- Cont.

School Name – School Counseling Department

Limitations, Lessons Learned, & Next Steps

- We have received positive feedback from math teachers about the lesson being engaging and containing important information.
- 9th grade families were sent a virtual letter about the graduation, extra-curricular, and college-eligibility requirements after students received the lesson.
- One math teacher forgot to administer the pre-test prior to the school counselors teaching the lesson, which may have impacted the results.
- We will continue to provide lessons to all students & intentional interventions for students who have a GPA below a 2.0.

Potter High – School Counseling Department

THANK YOU!!

Many thanks to administration, staff, and parents for contributions to these efforts and your support of the school counseling program!

School Name – School Counseling Department

The school counseling program is striving to guide all students to achieve their full potential & contributing to the academic success of all students.

Thank you to the staff, administration, & families for supporting & contributing to our program!!!

Potter High – School Counseling Department

ONE-PAGERS

Flashlight Presentation One-Pager

The Flashlight Presentation One-Pager is a one-page, double-sided tool that provides stakeholders with a lasting visual reference of the delivered Flashlight Presentation in a simple, summative format. The Flashlight Presentation One-Pager allows audience members to take notes directly as they are listening to the school counselor present and/or refer to the information at a later time.

The Flashlight Presentation One-Pager can be shared with stakeholders as a stand-alone document as well. Stakeholders who do not hear a live presentation from the school counselor can still reference the Flashlight Presentation One-Pager and easily understand the presented information. Additionally, this document can easily be distributed in staff mailboxes, emailed as an attachment, included in a newsletter, shared with the school board or parent teacher organization, posted on the school counseling program website, or issued at conferences when exhibiting your school counseling program.

A user-friendly reproducible template that sums up a Flashlight Presentation in a one-page, double-sided document is available on our website (see Figure 10.5). The template can easily be adapted—simply type over it and insert your text, graphs, and/or photos. Developing a Flashlight Presentation One-Pager to showcase your results has never been easier! See Figure 10.6 for an example.

Other One-Pagers

Another use for a one-pager is to highlight the work and results of one or more lessons or schoolwide activities. School counselors can include program descriptions, ASCA standards, testimonials, photographs, and data charts to share results. One-pagers allow school counselors to describe these schoolwide activities within their programs in a simple yet powerful way. The three examples shared in Figures 10.6, 10.7, and 10.8 are different ways to explain the school counseling lessons or programs while showcasing process, perception, and outcome data. School counselors can include student and teacher testimonials aligned with standards, results data, and photos to bring the school counseling activities to life. One-pagers can be distributed to teachers, families, and community partners to share the activities and successes within the school counseling program.

Figure 10.5   Flashlight One-Pager Template

[INSERT FLASHLIGHT PRESENTATION TITLE]
[INSERT SCHOOL NAME] SCHOOL COUNSELING PROGRAM

20XX-20XX

Abstract/Summary

Lorem ipsum dolor sit amet, consectetur adipiscing elit. Nam faucibus urna vitae pellentesque porta. Etiam tristique dapibus viverra. Maecenas rutrum nec eros eu varius. Suspendisse sit amet est justo. Vivamus sed facilisis purus. Donec laoreet nulla dui, ac sagittis mauris hendrerit vel.

Lorem ipsum dolor sit amet, consectetur adipiscing elit. Nam faucibus urna vitae pellentesque porta. Etiam tristique dapibus viverra. Maecenas rutrum nec eros eu varius. Suspendisse sit amet est justo. Vivamus sed facilisis purus. Donec laoreet nulla dui, ac sagittis mauris hendrerit vel. Lorem ipsum dolor sit amet, consectetur adipiscing elit. Nam faucibus urna vitae pellentesque porta.

Rationale and Need

- [Insert text]

- [Insert text]

- [Insert text]

- [Insert text]

- [Insert text]

School Counseling Program Activities

- [Insert text]

- [Insert text]

- [Insert text]

[Insert photo of counseling program at work or other image]

Mindsets & Behaviors/Standards
- **[Standard bullet point]**
  [Description/details]
- **[Standard bullet point]**
  [Description/details]
- **[Standard bullet point]**
  [Description/details]
- **[Standard bullet point]**
  [Description/details]

Competencies
- **[Competency bullet point]**
  [Description/details]
- **[Competency bullet point]**
  [Description/details]
- **[Competency bullet point]**
  [Description/details]
- **[Competency bullet point]**
  [Description/details]

Source: **From** *Hatching Results for Elementary School Counselling: Implementing Core Curriculum and Other Tier One Activities* (Hatch, T., Duarte, D., & De Gregorio, L. K., 2018).

Figure 10.5 Flashlight One-Pager (Continued)

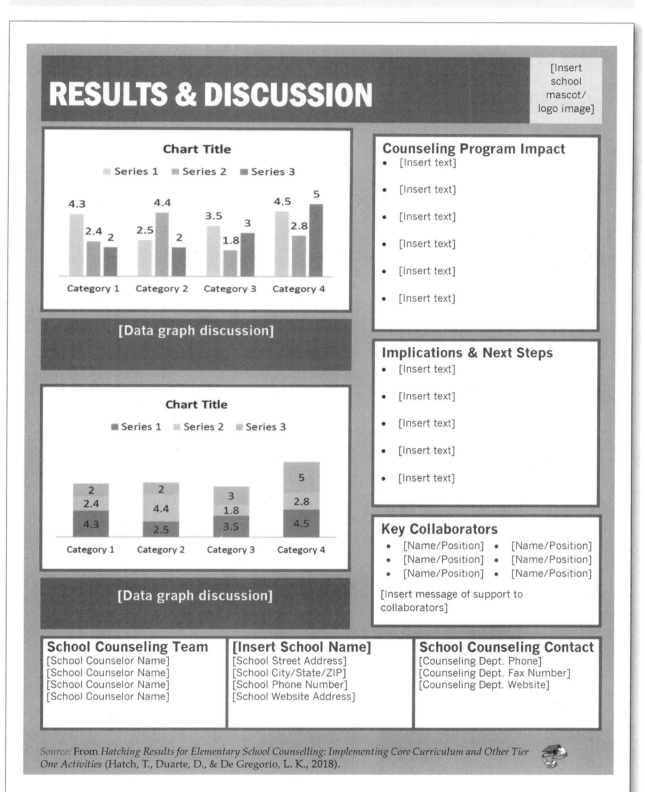

Source: From *Hatching Results for Elementary School Counselling: Implementing Core Curriculum and Other Tier One Activities* (Hatch, T., Duarte, D., & De Gregorio, L. K., 2018).

Figure 10.6 Flashlight One Pager Example: Las Flores Middle School End of Year Results (Front)

Las Flores Middle School Counseling Program
17/18 End of the Year Report

Data as of 6/11/18

Tier One – For ALL Students

School Counseling Core Curriculum Lessons

Topics Included:

6th – Working in Groups, Emotions Brains & Body, & Test Taking & Calming Down Strategies

7th – Working in Groups, Disagreeing Respectfully, Negotiating and Compromising, Giving & Getting Support, Responding to Bullying, Cyber Bullying, Signs of Suicide, Time Management & Learning Styles, Understanding Anger, Staying in Control, Coping with Stress, Substance Abuse Prevention – Myths & Facts & Making Good Decisions

8th – Leaders & Allies, Coping with Stress, Preparing for the High School Transition & De-escalating a Tense Situation

Number of Classrooms Visited

6th - 26

7th - 139

8th - 35

Tier Two – For SOME Students

Group Counseling Sessions

Topics: Stress Management, Self Regulation, Girls Group & Student Success Skills (6th & 7th/8th Grade)

Students Participating in Groups

Individual Counseling Sessions

38

51

778

Tier Three – For a FEW Students

Risk/Suicide Assessments

50

------------------------------ Data Driven Goals ------------------------------

Academic Goal

By the end of third quarter (March 16, 2018), students (grades 6-8) with 2 or more F from 1st quarter will reduce the number of F grades by 40% from 32 F grades in 1st quarter to 19 F grades in 3rd quarter.

How it was accomplished:

- Two small groups were run for students with failing grades, one group targeting 7th & 8th grades and another group targeting 6th graders
- Students were also seen individually by the school counselor, school counselor intern and their academic advisor.
- Of the 14 students with 2 or more F grades in 1st quarter, 12 of the students were referred to the Family School Partnership/Student Success Team Process
- 6 of the students were referred to the We STRIVE Mentor program
- 6 of the students were referred for Special Education Assessment - 5 have qualified and 1 is in the assessment process
- 1 of the students qualified for a 504 plan

ACADEMIC GOAL OUTCOME

The 14 students with 2 or more F grades in 1st quarter, decreased the number of F grades by 63%, from 32 F grades in 1st quarter to 12 F grades in 3rd quarter

F Grades.

■ 1st Quarter ■ 3rd Quarter

School Counselor: Alexis Goddard & School Counselor Intern: Brittney Pacini

Source: From Alexis Goddard and Brittney Pacini.

Figure 10.6 Flashlight One Pager Example: Las Flores Middle School End of Year Results (Back)

Las Flores Middle School Counseling Program
17/18 End of the Year Report

-------------------------- *Data Driven Goals* --------------------------

Behavior Goal

By June 2018, 7th grade students will decrease the number of office referrals by 30% from 93 office referrals for the 2016-2017 school year to 65 office referrals for the 2017-2018 school year.

How It Was Accomplished:

- 13 School Counseling Core Curriculum Lesson have been delivered to every 7th grade student
- Students with behavior referrals are seen 1 on 1 with the school counselor or school counselor intern
- Students with repeated (2 or more) behavior referrals were referred to Self Regulation Group (see attached)

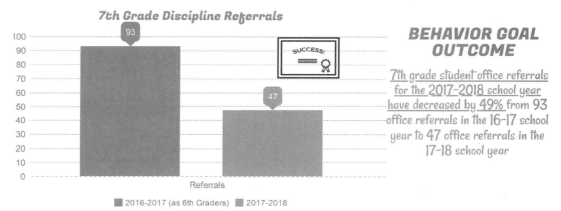

7th Grade Discipline Referrals

2016-2017 (as 6th Graders) — 2017-2018

BEHAVIOR GOAL OUTCOME

7th grade student office referrals for the 2017-2018 school year have decreased by 49% from 93 office referrals in the 16-17 school year to 47 office referrals in the 17-18 school year

Attendance Goal

By June 2018, LFMS students (grades 6-8) with 14 or more absences will decrease by 20% from 78 students in the 2016-2017 school year to 62 students for the 2017-2018 school year.

How it was accomplished:

- In September, the School Counselor met with 50 students who struggled with attendance the previous school year and try to get a better start
- 1 student was referred to the District Attorney's meeting as part of the SARB process.
- 20 of the 74 students are on a 504 or IEP - Case Carriers were notified and involved in process
- 10 Student Attendance Review Team Meetings with held with Assistant Principal, School Counselor and District Nurse
- Attendance Awareness Month was held in January. Daily attendance messages were made during morning announcements.

ATTENDANCE GOAL OUTCOME

The number of students missing 14 or more days has decreased by 9% for the 17-18 school year, from 78 students in the 16-17 school year to 74 students for the 17-18 school year

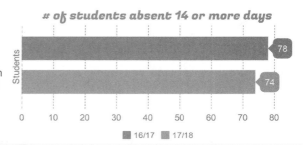

# of students absent 14 or more days

16/17 — 17/18

School Counselor: Alexis Goddard & School Counselor Intern: Brittney Pacini

Source: From Alexis Goddard and Brittney Pacini.

Activity 10.1

Consider the one-pagers presented in Figures 10.6, 10.7, and 10.8 here—what does each one teach the reader? What components are most powerful? What might you change? For what schoolwide counseling program or activity could you create a similar one-pager?

Figure 10.7, created by school counselors at Arroyo Vista Middle School, provides a snapshot of the 2017–2018 school counseling program results. The school counselors include the number of lessons they provided, describing lesson topics for each grade level. They also provide the number of individual counseling sessions, conflict mediations, parent events, and family contacts. The school counselors also present outcome data showing decreases in the number of students with D and F grades correlated with a school counseling program intervention. How could you use a one-pager like this to highlight your school counseling program?

Figure 10.7   Arroyo Vista Middle School Counseling Report

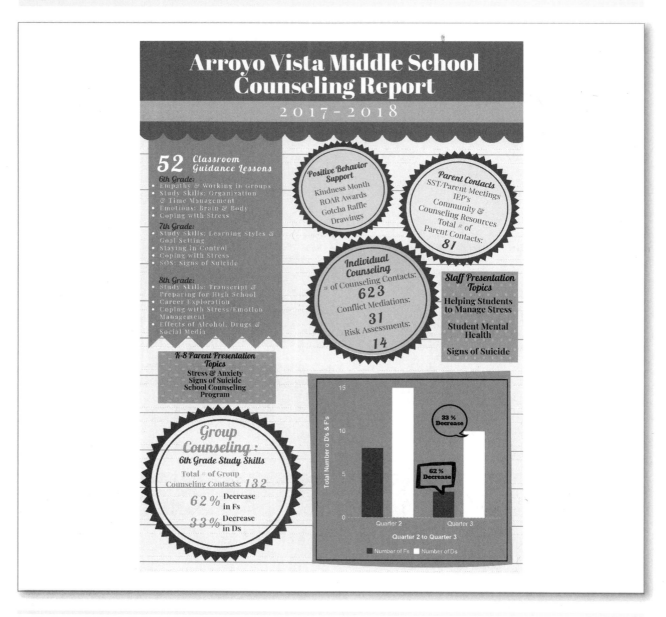

The one-pager shown in Figure 10.8 was created by middle school counselor Gayle Fleming to share an update of the counseling program. This document highlights both perception data (pre/post-test data) from a bullying prevention lesson and provides process data (number of lessons taught). Additionally, positive results from Tier 2 small groups and Tier 3 individual meetings are included. The newsletter is an excellent example of providing data along with critical information about bullying prevention. What impression does this newsletter give about the school counseling program? What kind of perception (attitudes, knowledge, and skills) and outcome (achievement-related and achievement) data might she include in her next edition?

Figure 10.9 presents a one-pager called a Support Personnel Accountability Report Card (SPARC) created by co-author Danielle Duarte and her school counseling teammate, Megan LaBare. This is a voluntary two-sided document on continuous improvement that focuses on key college and career readiness outcomes for students. Creating a SPARC at the secondary level can be used to accomplish the following:

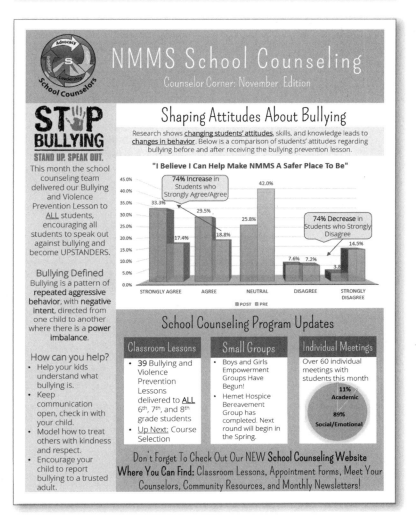

Figure 10.8 North Mountain Middle School School Counseling Bullying Prevention Update

- Demonstrate the school counselor's commitment to students' career and college readiness
- Describe alignment with local, state, and national career and college readiness initiatives
- Proactively promote the school counseling program to administrators, teachers, school boards, parents/guardians, community partners, businesses, and legislators

Schools in California that meet all SPARC submission requirements are recognized by receiving a SPARC Seal and Certificate of Participation from the California Department of Education. Other states have adopted similar documents under a different name; non-California schools can use the same components to create a document comparable to the SPARC. See www.sparconline.net for more information. What are the ways in which a school counselor could share this document with staff, administrators, families, and community members?

Figure 10.9 Support Personnel Accountability Report Card (SPARC) One-Pager Example

Potter Junior High School
2015 SPARC
Support Personnel Accountability Report Card
A continuous improvement document sponsored by the
California Department of Education

District: Fallbrook Union Elementary School District
Website: https://pjh.fuesd.org/
Principal: Mr. Leonard Rodriguez **School Counselors:** Danielle Duarte & Megan LaBare
Grade Levels: 7 & 8 **Enrollment:** 769

Principal's Message

Potter Junior High (PJH) School is a *Leadeein Me* school, committed to the following beliefs: all students will learn at a high level and achieve success, success breeds success, and we control the conditions of success. Our School Counseling Department uses the American School Counselor Association (ASCA) National Model as framework to support these school-wide goals and to ensure the development of all students in the college/career, academic, and social/emotional domains.

Students, parents, staff, and community members are involved in various programs to ensure a safe school climate, which remains a top priority. The SPARC is aligned to our School Site Improvement Plan. Our 2014-2015 focus-for-improvement goals

continue to be met by implementing Sean Covey's *7 Habits of Highly Effective Teens* into our weekly Leadership Program. Student connectedness has improved with the expansion of clubs and our mentorship program. In 2015-2016, our focus-for-improvement goals are to expand the AVID elective class and school-wide AVID strategies to increase rigor and support the implementation of Common Core across subject areas. Secondly, we plan to strengthen our high school transition to ensure all students are college ready. I am confident we will continue to provide a safe and supportive learning environment to ensure all students find the greatness within themselves.

Career and College Readiness Student Outcomes

The Potter School Counseling Department uses student outcome data in academic, career, and personal/social domains to evaluate and enhance support services, in alignment with the ASCA National Standards. This information is also used when evaluating the effectiveness of the Support Services Team in the three SPARC outcome categories: Career Readiness, College Readiness, and 21st Century Skills.

Career Readiness: The graph below highlights pre and posttest career readiness data of 8th grade students. After various career readiness activities, 89% of 8th graders can identify 2 careers of interest. The School Counseling Department promotes career readiness through core counseling curriculum classroom lessons and career exploration activities. Also, students are exposed to a variety of careers through College and Career Day when over 40 presenters share their experiences and career paths.

College Readiness: The School Counseling team at PJH makes it a priority to create a college-going mindset within all students. Core curriculum lessons are presented in the classroom by the school counselors and emphasize college planning. To additionally support the college-going environment, all students are given the opportunity to visit a college campus. In the chart below, you can see the percentage of 7th and 8th grade students who demonstrate knowledge of the A-G Course Requirements necessary for college.

21st Century Skills: All members of the team support the Fallbrook Union Elementary School District leadership initiative of implementing Stephen Covey's *7 Habits of Highly Effective Teens* into our school culture. School counselors create and present core counseling curriculum lessons around the 7 habits, respecting others, setting goals and making positive decisions. In their weekly leadership class, students complete lead journals, further developing these skills. As a result, 96% of our students report having goals for their futures.

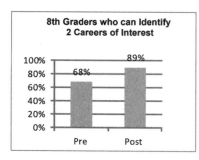

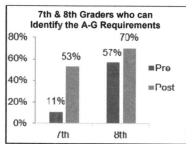

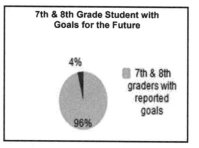

Additional achievements that document our career and college readiness efforts include:

- In 2014, 8th grade promotion rate was 98%
- In 2015, 98% of 8th graders completed a career interest inventory
- In 2015, 98% of 7th graders have visited at least one college campus
- in 2015, 100% of 8th graders will complete a 4-year high school plan

College and Career Readiness School Site Programs and Community Partnerships

The Potter Team collaborates with many outside resources and community based organizations to better serve our students and families. These partnerships provide our students with relevant and engaging college and career readiness opportunities. The following chart highlights many of our school programs and community partnerships that work together to provide valued services to directly help our students to become college and career ready.

School Site Programs
21st Century Skills Readiness Curriculum
- *The Leadeein Me* by Stephen Covey
- *7 Habits of Highly Effective Teens* by Sean Covey
- Safe School Ambassadors
College and Career Readiness Curriculum
- College and Career Day
- Homework Club
- Leadership Class
- California Junior Scholarship Federation (CJSF)
Parent Outreach
- Parent University/Parent Night (workshops)
- English Language Advisory Committee (ELAC)
Student Outreach
- Where Everyone Belongs Day (WEB)
- Student Forums
- Student Congress

Community Partnerships
Student Outreach
- Palomar Family Counseling
- San Diego State University School Counseling Interns
- Encuentros Youth Conference
- Latina Youth Leadership Conference through UCSD
- North San Diego County Fire Department
- Fallbrook Rotary Club
- Department of Migrant Education Services
Parent Support Services
- Parent Institute for Quality Education (PIQE)
- Cal State University, San Marcos—Early Outreach
After School Programs
- Boys and Girls Club
- After School Education & Safety Program

Student Support Team

The PJH Support Team continues to focus on a universal goal for all students to be college and career ready, while developing 21st century skills. The PJH Team works collaboratively to create, implement, and evaluate our support services to ensure their equability and effectiveness.

All of the members of the PJH Team are highly educated and qualified professionals. Each member holds valuable and unique experiences that benefit our students when working as a team. The Potter Team collaborates on a regular basis to fully serve the varying needs of our students.

The Potter school counselors play an integral role in the Student Support System. They actively contribute to the academic achievement, career development, and social/emotional competencies on a school-wide level. The school counselors constantly collect and analyze data to better support Potter students.

Members of our team are actively involved in various professional organizations including the American School Counselor Association, California Association of School Counselors, National Association of School Psychologists, and Association of California School Administrators.

Certificated Team Members		
Position	Academic Degree/Education	Years in Education
Principal	M.S. Administration	22
Assistant Principal	M.A. Business	16
School Counselors (2)	M.S. Counseling & M.A. Counseling	8 combined
School Psychologist (1 FTE)	M.A. School Psychology/School Counseling	20 Combined
Speech Therapist (1)	M.S. Communicative Sciences & Disorders & M.A. Education	16

Classified Team Members		
Position	Academic Degree/Education	Years in Education
Administrative Secretary (1)	B.A. Liberal Arts	14
Attendance Clerk (1)	A.A. Business Administration	35
Bilingual Clerk (1)	Secretarial Certificate	10
Counseling Clerk (1)	B.A. Spanish	7
Health Care Technician (1)	LVN License, B.A. in progress	5
School Counseling Interns (.8 FTE)	B.A., M.S. Counseling in progress	6 combined

Source: Created by Danielle Duarte and her school counseling teammate, Megan LaBare.

Percent Change Calculator

When sharing results with faculty, administrators, families, and other school stakeholders, it is important to accurately present the impact of the Tier 1 lessons and activities. Therefore, school counselors are encouraged to calculate improvements in pre- and post-assessment scores, attendance, behavior, or achievement using percentage change. In *The Use of Data in School Counseling* (Hatch, 2013), the following notes are included to describe percentage change:

One important point to remember is the distinction between the terms *increase* and *improvement*. For example, if someone had a quarter and was given an additional quarter, the increase would be 25 cents, but the improvement to the total amount of funds would be 100% because the total amount of money doubled. In the same way, if the percentage of correct responses on a test shifted from 25% to 50%, this represents an increase of 25% and an improvement of 100% (p. 230).

The book goes on to describe the mathematical formula used to calculate percentage change, but now school counselors can easily find percentage change online! Just by Googling "percentage change," multiple sites can be found. Figure 10.11 shows one located at www.percent-change.com. School counselors input the pre-assessment data in the "1st Value" box and the post-assessment data in the "2nd Value" box, click "Calculate," and the percentage change will be calculated!

Middle school counselor Jovianne Pereyra used the percent change calculator (see Figure 10.10) to assess the reduction in suspensions, comparing the current school year to the last school year. She found a 23% decrease in suspensions!

Figure 10.10   Percent Change Calculator Example: 23% Decrease in Suspensions

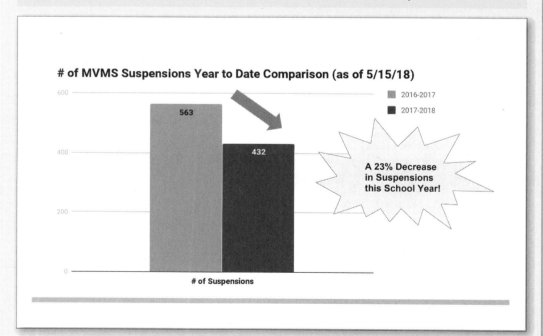

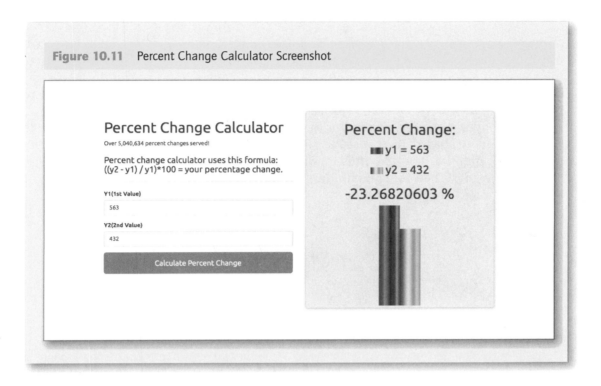

Figure 10.11   Percent Change Calculator Screenshot

PRESENTING RESULTS TO SPECIFIC STAKEHOLDERS

There are many forums to present your school counseling program results. The best practice is to regularly share your school counseling program results with all stakeholders (staff, students, families, community members, school board, and district leaders). This promotes their understanding the role of the school counselor as well as how the goals of the school counseling program align with the school/district goals. It also helps counselors advocate for the school counseling program.

In co-author Vanessa's district, San Jacinto Unified School District (SJUSD), school counselors work hard to ensure that all stakeholders are aware of the impact of the school counseling program. They have created systems to collect data for their comprehensive PreK–12 school counseling program, which includes a designated day of each month to review their data, and they create a results presentation at the end of the school year highlighting the goals, activities, and results of their school counseling program. As a result, SJUSD's comprehensive school counseling program has earned Riverside's Model of Excellence Award and the California State School Board Association (CSBA) Award, called the Golden Bell.

One strategy that the SJUSD PreK–12 school counseling program uses to share their results is that the district school counseling program leader asks each school counseling team to present their end-of-the-year results presentation at the last district school counselor meeting of the school year. This PreK–12 school counseling meeting is designed to celebrate the hard work that school counselors have done throughout the year and share the impact of their program. During this meeting school counselors provide feedback to each team and have the opportunity to share ideas for the next year. Each team of school counselors submits their results to the district leader, who oversees the school counseling program. The district leader combines all the results presentations to create one districtwide Flashlight Presentation, highlighting key outcomes of the PreK–12 school counseling program. The district school counseling presentation is shared with district leaders, school board members, cabinet members, and community groups.

The following shaded box includes examples of ways that school counselors in the SJUSD have shared their results. Their end-of-year results presentation is comprehensive, highlighting activities in all three tiers, and is used to create Flashlight Presentations designed for stakeholders, which makes it easier for school counselors to create a series of presentations.

San Jacinto Unified School District's (SJUSD) Results Presentations

Board Presentations

Two times a year the school counselors in SJUSD have the opportunity to share information and results of their school counseling program. These presentations are only 10 minutes long, requiring school counselors to be specific, concise, and selective about the information they will share. When school counselors present their data, it is critical to consider the following:

- Who is the audience you are presenting to?
- What data and information would that group be most interested in seeing?
- What story are you trying to tell?
- What is the goal of your presentation?

By considering the answers to all these questions, school counselors can be more strategic in creating their presentations. Table 10.1 is a presentation that was created for a team of state school board members who were visiting San Jacinto High School's Counseling Program to validate the Golden Bell Award for the outstanding work of the school counseling program.

Table 10.1   Next to each slide are talking points that school counselors used to highlight their program.

SLIDE	TALKING POINTS
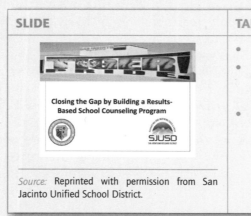 Closing the Gap by Building a Results-Based School Counseling Program	• Welcome and introductions • We are happy to share how our school counseling program results helped close some of our achievement gaps • The objective of the presentation today is to provide an overview of the development of our school counseling program, highlight some of our goals and program activities, and share some of our results

Source: Reprinted with permission from San Jacinto Unified School District.

SLIDE	TALKING POINTS
 The mission of San Jacinto Unified School District Counseling program is to ensure that all of our students receive equitable access to the attitudes, knowledge and skills necessary to achieve academic excellence, college/career readiness, personal growth, and social responsibility to become contributing members of society. *Source:* Reprinted with permission from San Jacinto Unified School District.	• Read our mission • Explain that our mission is the foundation of our counseling program • Highlight how important it is that our students receive *equitable* access
School Counseling in SJUSD **History of School Counseling** • Lack of leadership • Spending 90% of time dealing with 10% of population • Lack of team • Lack of a shared belief system • Lack of results • Clerical duties **Changes That Were Made** • Hired a consultant • Created a TK-12 lead counselor • Increased number of school counselors • Implemented ASCA National Model • LCAP • San Jacinto Difference • Focus on college and career	• To understand our school counseling program, it is important to understand our history • Over the last couple of years, we have transformed our school counseling program by implementing the ASCA National Model • Prior to implementing the ASCA National Model, the school counseling program lacked leadership and teamwork. School counselors were spending 90% of their time working with 10% of the population, providing no time to implement Tier 1 classroom lessons • Prior to implementing the ASCA National Model, the school counselor's role was undefined—they were spending much of their time doing clerical duties, and the program lacked results • Some of the changes made included our district hiring a consultant to help us evaluate and redesign the school counseling program • SJUSD created a lead counselor position to help guide the implementation of the ASCA National Model • Additional school counselors were hired, and the team aligned our school counseling program goals to the district and state goals and focused on college and career readiness
ASCA National Model  Domains: Academic, College/Career, Social/Emotional	• The ASCA National Model is a framework to guide the implementation of a comprehensive, data-driven school counseling program • Through implementing the ASCA National Model our school counseling program focused on three domains: academic, college/career, and social/emotional

(Continued)

Note: The ASCA National Model diamond used on this page represents the ASCA National Model, third edition. Readers are advised that the American School Counselor Association is revising the ASCA National Model, to be released June 2019, and are strongly encouraged to research and utilize the new version. The ASCA National Model is trademarked by the American School Counselor Association and reprinted with permission.

(Continued)

SLIDE	TALKING POINTS
Program Goals Driven by Data • Graduation rates • Completion of A-G courses • AP courses and exams • SAT scores and number of students taking it • California Healthy Kids Survey (CHKS) • Attendance rates • Suspensions and referrals • Community trends	• Our school counseling program is driven by data • Graduation rates, A–G (college preparation courses) completion rates, suspension, and attendance data are some examples of metrics that we examine to help create our school counseling program goals
 *Source:* Reprinted with permission from San Jacinto Unified School District.	• Based on our data we created six main program goals: 1) Implement the 8 Components of College and Career Readiness 2) Reduce the dropout rate 3) Prevent violence 4) Increase parent/family involvement 5) Improve student access to the school counseling program 6) Market and advertise our school counseling program • Each of our goals is linked to our district's Local Control Accountability Plan (LCAP) goals
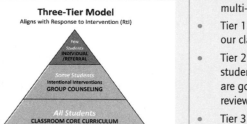 **Three-Tier Model** Aligns with Response to Intervention (RtI) *Few Students* INDIVIDUAL/REFERRAL *Some Students* Intentional Interventions GROUP COUNSELING *All Students* CLASSROOM CORE CURRICULUM	• Our school counseling program is designed using a multi-tiered approach • Tier 1 school counseling services are provided through our classroom lessons that all students receive • Tier 2 school counseling services are provided to students who need more support than Tier 1, and we are going to highlight some of these services when we review how we are closing the achievement gap • Tier 3 services are provided for students who need more individual support such as short-term one-on-one counseling
533 Lessons/Workshops in 2015–16 Over **1300** Lessons/ Workshops Over Last 3 Years! 	• Highlighting some of our Tier 1 data, we have provided 533 lessons in the last school year and over 1,300 lessons over the last 3 years

SLIDE	TALKING POINTS

SMART Goal: Increase A-G
 	
• College Kick Off
• National College Signing Day
• College and Career Making It Happen Lessons
• Course Selection Process
  – Video
  – Individual Meeting
• A-G Opt Letter
• Set High Expectations
• Transcript Analysis
• Course Recovery Options
 	
GOAL
	• Based on our school data, one area we wanted to focus on was increasing our A–G (college prep course completion) rate because less than 30% of our students were graduating eligible to apply for college in 2012–2013
	
	• Some of the activities we have implemented to improve A–G rates include implementing Tier 1 lessons titled College and Career: Making it Happen, highlighting the importance of meeting A-G requirements
	
	• We have also implemented systems to ensure that our students take A–G courses, such as requiring parents/guardians sign an opt-out form if their child wants to drop an A–G class
	
	• We conduct transcript analyses of the previous graduating class to identify trends that are preventing students from meeting the A–G requirements

A-G RATES BY YEAR San Jacinto HS <table><tr><td>Class</td><td>SJHS A-G</td><td>County A-G</td><td>CA. A-G</td></tr><tr><td>2012-13</td><td>28.4%</td><td>35%</td><td>39.4%</td></tr><tr><td>2013-14</td><td>37.4%</td><td>38%</td><td>41.9%</td></tr><tr><td>2014-15</td><td>40.3%</td><td>39.9%</td><td>43.9%</td></tr><tr><td>2015-16</td><td>45.7%</td><td>44.3%</td><td>45.4%</td></tr></table>	• As a result of implementing lessons and program activities to support our A–G SMART goal, we have increased our A–G rates significantly—a 61% increase over 3 years • Comparing SJHS to the county and state, last year our A–G rates were higher than both (Note: This is an example of outcome data. This slide demonstrates how you can use data over time to show growth. This slide also highlights comparison data, allowing counselors to compare SJHS's results to the county average and state average.)
SMART Goal: **65% of A-G Seniors will apply to one or more universities** • As of August 2016 **47.9%** of class of 2016 were on target for meeting A-G requirements • **81%** of Eligible A-G Seniors applied to one or more Universities—Goal EXCEEDED by 16% • **29% increase** in submitted university applications compared to class of 2015	• Another one of our school counseling program SMART goals is to increase the number of our seniors who apply to one or more universities • Many of our students are first-generation college students and in looking at our school data, we noticed that many of our students who met A–G requirements were not applying to a university • We decided to identify all of our A–G-eligible seniors and ensure that they applied to one or more universities • As a result, 81% of our eligible seniors applied to one or more universities, which is a 29% increase from the previous year

(Continued)

(Continued)

SLIDE	TALKING POINTS
Demystifying the College Process • College Parent Night– 100 parents attended • CASH for College Workshop • A-G Rallies (6) • College Application Workshops (38) • MSJC Workshops • University 101 • Student Intent to Register (SIR) Meetings- 190 meetings 	• As we mentioned earlier, our goal is to ensure that our students are college and career ready, and we used the College Board's 8 Components of College and Career Readiness to help us reach that goal • One of the Components of College and Career Readiness is to demystify the college process; we have done this by implementing activities such as A–G rallies, providing college application workshops, student intent to register for college meetings, and University 101 workshops for students and families
College Signing Day!  **210** Seniors symbolically committed to continuing their Post-Secondary education in the attendance of peers, parents and underclassmen!	• One of our favorite activities that we organize to create a college-going culture is our College Signing Day event, designed for seniors who have committed to attending college (community or university), enlisted in the military, or have committed to trade school • Representatives from each postsecondary group attend this event and congratulate the students • Families and underclassmen are invited to see the seniors sign a commitment and receive a medallion • This year 210 seniors attended College Signing Day, and we are going to show you a video highlighting this event (Note: Videos of school counseling events are an excellent tool to market your counseling program and share in presentations.)
2016 Postsecondary Plans 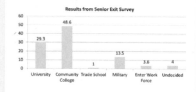	Our SMART goal was to increase college-going rates As a result of our school counseling team's effort, 29.3% of our seniors are attending a university Additionally, 92.4% of our seniors had a post-secondary plan

SLIDE	TALKING POINTS
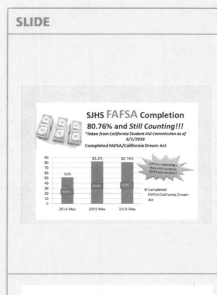	• Another school counseling program goal is to increase our FAFSA completion rate • In 2014 only 51% of seniors completed the FAFSA; currently, 80.7% of seniors completed their FAFSA • Although we are trending 2% lower than last year, we are still working hard to get all of our seniors to complete the application, and our school counseling team is examining what factors are contributing to the decline (Note: This data slide shows a decrease in FAFSA completion. It is okay to show data that are not improving or declining because they help school counselors examine causes for the decline. Additionally, sharing data that aren't perfect indicates that counselors are honest about program strengths and areas for growth.)
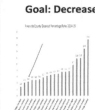	• We want to continue to decrease our dropout rate • Last year SJHS had the third-lowest dropout rate in the county • Some activities we implemented to address this goal included implementing a Tier 2 activity called Tiger Talks; during Tiger Talks school counselors meet with students who have multiple Fs and help them create a success plan to improve their grades • We also have systems in place to help students recover credits
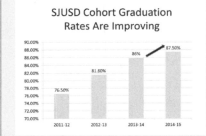	• Our graduation rates have been improving, from 76.5% to 87.5% in the last 4 years, but we still have a way to go
	• To reach our goals, we realize that we have to close our achievement gap • Through data, we realized that we need to provide more Tier 2 services to our English language learner (ELL) students and foster youth

(Continued)

(Continued)

SLIDE	TALKING POINTS
Creating Systems to Support ELL Students • ELL Student Focus Groups • ELL Student Surveys • ELL Graduation Talks for students deficient in credits • ELL Cohorts in Master Schedule • CELDT Talks • CELDT Lessons	• We created systems to support our ELL students • Some activities include providing California English Language Development Test (CELDT) Talks prior to the testing to help students understand why the test is important and how they can become reclassified as fluent English proficient • We also provide individual meetings with students to review their graduation plans and ways to make up credits • We held focus groups with ELL students to better understand areas that caused them struggle and asked for their input on ways to improve graduation rates for students with their backgrounds; based on the student feedback we advocated for more instructional aides to provide support in their core classes • We conducted a transcript analysis to identify patterns and trends for ELL students
Closing the GAP Action Plan: **English Language Learners** • **68%** of EL seniors completed FAFSA/CA.DREAM Act • **68%** of EL seniors graduated in 2016 • **8** classroom CELDT Talks • **50** individual CELDT Talks (the 2nd intervention) **44%** of ELLs who received the 2nd intervention passed CELDT	• Although there is much work to be done, we have started tracking the percentage of our ELL students who completed the FAFSA and graduated from high school • We provided eight CELDT lessons and 50 individual CELDT Talks—44% of students who received the intervention passed the CELDT
Creating Systems to Support Foster Youth • Grade Monitoring • Graduation Check Each Semester • AB216 Eligibility Review • Student Focus Groups • Connect to Support • Post-Secondary Planning • Guest Speaker	• Some of the activities we implemented to support our foster youth include academic monitoring every grading period and conducting focus groups with foster students for their suggestions about how school counselors can support them • One suggestion provided by the foster student focus groups was their desire to hear tips directly from former foster youth who are successful after high school, so we brought in one of our alumni who shared his success story
Closing the GAP Action Plan: **Foster Youth** • **100%** Completed the FAFSA • **67%** Graduated • **77%** On target to graduate	• We still have work to do with our foster students, but we are seeing an improvement in their graduation rates • We are also happy to report that 100% of foster youth seniors completed their FAFSA • In 2016 100% of foster youth seniors who graduated from high school applied to community college or university

SLIDE	TALKING POINTS
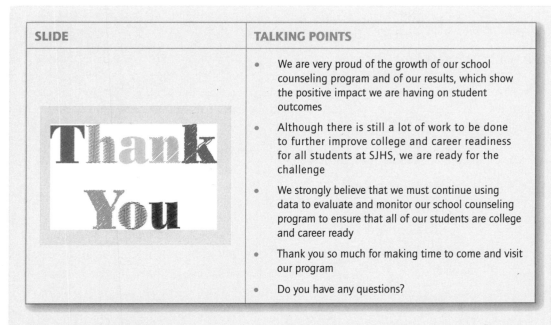	• We are very proud of the growth of our school counseling program and of our results, which show the positive impact we are having on student outcomes • Although there is still a lot of work to be done to further improve college and career readiness for all students at SJHS, we are ready for the challenge • We strongly believe that we must continue using data to evaluate and monitor our school counseling program to ensure that all of our students are college and career ready • Thank you so much for making time to come and visit our program • Do you have any questions?

District Presentations

SJUSD shares PreK–12 school counseling program results during general council monthly meetings (comprised of district leaders and principals of each site). Additionally, representatives from the school counseling team present their program results data at a school board meeting one to two times a year. The SJUSD superintendent presents school counseling results during her annual state of education presentation, which is in front of community, staff, and parent stakeholders. The annual state of education presentation highlights ways the district is reaching its goals. Because the school counseling program goals are aligned with the SJUSD Local Control Accountability Plan, called the San Jacinto Difference, school counseling results are also shared during the district's stakeholders quarterly meetings, called Vision 20/20.

Staff Meetings

School counselors also share their results during staff meetings. During one of the first staff meetings of the year, school counselors in SJUSD provide a 15- to 30-minute overview of their school counseling program including the program mission statement, information about the services they provide, a review of program goals and results, and a reminder about procedures for seeing a school counselor. These presentations help staff better understand the appropriate school counseling role as well as understand the why of their program and see the positive impact they are making aligning with student outcomes. Many school counselors have 5 to 10 minutes during staff meetings throughout the year to provide updates about what is going on with the school counseling program.

Site Administrator Beginning-of-the-Year Meeting

In SJUSD, school counselors and the district leader of the school counseling program meet with site administrators at the beginning of the year to present the previous year's

(Continued)

(Continued)

result report, discuss goals for the school counseling program, and review all ASCA documents, such as the annual agreement, core classroom action plan, closing the gap action plan, intentional intervention plan, and the yearly calendar. This important meeting enables site administrators and school counselors to communicate and discuss program goals.

School Counselor Advisory Council

School counselors in SJUSD conduct school counselor advisory council meetings two times a year comprised of administrators, teachers, students, certificated staff, parents/families, and community members. During these meetings school counselors share counseling program goals, activities, and results. They also solicit feedback from the participants for suggestions to help improve the school counseling program.

Creating Data Presentation Slides

There are a variety of ways to showcase data slides when creating Flashlight Presentations or other types. Review the following data slides from schools/ districts where Trish, Whitney, Danielle, and Vanessa have worked, which provide examples of ways to share data with school stakeholders. Figure 10.12 highlights classroom core curriculum lessons, providing information about the lesson, who received the lesson, and how many lessons were conducted (process data). In Figure 10.13 school counselors provide process and outcome data aligned with their *College Kick-Off* schoolwide event. Figure 10.14 provides an example of a pre/post-test (perception data) and highlights improvement using the percent change. San Jacinto high school counselors highlight one of their SMART goals in Figure 10.15, which is to increase FAFSA completion rates. Increasing FAFSA rates can reduce the financial barrier that may prevent students from continuing their education. This slide (one of two) provides a yearly comparison allowing the audience to see the growth from year to year. Figure 10.16 is the "show me the money" slide, which powerfully demonstrates the amount of money in grant funding students received.

NOTES

_____

_____

_____

Figure 10.12   Summary of One Core Lesson Providing Process Data

College & Career: Making It Happen!

An interactive lesson presented to every grade level!

- **Counselor-created video** that covered
  - Graduation and A-G requirements
  - All postsecondary education options (trade/technical, community college, & university)
  - Financial aid
- **Transcript review** that gave students an opportunity to evaluate their own
- Use of **Naviance** to complete a career cluster assessment and research careers that matched their interests

78 Classroom Lessons

954 Completed Career Cluster Assessments 9-11th grade

Figure 10.13   Summary of a Schoolwide Event: Notice how the school counselors described the activities and share the FAFSA rate after the event occurred

College Kick-Off

- 1,811 Students in 9-11th Grade took the PSAT
- Seniors Participated in:
  - FAFSA 101
  - Completing College Applications
  - Completing FAFSA/CA Dream Act Application
  - Military Preparation
  - Kick-Off Rally with Games & Give-a-ways

58% of the senior class submitted their FAFSA or CA Dream Act **THAT Day!**

Figure 10.14 Perception Data Slide—Pre/Post-Test with Percent Change

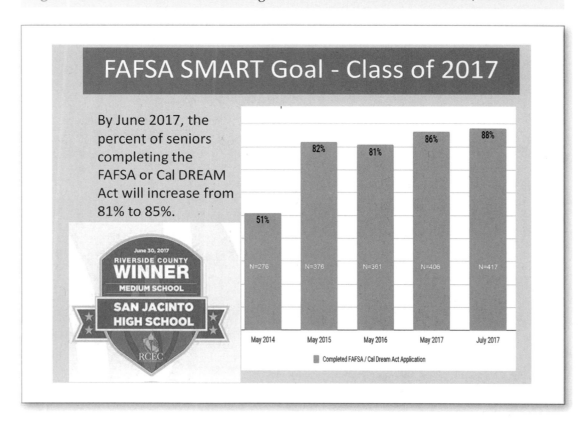

Figure 10.15 SMART Goal Showcasing FAFSA Achievement-Related Data, Slide 1 of 2

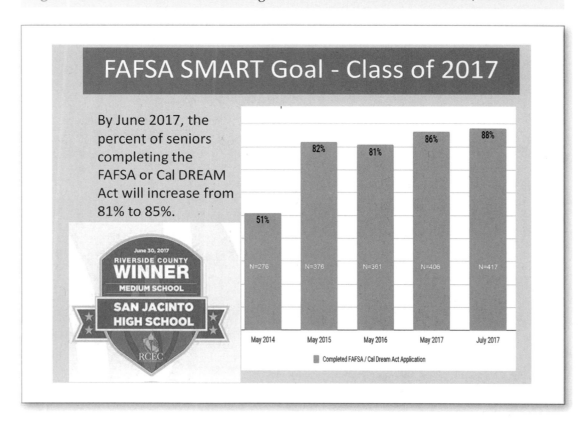

Notice how the school counselors used comparison data from previous years. The growth from 2014 to 2017 is a 73% increase in FAFSA completion! San Jacinto high school counselors also highlight how they received an award from Riverside County Office of Education for having the highest FAFSA completion rates. This is an example of a well-done slide marketing school counseling program results!

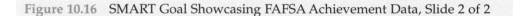

Figure 10.16   SMART Goal Showcasing FAFSA Achievement Data, Slide 2 of 2

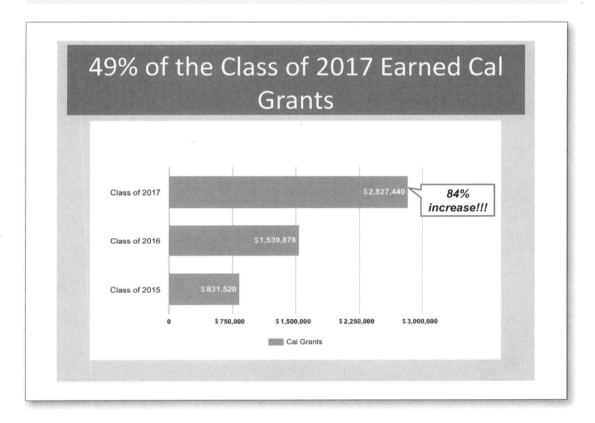

Figure 10.16 is the second slide that accompanies Figure 10.15. School counselors from San Jacinto High School not only tracked FAFSA completion but also calculated the number of seniors who earned California grants. There was an 84% increase compared to the previous year.

NOTES

Cautionary Tales of Data Gone Wrong

These slides depict exemplary ways to highlight school counseling program data. When creating results presentations, school counselors are encouraged to highlight process, perception, *and* outcome data in an equal way. Too much process data and not enough outcome data can weaken the impact of the presentation. Additionally, the way data are presented is also important to ensure the results are clear and easy to understand. Through providing professional development to school counselors throughout the United States, we find that presenting data in a thoughtful manner can be easier said than done. To help counselors avoid mistakes we have compiled some examples of common errors to learn from (which is a form of non-modeling, similar to modeling, described in Chapter 5). As you look through each slide, consider what could be done differently to improve the ease of understanding when showcasing the results. And feel reassured that we, too, have made data mistakes in the past!

Figure 10.17   Perception Data Gone Wrong

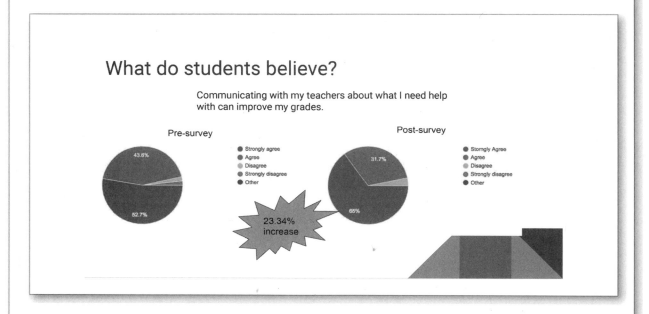

When you look at this data slide, how easy is it for you to read and understand? What could be done differently to highlight the data more clearly? When considering the type of chart to use when presenting data, think about which will be easiest for the audience to understand. This slide can be improved by using a bar graph instead of two pie graphs side by side. Additionally, the callout box (23.34% increase) can be improved by making it more clear—in what area, specifically, is there an increase? The counselor is trying to showcase the improvement in students who strongly agree that communicating with teachers can help them improve their grades, but this isn't clear. The *.34* can also be removed from the callout box; because school counselors are presenting basic results, this is unnecessary and may be distracting.

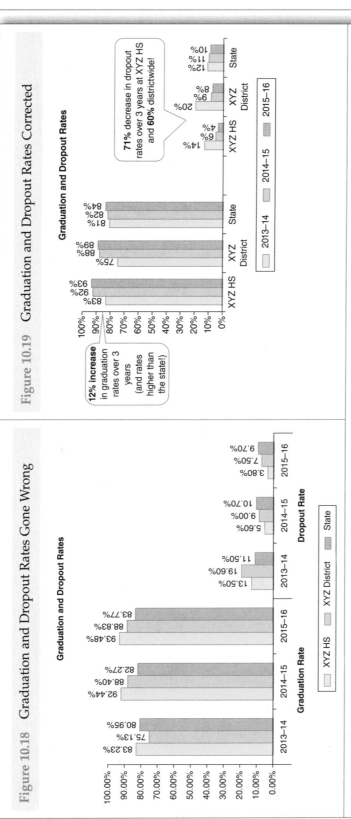

Figure 10.18   Graduation and Dropout Rates Gone Wrong

Figure 10.19   Graduation and Dropout Rates Corrected

When you look at the slide on the left (Figure 10.18), what do you see? Is it easy to understand? What do you think can be done to improve this slide? One of the first things we notice is that there is a lot of information on one slide. Although the school counselors are using comparison data, it is difficult to see changes because the data are presented by year rather than sorted by school, district, and state. When creating a data slide, it is helpful to ask yourself, "What do I want to highlight on this data slide?" In this case, we suggest showcasing the improvement in graduation rates and decrease in dropout rates at XYZ high school. The best way to present this information clearly is to include the yearly percentages for XYZ side by side (Figure 10.19). The percentages were also made larger and the decimal points removed to allow viewers to more easily focus on the whole numbers. Another key strategy to improve this slide is to add callout boxes highlighting the data being presented. Compare Figure 10.18 to 10.19 to see our upgrades to the data.

(Continued)

(Continued)

Figure 10.20   Perception Data (Attitudes) Gone Wrong

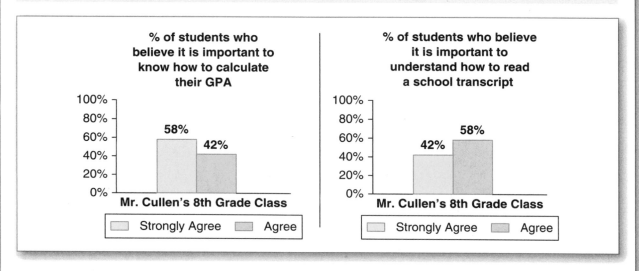

How can these attitudes slides be improved? These slides show responses to two different attitude questions. However, there are two main problems: 1) the slides do not indicate if these data are from a pre- or post-test and 2) when showcasing attitudes data, all student responses should be included to see the spectrum of answers (i.e., disagree and strongly disagree should be added to the slide). In addition, ideally the school counselors have both pre- and post-results from the lesson; if this is the case, it is suggested to compare the results within one slide, with pre- and post-percentages side by side. See the attitudes data presented within the Flashlight Presentation for an example (Figure 10.4).

Figure 10.21   More Perception Data (Attitudes) Gone Wrong

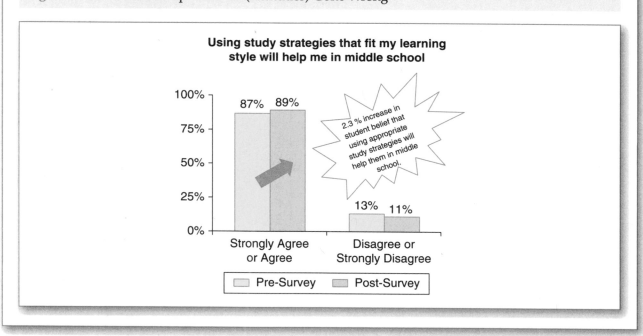

What would you change on this slide (Figure 10.21)? These results remind us to pay attention to what we are measuring and how we are showcasing improvement. A key feature of sharing students' attitudes is to see the shift between agree to strongly agree (or disagree to strongly disagree). This shift generally indicates behavior change as students are more likely to take action if they strongly agree (or strongly disagree). Therefore, clumping strongly agree and agree together does not show this possible shift. In addition, although an improvement in graduation rates from 87% to 89% is positive, a two percentage point increase within perception data is neutral. Therefore, we suggest the callout box be removed and saved for times when improvements are large.

Figure 10.22   Perception Data (Knowledge) Gone Wrong

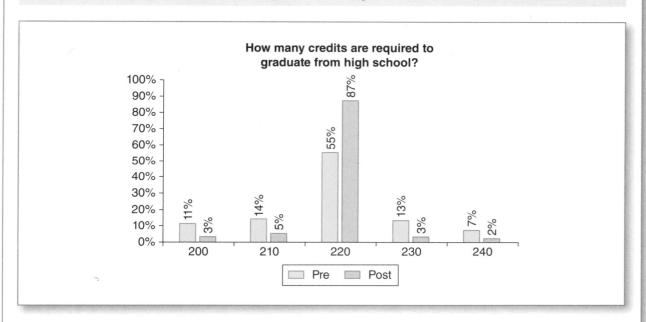

What upgrades would you make to this presentation of data? For attitude questions, there is not a right or wrong answer (even though we often hope students will respond in a "right" way); therefore, sharing all student responses is useful for the audience. However, for knowledge and skills questions, usually only one answer is correct. Displaying incorrect responses within results presentations detracts from showcasing the improvement students (hopefully) showed. This slide can be modified to only include the pre- and post-results of the correct answer.

Tools to Create Results Reports and Presentations

Different software programs with a variety of features are available to help school counselors present their results effectively. Although PowerPoint and Google Slides are often used, there are other options to consider that offer varying levels of ease of use, cost, and so on. School counselors may choose programs readily available at their workplace or may want to look at the alternatives listed in Table 10.2.

Table 10.2   Program Results Presentation Software

Software	Description	Cost
Prezi https://prezi.com	This visual storytelling software features a map-like, schematic overview that lets users pan between topics at will, zoom in on desired details, and pull back to reveal context. This freedom of movement enables a conversational presenting style in which presentations follow the flow of dialogue instead of vice versa.	Free public account (limited); 14-day free trial; three monthly subscription plans with additional features at a cost
Google Slides https://www.google.com/slides/about	Praised for its simplicity and frequent product updates, this presentation program offered by Google within its Google Drive service allows users to create and edit files online while collaborating with other users in real time.	Free
Piktochart https://piktochart.com	This web-based infographic application allows users to easily create professional designer-grade infographics using themed templates. It features HTML publishing capability, which generates infographics that are viewable online with multiple clickable elements, such as videos, hyperlinks, and charts for users.	Free lifetime account, with options to upgrade anytime to access additional features
(Apple) Keynote https://www.apple.com/keynote	This presentation software application includes beta release so that your team can work together collaboratively in real time on a Mac, iPad, iPhone, or even on a PC using iWork for iCloud. With Keynote Live, many people in different places can be invited to watch your presentation.	Included in the iWork productivity suite by Apple Inc.; cost varies for Mac OS or iOS
Visme https://www.visme.co	This is a one-stop shop for all visual design needs to develop engaging content in the form of presentations (online and off-line), infographics, reports, web products, etc.	Basic plan (limited) is free; monthly subscription plans with premium features available at a cost with student and teacher discounts available
Presbee https://presbee.com/index	This tool is simple to use, with full multimedia functionality, including live websites, streamed video, timing controls, full analytics, nonlinear presentations, pre-styled tables and data charts, and remote meetings.	Free (limited) for beginners, with two subscription plan options for professionals or teams needing additional features

USING NATIONAL SCHOOL COUNSELING WEEK AND OTHER OPPORTUNITIES TO SHARE SCHOOL COUNSELING PROGRAM RESULTS

National School Counseling Week (NSCW), celebrated annually during the first week of February, focuses public attention on the unique contribution of school counselors within the school system and how students improve as a result of school counselors' work. ASCA (2018a) states that NSCW "exists to focus public attention on the unique contribution of school counselors within U.S. school systems." NSCW is a wonderful opportunity for school counselors to promote the services and outcomes of their school counseling program while also thanking the school staff for their support. What follows are different ways in which secondary school counselors have shared results during NSCW.

Transforming Our Thinking About NSCW: Overcoming a Common Misconception

School counselors (and others) sometimes view National School Counseling Week (NSCW) similarly to Teacher Appreciation Week—both as weeks designed to honor and celebrate educators. They see NSCW as simply a week to thank school counselors for the work that they do. It's even common to hear the phrase, "Happy School Counselor Week"—although it has intentionally been named National School Counseling Week to place emphasis on the school counseling *program* instead of the *person*. These views are not necessarily wrong, but they do miss the intention and spirit that are central to NSCW, which was designed to be a systemized opportunity for us to educate key stakeholders about school counseling.

Quite simply, NSCW is a *vehicle for professional advocacy*. For school counselors to effectively support students, it is critical that stakeholders fully understand and buy into the breadth and depth of what it is that transformed school counselors do, including the impact that our actions have on our students. Because we've chosen to be a part of a young, evolving profession, we also have a responsibility to contribute to the building of its legitimacy through advocacy for the betterment of our students. NSCW is a phenomenal opportunity for us to contribute to the legitimacy of our profession. It gives us a great excuse to pause, reflect on our own unique contribution, and then share it with our school community! In so doing, we build the capacity of our stakeholders to understand the role and function of a transformed school counselor that impacts student success. *Greater understanding of the school counselor role results in better supports for our students and a larger impact on student success.*

Professional advocacy is not about school counselors—it's about students. Although we should absolutely celebrate and thank school counselors (#SchoolCounselorsRock!) during NSCW, our primary focus should be on *educating* administrators, staff, students, families, and community partners about the role of today's transformed school counselors in impacting student success. So let's roll up our sleeves, put on our "advocate hats," and utilize NSCW to be *change agents for our profession* (#AdvocacyWorks)!

School Counseling Trivia Contest

One activity that school counselors have utilized is having a trivia contest at their site to increase awareness of the comprehensive school counseling program. School counselors create questions about the school counselor role and/or data related to school counseling program results that are announced daily. Students and staff make guesses about correct answers in the counselor office and staff lounge. A winner is drawn, and an announcement over the intercom is made at the end of the day providing the correct information and the name of the winner. Trivia questions can include: "How many classroom lessons have the school counselors provided this year?", "Can you name three lessons the school counselors have provided?", and so on.

Results and Treats

Co-author Danielle Duarte used NSCW to celebrate her counseling program through sharing treats and data (see Figures 10.23, 10.24, and 10.25). Each year, Danielle created a PowerPoint highlighting program information and results, including those from Tier 1, in an easy-to-read format. On the first day of NSCW, Danielle and her counseling team set up a table in the staff lounge decorated with printed-out school counseling program slides and also set out cookies and candy. The counseling team sent an email to the staff thanking them for their support of school counseling and inviting them to enjoy treats in celebration of NSCW during lunch. At the end of the day, they sent another thank-you email to the staff with the PowerPoint presentation attached so that all staff had access to the information. Additionally, Danielle and her team created an NSCW lunchtime activity for students, asking them to write down how their school counselors help them succeed. Student quotes were shared with faculty and on the school website.

Figure 10.23   Danielle's NSCW Celebration

Figure 10.24   NSCW Student Lunchtime Activity

Figure 10.25   NSCW Program Highlight Slides

Happy National School Counseling Week!

We ♥ your support!!!

Please enjoy some treats in celebration of the week! ☺

~The Potter School Counseling Department

My school counselor helps me succeed by...

"...helping me be happier and encouraging me"

"...being proactive"

"...helping me with my grades and problems"

"...making school a fun and safe place."

"...educating us about preparing for a bright future!"

"...helping us make good decisions."

Intentional Guidance: Academic Interventions

▸ **Programs & Activities***
  ◦ Grades Check Lunch Workshops
  ◦ Academic-Focused Small Groups
  ◦ 8th Grade *7 Habits* Summer Workshop
  ◦ School Counseling Intern Mentoring
  ◦ Study Skills Support
  ◦ Parent Contact & Meetings
  ◦ Progress Monitoring
  ◦ Lunch Tutoring

"One thing I learned during the group is to never give up and just keep trying no matter what"

*Additionally, ALL students received instruction on how to check their grades online

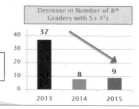

Decrease in Number of 8th Graders with 5+ F's

37	8	9
2013	2014	2015

Thank you for your support of Potter Junior High's School Counseling Program & activities like College & Career Day.

American School Counselor Association Standards related to **College & Career Readiness**

Standard C: Students will understand the relationship between personal qualities, education, training and the world of work.

C:C1.1 Understand the relationship between educational achievement and career success

C:C2.1 Demonstrate how interests, abilities and achievement relate to achieving personal, social, educational and career goals

Core Counseling Curriculum:
College & Career Readiness

▸ **Programs & Activities**
- College & Career Day
- 7th Grade College Field Trip
  - Career & College Exploration
  - 4 Year HS Plans
  - Computer-Based Career Exploration Assessment
- Core Counseling Classroom Lessons
- College Trips
- College Shirt Thursdays
- Lunch with a College Student
- Parent Workshops
- Articulation with Fallbrook HS
- Promote Upward Bound & AVID at HS

Percent of Students Who Know the A-G College Requirements

100%
80% — 71% 77%
60% — 63%
40% — 14%
20%
0%
    7th   8th

*As 7th graders, only 10% knew the A-G Requirements

Our students are learning about CSUSM 4 U!

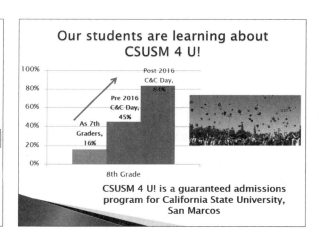

100%
80% — Post 2016 C&C Day, 84%
60% — Pre 2016 C&C Day, 45%
40% — As 7th Graders, 16%
20%
0%
        8th Grade

CSUSM 4 U! is a guaranteed admissions program for California State University, San Marcos

The Potter School Counseling Program received the Recognized ASCA Model Program (RAMP) designation for creating comprehensive, data–driven academic, social/emotional, & college and career readiness services for all students.

Only five other schools in California have received this distinction!

Note: The ASCA National Model diamond used on this page represents the ASCA National Model, third edition. Readers are advised that the American School Counselor Association is revising the ASCA National Model, to be released June 2019, and are strongly encouraged to research and utilize the new version. The ASCA National Model is trademarked by the American School Counselor Association and reprinted with permission.

For additional ideas for celebrating NSCW, listen to Episode 4 of the Hatching Results Podcast, available at www.hatchingresults .com/podcast stitcher.com/podcast/hatching-results-podcast.

Activity: After listening to the podcast, reflect on the variety of ways to share your program results. What do you like about them? How can you modify one of these examples or create your own to showcase the work you are doing in your own school counseling program?

ADDITIONAL IDEAS FOR SHARING RESULTS

There are many ways to share school counseling program results throughout the year. What follows are some suggested activities and strategies. Which opportunities fit your skills, level of comfort in public speaking and use of technology, and available resources best? Making a commitment to sharing program results benefits both the school counseling program and the entire profession.

- Contact the local newspaper before a schoolwide activity, such as College Signing Day or College and Career Day, and ask the paper to cover the event. If a reporter is unable to attend, the newspaper often allows stories and photos to be submitted. You can also submit a press release (see Figure 10.26).
- Publicize a few highlights of the school counseling program process, perception, and/or outcome data in a regular school or counseling program newsletter for families and staff.
- Display a summary of counseling activities and outcomes on the school counseling program's or the school's website. Figure 10.27 provides examples of exemplary school counselor websites.
- Present a report to the local school council, school site council, or the parent–teacher association.
- Share about the school counseling program during open sessions of district school board meetings. Anyone from the public is welcome to attend and share at these meetings with a written request before the meeting begins. Generally, the time allotted to speak is 3 to 5 minutes. Prepare a brief statement, and bring a Results Report or other program information (see Figure 10.28) and outcomes to share with those in attendance (note: be sure to discuss this presentation with site administrators beforehand for approval).
- Email staff and students brief data points, and advertise in the announcements.
- Share results with other school counselors by presenting a workshop session at state and national conferences.
- Invite school board members to visit your site, and use the opportunity to share program activities and results (remember to always discuss this idea with your administrators first).

- Submit photos and achieved results to state, national, and/or district offices seeking good news stories and articles for publication.
- Create a video showcasing the school counselor department's role on campus (see Figure 10.29).
- Utilize social media to share your data, and market your school counseling program.
- Participate in a district or conference poster exposition featuring school counseling program services and outcomes.
- Network with other counselors using social media exchanges and blogs—share program results and activities with them virtually.
- Create an end-of-the-year bulletin board or other visual display stating "Thanks for a great year!" with highlights of the program's impact that school year.
- Create a school counselor program profile, which is a summary of what your school counseling program offers, and post it on your website (see Figure 10.30).

Figure 10.26 Sample press release that can be mailed to newspapers prior to your event—always contact your district's public relations officer to get permission.

FOR IMMEDIATE RELEASE

Date: October 11, 2017

Contact: Suzy Que, School Counselor, XYZ School District
(XXX) XXX-XXXX ext. XXXX

XYZUSD Celebrates Countywide College Kick-Off Event Districtwide

XYZ High School will hold a College Kick-Off Day on Wednesday, October 14, 2017; the focus of this event is to focus on college and career readiness. The _____ County Office of Education challenged each school district to implement activities for students, parents and community partners to explore and emphasize the importance of planning for postsecondary education, including two and four-year college, trade school and/or the military.

"This is the time of year we promote the college application process, and XYZ High School will administer the Pre-Scholastic Assessment Test (PSAT) to all students in grades 9 through 11, while seniors will complete their FAFSA application and college applications," said Suzy Que, school counselor at XYZ High. Last year, XYZ high school had a 96% graduation rate, far surpassing the countywide average, and also had the highest growth in _____ County for completing the FAFSA (Free Application for Federal Student Aid) at 86%. In 2016, 83% of XYZ High students attended a two- or four-year college.

On College Kick-Off Day students and staff will adorn their favorite college shirts, colors and career attire and attend lunchtime pep rallies; there will be a college essay contest, and decorated office/classroom doors, just to name a few activities that will be held on College Kick-Off Day. "We are committed to promoting college and career readiness," said Jane Doe, XYZ superintendent. The school counselors will be facilitating college application workshops and financial aid applications to ensure that their students are prepared for postsecondary options.

###

"All Students College & Career Ready"

Figure 10.27   Exemplary Websites and Activity

School Counseling Program
Website Activity and Exemplar Websites

Activity:

Imagine you are a parent of a middle school or high school student. What information would you want to know about your student's school counseling program?

Important Items to Include on Your Website:

- School counselor information (name, brief biography, picture, specializations, contact information, and caseload information)
- School counseling program mission
- Description of the school counseling program
- Core classroom lessons provided and actual lessons posted
- Resources for academic, college/career, and social/emotional
- How to contact or make an appointment with school counselors
- Calendar
- Upcoming events
- Results
- Photos of school counseling activities

Exemplar School Counseling Websites*:

High School	Middle School
Orange Glen Escondido, CA	Rensselaer Central Albinrcms.weebly.com
Cactus Shadow Cave Creek, AZ	Hillview Jr High Pittsburg, CA
San Jacinto San Jacinto, CA	Potter Jr High Fallbrook, CA
San Mateo San Mateo, CA	Monte Vista Middle School San Jacinto, CA
Pittsburg Pittsburg, CA	
Brea Olinda Brea, CA	

*As of the time of this book's publication.

Figure 10.28 Semester 1 Summary of School Counseling Program Activities

San Jacinto High School

School Counseling Update

"Our School, Our Education, Our Future, Our Responsibility."

Semester One Update

"Be the change that you wish to see in the world." Mahatma Gandhi

Academic
- Counselors referred 120 students to Mountain View to recover credits towards graduation.
- 88 Tiger Talk Small Group Interventions. Met with 10th and 11th grade students who are behind in credits and created an academic success contract with each student. Discussed strategies to improve grades, goals and opportunities to make up credits
- 33 Tiger Talk Student Skills Group Intervention. Met with 10th and 11th grade students to provide study skills for success.
- 3 AVID SAT Preparation Presentations
- 2 ELD SAT Preparation Presentations
- 35 ELL CELDT Test preparation meetings with intermediate students
- Bi-Weekly 9th Grade Tiger Student Success Meetings. On-going meetings with students who have 3+ F's. Contribute a positive attribute to students, review grades, attendance, identify at least two goals per course, plan for success, tutoring, Saturday Scholars, supplies and campus connectedness
- Ongoing student meetings to discuss academic achievement
- Counselors meet with students and parents before referral to Mountain Heights Academy.

College/Career
- ROTC junior flight Career Exploration Lesson
- 67 College and Career Lessons provided to all students in grades via English 1 and the Social Science Department
- "College Rush" held during lunch for grades 9-12 on 10/21/14 and recruiters from UCI, UCR, UCSB, MSJC, CSUSB, PLNC, ITT, UCD, GCU, and UCM provided information for all students
- 6 "A-G Rallies" offered for the 250 A-G eligible seniors who meet the A-G requirements
- 22 University Application Workshops conducted for 12th grade students various times in the school day. The deadline for the UC/CSU application is November 30th for students to be admitted during the next school year.
- Over 200 students participated in taking the PSAT held on 10/18
- 3 Scholarship workshops held for12th grade students
- School Counselor attended the collaborative planning meeting for annual Career Business Summit. The Business Summit is a career focused event for 12th grade students. Students receive workshops on resume writing, grooming, interviewing, job search assistance, professionalism and more.
- School counselor met with 19 non A-G seniors to discuss career options and preparation for the Business Summit
- Military Day was held during lunch at SJHS of all students on November 6th. Recruiters from the Navy, Marines, Army, National Guard, and Air Forces attended and provided information for all students.
- School Counselors visited that San Diego Military Processing Station to MEPS
- School Counselors were summoned to the White House School Counseling Forum at SDSU.
- Ongoing student meetings to discuss College and Career options after high school
- 1 workshop for ELD 2 students on Naviance Navigation
- Counselors attended the CSU/UC counselor conferences during the school year.

Personal/Social
- 12 Bullying Guidance Lessons conducted for all 9th grade students during their physical education class. During this lesson, students learned the how to identify bullying, what to do if they were being bullying, and how to stop bullying by using Stop.. Walk.. Talk (SWT)
- 11 Early Warning Signs of Violence (CC Linked Lessons) conducted for 10th grade students in English 2.
- 33 students evaluated for suicidal ideation and/or plans
- 17 students evaluated for self injury
- 20 students were referred to the Riverside County Probation Youth Accountability Team (YAT)
- Ongoing student crisis response for grief, stress, family support, friendship, anger management, and suspension reflections
- Intake for group counseling for Alcohol, Tobacco, and Other Drugs (ATOD) group, Anger Management, Boys Leadership, and Girls Leadership

Parent Connection
- Over 100 parents attended "Parent College Night" held on 10/2
- 9th Grade new student Parent Meeting held on 8/7
- 4 ELAC Parent presentations
- On-going parent meetings to discuss academic achievement, behavioral, attendance, and personal/social
- On-going parent home visits to discuss attendance

Campus Connectedness
- Counselors are involved in advising or co-advising the following student clubs: Mecha, Interact, and Active Minds
- Counselor participation in the district counselor meetings, CTE, safety committee, leadership team meetings, administration meetings

To learn more about the role of a high school counselor visit: http://www.schoolcounselor.org/school-counselors-members/careers-roles/why-secondary-school-counselors

For more information about the SJHS school counseling program visit: http://sjhs-sjusd-ca.schoolloop.com/counseling

The mission of San Jacinto High School Counseling program is to ensure that all of our students receive equitable access to the knowledge, attitudes and skills necessary to achieve academic excellence, college/career readiness, personal growth and social responsibility to become contributing members of their world community.

Figure 10.29   Video School Counseling 101—to watch the video go to https://youtu.be/ryTjcHLm2uQ

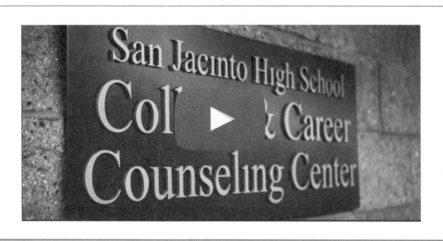

Figure 10.30   Vintage High School Counselor Profile

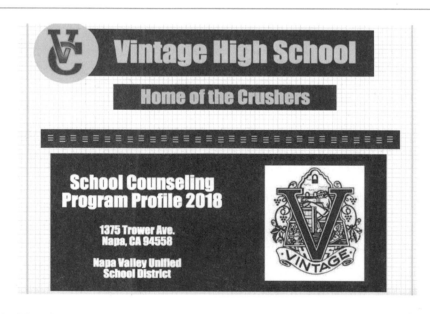

To view the full profile, go to https://create.piktochart.com/output/29112348-copyvintage-high-school-school-counseling-profile-2018-copy.

Sharing school counseling program results is an essential component of a school counseling program. Whether presented through a Flashlight Presentation, a one-pager, or a newsletter article, there are a variety of ways to showcase the work of secondary school counselors. Sharing results increases the understanding among faculty and families of the importance of the role of the school counselor and contributes to garnering buy-in for the program. Through highlighting the successes supported by their work, school counselors build program credibility, sustainability, and, hopefully, growth (Duarte & Hatch, 2014). As you reflect on your program and the desired effect of sharing counseling program outcomes, consider the following:

- How will your experience documenting your work using the School Counseling Core Curriculum Results Template help your practice?
- How will you commit to sharing and celebrating your program successes with others?
- What audience most needs to hear about your school counseling activities and outcomes?
- Based on your results, what are the future implications and next steps for counseling program goals for your next school year?)

11

Supporting Successful Tier 1 Teams and Systems

TRISH'S STORY

I often ask at trainings, "If your whole team won the lottery and quit, how would the new school counseling team know what to do?" Last year while telling this story to a room full of school counselors in Shasta County, a group raised their hands and said, "That actually happened here!" Sure enough, "The Shasta Lake 15," a group of educators from the Gateway Unified School District in California, won the $76 million jackpot in the California Superlotto Plus Lottery (see http://www.shastalake.com/lotto/). I tell this story because it can actually happen!

In all seriousness, effective management systems are important in ensuring that the school counseling program will continue to run in the event that the school counselor wins the lottery, transitions to another position or school building, goes out on leave, or otherwise is unavailable to implement the program. Management systems also ensure that school counselors spend their time effectively and efficiently, prioritizing the most important activities based on student needs.

EFFECTIVE SYSTEMS

School counselors often report that they spend far too much time responding to unexpected crises and "putting out fires." Although it is true that school counselors are often first responders to crisis situations, best practice is to "happen to your day" as opposed to having "your day happen to you" (Hatch, 2013). Calendaring a daily, weekly, monthly, and annual schedule is key to ensuring that proactive management systems are in place for students.

The average counselor-to-student ratio is 1:482, which can make it difficult to meet the needs of every student (ASCA, n.d.). In addition to serving *all* students, school counselors are also expected to provide support for staff, parents, and other stakeholders. Therefore, creating systems that allow school counselors to use their time efficiently is crucial.

Proactive school counselors do not sit in their offices and wait for students or staff to come to them. Rather, they create an annual and weekly calendar that outlines all school counseling program activities; this also sends a message to stakeholders that counselors are not always available and that those in need of school counseling support may have to schedule an appointment, as is the case with other professionals. Developing effective management systems ensures that students receive prescheduled and consistent preventative school counseling services, such as core curriculum classroom lessons. By maintaining a strong time-management system, school counselors will be less likely to be asked to engage in non–school counseling activities (Figure 11.1) that are often incorrectly deemed fair-share responsibilities, such as proctoring state testing, supervising the playground, substitute teaching, disciplining students, or providing long-term therapy in the school setting.

Fair Share Duties

Fair share duties are activities that all members of the school staff take equal *turns doing to ensure the school's smooth operation. When an activity falls heavier on school counselors than other school staff, it is no longer a fair share activity. In this case, the duty should be reallocated equally among school staff or reassigned altogether such that the school counseling program is not negatively affected.*

Organizational Audit

As part of our comprehensive districtwide trainings, we often provide organizational audits as well as site visit audits to review policies, practices, procedures, job descriptions, interview questions, evaluations tools, handbooks, websites, and other components of the school counseling program. We often do this because we find that districts that have these in place have not updated them in decades and others don't have them at all. To conduct your own organizational audit, you can use the one provided here. High school counselors are also encouraged to visit each other's school sites to provide an outsider perspective during audits (plus it helps school counselors network with one another within a district or geographical area!).

Figure 11.1   ASCA List of Appropriate and Inappropriate School Counselor Activities

Appropriate Activities for School Counselors

- individual student academic program planning
- interpreting cognitive, aptitude and achievement tests
- providing counseling to students who are tardy or absent
- providing counseling to students who have disciplinary problems
- providing counseling to students as to appropriate school dress
- collaborating with teachers to present school counseling core curriculum lessons
- analyzing grade-point averages in relationship to achievement
- interpreting student records
- providing teachers with suggestions for effective classroom management
- ensuring student records are maintained as per state and federal regulations
- helping the school principal identify and resolve student issues, needs and problems
- providing individual and small-group counseling services to students
- advocating for students at individual education plan meetings, student study teams and school attendance review boards
- analyzing disaggregated data

Inappropriate Activities for School Counselors

- coordinating paperwork and data entry of all new students
- coordinating cognitive, aptitude and achievement testing programs
- signing excuses for students who are tardy or absent
- performing disciplinary actions or assigning discipline consequences
- sending students home who are not appropriately dressed
- teaching classes when teachers are absent
- computing grade-point averages
- maintaining student records
- supervising classrooms or common areas
- keeping clerical records
- assisting with duties in the principal's office
- providing therapy or long-term counseling in schools to address psychological disorders
- coordinating schoolwide individual education plans, student study teams and school attendance review boards
- serving as a data entry clerk

AMERICAN
SCHOOL
COUNSELOR
ASSOCIATION

1101 King St., Suite 625, Alexandria, VA 22314 ■ Phone: 703 683 ASCA ■ *www.schoolcounselor.org*

School Counseling Program Organizational Questionnaire

When consulting with a school district, I often begin with a questionnaire designed to quickly gather a large amount of information regarding the organizational systems and functionality of the program. The questions that follow are not by any means an exhaustive list, as typically many more emerge once we begin, but they do provide a reference point for beginning conversations and a window into the policies, practices, and procedures that are working well in addition to those that might benefit from revision during the training process. How might you answer them for your school?

1) How many credentialed school counselors are at your site?

2) How are caseloads organized (alphabetically, grade level, domain, etc.)?

3) What is the student-to-counselor ratio?

4) What other student support service professionals are at your site (e.g., school social worker or school psychologist)?
   a) What are their ratios or days of service?
   b) Have you delineated roles and responsibilities?

5) Do you have a school counseling program assistant, clerk, or secretary?
   a) Who determines the responsibilities of the classified support for the school counseling program?
   b) Who does the classified person primarily work for?
   c) Do school counselors have input into the selection, training, mentoring, or evaluation of the classified person?

6) Do you have a person assigned to the career center (clerical or certificated)?

7) Do you have a schoolwide curriculum action plan?

8) Do you have a set counseling curriculum? Do you have any assessment tools (pre/post) for it?

9) Who delivers the school counseling curriculum?

10) Do you have teacher advisory programs (model)?
    a) What role does advisory play in delivering school counseling curriculum?
    b) What role do the school counselors play in the delivery of advisory curriculum?

11) Do you run groups?
    a) What types (intervention groups, study skills, life issues, or crises)?
    b) How often do you run groups, and how many sessions are typically held?
    c) How are students in group counseling referred to or identified?
    d) What curriculum do you use, and how was it selected?
    e) How do you evaluate groups?

12) Does each student have a 4-year plan (or learning plan) on file?
    a) When do students first create their plan?
    b) How often is it reviewed and revised? What is the process?
    c) Are parents included, invited, and expected to attend these meetings?
    d) What is the content of the meeting? How long is it scheduled for?

13) Do you provide parent evening presentations?

    a) How many are held?

    b) What topics are covered?

    c) Are the topics the same each year?

    d) When are presentations held?

    e) Do all school counselors participate?

    f) What is your rate of parent attendance?

14) May I see your yearly, monthly, or weekly calendar?

    a) Who has access to your calendar?

    b) Who can make appointments on your calendar?

    c) How are decisions made about what will be scheduled on your calendar?

15) How do you use data to drive student interventions?

16) How do you use data to inform closing-the-gap activities?

17) How do you demonstrate accountability?

18) What results do you collect and/or share?

19) With whom do you share results?

20) What marketing strategies do you use to promote your program?

21) How do students let you know that they want or need to see you?

22) How do teachers or parents refer students to the school counselor?

23) What is your role in student discipline?

24) What is your role in the development of the master schedule?

25) What is your role in registering students for classes?

26) What is your role in testing (e.g., standardized, ASVAB, PSAT, AP, SAT, ACT)?

27) What is your role on the IEP team? Do you provide DIS counseling? What is the typical length of time you provide counseling (individual, group, etc.) to students on IEPs?

28) May I see your school counseling program brochure?

29) May I see your website (review for depth, breadth, user friendliness, etc.)?

30) What is your role on the site leadership or management team?

31) Who supervises you? Do you have a job description?

32) Do you have an evaluation that reflects your responsibilities?

33) When is the last time you attended professional development? Why did you attend?

34) Are you a member of your state and national professional association?

35) Do you attend regularly or have you attended a state or national conference? Why or why not?

Program Handbook

Just as teachers have a teaching manual and districts have crisis response manuals and protocols, so too should there be a program handbook for school counseling so that counselors and others are clear on their roles and responsibilities. Otherwise, school counselors might be easily influenced by their administrator to perform inappropriate duties that, for instance, the previous school counselor performed. For example, lacking a program handbook, the school counselor for last names A–E might counsel their students individually, whereas the counselor for F–L might wait for students to come to them. This becomes an equity and access issue because students are not receiving consistent services from counselor to counselor. Curriculum, Individual Learning Plans, annual agreements, schoolwide activities—all of these should be franchised by their inclusion in the program handbook, which is ideally shared with all stakeholders.

Annual Agreements

To create an effective management system for your school counseling program, administrator support and a clear understanding of counseling tasks are essential. One useful tool to develop a coordinated plan between school counselors and administrators as well as clarify expectations related to formal performance evaluations is the annual agreement. Ideally developed in collaboration with and approved by administrators, the annual agreement is an organizational tool provided by the American School Counselor Association (ASCA) that outlines the roles and responsibilities of the school counselor. The authors recommend developing the annual agreement *prior to the start of the school year* so that both the school counselor and administrator are clear on roles, responsibilities, and program goals from day one.

This tool promotes articulation between counselors and administrators as the components prompt questions about effective use of the school counselor's time, ways in which the school counseling program is organized, alignment of goals to the school's mission, professional growth needs, and opportunities for collaboration with other stakeholders. Current needs data and previous results can be shared by the school counselor, along with relevant materials (Results Reports, ASCA executive summary, lesson plans, etc.) to increase administrator awareness and garner support for the school counseling program. The annual agreement can also be used to advocate for the school counselor to spend time engaging in activities that will impact student achievement in clear and measurable ways.

It is important to note that the tone and body language of collegial conversation matters as much as the content, so school counselors are encouraged to begin the meeting with the administrator with a tenor of mutual respect. What follows is a list of talking points to enlist support for Tier 1 activities and interventions when discussing the annual agreement with administrators:

- Ways in which the school counseling program's mission statement supports the school's mission and how the school counseling program's goals support the school's and district's goals

- Development of an annual calendar, including schoolwide activities, core curriculum lessons, and small group services

- A plan for ensuring each student has an Individual Learning Plan

- Agreement on the school counselor referral system and process

- Collaboration efforts with other school staff, community partners, and families to implement Multi-Tiered, Multi-Domain System of Supports (MTMDSS)

- Curriculum and materials needed to provide all students with a standards-based school counseling core curriculum to address universal academic, college/career, and social/emotional development

- The difference between direct and indirect services and the amount of time recommended for classroom lessons (15–25% at the high school level and 25–35% at the middle school level [ASCA, 2005])

- The list of inappropriate and appropriate duties in the ASCA National Model to explore the reassignment of duties that are not in line with best practices; find this in the executive summary at https://schoolcounselor.org/Ascanationalmodel/media/ANM-templates/ANMExecSumm.pdf (ASCA, 2012)

ASCA's annual agreement template can be modified to include the site- and counselor-specific details most relevant to each school counseling program (see our website for an example). Find the most up-to-date annual agreement template at www.schoolcounselor.org/school-counselors/recognized-asca-model-program-(ramp)/ramp-application-templates.

Just like principals develop their school improvement plans and teachers complete their lesson/unit plans before the school year begins, school counselors must also have a plan in place *before* students arrive so that they are ready to go on day one! Chicago Public Schools' Evidence-Based Implementation Plan supports school counselors in developing a structured, intentional, systematic approach to address the academic, career, and social/emotional development of all of their students. It also helps them develop a plan for collecting data and sharing the impact of their school counseling program with key stakeholders. Consisting of components such as the annual agreement, program calendar, SMART goals, and action plans, the evidence-based implementation plan helps school counselors not only plan for the upcoming school year but also demonstrate to school administration that planning and their program alignment to the schoolwide mission and goals. View the evidence-based implementation plan on our website.

School Counselor–Administrator Meetings

In addition to the annual agreement meeting, secondary school counselors should schedule a consistent and regular meeting time with administrators. This promotes the success of school counselors, as the time to communicate and collaborate ensures that everyone is on the same page and support is provided as necessary. During these meetings, school counselors can present their weekly calendar, discuss current Tier 1 activities, and strategize solutions regarding classroom management, scheduling, or other issues impacting the effective delivery of core curriculum. Keeping in mind that the administrator's priority is academic instruction, make connections between what is being taught through the school counseling core curriculum and how it impacts academics with collected data so that the value of the counseling lesson is seen to be worth the resource of time. School counselors may also want to use this time to discuss logistics and planning for schoolwide activities and/or parent events.

Scheduling Core Curriculum

To make the process of collaborating with teachers to schedule core curriculum counseling lessons most efficient, work with administrators *well in advance* (i.e., immediately after the master schedule is created in the spring) to identify times to visit teachers' classrooms for the upcoming school year or other creative ways for becoming part of the master schedule. School counselors might also consider giving teachers a targeted and timely list of dates for lessons they will be delivering and ask for the teachers' input on which dates work best. It is important to note, however, that school counselors ensure the fidelity of the scope and sequence of the core curriculum and teach lessons in a reasonable and developmentally appropriate order.

For example, the school counselor might give the junior English teacher a list of a few possible dates for co-teaching a lesson on writing personal statements during the month of May. However, such a lesson might not be appropriate to teach in November or December once college applications are well underway, so those dates would be avoided when asking for teacher feedback.

Using a sign-up sheet for school counseling lessons, whether paper or electronic, could allow teachers the option of not signing up at all. However, if the school counselor is clear that all teachers will have school counseling lessons and then follows up with individuals who did not sign up, there is a system of accountability. One way to promote sign-up is to implement a "freedom within limits" approach, such as "Would you prefer your lessons in October or November?" Note that in this case, the lesson delivery itself is not an option; rather, the month of delivery is negotiated. If possible, schedule all class lessons for a specific grade level on the same day so that you teach the same lesson plan repeatedly throughout a single day and avoid having to "rewire" your brain for different lessons. Additionally, keep in mind the time needed in between lessons to set up and put away materials, travel between classrooms, and prepare yourself for the next class.

TRISH'S STORY

One of my favorite trainings I went to as a school counselor was Love and Logic, by Jim Fay. It was helpful not only in my role as a school counselor but also as a parent. In one particular training, Fay talked about the "freedom within limits" approach (Cline & Fay,

2014). I used that technique more often than I can say, not only professionally but also in my parenting. For instance, I used it with my sons when it was time to go out to dinner or to visit relatives. I would say, "You can pick any shirt in the closet you want to wear; it's your choice, your decision—the only requirement is that it has to have a collar." With this approach, my sons were able to feel completely in control, and I was able to have what I needed, which was a shirt with a collar. In the same way, I would suggest that school counselors say to teachers when they are scheduling their core curriculum lessons, "You can have your lesson any day of the week or any time you like as long as it's during the month of October."

LaNedra was a new school counselor at King High School. Prior to her arrival, the school did not have a comprehensive school counseling program. Once LaNedra was hired, she recognized the need to do the following:

1) Meet with the administration to gain support for the delivery of school counseling core curriculum lessons and input about the best way to deliver them based on the master schedule.

2) Review the schedule of existing school activities (such as non–student attendance days, exam weeks, spirit week, and other events and activities that might impact the delivery of school counseling lessons).

3) Educate the staff on the nature of a comprehensive school counseling program, and explain the purpose and goals of core curriculum classroom lessons, including how topics are developed and selected based on data-driven needs.

4) Collaborate with staff to solidify a schedule for core curriculum, ensuring the "freedom within limits" strategy through a sign-up sheet with predetermined time slots for each topic.

5) Upload the core curriculum class lesson schedule to the general school calendar to ensure that reminders would be sent to teachers prior to the lessons.

By offering open time slots and asking teachers to sign up for one of those available times, LaNedra sent the message that core curriculum is a necessary and integral part of a student's learning environment. Providing teachers this "freedom within limits" allowed them to be involved in the process and also ensured that the times selected fit within LaNedra's schedule.

Calendars

As school counselors schedule core curriculum and other program activities, calendars are a vital component in planning and ensuring appropriate allocation of time and services. School counselors utilize their calendars as marketing tools to keep stakeholders and administrators informed of their school counseling program and encourage active participation in activities throughout the year. Additionally, a well-planned calendar puts school counselors in the driver's seat by allowing them to control the direction and implementation of their program, protecting counselors' time for their work, and providing programmatic legitimacy. Within the Tier 1 system, calendars allow scheduling of core curriculum lessons and schoolwide activities in a systematic manner that guarantees consistent instruction for all students.

Sharing the school counseling calendars with teachers, families, administrators, community members, and students is a critical aspect of ensuring buy-in and support for the school counseling program. Calendars also invite family and community involvement beyond the school staff and foster partnerships with additional resources. Some common ways in which school counselors share their calendars are through the following:

- School counseling websites
- Weekly, monthly, or quarterly newsletters
- Bulletin boards
- Email
- Shared Google Calendars
- Printouts posted outside the counseling office

Tips for creating school counseling program calendars:

- Create complete, timely, visually appealing, and organized calendars.
- Format calendars for ease of understanding, with attractive design, color, and detail.
- Identify grade level, dates, and activities.
- Distribute calendars to appropriate stakeholders.
- Use a template that resonates best with you.

Annual Calendars

Annual calendars (Figure 11.2) are comprehensive and identify all Tier 1 activities, including schoolwide programs and the full scope and sequence of lessons and activities scheduled for delivery. Although not the focus of this text, Tier 2 and 3 activities (such as small counseling groups and individual sessions) would also be calendared.

When creating an annual calendar, school counselors collaborate with all stakeholders to ensure that core curriculum lessons, individual student planning, and schoolwide programs and activities are developed and delivered in a purposeful way. For example, when determining which core

Figure 11.2   Annual Calendar Contents

Annual Calendars

The annual calendar communicates school counseling program priorities for the entire school year.

It includes all major activities delivered or coordinated by the school counselor(s) and should be widely shared with stakeholders.

Examples to include:

- Core curriculum lessons/units
- Back-to-school nights, open houses, orientations
- Postsecondary fairs and tours
- Family workshops
- National awareness dates
- Family–teacher conference dates
- Assembly dates
- Major postsecondary deadlines

curriculum lessons to teach 11th grade students in January, FAFSA completion would not be included because the timing would not be appropriate. Rather, providing such lessons in September (or better yet, the spring of junior year) is more logical. In addition, school counselors will want to consider national awareness campaigns (see Chapter 8) when planning the annual calendar.

School counseling calendars convey professionalism through visual appeal and ease of reading. Although there is no specified format to use, school counselors should create a calendar that fits their needs and keeps them on track. While some go so far as to color-code activities per type of direct or indirect counseling service to assist in giving a visual picture of the amount of time spent in different activities, or color-code according to the school counseling program SMART goals, the calendar should help, not hinder you.

See Figures 11.3 and 11.4 for examples of annual calendars, noting the differences. Figure 11.3, provided by high school counselor Karen Devine, is an example of an annual calendar in a linear monthly list view. Figure 11.4, provided by high school counselor Heidi Truax, is an example of an annual calendar that is broken down by ASCA National Model components. Both of these schools have earned the distinction of being Recognized ASCA Model Schools at the time of publication.

To market your parent education program, create a monthly calendar of activities, and post on your school's website (e.g., see our website). Figure 11.5 is an excerpt from an annual school counseling calendar template that can be modified for your use, available on our website.

Figure 11.3   Annual Calendar Example—Taft High School

AUGUST
• Freshman Connection: Aug 15–17: Executive functioning, Digital Doings, Study Skills, Self-Care, Advocacy
• Academic Center Connect: Aug 16–17: Executive functioning, Digital Doings, Study Skills, Self-Care, Advocacy
• Jump Start to College: Aug 1–2: Postsecondary Prep
• College Camp for Pre-Teens & Teens: Aug 22–23
• Online recovery classes Mon–Fri mornings

SEPTEMBER
• Naviance lessons for all grades to introduce contracts and task completion.
• Navigate Naviance: Sept 13, 14, 20, 21, 27, 28
• Academic Success Lessons with 10th Grade: Sept 18, 19
• Café Connection & GPA activity with 7th–9th: Sept 25, 26
• College 101 with 12th graders: Sept 15, 22

(Continued)

Figure 11.3 (Continued)

- Get interest & referrals from students, parents, teachers, BHT for:

  Coping Skills

  Grief Groups

  Anger Group

  ID Group
- Reshaped Family Group
- During classroom instruction: present groups & complete confidential surveys for interest and need
- DP Drips (IBDP parents)
- AC/Frosh Cafés (monthly topical coffee for parents from 7:45am–8:45am in APR)
- Parent/Guardian/Staff Food Truck Fest Get-Together: Sept 21, 6–8 pm
- College Fair and Back-to-School Parent/Student Night: Sept 25, 6–8 pm

OCTOBER

- On the Edge Minute Meeting with Frosh/Sophs: Oct 13, 20
- Coping Skills Group
- Grief Group
- Anger Group
- ID Group
- Reshape Family Group
- Silent Mentorship for Identified Students
- DP Drips
- AC/Frosh Cafés (monthly topical coffee for parents from 7:45 am–8:45 am in APR)
- Stall Street Journal in restrooms: Oct 2
- PSAT: Oct 2017
- FAFSA completion workshop for families: Oct 1
- Raise the Grade Saturday Tutoring & Support event: Oct 14
- Online recovery classes Mon & Wed, 3:15 pm–5:15 pm

NOVEMBER

- Expect Respect Lessons 7th–9th grade: Nov 16, 17
- Naviance Task Completion Lessons for *all* grades: Nov 20, 21
- Coping Skills Group
- Grief Group
- Anger Group
- ID Group
- Reshape Family Group
- Silent Mentorship for Identified Students
- DP Drips
- AC/Frosh Cafés (monthly topical coffee for parents from 7:45 am–8:45 am in APR)

- Online recovery classes Mon & Wed, 3:15 pm–5:15 pm
- Credit Recovery Workshop at RCPU: Nov 16

DECEMBER

- Senior Sit-Down Lessons: Dec 18, 19
- Half-Cap Graduation Lessons 10th graders: Dec 20, 21
- Silent Mentorship for Identified Students
- DP Drips
- AC/Frosh Cafés (monthly topical coffee for parents from 7:45 am–8:45 am in APR)
- Raise the Grade Saturday Tutoring & Support event: Dec 9
- Online recovery classes Mon & Wed, 3:15 pm–5:15 pm
- Stall Street Journal in restrooms: Dec 4

JANUARY

- Naviance Task completion lessons for *all* grade levels: Jan 8–12
- Street Management Lesson for 7th–9th grades: Jan 17, 18
- Regroup & launch second sem. groups
- Silent Mentorship for Identified Students
- DP Drips
- AC/Frosh Cafés (monthly topical coffee for parents from 7:45 am–8:45 am in APR)
- Raise the Grade Saturday Tutoring & Support event: Jan 13
- Online recovery classes Mon & Wed, 3:15 pm–5:15 pm

FEBRUARY

- Scholarship & Financial Aid Lessons for seniors: Feb 14, 15
- Coping Skills Group
- Grief Group
- Anger Group
- ID Group
- Reshape Family Group
- Silent Mentorship for Identified Students
- DP Drips
- AC/Frosh Cafés (monthly topical coffee for parents from 7:45 am–8:45 am in APR)
- Raise the Grade Saturday Tutoring & Support event: Feb 5
- Online recovery classes Mon & Wed, 3:15 pm–5:15 pm
- IBDP Informational Session: Feb 9

MARCH

- Naviance Task Completion Lessons for *all* grades: Mar 19–13
- Coping Skills Group
- Grief Group
- Anger Group
- ID Group

(Continued)

Figure 11.3 (Continued)

- Reshape Family Group
- Silent Mentorship for Identified Students
- DP Drips
- AC/Frosh Cafés (monthly topical coffee for parents from 7:45 am–8:45 am in APR)
- Raise the Grade Saturday Tutoring & Support event: Mar 10
- Online recovery classes Mon & Wed, 3:15 pm–5:15 pm

APRIL

- Test Prep Tips Lessons for JRs: Apr 4, 5
- Coping Skills Group
- Grief Group
- Anger Group
- ID Group
- Reshape Family Group
- Silent Mentorship for Identified Students
- DP Drips
- AC/Frosh Cafés (monthly topical coffee for parents from 7:45 am–8:45 am in APR)
- Raise the Grade Saturday Tutoring & Support event: May 2
- Online recovery classes Mon & Wed, 3:15 pm–5:15 pm
- National College Fair Visit: Apr 13
- PSAT/SAT: TBD

MAY

- Naviance Task Completion Lessons for *all* grades: May 7–11
- Silent Mentorship for Identified Students
- Raise the Grade Saturday Tutoring & Support event: May 2
- Online recovery classes Mon & Wed, 3:15 pm–5:15 pm

JUNE

- College 101 for juniors: June 11–13
- Silent Mentorship for Identified Students
- DP Drips
- AC/Frosh Cafés (monthly topical coffee for parents from 7:45 am–8:45 am in APR)
- Online recovery classes Mon & Wed, 3:15 pm–5:15 pm
- NavigaTEEN workshop: June 26, 27
- Positive ParenTEEN Workshop: June 28
- College Knowledge for Parents: June 27
- College/Postsecondary Workshop Day for juniors: June 15

JULY

- Online recovery classes Mon–Fri mornings

Source: Taft High School Annual School Counseling Program Calendar.

Figure 11.4   Annual Calendar Example—Marine Leadership Academy

Month	Direct Student Services			Indirect Student Services	Program Planning and School Support
	School Counseling Core Curriculum & Events	Individual Planning	Responsive Services	Referrals, Collaboration, Consultation	Foundation, Management, Accountability
Ongoing Services	• Know Your Numbers Campaign in Advisory–Students get biweekly report out of 6 of their data points: GPA, Test Scores, Attendance %, Behavior (Infractions, Merits & Demerits), College Cohort, BAG Report Tier Total, # of Ds & Fs (All) • Social Emotional Learning in Advisory (all themes identified below by months) • One Goal Curriculum through Junior Seminar (1 Junior Cohort) • College Possible Curriculum and Support (1 Senior Cohort)	• Transfer student transition planning and academic advising • Assist students with academic planning • High-alert student academic and attendance data identified individual interventions	• Referrals accepted • Open office hours during lunch and before and after school • Emergency availability • Student newsletter hung in bathroom stalls • Restorative practices (peace circles, conflict mediation, re-engagement post-suspension) • High-alert student data identified individual interventions • Peer-to-Peer Mentoring (Upper to Lower Classmen)	• School Committee Meetings—Instructional Leadership Team, School Leadership Team (with Teachers and Admin; Biweekly) • Postsecondary Leadership Team (with Teachers & Admin; Monthly) • Assigned Counselor with Assigned Grade Level Team Meeting (with Teachers; Biweekly) • Behavioral Health Team Meeting (with Case Manager & School Social Worker; Biweekly) • Multi-Tiered Systems of Support Meeting (with Deans, Military Leadership, Admin, Caseworker, & Attendance Clerk; Biweekly) • Network Postsecondary Leadership Team (with Network Leaders, College Coaches from Network; Monthly) • Multi-Tiered System of Support (MTSS) Network/District PD (District & Network Leaders, School Counselors from Other Schools; Monthly) • Behavioral Health Team (BHT) Network/District PD (District & Network Leaders, School Counselors & Clinicians from Other Schools; Quarterly)	• Team Counseling Meeting (Biweekly) • RAMP Preparation Meeting (Biweekly) • Site Supervisor Meeting with Counseling Intern (Weekly)
August	• Student Registration (All); *August 30, 2016, 11am–3pm* • Postsecondary Transition Support (Outgoing Students)	• POSSE Foundation Scholarship communication with senior applicants		• OSCPA Summer Counseling Institute • Facilitate MLA Staff Professional Development (District Leadership, Community Partners, School Counselors from Other Schools; Annual) • MTSS Workshop (District Leadership, School Counselors from Other Schools; 1 Time)	• School Year Planning & Preparation (1 time)
September	• Orientation of New/Absent Students (7th–9th); *first two weeks of school* • Back-to-School Night Parent Info Session (All); *September 27, 2016, 5–7pm* • High School Fairs/Recruitment (Incoming); *ongoing through fall* • ISAC/NACAC College Fair (11th & 12th); *September 30, 2016, 8–1:30pm* • Executive Functioning Development in Advisory (7th–9th) • College Match Lesson (Test Scores and GPA, 12th) • College Fit Lesson (What Is Best for You?, 12th) • What Are You Looking for in a College Lesson (12th) • College Night Parent Meeting (12th) • Policies, Procedures, and Team Building in Advisories (All) • Community Day (All); *September 30, 2016, 8:15–3:30pm* • Ally Week Lesson Plan through Advisory (All)	• Registration of New/Absent Students (7th–9th, as Needed) • Scheduling Support & Course Corrections (All, as Needed) • Credit Recovery Application Facilitation (All, as Needed) • Dual-Enrollment College Application Completion (11th & 12th) • Scholarship Application Completion (12th) • College Application Completion (12th) • Transcript Audits (12th)		• Quarter 1 Office of School Counseling and Postsecondary Advising Network/District Professional Development (District Leadership, Community Partners, School Counselors from Other Schools; Quarterly) • Ally Week Lesson Plan PD (Teachers & Admin)	• Beginning of Year Prep Meeting (1 time)

(Continued)

Figure 11.4 (Continued)

Month	Direct Student Services			Indirect Student Services	Program Planning and School Support
	School Counseling Core Curriculum & Events	Individual Planning	Responsive Services	Referrals, Collaboration, Consultation	Foundation, Management, Accountability
October	• Grade Transition Support Guidance Lesson (7th & 9th) • Planning for Academic Success (9th) • High School Fairs/Recruitment (Incoming); *ongoing through fall* • Feeder School Visits to MLA (Incoming); *ongoing through fall* • Information Session (Incoming) • MLA IACAC College Fair (All); *October 6, 2016, 12–2:30pm* • Decisions, Decisions (College Planning, 12th) • Managing Stress Lesson (9th) • Anti-Bullying Month Activities and Curriculum (All)	• FAFSA Completion Begins (12th) • Scholarship Application Completion (12th) • Résumé Completion (11th & 12th) • College Application Completion (12th) • Transcript Audits (10th–11th)	• Genders and Sexualities Alliance (GSA) Small Group (Biweekly) • Sexual Assault Survivor Support (SASS) Small Group (Weekly)		
November	• High School Fairs/Recruitment (Incoming); *ongoing through fall* • Feeder School Visits to MLA (Incoming); *ongoing through fall* • Information Session (Incoming) • Military Probation Intervention Advisory (14 students on probation) • Military Appreciation Lessons & Celebration (All) • College Campus Visit (12th); *November 16, 2016*	• FAFSA Completion Continues (12th) • Scholarship Application Completion (12th) • Résumé Completion (11th & 12th) • College Application Completion (12th)	• GSA Small Group (Biweekly) • SASS Small Group (Weekly) • Military Probation Individual Interventions (Weekly)	• Counseling Advisory Board Meeting (Parents, Students, and Community Partners) • Report Card Pick-Up Day (Parents, Students and Community Partners; Biannual) • District Office of School Counseling and Postsecondary Advising Tool Kit (District Leadership, Community Partners, School Counselors from other Schools; Biannual) • District HS Achievement Summit with University of Chicago Consortium	
December	• Planning for Academic Success (8th) • Information Session (Incoming) • Community Day (All); *December 23, 2016, 8:15–3:30pm* • Military Probation Intervention Advisory (14 students on probation) • Human Rights Advisory Lessons (All) • College Campus Visit (12th); *December 8, 2016*	• FAFSA Completion Continues (12th) • Scholarship Application Completion (12th) • Résumé Completion (11th & 12th) • College Application Completion (12th)	• GSA Small Group (Biweekly) • SASS Small Group (Weekly) • Military Probation Individual Interventions (Weekly)	• Partner Building Meeting with the YMCA (Community Partners, Admin; 4 Total)	
January	• What Are You Looking for in a College? Lesson (7th–10th) • Military Probation Intervention Advisory (14 students on probation) • Gender Equality Advisory Lessons (All) • Core Values & Team Building Advisory Lessons (All) • College Bridge Program Presentation (9th)	• FAFSA Completion Continues (12th) • Scholarship Application Completion (12th) • Résumé Completion (11th & 12th) • College Application Completion (12th)	• Student Needs Assessment (All) • GSA Small Group (Biweekly) • Attendance Intervention Small Groups (Weekly) • YMCA Peace Circles (Weekly) • Military Probation Individual Interventions (Weekly)	• Q2 Office of School Counseling and Postsecondary Advising Network/District PD (District Leadership, Community Partners, School Counselors from Other Schools; Quarterly)	

	Direct Student Services			Indirect Student Services		Program Planning and School Support
Month	School Counseling Core Curriculum & Events	Individual Planning	Responsive Services	Referrals, Collaboration, Consultation		Foundation, Management, Accountability
February	• What Are You Looking for in a College Lesson (11th) • Credit Recovery Application Facilitation (9th–12th) • On Track & Award Celebrations for students with 3.0+, 95%+ attendance, & honorable behavior (All); *week of February 13–17, 2017* • Black History Month & Digital Citizenship Advisory Lessons (All) • College Bridge Program Presentation (9th)	• FAFSA Completion Continues (12th) • Scholarship Application Completion (12th) • Résumé Completion (11th & 12th) • College Application Completion (12th) • Credit Recovery Application Facilitation (All, as Needed) • Transcript Audits (9th–12th)	• GSA Small Group (Biweekly) • Attendance Intervention Small Groups (Weekly) • YMCA Peace Circles (Weekly)	• District HS Achievement Summit with University of Chicago Consortium • Partner Building Meeting with the Hartgrove Hospital (Community Partners, Admin; 1 Time)		
March	• College Madness Month Activities (All) • College Day (All) • Closing the Gap 7th Grade on Track Intervention (Off Track 7th graders—fluctuating list of 45–60 students) • Military Probation Intervention Advisory (48 students on probation) • College Campus Visits (All); *several throughout the month* • College Going and Healthy Relationship Advisory Lessons (All)	• Scholarship Application Completion (12th) • Financial Aid Award Letter Review (12th) • SAT Registration (11th) • Admission Selections, Letters, and Responses • Summer Enrichment Program Application Completion (All)	• GSA Small Group (Biweekly) • Attendance Intervention Small Groups (Weekly) • YMCA Peace Circles (Weekly) • Prime Care Anger Management Group (Weekly) • Military Probation Intervention Group (Weekly) • Military Probation Individual Interventions (Weekly)	• Counseling Advisory Board Meeting (Parents, Students and Community Partners; Biannual) • Report Card Pick-Up Day (Parents, Students, and Community Partners; Biannual) • Q3 Office of School Counseling and Postsecondary Advising Network/District PD (District Leadership, Community Partners, School Counselors from other Schools; Quarterly) • College Resource Night (Parents, Families, & Students; 1 Time) • Youth Mental Health First Aid (YMHFA) Training (Community Partners, School Counselors from Other Schools; 1 Time)		
April	• Career Month Activities & Advisory Lessons (All) • Closing the Gap 7th Grade on Track Intervention (Off Track 7th graders—fluctuating list of 45–60 students) • Military Probation Intervention Advisory (48 students on probation) • Application/Testing for incoming applicants (56 applicants); *April 18, 2016, 11–2pm.*	• Scholarship Application Completion (12th) • Financial Aid Award Letter Review (12th) • Admission Selections, Letters, and Responses • Summer Enrichment Program Application Completion (All)	• GSA Small Group (Biweekly) • Military Model Probation Small Groups (Weekly) • YMCA Peace Circles (weekly) • Prime Care Anger Management Group (Weekly) • Military Probation Intervention Group (Weekly) • Military Probation Individual Interventions (Weekly)	• Illinois School Counselor Association Conference (Professional Leaders, Fellow School Counselors throughout the State) • District HS Achievement Summit with University of Chicago Consortium • Counseling Advisory Board Meeting (Parents, Students, and Community Partners; Biannual) • Report Card Pick-Up Day (Parent's, Students, and Community Partners; Biannual)		• Evidenced-Based Intervention Plan Working Meeting (Twice This Month at 4–6 Hours Each)

(Continued)

Figure 11.4 (Continued)

Month	Direct Student Services			Indirect Student Services	Program Planning and School Support
	School Counseling Core Curriculum & Events	Individual Planning	Responsive Services	Referrals, Collaboration, Consultation	Foundation, Management, Accountability
May	• SMART Goals for Next School Year Lesson (All) • Closing the Gap 7th Grade on Track Intervention (Off Track 7th graders—fluctuating list of 45–60 students) • Military Probation Intervention Advisory (48 students on probation) • High School Success Lesson (8th) • Mental & Physical Health Advisory Lessons (All)	• Financial Aid Award Letter Review (12th) • Summer College Dual-Enrollment Registration (Incoming 11th and 12th) • SAT Score Interpretation Conferences (11th)	• GSA Small Group (Biweekly) • Military Model Probation Small Groups (Weekly) • YMCA Peace Circles (Weekly) • Prime Care Anger Management Group (Weekly) • Military Probation Intervention Group (Weekly) • Gang Prevention & Awareness Event (Self-Identified & Needs Assessment Identified, Open to All) • Military Probation Individual Interventions (Weekly)	• College Decision Day! (Parents, Families, & 12th grade students; Annual) • College Prep Parent Meeting (11th grade Students, Parents, Families; Annual)	
June	• Parent/Student Orientation (Incoming); *June 27, 2017, 9–3pm* • Closing the Gap 7th Grade on Track Intervention (Off Track 7th graders—fluctuating list of 45–60 students) • Military Probation Intervention Advisory (48 students on probation) • High School Success Lesson (8th) • Nutrition Advisory Lesson (All) • Community Day (All)	• Summer College Dual-Enrollment Registration (Incoming 11th & 12th) • Credit Recovery Application Facilitation (All, as Needed) • Financial Aid Award Letter Review (12th)	• GSA Small Group (Biweekly) • Military Model Probation Small Groups (Weekly) • YMCA run Peace Circles (Weekly) • Military Probation Intervention Group (Weekly) • Military Probation Individual Interventions (Weekly)	• Q4 OSCPA Network/District PD & Awards Celebration (District Leadership, Community Partners, School Counselors from Other Schools; Quarterly) • Parent Orientation (Incoming)	
July	• Recruitment/Enrollment/ Interviewing (Incoming) • Summer Transition Counseling (Outgoing)				

Figure 11.5   Annual School Counseling Calendar Template

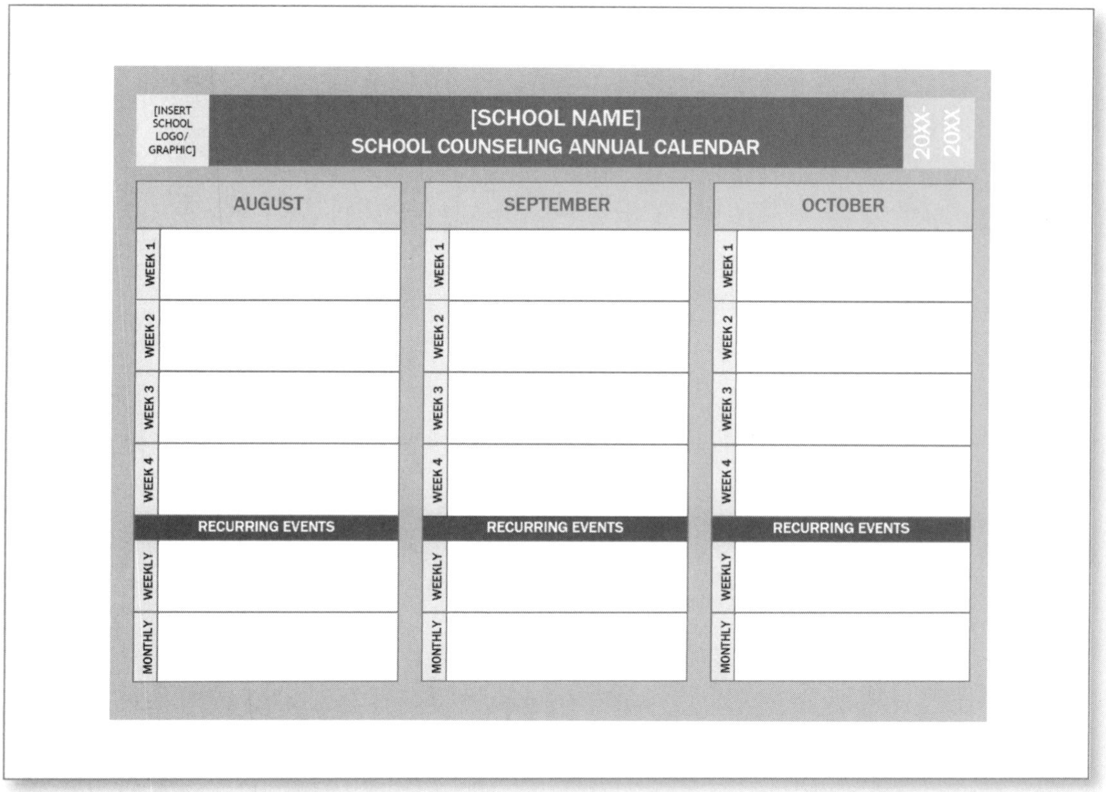

Weekly Calendars

The weekly calendar (Figures 11.6 and 11.7) keeps the secondary school counselor organized and communicates general whereabouts and availability daily. Although

online resources

the weekly calendar provides a detailed plan of the school counselor's activities, it is important that stakeholders understand that the calendar is somewhat flexible, based on the possibility of needing to deal with crises or other situations that may require immediate attention. See the online appendix for samples of weekly calendars as well as a template.

Figure 11.6   Weekly Calendars

Weekly Calendars

A weekly calendar provides a detailed plan of the school counselor's activities for the week. It is somewhat flexible due to crisis response or immediate need situations. It should be shared with the supervising administrator and care should be taken to protect students' confidentiality.

Examples to include:

- Core curriculum lessons
- Small group lessons
- Individual counseling
- Committee/team meetings
- Collaboration or data analysis time
- Meetings with families and external partners
- Fair-share responsibilities

Figure 11.7 School Counseling Weekly Calendar Template

[INSERT SCHOOL LOGO/ GRAPHIC]	**[SCHOOL NAME]** [SCHOOL ADDRESS] • [SCHOOL CITY/STATE/ZIP] • [SCHOOL PHONE NUMBER] *[Name of principal]* • *[Name of assistant principal]* • *[Name of school counselor]*				20XX– 20XX

SCHOOL COUNSELING WEEKLY CALENDAR

	MONDAY	TUESDAY	WEDNESDAY	THURSDAY	FRIDAY
8:00 to 8:30 am					
8:30 to 9:00 am					
9:00 to 9:30 am					
9:30 to 10:00 am					
10:00 to 10:30 am					
10:30 to 11:00 am					
11:00 to 11:30 am					
11:30 to 12:00 pm					
12:00 to 12:30 pm					
12:30 to 1:00 pm					
1:00 to 1:30 pm					
1:30 to 2:00 pm					
2:00 to 2:30 pm					
2:30 to 3:00 pm					
3:00 to 3:30 pm					
LEGEND:		**DIRECT**	**INDIRECT**	**STUDENT SUPPORT**	

Figure 11.8 Don't forget to talk to your administrator about flexing your schedule if you need to attend your own child's awards ceremony! And remember to attend your School Counselor in the '90s Conference! LOL!

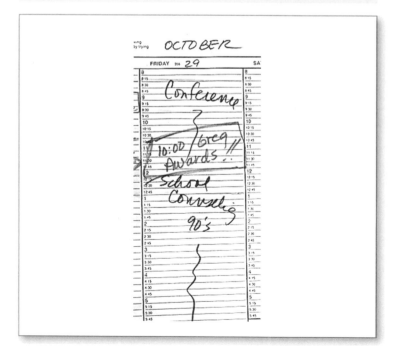

Monthly Planning Guides

A monthly planning guide of suggested school counseling activities, when reviewed and updated each year, is helpful to ensure that school counselors keep in mind the rhythm of regular events and action items throughout the academic school year when creating their calendars. The sample that follows has been updated since Trish's use of a hardcopy planner with her district in the 1990s (see Figure 11.8). Note that the guide presented here doesn't include state or local activities, which school counselors can add themselves.

Sample Year-at-a-Glance Planning
Guide of Secondary School Counselor Activities

August (Before the Start of the School Year)

- Revise and publish the school counseling annual calendar to administration, staff, and families (be sure to include your Tier 1 school counseling core curriculum and schoolwide activities!).
- Locate the updated national and local campaigns and awareness events (see www.schoolcounselor.org in August for a list).
- Review data (attendance, behavior, grades, etc.), and create SMART goals with tiered prevention and intervention lessons and activities to support the goals.
- Create core curriculum (Tier 1) and intentional action plans (Tiers 2 and 3).
- Determine which core curriculum lessons and interventions will be measured and reported.
- Create an annual agreement and review it with your administrator before the first day of school.
- Identify subpopulations that will require regular monitoring (e.g., severely credit deficient students).
- Review students with Individualized Education Plans (IEPs), and consult with support staff to determine appropriate counseling services.
- Check supplies and order materials for core curriculum and small groups.
- Design or update the school counseling page on the school's website, including an overview of the school counseling program, a school counselor bio and photo, confidentiality statement, resources, contact information, and core curriculum lessons to be taught.
- Ensure that the student referral form is available to staff and students and that they know how to appropriately use it.
- Update your list of referral services for students and families, and post in a centralized location (i.e., school website).
- Create or update the school counseling program brochure, and deliver a stack to the main office.
- Schedule and begin planning topics for family workshops for the year, and publicize them.
- Update membership in state and national school counseling associations, and register for annual conference(s).
- Identify professional development opportunities and dates for the year, including any required district meetings for the year.
- Evaluate your current school counseling program management systems, and determine if tweaks or changes should be made to help things run more smoothly (e.g., office hours for walk-ins, time tracking, referral process, record keeping, teaming, etc.).
- Meet with administrators to review action plans, calendars, and so on, and discuss next academic year planning.
- Participate in student and family orientations.

(Continued)

(Continued)

- Present information about the school counseling program at a staff meeting, including program goals, core curriculum lessons, and activities for the year (also consider presenting to the parent–teacher association and school site council!).

August/September (First Month of School)

- Participate in Back-to-School Night.
- Provide orientation for students and families that are new to the school.
- Finalize dates and times for classroom lessons with teachers as well as family workshops, and publicize.
- Support freshman transition (for students and families).
- Send a letter (or newsletter) to families describing your program and goals for this year, and post it on your website.
- Connect students experiencing adjustment challenges to resources and support (e.g., a peer mentor or group).
- Attend state university counselor conferences and articulation meetings to get important updates on admissions procedures.
- Collaborate with the coaches to set up an NCAA meeting with all potential college athletes and their parents to discuss expectations and requirements.
- Start core curriculum lessons, especially around transitioning to high school (for freshmen) and FAFSA (for seniors).
- Assist students with credit deficiencies in getting registered for credit recovery.
- Advertise college fairs, especially targeting special and underrepresented populations.
- Remind male seniors of the selective service requirement for those seeking financial aid for college.
- Convene (or collaborate to establish) a postsecondary leadership team, a scholarship committee, and the senior activities team, and set dates for regular meetings throughout the year.
- Meet with local college access partners that work directly with students and families in the postsecondary planning process to establish processes, procedures, and expectations for effective collaboration.
- Complete senior credit checks.
- Meet with English Department to discuss plans for supporting students around college essays, scholarship essays, portfolios, and so on.
- Set up group meetings with students who are considering applying under early decision or early action.
- Set up group meeting for your undocumented and underrepresented populations and their families around the FAFSA and alternative sources of financial aid for postsecondary education.
- Publicize scholarship information and college application deadlines widely, especially targeting underrepresented populations and their families.
- Track your use of time.
- Collaborate to set up a voter registration drive for eligible seniors.
- Attend Student Support Teams (SSTs), IEPs, 504s, and so on as appropriate.

October

- Make the staff and families aware of school counseling program activities for October.
- Continue teaching core curriculum lessons and implementing schoolwide activities and programs.
- Monitor progress toward your established school counseling SMART goals.
- Analyze grades, behavior, and attendance to determine students in need of Tier 2 interventions, and begin setting up schedules for groups and check-in/check-out.
- Remind students to complete the FAFSA as soon as possible after October 1 for the most access to state and institutional aid.
- Assist students in completing the FAFSA, and frequently track submission and completion, following up with students who are lagging behind or flagged for verification.
- Write letters of recommendation, giving priority to students applying for early decision or early action.
- Remind students of SAT/ACT deadlines for retakes.
- Remind English as a second language students to register for the Test of English as a Foreign Language (TOEFL).
- Review college choices with seniors to ensure they have a balanced list of match, reach, and safety schools.
- Market college and career fairs and tours, especially to underrepresented students and families.
- Assist freshmen in joining extracurricular activities and clubs.
- Be available for parent–teacher conferences at report card time.
- Facilitate family workshops.
- Track your use of time.
- Attend team meetings, SSTs, IEPs, 504s, and so on as appropriate.

November

- Make the staff and families aware of school counseling program activities for November.
- Continue teaching core curriculum lessons and implementing schoolwide activities and programs.
- If your students participated in fall testing, help them make sense of their test results (great classroom lesson!).
- Use the report card (end-of-quarter data) to determine which students will receive Tier 2 interventions (i.e., students with five or more office referrals for the second quarter are targeted to receive a behavior group intervention, whereas students currently participating in the group with no referrals for the second quarter are transitioned out of the behavior group).
- Begin to prepare for the closure of first quarter groups.
- Continue assisting students in completing the FAFSA, and frequently track submission and completion, following up with students who are lagging behind or flagged for verification.

(Continued)

(Continued)

- Write letters of recommendation, giving priority to students applying for early decision or early action.
- Consult with teachers regarding student attendance or behavior challenges.
- Collaborate with school staff, the parent–teacher association (PTA), and community organizations to help coordinate donations for Thanksgiving and other winter holidays for low-income families served by your school.
- Hold special workshops for student athletes, fine/performing arts students, and those with disabilities regarding the college application process.
- Remind seniors to request college housing applications.
- Continue writing letters of recommendation and remind teachers and staff to complete them. Hold workshops or drop-in hours for faculty who may need additional assistance or guidelines.
- Continue scheduling visitations from college representatives.
- Facilitate family workshops.
- Monitor progress toward your established school counseling SMART goals.
- Track your use of time.
- Attend team meetings, SSTs, IEPs, 504s, and so on as appropriate.

December

- Make the staff and families aware of school counseling program activities for December.
- Continue teaching core curriculum lessons and implementing schoolwide activities and programs.
- Develop and/or revise lessons for the remainder of the year.
- Be on the lookout for students with holiday crisis issues.
- Prepare for college applications due in January.
- Remind seniors to have scores sent from testing organizations to colleges.
- Plan senior rap sessions—have alumni return during their winter break to share their first-semester experiences with students, taking special care to ensure underrepresented populations are represented among both the speakers and attendees.
- Help any seniors who have not yet taken the SAT/ACT to register for a test date.
- Create an informative, professional, and friendly out-of-office email and voicemail for winter break.
- Monitor progress toward your established school counseling SMART goals.
- Continue facilitating groups.
- Track your use of time.
- Attend team meetings, SSTs, IEPs, 504s, and so on as appropriate.

January

- Make the staff and families aware of school counseling program activities for January.
- As soon as they return from break, be on the lookout for students with holiday crisis issues.
- Begin planning for National School Counseling Week (first full week in February—visit www.schoolcounselor.org for ideas).

- Continue teaching core curriculum lessons and implementing schoolwide activities and programs.
- Use the end-of-semester data to determine which students will receive Tier 2 interventions or transition out of Tier 2 interventions.
- Begin to prepare for the closure of second quarter groups.
- Complete an end-of-first-semester transcript review.
- Assist students with any credit deficiencies in getting registered for credit recovery opportunities.
- Address any potential cases of "senioritis," collaborating with appropriate stakeholders to assist.
- Create a We Got In! bulletin board or wall for posting college and other postsecondary acceptance letters for all to see.
- Begin requesting copies of seniors' scholarship award letters, and track dollars earned by the senior class.
- Continue facilitating family workshops.
- Plan activities for National School Counseling Week (the first week in February).
- Continue assisting students with FAFSA completion, especially those flagged for verification.
- Help students and families make sense of their Student Aid Reports.
- Finish and evaluate groups from the second quarter (or first semester), and review data to determine groups for the third quarter.
- Monitor progress toward your established school counseling SMART goals.
- Track your use of time, and share with your administrator after the first semester.
- Attend team meetings, SSTs, IEPs, 504s, and so on as appropriate.

February

- Make the staff and families aware of school counseling program activities for February.
- Celebrate National School Counseling Week—inform, advertise, and promote stakeholder awareness!
- Develop a wish list to spend all your program money (or request any needed supplies) by March 1.
- Continue teaching core curriculum lessons and implementing schoolwide activities and programs.
- Begin facilitating a new round of groups for students who meet semester criteria for intentional (Tier 2) intervention.
- Publicize spring college and career tours, especially to those from underrepresented populations.
- Coordinate a college night for students and families.
- Continue requesting copies of seniors' acceptance letters for the We Got In! wall as well as scholarship award letters and publicize a running total of dollars earned.
- Begin test preparation classroom lessons.
- Help students and families make sense of their Student Aid Reports.
- Remind students and families of deadlines for college and postsecondary programs, tuition deadlines, and campus housing applications.

(Continued)

(Continued)

- Begin postsecondary transition workshops to discuss student support services on 2- and 4-year college campuses, service year programs, military, and work or career options.
- Begin core curriculum classroom lessons on course selections for next year's classes, and discuss promotion and graduation requirements.
- Deliver family workshops.
- Present a Flashlight Presentation to stakeholders on core curriculum from the fall.
- Monitor progress toward your established school counseling SMART goals.
- Track your use of time.
- Attend team meetings, SSTs, IEPs, 504s, and so on as appropriate.

March

- Make the staff and families aware of school counseling program activities for March.
- Schedule spring break massage! :)
- Continue teaching core curriculum lessons and implementing schoolwide activities and programs.
- Infuse content about spring break safety and extracurricular opportunities into the core curriculum lessons.
- Continue monitoring grades, attendance, behavior, credits earned, FAFSA completion, and other postsecondary readiness data, and move students in and out of intervention groups as appropriate.
- Begin to prepare for the closure of third quarter groups.
- Publicize summer internship, job, and extracurricular opportunities, and collaborate with external partners to facilitate workshops on résumé writing, interviewing, professional dress, and other workplace skills.
- Modify senior contracts as needed.
- Contact the feeder middle schools to arrange a date, time, and schedule for an orientation and course selection presentation and/or school visit in May.
- Continue requesting copies of seniors' acceptance letters for the We Got In! wall, as well as scholarship award letters, and publicize a running total of dollars earned.
- Continue test preparation classroom lessons.
- Help students and families make sense of their Student Aid Reports.
- Monitor progress toward your established school counseling SMART goals.
- Track your use of time.
- Attend team meetings, SSTs, IEPs, 504s, and so on as appropriate.

April

- Make the staff and families aware of school counseling program activities for April.
- Continue teaching core curriculum lessons and implementing schoolwide activities and programs.
- Continue monitoring grades, attendance, and behavior data, and move students in and out of intervention groups as appropriate. Begin to prepare for the closure of groups.
- Communicate with faculty regarding the importance of the senior final failure list and the importance of submitting names and reasons for failures by the requested deadline.

- Begin May 1 College Signing/Decision Day preparation, and meet with seniors to finalize postsecondary plans. Remind students to send their letter of intent to one and only one institution by May 1.
- Remind seniors to complete their college placement exams.
- Collaborate in the planning of the graduation ceremony, submitting appropriate information as needed (i.e., list of scholarship recipients, top 10 list, and special awards recipients).
- Infuse content about prom safety into core curriculum lessons for the appropriate grade levels.
- Continue requesting copies of seniors' acceptance letters for the We Got In! wall, as well as scholarship award letters, and publicize a running total of dollars earned.
- Continue financial aid and postsecondary transition counseling.
- Identify students to serve as peer mentors in freshman transition activities (e.g., orientation and Freshman Connection).
- Meet with teachers and families of students who are in danger of retention (Tier 3).
- Be aware of standardized test dates—support student attendance during these times.
- Monitor progress toward your established school counseling SMART goals.
- Track your use of time.
- Attend team meetings, SSTs, IEPs, 504s, and so on as appropriate.

May/June (Last Month of the School Year)

- Make the staff and families aware of school counseling program activities for May/June.
- Facilitate final core curriculum classroom lessons.
- Facilitate May 1 College Signing/Decision Day activities, and remind seniors to submit their letters of intent to one institution.
- Participate in middle to high school orientation activities.
- Participate in awards ceremonies.
- If your students participated in spring standardized testing, help them make sense of their test results.
- Distribute a senior exit survey to assess seniors' experience and perceptions of the school's support services.
- Ensure every single senior has a completed, concrete postsecondary plan and is submitting proof of those plans (i.e., college course schedule or paid housing deposit, enlistment or boot camp letter, acceptance letter from a public service or gap year program, or verification letter of full-time employment).
- Ensure all students have a complete Individual Learning Plan.
- Encourage students and families to visit colleges over the summer, especially those from underrepresented populations.
- Continue requesting copies of seniors' acceptance letters for the We Got In! wall, as well as scholarship award letters, and publicize a running total of dollars earned.
- Attend SSTs, IEPs, 504s, and so on as appropriate, including transition meetings for students moving from middle to high school and seniors transitioning to postsecondary.

(Continued)

(Continued)

- Notify students and families of summer school opportunities and summer educational activities (such as summer reading programs at the local library).
- Begin summer melt tasks and activities.
- End and evaluate small groups.
- Collaborate with administration to contact families of seniors who are no longer eligible for graduation. Discuss next steps, options, and encourage, encourage, encourage!
- Discuss summer school and other credit recovery options for students with credit deficiencies, and collaborate to design their fall schedules.
- Ensure that seniors are submitting final transcript requests for enrollment in college.
- Conduct final transcript audits.
- Write thank-you notes to administration and key partners that supported the success of the school counseling program this year.
- Evaluate the effectiveness of the school counseling program—survey teachers, administrators, students, and families. Reflect on successes and areas of thoughtfulness from the past year. Take notes on ways to improve the school counseling calendar next year. Prepare any final reports for sharing with stakeholders.
- Report to administration the results of the comprehensive school counseling program, including your use of time throughout the school year. Present a Flashlight Presentation to staff and other stakeholders.
- Participate in graduation and *celebrate*!
- Secure any records.
- Prepare your office for next year.
- Begin drafting your annual agreement, calendar, SMART goals, and action plans for the upcoming year.
- Schedule end-of-year massage! :)

June/July

- Attend the American School Counselor Association (ASCA) Annual Conference to network, gain new ideas, and refresh!
- Take a vacation where there are no emails to open and no phones to answer, and pamper yourself for a week or two!
- Take a deep breath, and get ready to begin a new school year!

Systematic Referral Process

School counselors at the high school level are encouraged to spend approximately 15% to 25% of their time providing core curriculum lessons (formerly called "guidance curriculum" in the second edition of the ASCA National Model; ASCA, 2005; see Figure 10.12), whereas middle school counselors are encouraged to spend approximately 25% to 35% of their time providing core curriculum lessons (Figure 11.9). Although the focus of this book is Tier 1, counselors may have a high number of individual student referrals, which may not allow them to

Figure 11.9   ASCA National Model Suggested Use of Time

ASCA National Model Suggested Use of Time

	Delivery System Component	Elementary School % of Time	Middle School % of Time	High School % of Time	ASCA Recommendation
Direct Services	Core Curriculum (Tier 1)	35%	30%	20%	80% or more
	Individual Student Planning (Can be Tier 1/2/3)	5%	15%	25%	
	Responsive Services (Can be Tier 1/2/3)	25%	20%	20%	
Indirect Services	Referrals, Consultation, Collaboration (Can be Tier 1/2/3)	20%	20%	20%	
	System Support (Can support Tiers 1/2/3)	15%	15%	15%	20% or less

Source: Adapted from Gysbers & Henderson (2000).

effectively implement Tier 1 core curriculum services. One way to address this challenge is to ensure that a systematic referral process is in place.

Similar to creating a structured calendar, school counselors are encouraged to develop and implement a systematic referral process to ensure that students are being identified for Tier 2 and 3 supports using data (Chapter 1) rather than teacher referrals. One important exception to consider is students who have had an extreme change in behavior, attendance, affect, or academic achievement. These students may need immediate support and may not be identified via the data. For example, Justice's father recently committed suicide, and her teacher has noticed that she has been extremely angry and withdrawn; Luisa is exhibiting isolating behaviors that would not be recognized through discipline referrals; Tyson is normally happy and energetic but has been extremely sullen and lethargic during the last 2 weeks. In addition, unless a student's mood is causing their grades to drop dramatically and suddenly, data would not be a useful tool to identify that these students need support. Therefore, creating a referral form for teachers to complete in extraordinary situations, such as those listed previously, ensures that students in need of immediate support are serviced. Refer to the sample on page 131 of *The Use of Data in School Counseling: Hatching Results for Students, Programs, and the Profession* (Hatch, 2013). Utilizing a systematic referral process is vital for effective time management within a tiered school counseling program.

Marketing and Branding the School Counseling Program and Tier 1 Services

"Marketing is what you say about your program. Branding is what people say about your program when you are not in the room." (adapted from Jeff Bezos, founder of Amazon.com)

Activity: Watch this 3-minute video, and reflect on how marketing and branding are different, as they relate to your school counseling program: http://bit.ly/BrandingVid.

–Adapted from a phenomenal presentation from school counselors Jeff Ream, aka "The Counseling Geek," and Jeremy Goldman

With access to technology at school counselors' fingertips, it is easier than ever to inform families, students, staff, and the school community about core curriculum lessons and schoolwide activities. Marketing yourself and the program is essential in providing professional legitimacy and inciting participation from others. Introductory letters, counseling program brochures, and websites provide a clearer understanding of how school counselors support students, families, and the entire school community.

School counselors can also seek opportunities to discuss the counseling program during staff, local school council, parent–teacher association, or board meetings and family events. Be sure to get on the agenda of the initial staff meeting for each new school year. School counselors who work in diverse schools are encouraged to translate family information into their community's native language(s).

School counselors are also encouraged to seek to keep stakeholders engaged in up-to-date information through district-approved social media accounts. Using multiple modalities and avenues for engaging stakeholders helps school counselors to not only market their program but brand it too!

School counselors can also brand schoolwide programs or activities. For example, co-author Whitney would frequently use the same free clipart graphic for her Freshman on Track initiative. She ensured that the same image appeared in her core curriculum classroom lessons, posters around the school, letters home, Flashlight Presentations, and school website whenever the content included Freshman on Track. Branding the on-track initiative helped her students, families, and staff to easily and quickly recognize the content and gave it an added layer of professionalism and legitimacy.

Activity 11.1

Figures 11.10 through 11.13 show examples of a school counselor's welcome letter, brochure, website, and other promotional materials. What do you like about each one? What might you change? How can you use and adapt the different examples to market your own school counseling program and role in the school?

One of the ways co-author Whitney introduced herself to the families at Pine Lake Preparatory School was through an introduction letter (see Figure 11.10). Because the school previously did not have a high school counselor, explaining her role and services was especially important to bring clarity to her position and begin gaining buy-in.

Figure 11.10 Whitney's School Counselor Introduction Letter

Dear PLP Community,

Welcome to a new school year! I wanted to take a second to introduce myself. My name is Whitney Triplett and I am so excited to join the PLP community as the new (and first!) Upper School Counselor this year!

Whitney Triplett, M.A., NCC
Upper School Counselor

About me:

* I'm passionate about helping teenagers and believe that ALL students can succeed in school and life when given the proper support
* Originally from "all over NC," I've lived in 12 NC cities + Chicago, IL and have been so fortunate to work with amazing, resilient, driven, talented teenagers and their families
* Alumnus of AppState and UNC Charlotte with degrees in Anthropology and Counseling
* Love Tarheel b-ball, reading, hiking, and spending time with my hubby, our 8-month-old son, and lab!

So what does a school counselor DO exactly?

Gone are the days of reactive "guidance counselors" who just meet with students in crisis. Today's "school counselors" are collaborators, leaders, advocates, and change agents in schools, working to impact the achievement and holistic development for ALL students. We use data to monitor and measure the results of our programs and partner with everyone to improve student outcomes. Some of the services I provide:

→ **Core Curriculum Classroom Lessons:** Provided to all students in the classroom, topics include those that are relevant to all students' developmental needs such as social skills, conflict resolution, study skills, and postsecondary readiness.

→ **Schoolwide Programs and Activities:** Such as college and career fairs, postsecondary tours and site visits, orientations, national and local awareness events, and much more!

→ **Small Groups:** Provide extra support for students who may be having difficulty in a specific area.

→ **Individual Support:** Short-term, goal-focused individual services for students as appropriate.

→ **Consultation, Collaboration, and Referrals:** Working together with other partners helps to ensure that our students receive the best supports!

My overarching tasks over the next year:

→ Begin development of an upper school counseling program that is aligned to PLP's mission and goals, the American School Counselor Association National Model, and state and national standards

→ Ensure the school counseling program is culturally sensitive, comprehensive in scope, preventative in design, developmental in nature, and an integral part of the total PLP educational program

→ Utilize input from the entire PLP community in tailoring the program elements and services to our students' unique needs

A high-quality school counseling program takes time to build and feedback from many different voices. I look forward to working with you to create the best possible school counseling program for PLP students and families. It's gonna be an awesome year!!

-Whitney Triplett, M.A., NCC
Pine Lake Preparatory Upper School Counselor

Figure 11.11 School Counseling Program Brochure Sample

Our Philosophy...

The School Counseling Office is delighted to welcome families and students to Hanover High School. We look forward to working with you as you move through high school and begin planning for a career, school courses, or college applications. We believe that with the proper support, high school students can make important decisions about managing their school lives and can learn to act responsibly and maturely by having the opportunity to make their own decisions. We are also here to support students and families through times when things seem overwhelming and stressful.

Confidentiality Statement...

As school counselors, we maintain strict confidentiality in all of our interactions. All meetings held with the school counselor will remain confidential unless student gives permission to share information with related parties.

However, circumstances do arise when we must disclose information to appropriate professionals based on NH state law and Hanover School District Policy. Our goal is to keep all members of the HHS community safe from harm.

Reasons for reporting include, but are not limited to: a student is in danger of harming him or herself, another individual, or if a student is in danger of being harmed by others.

Contact Your Counselor!

Hello

Ms. Koppenheffer
Room 104B

During busy times, you may have to make an appointment. Be sure to tell the receptionist if it is an emergency.

<u>Make A Referral</u>

Introducing your...

Hanover High School

School Counseling Program

Our Mission Statement...

The Hanover High School Counseling staff collaborates with students, parents, and staff members to prepare and inspire all students to achieve standards of excellence. We provide a comprehensive developmental program that addresses the academic, social/emotional and college/career preparatory needs of our diverse student body. By empowering students to achieve their current and future goals, we encourage student self-advocacy and accountability. We promote the development of citizenship that embraces excellence of character.

Our Vision Statement...

The vision of the Hanover High School Counseling Staff is for all students to achieve their maximum potential in the areas of academic achievement, social/emotional development, and post-secondary planning through data driven programs which promote personal responsibility, integrity, respect, compassion, and commitment and service to others.

THE SCHOOL COUNSELORS AT HANOVER HIGH SCHOOL BELIEVE all students can learn and will be encouraged to pursue lifelong learning, all students have dignity and worth and the right to access counseling services, all students are individuals with varied learning styles and abilities, and all students should strive towards healthy relationships.

Menu of Services...

School counseling services are available to all students through structured core curriculum lessons, and other services are available on an as-needed basis.

Academic Advising: Assistance in designing meaningful and challenging academic programs.

College/Career Advising: Assistance exploring and developing career plans, setting goals, and planning for college and work.

Social/Emotional Support Services: Assistance dealing with social, emotional, and personal concerns.

Core Curriculum Lessons: 9th graders meet with counselors in the fall to learn about counseling services and to discuss concerns or questions about high school. Sophomores meet with counselors during the fall and winter to learn about career opportunities, career decision-making, and junior and senior year academic opportunities. Juniors meet in the spring for college and post-secondary planning. Seniors meet in the fall to go over college and future plans. The department also organizes an orientation for new students, works with middle schools to facilitate the transition to high school, and assists with career and college planning, as well as course selection and registration.

As-Needed Services: In addition to regularly scheduled core curriculum activities, students may receive additional services as needed.

Community-Based Resources...
Always call 911 in an emergency

National Youth Crisis Hotline
1-800-442-4673

Alcoholics Anonymous
1-800-344-2666
www.al-anon.alateen.org

Domestic Abuse Reporting
1-800-894-5533 *from NH phones only

WISE Crisis Line
603-448-5525 or 1-866-348-9473
www.wiseoftheuppervalley.org

National Runaway Switchboard
1-800-786-2929

Sexual Concerns
ACORN - A Community Resource Network
603-448-8887 or 1-800-816-2220
www.acornvtnh.org

Gay & Lesbian National Hotline
1-888-843-4564
www.glnh.org

Planned Parenthood of Northern New England
1-800-230-7526
www.ppnne.org

National Hopeline Network for Suicide Concern
1-800-784-2433

Source: Created by Araminta Koppenheffer.

Figure 11.12 School Counseling Program Brochure Sample

How and **why** families contact the school counselor:

*Concerns over student achievement

*Course selection and college planning

*Standardized test interpretation

*Early discussion of potential crisis

*Family difficulties or concerns

Parents can email or call the school counselor to set up an appointment

How students see the school counselor:

*Automatically, in the classroom for core curriculum lessons

*At schoolwide events

*Group or individual counseling

*By referral as appropriate

Make an appointment today:
Referral Form

Text the district's crisis line in case of emergency outside of school hours

School Counseling Mission:

The Tualatin High School Counseling Department's mission is to provide support, resources and opportunities that will empower all of our students to develop and demonstrate the **knowledge, skills, abilities** and **character** to pursue their individual plans and goals as they move beyond high school and become contributing members of our society.

School Counseling Vision:

Tualatin High School graduates will be college and career ready and will have the skills needed to maximize their academic success and social/emotional development. The comprehensive school counseling department supports students through rigorous curriculum while providing a variety of opportunities for self-directed growth to become contributing members of a competitive global society. We believe that every student can learn and achieve their goals.

TuHS School Mission Statement:
Educate every child

Introducing your...

School Counseling Department

Tualatin High School

Contact:
Shannon Messenger

CRISIS TEXT LINE |

Crisis Text Line serves anyone, in any type of crisis, providing access to free, 24/7 support and information via the medium people already use and trust: text. Here's how it works:

Text **HOME** to **741741** from anywhere in the US, anytime, about any type of crisis.

A live, trained Crisis Counselor receives the text and responds quickly, all from our secure online platform.

The volunteer Crisis Counselor will help you move from a hot moment to a cool moment.

"People will forget what you said, people will forget what you did, but people will never forget how you made them feel" -Maya Angelou

Counseling services provided all year:

*Classroom core curriculum lessons and schoolwide activities for ALL students

*Small group counseling

*Crisis intervention/response

*Consultation with families and teachers

*Referrals to community services

Tualatin Community Resources

FOR EMERGENCY ASSISTANCE, CALL 911

Washington County Child Abuse 24-hour Reporting Hotline: (503) 681-6917

Washington County Non-Emergency Police: (503) 629-0111

Alcohol and Substance Helpline:
1-800-923-4357
Spanish: 1-877-515-7848

Poison Control (overdose of drugs or alcohol):
1-800-222-1222

Washington County Mental Health 24-Hour Crisis Line: (503) 291-9111

Portland Women's 24-hour Crisis Line:
(503) 235-5333 , www.pwcl.org

National Parent Helpline: 1-855-427-2736

Confidentiality Statement

Information students share with the school counselor is confidential. The student's right to privacy is guarded as much as permitted by law, ethics and school rules. The school counselor is obligated to break confidentiality when there is a potential harm to the student or others, concern of neglect or abuse, or a court of law that requires testimony or student records. The school counselor often consults with other school professionals, but only shares information necessary to achieving the goals of the consultation.

Source: Created by Shannon Messenger.

Figure 11.13   School Counseling Program Website Example

EFFECTIVE TEAMING

Collaboration is such an important role of the school counselor that it is one of the four themes depicted around the frame of the ASCA National Model. It is given such prominence because effective school counselors must proactively engage with stakeholders both inside and outside of the school to successfully meet the needs of all students, particularly around the implementation of Tier 1 school counseling core curriculum and schoolwide activities.

Collaboration With Administrators

The influence and expectations of administrators, their knowledge of the role of the school counselor, and their understanding of program development and implementation have been identified as significant factors affecting the development of exemplary school counseling programs (Ponec & Brock, 2000) and as aspects of school counselor efficacy (Sutton & Fall, 1995). Often, administrators have not been trained in the role of the school counselor. Therefore, the school counselor plays a critical role in educating the administration about the proper role and most impactful model of school counseling. Supporting the improvement of the principal–school counselor relationship is vitally important in developing the school counseling program.

In *A Closer Look at the Principal–Counselor Relationship: A Survey of Principals and Counselors* (Finkelstein, 2009), the College Board holds that the principal–counselor relationship is dynamic and evolves over time in response to the ever-changing needs of a school. Effective principal–counselor relationships are used to collaboratively lead school reform efforts to increase achievement for all students. Review Figure 11.14 and assess which of the characteristics of an effective counselor–principal relationship are currently in place in your school.

Figure 11.14   10 Characteristics of an Effective Principal–Counselor Relationship

10
Characteristics of an Effective Principal–Counselor Relationship*

1. Open communication that provides multiple opportunities for input to decision making

2. Opportunities to share ideas on teaching, learning and schoolwide educational initiatives

3. Sharing information about needs within the school and the community

4. School counselor participation on school leadership teams

5. Joint responsibility in the development of goals and metrics that indicate success

6. Mutual trust between the principal and school counselors

7. A shared vision of what is meant by student success

8. Mutual respect between the principal and school counselors

9. Shared decision making on initiatives that impact student success

10. A collective commitment to equity and opportunity

* The questions on the national survey of principals and counselors, including the characteristics of effective principal-counselor relationships, were suggested by experts at the College Board, ASCA and NASSP. While this is not an exhaustive list and there may be additional important characteristics of these relationships, all 10 presented here were endorsed by both principals and counselors as important characteristics of an effective principal-counselor relationship.

8   **Finding a Way:** Practical Examples of How an Effective Principal-Counselor Relationship Can Lead to Success for All Students

Several examples from Shasta County, California, are provided throughout this text. Figure 11.15 is a word cloud that Superintendent Judy Flores says came from an activity where the school counselor and administrators were asked to share words as the reasons for our success this year. The larger the word, the more often that word was mentioned.

Figure 11.15   Shasta County Word Cloud

WHITNEY'S STORY

True Collaboration Isn't Easy

When my sons Grady and Everson were ages 5 and 4, they enjoyed playing Super Mario Brothers U together as a family. I liked to use the opportunity to teach them how to work through conflicts with one another and work together as a team because everyone could play at one time and they would have to collaborate and coordinate with one another to win each level (plus, sometimes I needed the practice myself as I can be competitive—ha!).

On one particularly contentious evening of gaming, I was trying to teach Grady the importance of not going too far ahead so the other three wouldn't get left behind. I explained that "we have to learn to work together as a team or we won't be able to win," which wasn't sinking in. Out of patience, I turned off the game for a cool-down break and said angrily, "We obviously haven't mastered working together yet." To which Grady, in all of his 5-year-old wisdom, replied under his breath, "Well, *I have!*" (my attitude in this situation displayed the exact same sentiment at the time, lol).

Really, even as adults, it is common to take this approach to collaboration in which we feel the other party is the problem and we are doing what we can to accomplish the task. However, true collaboration is a two-way street (or three, four, or five+ parties). The reality is that if a collaborative relationship is not accomplishing the tasks at hand, in our case, serving students effectively, school counselors are encouraged to take another look at how to approach the relationship. Collaboration isn't easy, but school counselors have a unique set of skills to broker productive conversations even in the toughest situations and build relationships such that students have greater opportunity.

Collaboration With Staff

Secondary school counselors are leaders, advocates, and change agents, which often involves being a coach or consultant. Consistent communication, accessibility, and visibility are vital to enhancing relationships with staff and faculty. Teachers must have explicit means and methods to approach, communicate with, and share feedback and concerns with the school counselor, whether via drop-in office hours, an online appointment calendar for conferences that displays available time slots, an advisory council for your school counseling program, or feedback forms for the school counseling core curriculum lessons. Be mindful of providing clear instructions when issuing forms or sign-up sheets, include deadlines, and give plenty of advanced notice whenever possible. Remember that buy-in from the faculty is important to the successful implementation of the Tier 1 school counseling core curriculum and schoolwide activities.

It is also important that the school counselor participate on school leadership teams. Uniquely suited to understand and address the developmental needs of students, school counselors can contribute a great deal to school-based teams and committees while leveraging their support in implementing strong Tier 1 programs and activities. Additionally, the school counselor's ability to facilitate conversations, diffuse difficult situations, and promote student-centered, data-informed thinking is a huge asset on school teams.

Here are examples of teams with which school counselors can collaborate to implement Tier 1 programs and activities:

- Instructional leadership team
- School improvement plan committee
- Crisis response team
- Grade level teams
- Data teams
- Sexual health team
- Postsecondary leadership teams
- Freshman transition teams
- Culture and climate team
- Behavioral health team
- Senior activity committee
- Parent or family advisory committee

The University of Chicago's Network for College Success has published a great deal of free resources to help school teams flourish. Adaptable to any school-based team, this tool kit includes a wealth of samples, templates, examples, and research that can be very useful to school counselors in teaming with others, including the following:

- Protocols for guiding conversations around data
- Strategies for effective adult teaming
- Building community within adult teams
- Videos of school teams engaging in successful, goal-driven meetings

Access the full tool kit here: https://ncs.uchicago.edu/page/resources (click on either "Freshman On-Track Toolkit" or "Postsecondary Success Toolkit").

Collaboration With External Partners

It is vital that school counselors collaborate and consult with external partners in an effort to provide the best services to students (i.e., college access partners, student financial assistance organizations, sexual health experts, and test prep specialists). Partnering helps the school counselor expand opportunity and support to students and families within Tier 1 and within each of the three domains. When school counselors fail to communicate with external partners about their programs, others might think they should be performing actions of a school counselor providing lessons on college and career to students. Instead, school counselors must lead this work and collaborate with partners to ensure seamless opportunities and a consistent message for all students. In "Fun Story From a School Counselor," below, we read the pride the counselor feels that they are now delivering their own lessons. In this case, the external partner can now support the counselors by assisting students in filling out FAFSAs, and together they can accomplish more!

Fun Story From a School Counselor

Today was a good day at our school when an external partner came in to give our office posters for a FAFSA workshop that they are holding in the next few weeks. She also asked to come in and speak to some seniors because "they don't even know what the FAFSA is."

Well, I set her straight when I said, "No, actually our students *do* know what the FAFSA is because we just held classroom lessons with our seniors specifically on the FAFSA with a pre-test and post-test to make sure they learned what they needed to know. So, we actually have data to prove that our kids know what the FAFSA is and how to access it."

Do you know how great it felt to say that? :) I just felt like we were the best school counseling office in the state because this partner had been to other districts that had not done what we did.

Hope this puts a smile on your face!

External partners collaborate under the umbrella of the school counseling program and are overseen by a school counselor who ensures that the content of the lessons and activities provided are accurate, current, and aligned with the needs of the students and the philosophy and goals of the school. School counselors take a proactive role to ensure that their administrators are educated about the vital role of external partners. School counselors collaborate with their administrators when writing grants or memorandums of understanding (MOUs), ensuring external partners are not working outside of (separate silo) but rather *within* the comprehensive program. Additionally, school counselors and administrators ensure external partners provide evidence that their services produce the intended effects, as outlined in a written contract or MOU developed prior to the partners' service delivery. These strategies for collaboration and coordination ensure that external partnerships happen *with* school counselors, not *to* them.

Advisory Councils

An advisory council is a representative group of stakeholders that meets to review and provide feedback on the school counseling program mission, goals, activities, outcomes, and general implementation. Potential members may include students, parents, teachers, staff, community members, and administrators. The advisory council ideally meets each semester and helps counselors ensure that the school counseling program is consistent with the needs of the students and is impacting student success. Advisory councils can be a great resource for school counselors, especially those in solo-counselor buildings, acting as sounding boards and garnering support for the school counseling program. It is important to note that advisory councils are required for schools planning to apply for the Recognized ASCA Model Program (RAMP) recognition. Please visit the following resources for more information:

- **ASCA National Model: A Framework for School Counseling Programs, 3rd Edition:** https://www.schoolcounselor.org/school-counselors/asca-national-model/purchase-the-books
- **Advisory Council Meetings (ASA Institute)—includes samples, templates, and examples:** http://www.asainstitute.org/schoolcounseling/advisory-council.html
- **Advisory Council (Counselor Up Blog)—includes templates:** https://www.counselorup.com/blog/asca-national-model-advisory-council
- **Advisory Council (Happy School Counselor Blog)—includes samples:** http://happyschoolcounselor.blogspot.com/2014/09/advisory-council.html
- **Starting a School Counseling Advisory Council (Exploring School Counseling Blog):** http://exploringschoolcounseling.blogspot.com/2016/02/starting-school-counseling-advisory.html

---

Master School Counselor Advisory Council

The advisory council concept can also be applied to the district level. For example, Chicago Public Schools (CPS) has developed an exemplary Master Counselor Advisory Council, which is a representative group of highly skilled and competitively selected school counselors from across the district who ensure that the school counselor voice is represented during the development of district policies, procedures, and initiatives. Originally created by Barbara Karpouzian, then–executive director of the Office of School Counseling and Postsecondary Advising for CPS, the master counselors (MCs) are critical partners to the district office in the following ways:

- Facilitating professional learning sessions for their peers
- Serving as mentors for new or struggling school counselors
  - Co-facilitating one-on-one and small group support sessions
  - Offering up their schools as shadow sites
  - Serving as "consulting educators" to help school counselors improve their practice and performance evaluation scores
  - Answering questions that may arise from other school counselors about practices and procedures and helping them troubleshoot problems

- Participating on cross-functional teams and working groups at central office to inform policy, procedure, and initiative development

(Continued)

(Continued)

- Garnering buy-in among school counselors for new initiatives (via social media, workshops, word-of-mouth, etc.)
- Serving as a trusted on-the-ground listening ear and conduit for school counselors to voice concerns to the district office
- Brainstorming and implementing solutions to problems that school counselors face or ineffective systems that negatively impact student success
- Reviewing results data on the impact of the school counseling program districtwide and providing feedback to the district office

Later, co-author Whitney led the MCs in developing their own mission and vision statements and core principles to drive their work:

MC Mission

The Master Counselor Advisory Council leads, advocates, collaborates, and effects systemic change such that all CPS school counselors and postsecondary advisors are fully equipped and supported to implement comprehensive, student-centered, data-informed school counseling programs that significantly impact students' academic, social/emotional, and postsecondary success.

MC Vision

That every CPS student has access to a school counselor that is:

- Effectively planning, implementing, evaluating, and enhancing their comprehensive, student-centered, data-informed school counseling program.
- Staffed at a maximum school counselor-to-student ratio of 1:250.
- Engaged only in activities that are fully aligned to the ASCA National Model and REACH Framework for School Counselors.
- A leader, advocate, collaborator, and an agent of systemic change that promotes the equity and access of all students.

MC Core Principles

- Ensure that student achievement is at the center of our work as school counselors/coaches.
- Foster school counselor and coach leadership across the district.
- Develop a culture of collaboration.
- Engage in collective inquiry that is action oriented and results focused and promotes best practices in the district.
- Ensure that the school counselor or coach voice is represented in the development of district policies, procedures, and initiatives.

This model is recommended for any school district but especially those that are larger as it helps foster and distribute leadership. Whitney shares that policies, procedures, and initiatives coming out of the CPS central office are so much stronger and have greater buy-in when the representative voices have shared in their development.

RECOMMENDATIONS FOR NEW SCHOOL COUNSELORS RELATED TO DELIVERY OF TIER 1 SERVICES

As new school counselors begin their work, the success of implementing core curriculum and other Tier 1 activities can be enhanced through learning about the school culture, building relationships, and creating effective systems. What follows are some tips for new school counselors:

- Schedule a meeting with administrators to develop a collaborative relationship, learn about the school's goals, and discuss school counseling program services such as core curriculum. New school counselors may want to share educational literature such as ASCA's "The Role of the School Counselor" document (see https://www.schoolcounselor.org/asca/media/asca/Careers-Roles/RoleStatement.pdf).
- Build relationships with teachers; visit their classrooms to learn about expectations, observe their student engagement and classroom management styles; and get to know students. School counselors can learn from great teachers and incorporate this knowledge into their style as they teach core curriculum.
- Begin by teaching lessons on specific topics to a few grade levels, ask for feedback, and then incorporate additional lessons as confidence and skills build.
- Consider the number of lessons to be provided and scheduling—try not to schedule more than three to four lessons per day, and allow for at least 15 minutes in between sessions to account for unexpected occurrences and time to set up and clean up.
- Know your boundaries. From time to time, a teacher may ask you to teach a lesson that is specific to a classroom issue, but it is important for school counselors to balance scheduled and developmentally appropriate core curriculum with supporting specific teacher needs. Use professional wisdom to set appropriate boundaries to prioritize core curriculum while supporting needs and building relationships.
- Remember to dress for success and demonstrate confidence when entering classrooms, building your credibility by showing your professionalism outwardly. Arrive early to set up, and support the teacher in transitioning instruction to the school counselor.

CLOSING

The goal of this book is to provide a practical hands-on guide to creating and implementing a high-quality Tier 1 school counseling system of supports with a focus on *effective teaching strategies* and the *use of measurement tools*. As authors, we set out to include best practices, examples, and resources from secondary school counselors across the country that have been proven to be effective.

Throughout this text, we have shared with you the knowledge, attitudes, skills, and behaviors recommended for school counseling best practices in implementing

Tier 1 core curriculum, individual student planning, and schoolwide activities within a secondary school counseling program.

This text is written by four authors who have not only been secondary students (see Figure 11.16) but have also served as secondary school counselors in different parts of the country at different times and even within different generations. Although each of us may have operationally approached the work in different ways, we are in fundamental agreement about how to structure a school counseling program aligned with the ASCA National Model and a Multi-Tiered, Multi-Domain System of Supports.

We have combined our art with science, thereby developing our wisdom within the work. *And now it is your turn!* We hope this text will help you blend your art and science, develop your wisdom, and grow as a professional school counselor. It is our hope that you will identify new or innovative ways to improve outcomes for students as you collect and share results to improve your program. We look forward to your stories regarding the outcomes you achieve, both professionally and personally. We hope you will share your data, your courageous moments, and your wisdom with other secondary school counselors at local, state, and national conferences. The profession truly needs this.

Finally, we hope that you will share your feedback with us. If you have any suggestions for ways in which we might improve this text or recommendations for the online appendix, please contact us at office@hatchingresults.com.

Figure 11.16

| Trish Hatch | Whitney Triplett | Danielle Duarte | Vanessa Gomez |

Watercolor on facing page is by coauthor Whitney's mother, Debra Danner.

"Taking Flight"

References

Action Learning Systems. (2012). *Direct interactive instruction.* Pasadena, CA: Author.

Allensworth, E., & Easton, J. Q. (2005). *The on-track indicator as a predictor of high school graduation.* Chicago, IL: University of Chicago Consortium on Chicago School Research.

Allensworth, E., & Easton, J. Q. (2007). *What matters for staying on-track and graduating in Chicago Public Schools: A close look at course grades, failures, and attendance in the freshman year.* Chicago, IL: University of Chicago Consortium on Chicago School Research.

American School Counselor Association (ASCA). (2003). *ASCA National Model: A framework for school counselling programs* (2nd ed.). Alexandria, VA: Author.

American School Counselor Association (ASCA). (2005). *ASCA National Model: A framework for school counselling programs* (2nd ed.). Alexandria, VA: Author.

American School Counselor Association (ASCA). (2010). The school counselor and discipline. Position statement. Retrieved from https://www.schoolcounselor.org/asca/media/asca/PositionStatements/PS_Discipline.pdf

American School Counselor Association (ASCA). (2012). *ASCA National Model: A framework for school counselling programs* (3rd ed.). Alexandria, VA: Author.

American School Counselor Association (ASCA). (2013). The school counselor and discipline. Retrieved from https://www.schoolcounselor.org/asca/media/asca/PositionStatements/PS_Discipline.pdf

American School Counselor Association (ASCA). (2014). *Mindsets and behaviors for student success: K–12 college- and career-readiness standards for every student.* Alexandria, VA: Author.

American School Counselor Association (ASCA). (2016). *ASCA ethical standards for school counselors.* Alexandria, VA: Author. Retrieved from https://www.schoolcounselor.org/asca/media/asca/Ethics/EthicalStandards2016.pdf

American School Counselor Association (ASCA). (2017a). ASCA National Model delivery. Retrieved from https://www.schoolcounselor.org/school-counselors/asca-national-model/delivery

American School Counselor Association (ASCA). (2017b). The school counselor and career development. Position statement. Retrieved from https://www.schoolcounselor.org/asca/media/asca/PositionStatements/PS_CareerDevelopment.pdf

American School Counselor Association (ASCA). (2018a). National school counseling week. Retrieved from https://www.schoolcounselor.org/school-counselors-members/about-asca-(1)/national-school-counseling-week

American School Counselor Association (ASCA). (2018b). The school counselor and multitiered system of supports. Position statement. Retrieved from https://www.schoolcounselor.org/asca/media/asca/PositionStatements/PS_MultitieredSupportSystem.pdf

American School Counselor Association (ASCA). (2018c). The school counselor and test preparation programs. Position statement. Retrieved from https://www.schoolcounselor.org/asca/media/asca/PositionStatements/PS_TestPrep.pdf

American School Counselor Association (ASCA). (n.d.). *Student-to-school-counselor-ratio 2015–2016.* Retrieved from https://www.schoolcounselor.org/asca/media/asca/home/Ratios15-16.pdf

Anderson, C. M., & Borgmeier, C. (2010). Tier II interventions within the framework of school-wide positive behaviour support: Essential features for design, implementation, and maintenance. *Behavior Analysis in Practice, 3*(1), 33–45. doi:10.1007/bf03391756

Armstrong, P. (n.d.). *Bloom's taxonomy.* Retrieved from https://cft.vanderbilt.edu/guides-sub-pages/blooms-taxonomy

ASCD. (2019). School culture and climate. Retrieved from http://www.ascd.org/research-a-topic/school-culture-and-climate-resources.aspx

Bloom, B., Englehart, M., Furst, E., Hill, W., & Krathwohl, D. (1956). *Taxonomy of educational objectives: The classification of educational goals. Handbook I: Cognitive domain.* New York and Toronto: Longmans, Green.

Bowen, W., Chingos, M., & McPherson, M. (2009). *Crossing the finish line: Completing college at America's public universities.* Princeton, NJ: Princeton University Press.

Bowman, S. L. (1997). *Presenting with Pizzazz.* Glenbrook, NV: Bowperson Publishing Company.

Boyko, T. (2016). *AVID culturally relevant teaching: A schoolwide approach.* San Diego, CA: AVID Press. Retrieved from https://books.google.com/books/about/AVID_Culturally_Relevant_Teaching.html?id=i9OTnQAACAAJ

Bruce, M., Bridgeland, J., Fox, J., & Balfanz, R. (2011). *On track for success: The use of early warning indicator and intervention systems to build a grad nation.* Washington, D.C.: Civic Enterprises.

Campbell, C. A., & Dahir, C. A. (1997). *Sharing the vision: The ASCA national standards for school counselling programs.* Alexandria, VA: American School Counselor Association.

Canter, L. (2010). *Assertive discipline: Positive behavior management for today's classroom.* Bloomington, IN: Solution Tree Press.

Castleman, B. L., & Page, L. C. (2014). A trickle or a torrent? Understanding the extent of summer "melt" among college-intending high school graduates. *Social Science Quarterly, 95*(1). Southwestern Social Science Association. Retrieved from https://pdfs.semantic-scholar.org/3cde/fef59be6d5bb61b2eca5ffbe3b5185d2708e.pdf

Castleman, B. L., Page, L. C., & Snowdon, A. L. (2013). *SDP summer melt handbook: A guide to investigating and responding to summer melt.* Center for Education Policy Research, Harvard University. Retrieved from https://www.acenet.edu/news-room/Documents/SDP-Summer-Melt-Handbook.pdf

Classroom management skills: From chaos to calm, from inattentive to inspired. (2016). *ASCA School Counselor, 53*(6) [Special issue].

Cline, F., & Fay, J. (2014). *Parenting with love and logic.* Colorado Springs, CO: NavPress.

College Board. (2012). *Elementary school counselor's guide: NOSCA's eight components of college and career readiness counseling.* New York, NY: Author. Retrieved from https://secure-media.collegeboard.org/digitalServices/pdf/advocacy/nosca/11b-4383_ES_Counselor_Guide_WEB_120213.pdf

Córdova, T. L., & Wilson, M. D. (2016). *Lost: The crisis of jobless and out of school teens and young adults in Chicago, Illinois and the U.S.* Great Cities Institute, University of Illinois at Chicago: Chicago, IL.

Cowan, K. C., Vaillancourt, K., Rossen, E., & Pollitt, K. (2013). *A framework for safe and successful schools* [Brief]. Bethesda, MD: National Association of School Psychologists.

Dearden, J. A., Li, S., Meyerhoefer, C. D., & Yang, M. (2017). Demonstrated interest: Signaling behavior in college admissions. *Contemporary Economic Policy, 35*(4), 630–657.

Dimmitt, C., Carey, J. C., & Hatch, T. (2007). *Evidence-based school counseling: Making a difference with data-driven practices.* Thousand Oaks, CA: Corwin.

Driscol, M. P. (20005). *Psychology of learning for instruction.* Boston, MA: Pearson Education.

Duarte, D., & Hatch, T. (2014). Successful implementation of a federally funded elementary school counseling program: Results bring sustainability. *Professional School Counseling, 14*(1).

Duncan, A. (2015). Duncan: Colleges are falling short for millions of students. Debt-free degrees are just part of the solution. *Washington Post.* Retrieved from https://www.washingtonpost.com/news/grade-point/wp/2015/07/27/duncan-colleges-are-falling-short-for-millions-of-students-debt-free-degrees-are-just-part-of-the-solution/?noredirect=on&utm_term=.9b21957dca36

Durlak, J. A., Weissberg, R. P., Dymnicki, A. B., Taylor, R. D., & Schellinger, K. B. (2011). The impact of enhancing students' social and emotional learning: A meta-analysis of school-based universal interventions. *Child Development, 82,* 405–432. doi:10.1111/j.1467-8624.2010.01564.x

Easton, J., & Engelhard, G. (1982). A longitudinal record of elementary school absence and its relationship to reading achievement. *The Journal of Educational Research, 75,* 269–274. doi: 10.1080/00220671.1982.10885393

Easton, J., Johnson, E., & Sartain, L. (2017). *The predictive power of ninth-grade GPA.* Chicago, IL: University of Chicago Consortium on Chicago School Research.

Education Trust. (2011). Poised to lead: How school counselors can drive college and career readiness. Retrieved from http://www.edtrust.org/dc/publication/poised-to-lead

Evertson, C. M., & Weinstein, C. S. (Eds.). (2013). *Handbook of classroom management: Research, practice, and contemporary issues.* New York, NY: Routledge.

Farrington, C. A., Roderick, M., Allensworth, E., Nagaoka, J., Keyes, T. S., Johnson, D. W., & Beechum, N. O. (2012). *Teaching adolescents to become learners: The role of noncognitive factors in shaping school performance: A critical literature review.* Chicago, IL: University of Chicago Consortium on Chicago School Research.

Finkelstein, D. (2009). *A closer look at the principal–counselor relationship: A survey of principal and counselors.* New York, NY: College Board Advocacy & Policy Center.

Gay, G. (2010). *Culturally responsive teaching: Theory, research, and practice.* New York, NY: Teachers College Press.

Gesek, T. (n.d.). Fight or flight: Anxiety in the classroom. *Special Education Advisor.* Retrieved from http://www.specialeducationadvisor.com/fight-or-flight-anxiety-inthe-classroom

Gettinger, M., & Kohler, K. M. (2006). Process-outcome approaches to classroom management and effective teaching. In C. M. Evertson & C. S. Weinstein (Eds.), *Handbook of classroom management: Research, practice, and contemporary issues* (pp. 73–95). New York, NY: Routledge.

Greenberg, M. T., Weissberg, R. P., O'Brien, M. U., Zins, J. E., Fredericks, L., Resnik, H., & Elias, M. J. (2003). Enhancing school-based prevention and youth development through coordinated social, emotional, and academic learning. *American Psychologist, 58*(6–7), 466.

Gysbers, N. C. (2008). Individual student planning in the United States: Rationale, practices, and results. *Asian Journal of Counseling, 15*(2), 117–139.

Hatch, T. (2005, June). *Data made easy: Using data to effect change.* Paper presented at the American School Counselor Association, Orlando, FL.

Hatch, T. (2013). *The use of data in school counseling: Hatching results for students, programs, and the profession.* Thousand Oaks, CA: Corwin.

Hatch, T. (2017, March 8). *Multi-tiered, multi-domain system of supports by Trish Hatch, PhD.* Retrieved from https://www.hatchingresults.com/blog/2017/3/multi-tiered-multidomain-system-of-supports-by-trish-hatch-phd

Hatch, T., Duarte, D., & De Gregorio, L. (2018). *Hatching results for elementary school counseling: Implementing core curriculum and other Tier 1 activities.* Thousand Oaks, CA: Corwin.

Hawken, L., Vincent, C., & Schumann, J. (2008). Response to intervention for social behavior: Challenges and opportunities. *Journal of Emotional and Behavioral Disorders, 16,* 213–225.

Hurwitz, M., & Howell, J. (2013). *Measuring the impact of high school counselors on college enrollment.* College Board Advocacy and Policy Center. Retrieved from http://media.collegeboard.com/digitalServices/pdf/advocacy/policycenter/research-brief-measuring-impact-high-school-counselors-college-enrollment.pdf

Illinois State Board of Education. (2010). *Understanding RtI/MTSS: Multi-tiered system.* Retrieved from http://www.illinoisrti.org/i-rti-network/for-educators/understanding-rti-mtss/multi-tiered-system

Individual Learning Plan. (2018). In *Wikipedia*. Retrieved from https://en.wikipedia.org/wiki/Individual_Learning_Plan

Input. (n.d.). In *Merriam-Webster online*. Retrieved from http://www.merriam-webster.com/dictionary/input

Kennelly, L., & Monrad, M. (2007). *Approaches to dropout prevention: Heeding early warning signs with appropriate interventions*. Washington, DC: National High School Center. Retrieved from http://files.eric.ed.gov/fulltext/ED499009.pdf

Kentucky Department of Education. (2018). Individual Learning Plan. Retrieved from https://education.ky.gov/educational/compschcouns/ILP/Pages/default.aspx

Killian, S. (2015, August 28). *The I do WE do YOU do model explained*. Australian Society for Evidence Based Teaching. Retrieved from http://www.evidencebasedteaching.org.au/the-i-do-we-do-you-do-model-explained

Lemov, D. (2015). *Teach like a champion 2.0: 62 techniques that put students on the path to college*. San Francisco, CA: Wiley.

Lopez, C., & Mason, E. (2018). School counselors as curricular leaders: A content analysis of ASCA lesson plans. *Professional School Counseling*. Retrieved from https://doi.org/10.1177/2156759X18773277

Lorette, K. (n.d.). Definition of a franchise business. *Houston Chronicle*. Retrieved from http://smallbusiness.chron.com/definition-franchise-business-4467.html

Mason, E. C., Ockerman, M. S., & Chen-Hayes, S. (2013). Change-Agent-for-Equity (CAFE) Model: A framework for school counselor identity. *Journal of School Counseling, 11*(4). Retrieved from https://files.eric.ed.gov/fulltext/EJ1012301.pdf

Mayer, P. (2017, December). *Effective parent engagement strategies*. Presentation made at the 2017 AVID National Conference, Orlando, FL.

Missouri Department of Education. (2017). School counseling. Retrieved from https://dese.mo.gov/college-career-readiness/school-counseling#mini-panel-school-counseling7

Missouri School Counselors and Educators. (2015). *School counselor's guide to the K–12 individual student planning process*. Retrieved from https://dese.mo.gov/sites/default/files/cnsl-isp-guide-k-12.pdf

Mitchell, M. M., & Bradshaw, C. P. (2013). Examining classroom influences on student perceptions of school climate: The role of classroom management and exclusionary discipline strategies. *Journal of School Psychology, 51*(5), 599–610.

O'Brennan, L., & Bradshaw, C. (2013, November). Importance of school climate. National Education Association Research Brief no. 15584. Retrieved from https://www.nea.org/assets/docs/15584_Bully_Free_Research_Brief-4pg.pdf

Ockerman, M. S., Mason, E. C., & Chen-Hayes, S. F. (2013). School counseling supervision in challenging times: The CAFE supervisor model. *The Journal of Counselor Preparation and Supervision, 5*(2). Retrieved from http://dx.doi.org/10.7729/51.0024

Ockerman, M.S., Mason, E.C., & Feiker-Hollenbeck, A. (2012) Integrating RTI with school counseling programs: Being a proactive professional school counselor. *Journal of School Counseling, 10*(15).

Patrikakou, E., Ockerman, M.S., & Hollenbeck, A. F. (2016). Needs and contradictions of a changing field: Evidence from a national response to intervention implementation study. *The Professional Counselor, 6*(3).

Pickeral, T., Evans, L., Hughes, W., & Hutchison, D. (2009). *School climate guide for district policymakers and educational leaders*. New York: Center for Social and Emotional Education (www.schoolclimate.org). Retrieved from https://www.schoolclimate.org/themes/schoolclimate/assets/pdf/policy/district-guide-csee.pdf

Ponec, D. L., & Brock, B. L. (2000). Relationships among elementary school counselors and principals: A unique bond. *Professional School Counseling, 3*(3), 208.

Reeves, R., & Guyot, K. (2018, July). REPORT: FAFSA completion rates matter: But mind the data. The Brookings Institution. Retrieved from https://www.brookings.edu/research/fafsa-completion-rates-matter-but-mind-the-data/

Roderick, M., Kelley-Kemple, T., Johnson, D., & Beechum, M. (2014). *Preventable failure: Improvements in long-term outcomes when high schools focused on the ninth grade year.* Chicago, IL: University of Chicago Consortium on Chicago School Research.

Roderick, M., Nagaoka, J., Coca, V., & Moeller, E. (2008). *From high school to the future: Potholes on the road to college.* Chicago, IL: University of Chicago Consortium on School Research.

Sackett, D. L., Straus, S. E., Richardson, W. S., Rosenberg, W., & Haynes, R. B. (2000). *How to practice and teach EBM.* Edinburgh, Scotland: Churchill Livingstone.

Schunk, D. H. (2012). *Learning theories: An educational perspective.* Boston: Pearson.

Seattle Public Schools. (n.d.). *Curriculum alignment.* Retrieved from https://www.seattle schools.org/cms/one.aspx?portalId=627&pageId=16664

Shapiro, E. S. (n.d.). Tiered instruction and intervention in a response-to-intervention model. *RTI* Action Network. Retrieved from http://www.rtinetwork.org/essential/tiered instruction/tiered-instruction-and-intervention-rti-model

Siegle, D. (2010). University of Connecticut. *Likert scales.* Retrieved from http://researchbasics .education.uconn.edu/likert_scales

Siegler, R. S., & Alibali, M. W. (2005). *Children's thinking* (4th ed.). Englewood Cliffs, NJ: Prentice Hall.

Simonsen, B., Fairbanks, S., Briesch, A., Myers, D., & Sugai, G. (2008). Evidence-based practices in classroom management: Considerations for research to practice. *Education and Treatment of Children, 31*(3), 351–380.

Sink, C. A., & Ockerman, M. S. (2016). School counselors and a multi-tiered system of supports: Cultivating systemic change and equitable outcomes. *The Professional Counselor, 6*(3).

Solberg, S., Martin, J., Larson, M., Nichols, K., Booth, H., Lillis, J., & Costa, L. (2016). *Promoting quality individualized learning plans throughout the lifespan: A revised and updated "ILP how to guide 2.0."* Retrieved from http://www.ncwd-youth.info/wp-content/ uploads/2018/03/Promoting-Quality-ILPs-Throughout-the-Lifespan-WEB.pdf

Solberg, V. S., Willis, J., Redmond, K., & Skaff, L. (2014). *Use of Individualized Learning Plans: A promising practice for driving college and career readiness efforts. Findings and recommendations from a multi-method, multi-study effort.* Washington, DC: National Collaborative on Workforce and Disability for Youth, Institute for Educational Leadership. Retrieved from http://www.ncwd-youth.info/wp-content/uploads/2018/03/ILPs-A-Promising-Practice-for-Driving-College-and-Career-Efforts.pdf

Sparks, E., & American School Counselor Association. (n.d.). *ASCA Mindsets & Behaviors for Student Success: K–12 college- and career-readiness standards for every student* [PowerPoint slides]. Retrieved from https://www.schoolcounselor.org/asca/media/webinars/Mindsets-Beh-Presentation.pdf

State of Washington, Office of Superintendent of Public Instruction. (n.d.). Graduation requirements. Retrieved from http://www.k12.wa.us/GraduationRequirements/Requirement-HighSchoolBeyond.aspx

Sutton, J. M., & Fall, M. (1995). The relationship of school climate factors to counselor self-efficacy. *Journal of Counseling & Development, 73*(3), 331–336.

Toward a new focus on outcomes in higher education. (2015, July 27). Remarks by Secretary Arne Duncan at the University of Maryland Baltimore County (UMBC). Retrieved from http://www.ed.gov/news/speeches/toward-new-focus-outcomes-higher-education

Triplett, W. (2017). Utilizing a multi-tiered system to implement your school counseling program [PowerPoint slides]. Created for Chicago Public Schools.

U.S. Department of Education. (2002). *Education longitudinal study of 2002* (ELS:2002/06). National Center for Education Statistics. Retrieved from https://nces.ed.gov/surveys/ els2002/tables/table_01.asp

U.S. Department of Education Office for Civil Rights. (2014, March 21). Civil rights data collection data snapshot. Retrieved from https://ocrdata.ed.gov/downloads/crdc-school-discipline-snapshot.pdf

Vavrus, M. (2008). Culturally responsive teaching. In T. L. Good (Ed.), *21st century education: A reference handbook* (vol. 2, pp. 49–57). Thousand Oaks, CA: Sage.

Velez, E. D. (2017). How can high school counseling shape students' postsecondary attendance? National Association for College Admission Counseling. Retrieved from https://www.nacacnet.org/globalassets/documents/publications/research/hsls-phase-iii.pdf

Walker, T. (n.d.). Legal controversy over lesson plans. National Education Association. Retrieved from http://www.nea.org/home/37583.htm

Weinstein, C., Curran, M., & Tomlinson-Clarke, S. (2003). Culturally responsive classroom management: Awareness into action. *Theory Into Practice, 42*(4), 269–276.

Wesson, K. (2018, September 9). Education for the real world: 6 great ideas for parents and teachers. *Brainworld*. Retrieved from https://brainworldmagazine.com/education-for-the-real-world-6-great-ideas-for-parents-and-teachers/

Willis, J. (2006). *Based strategies to ignite student learning: Insights from a neurologist and classroom teacher*. ASCD.

Wilson, D. (2004). The interface of school climate and school connectedness and relationships with aggression and victimization. *Journal of School Health, 74*, 293–299. doi:10.1111/j.1746-1561.2004.tb08286.x

Ziomek-Daigle, J., Goodman-Scott, E., Cavin, J., & Donohue, P. (2016). Integrating a multi-tiered system of supports with comprehensive school counseling programs. *The Professional Counselor, 6*(3), 220-232. https://files.eric.ed.gov/fulltext/EJ1115900.pdf

Zyromski, B., & Mariani, M.A. (2016). *Facilitating evidence-based, data-driven school counseling: A manual for practice*. Thousand Oaks, CA: Corwin.

Index

Figures and tables are indicated by f or t following the page number.

CORWIN
A SAGE Publishing Company

CORWIN HAS ONE MISSION: to enhance education through intentional professional learning.

We build long-term relationships with our authors, educators, clients, and associations who partner with us to develop and continuously improve the best evidence-based practices that establish and support lifelong learning.

Solutions YOU WANT | Experts YOU TRUST | Results YOU NEED

EVENTS

>>> **INSTITUTES**

Corwin Institutes provide large regional events where educators collaborate with peers and learn from industry experts. Prepare to be recharged and motivated!

corwin.com/institutes

ON-SITE PD

>>> **ON-SITE PROFESSIONAL LEARNING**

Corwin on-site PD is delivered through high-energy keynotes, practical workshops, and custom coaching services designed to support knowledge development and implementation.

corwin.com/pd

>>> **PROFESSIONAL DEVELOPMENT RESOURCE CENTER**

The PD Resource Center provides school and district PD facilitators with the tools and resources needed to deliver effective PD.

corwin.com/pdrc

ONLINE

>>> **ADVANCE**

Designed for K–12 teachers, Advance offers a range of online learning options that can qualify for graduate-level credit and apply toward license renewal.

corwin.com/advance

Contact a PD Advisor at (800) 831-6640 or visit www.corwin.com for more information